Reclams Grund- und Aufbauwortschatz Englisch

Fremdsprachentexte | Englisch

Reclams Grund- und Aufbauwortschatz Englisch

Von Herbert Geisen

Reclam

Muttersprachliche Beratung: Peter Russell

RECLAMS UNIVERSAL-BIBLIOTHEK Nr. 19872
2018 Philipp Reclam jun. GmbH & Co. KG,
Siemensstraße 32, 71254 Ditzingen
Gestaltung: Cornelia Feyll, Friedrich Forssman
Druck und Bindung: Canon Deutschland Business Services GmbH,
Siemensstraße 32, 71254 Ditzingen
Printed in Germany 2018
RECLAM, UNIVERSAL-BIBLIOTHEK und
RECLAMS UNIVERSAL-BIBLIOTHEK sind eingetragene Marken
der Philipp Reclam jun. GmbH & Co. KG, Stuttgart
ISBN 978-3-15-019872-8

Auch als E-Book erhältlich

www.reclam.de

Inhalt

Hinweise zur Benutzung

Reclams Grund- und Aufbauwortschatz Englisch wurde völlig neu erstellt auf der Grundlage von Frequenzlisten (Listen, in denen die Wörter nach der Häufigkeit ihres Vorkommen geordnet sind) und von Vokabellisten der wichtigsten Englisch-Lehrwerke. Dabei haben wir besonders auf Begriffe geachtet, die Ihnen im Englischunterricht in Schule und Universität und bei Reisen ins englischsprachige Ausland begegnen. Ein weiterer Schwerpunkt sind Begriffe aus den für die Geschäftskommunikation so wichtigen Bereichen Wirtschaft und Industrie.

Der gesamte hier enthaltene Wortschatz umfasst etwa 3000 Wörter Grundwortschatz und 4000 Wörter Aufbauwortschatz. Bei der Auswahl und Einordnung der Wörter sind die Vorkenntnisse, die deutschsprachige Lernerinnen und Lerner aufgrund der Verwandschaft der beiden Sprachen haben, besonders berücksichtigt worden.

Die Wörter sind nach Sachgruppen angeordnet, innerhalb der Sachgruppen alphabetisch, und zwar zunächst der Grundwortschatz, fett gedruckt, dann der Aufbauwortschatz. Die wichtigsten 1000 Wörter sind grau unterlegt, damit Sie schnell einen Grundstock nützlicher Wörter erwerben können.

Die Einträge folgen dem Schema englisches Wort – deutsche Übersetzung – Beispielsatz:

to finish ▪ beenden, abschließen
Next summer my daughter is going to finish school.

Bei einem Wort, das mehrere Bedeutungen hat, werden auch mehrere Beispielsätze gegeben:

to push ▪ drücken; drängen; schieben
Don't pull the door, push it.
Don't push ahead of me, please.
He pushed his bike because the hill was too steep.

Bei unregelmäßigen Verben sind zusätzlich die Stammformen Präteritum und Partizip Perfekt angegeben;

to give (gave, given) ▪ geben, schenken
What has your brother given you for your birthday?

und bei Verben auf -y die 2. Person Singular und das Partizip Präsens:

to fly (flew, flown; flies; flying) ▪ fliegen
It's always been one of mankind's dreams to fly like birds.

Die sogenannten Hilfsverben (Auxiliaries oder Auxiliary Verbs) sind unterstrichen und stehen ohne »to«, um sie von den Vollverben zu unterscheiden:

can (could, could) ▪ können
Of course I can swim.

Bei den Substantiven ist bei unregelmäßiger Pluralbildung auch die Pluralform angegeben:

tooth (Pl.: teeth) ▪ Zahn
Most adults have 32 teeth.

In allen Fällen, in denen die Aussprache Schwierigkeiten bereiten könnte, stehen Ausspracheangaben nach dem Internationalen Phonetischen Alphabet:

to laugh [lɑːf] ■ lachen
This type of joke doesn't really make me laugh.

Dort, wo es leicht zu Fehlern – etwa bei der Aussprache oder der Übersetzung – kommen kann, steht ein Warnzeichen:

iron ⚠ ['aɪən] ■ Eisen
Iron is required for the production of steel.

Nützliche Wendungen sind als Untereintrag, versehen mit einem Pfeil, angegeben:

hand ■ Hand
One of the Beatles' songs was "I Want To Hold Your Hand".
▸ **give me a hand** ■ hilf mir doch mal
▸ **to shake hands** ■ sich die Hand geben

In Kapiteln, in denen zahlreiche Wörter im Englischen und im Deutschen gleich oder sehr ähnlich sind, haben wir aus Gründen der Übersichtlichkeit auf Beispielsätze verzichtet. Dies betrifft die Kapitel 1.2, 3.6, 8.3, 10.1, 10.4 und 16.4. Sie werden feststellen, dass bei diesen Themen besonders schnelle Lernfortschritte möglich sind.

Die folgenden Abkürzungen werden verwendet:

Adj.	Adjektiv
Adv.	Adverb
AE	American English
Akk.	Akkusativ
BE	British English
Lat.	Latein
Pl.	Plural

1. Mensch

1.1 Allgemeine Angaben

adult ['ædʌlt] ■ Erwachsene(r)
Once you are eighteen you are legally an adult.

age ■ Alter
What's your age? – I'm sixteen.

baby ■ Baby, Säugling; Schatz, Liebling
Little babies sleep a lot.
Ooh, I love you, baby, I love you night and day.

to be born (was, been) ■ geboren sein, geboren werden
Barack Obama was born in Honolulu, Hawaii.

birth ■ Geburt
After his birth, John's parents moved into a new house.

birthday ■ Geburtstag
My mother's birthday is 12 May 1980.

boy ■ Junge
"I've loved football ever since I was a little boy", Lionel Messi said.

female ■ weiblich; Frau
He looks very female although he is not a female.

first name ■ Vorname
Shakespeare's first name was William.

gentleman (Pl.: -men) ■ Herr, Gentleman
Would the gentlemen please make room for the ladies?

girl ■ Mädchen
Two of Liz's children are girls.

kid ■ Kind
When I was a kid I liked to play in our garden.

lady ■ Dame; (adlige) Lady
A real lady never talks about shocking things.
May I introduce Lord and Lady Wilberforce?

last name ■ Nachname, Familienname
I know "Mary" is your first name. But what is your last name?

lord ■ Lord (englischer Adelstitel)
The lord opened his castle to the public.

▸**the Lord** ■ Gott

male ■ männlich; Mann
In mathematics the number of male students is often bigger than that of female students.
In Britain, "Evelyn" can be the name of a male.

man [mæn] (Pl.: men [men]) ■ Mann
The novelist Evelyn Waugh was a man, not a woman.

name ■ Name
Lady Gaga's real name is Stefani Joanne Angelina Germanotta.

old ■ alt
How old are you? – I'm sixteen.

person ■ Person, Mensch
This room may be used for a maximum of thirty persons.

race ■ Rasse
The relationship between the various races in this country has always been difficult.

sex ■ Geschlecht
The sex of our baby? – It's male.

single ■ ledig
Are you single or married?

teenager ■ Teenager
Young people between 13 and 19 are called teenagers.

title ▪ Titel

What's the title of the book you are reading?

In Britain academic titles are added after the name, as in Arthur Dundas, PhD.

widow ▪ Witwe

My mother became a widow at the age of 54.

widower ▪ Witwer

He did not remain a widower long but married again.

woman ['wʊmən] (Pl.: women ['wɪmɪn]) ▪ Frau

According to the bible Eve was the first woman on earth.

young ▪ jung

He is already a young man, not a boy any longer.

youth ▪ Jugendliche(r); Jugend

He was a youth of eighteen years.

In her youth she was an excellent sprinter.

---

aged ▪ im Alter von

My daughter has two children aged 7 and 5.

alike ▪ ähnlich, gleich

Twins are alike only if they are identical twins.

duchess ▪ Herzogin

A woman who is a duchess holds the same rank as a man who is a duke.

duke ▪ Herzog

The Duke of Edinburgh is Queen Elizabeth's husband.

earl ▪ Graf

In the UK, an earl holds a rank below that of a queen or king, duke and marquess.

ethnic ▪ ethnisch, Volks…

Many people of different ethnic origins live in our country.

gender ▪ Geschlecht

Which gender is the baby, please?

human ▪ Mensch
According to research all modern humans descended from the same small group of people.

ID ▪ Ausweispapier(e)
If you cannot show your passport your driver's licence will be enough as an ID.

identification ▪ Identifikation, Ausweis
Could I see your identification, please?

to identify (-fies; -fying) ▪ identifizieren, erkennen
The police identified the dead body as that of Mr Myers.

identity ▪ Identität
In their youth many people undergo some sort of identity crisis.

infant ▪ Kleinkind; Säugling; Kindes…
"Infant" is the more formal term for "baby".
Infant mortality has dropped sharply in the past century.

junior ▪ Jüngere(r, s); Junior
Instead of saying that Margaret is younger than her sister, you can also say that she is her sister's junior.
Mr Bush junior was less popular than his father.

lad ▪ Junge, Bursche
A couple of lads were playing football on the field.

minor ▪ Minderjährige(r)
As a minor you are not served any alcohol in the USA.

native ▪ einheimisch, heimatlich; gebürtig
My aunt is a native speaker of English.
The English novelist Joseph Conrad was a native Pole.

nickname ▪ Spitzname
Henry's nickname was "Professor" because he was so good at school.

peer ▪ Angehörige(r) des britischen Hochadels
Some examples of peers in Britain are dukes and earls.

to register ▪ (sich) anmelden; registrieren
If you move to Britain from abroad you must register with the police.
I would like to register my son for the football club.

register ▪ Register, Verzeichnis
This is a register of schools and colleges in England.

reputation ▪ Ruf, Reputation
John has a good reputation. Nobody has ever said anything negative about him.

residence ▪ Wohnsitz
Please indicate your place of residence.

resident ▪ Bewohner(in)
Are you a resident of this city?

self (Pl.: selves) ▪ Selbst, Ich
Since the death of their mother Carol and Mike have never been their usual selves.

senior ▪ Ältere(r, s); Senior
Michael is older than John, i.e. he is John's senior.
Mr Bush senior was more popular than his son.

surname ▪ Familienname
Could you spell your surname please, Mr Dalyell?

1.2 Körper und äußere Erscheinung

appearance ▪ Aussehen
He had the appearance of an athlete.

arm ▪ Arm
She broke her arm when she fell off a tree.

attractive ▪ attraktiv, anziehend
He struck everyone by his attractive appearance.

back ▪ Rücken
Oh dear, my back has been hurting for days.

barefoot ■ barfuß
He doesn't like shoes and socks. That's why he always goes barefoot.

to be (was, been) ■ sein
She is a very tall girl.

▸ **to be at …** ■ beschäftigt sein mit
He's been at this job for a couple of hours.

▸ **to be up** ■ auf sein
It was nine o'clock, but John wasn't up yet.

beard ■ Bart
My brother grew a beard when he was only fifteen.

beautiful ■ schön
It's a beautiful weather today, isn't it?

beauty ■ Schönheit
The new Miss World is a real beauty.

big ■ groß
It was a big surprise when my sister announced her wedding.

body ■ Körper
Trust your feelings and your body.

bone ■ Knochen
There are more than 200 bones in the human body.

brain ■ Gehirn
The brain is a very complex organ, and one of the largest in the human body.

breast [brest] ■ Brust
He pressed his hand to his breast and said: "I am not lying!"

breath [breθ] ■ Atem; Atemzug
He had run so fast that he was quite out of breath.

cheek ■ Backe, Wange
Babies often have fat cheeks.

ear ■ Ohr
Dogs have much better ears than human beings.

elbow ■ Ellenbogen
Many tennis players have occasional problems with their right – or left – elbow.

eye ■ Auge
His eyes were as good as an eagle's.

face ■ Gesicht
His face was covered with tears.

fair ■ blond, hell
She had long, fair hair.

finger ■ Finger
When I use a keyboard to write a letter I only use two fingers.

to fit (fitted, fitted; AE: fit, fit) ■ passen
Oh dear, my pants don't fit any more.

foot (Pl.: feet) ■ Fuß
Those feet are made for walking.

forehead ['fɒrəd, 'fɔːhed] ■ Stirn
A golf ball hit him right on the forehead.

hair ■ Haar
I wash my hair every other day.

hand ■ Hand
One of the Beatles' songs was "I Want To Hold Your Hand".

▸ **give me a hand** ■ hilf mir doch mal

▸ **to shake hands** ■ sich die Hand geben

handsome ■ gut aussehend
George is a very handsome man.

to have (had, had) ■ haben, besitzen
Emma has three cats.

▸ **to have s.th. done** ■ etwas machen lassen
He had his hair cut.

head [hed] ■ Kopf
Cristiano Ronaldo hurt his head and immediately left the game.

heart [hɑːt] ■ Herz
My father never had problems with his heart.

human ■ menschlich
The human body is highly developed.

image ■ Bild
Little Sylvia is the image of her mother as a young girl.

internal ■ innere(r, s)
The heart is a very important internal organ.

joint ■ Gelenk
I can't go for long walks anymore because my knee joints begin to hurt after only ten minutes.

knee [niː] ■ Knie
After the accident my father had difficulties bending his knees.

large ■ wohlbeleibt
He was rather a large man.

leg ■ Bein
The guitarist broke his right leg when he fell off the stage.

lip ■ Lippe
Red lips are a classic beauty trend.

little (smaller, smallest) ■ klein
Jacob was quite little when he was born but his brother was even smaller.

▸ **a little** ■ ein bisschen
We should have known this a little earlier.

liver ■ Leber
In Shakespeare's time the liver was believed to be the seat of love and passion.

lovely ■ schön, reizend, nett
Mary is a lovely little girl.

lung ■ Lunge
He filled his lungs with air and dived into the water.

mark ■ Fleck, Zeichen
She had a dark mark on her right cheek.

mouth ■ Mund
The actor has a very large mouth.

naked ■ nackt
We are born naked.

neck ■ ⚠ Hals
She put her arms around my neck.

nice ■ schön, angenehm
Margaret was a nice little girl with her pretty smile and blue eyes.

nose ■ Nase
The boxer's nose started to bleed after he had been hit.

▸ **to blow one's nose** (blew, blown) ■ sich die Nase putzen, sich schnäuzen

powerful ■ stark
Doing a lot of sports has made him even more powerful.

pretty ■ hübsch
I like the pretty old villages on the Isle of Wight very much.

pupil ['pju:pəl] ■ Pupille
The darker it gets the larger your pupils.

sense ■ Sinn
Human beings have five senses: touch, sight, hearing, smell, and taste.
She's got a very strong sense of responsibility.

short ■ klein
He is rather a short person.

shoulder ■ Schulter
Bob, you are a big boy. I can't carry you on my shoulders.

skin ■ Haut
Little Mary has very smooth skin.

slim ■ schlank, dünn, mager
I'm not as slim as I used to be.

small ▪ klein
He is rather small for his age.

strength ▪ Kraft, Stärke
Hercules was known for his great strength.

strong ▪ stark, kräftig
He is as strong as a horse.

tall ▪ groß
At 7 feet Dirk is very tall.

thick ▪ dicht
Anne has thick hair.

thin ▪ dünn
Many models have very thin arms and legs.

tiny ▪ winzig, klein
Babies have tiny fingers and toes.

tiptoe: on tiptoe ▪ auf Zehenspitzen
Little Peter had to stand on tiptoe to open the door.

toe ▪ Zeh
Human beings have ten toes and ten fingers.

tongue [tʌŋ] ▪ Zunge
My aunt could touch her nose with her tongue.

tooth (Pl.: teeth) ▪ Zahn
Most adults have 32 teeth.

ugly ▪ hässlich
Frankenstein's monster was rather ugly.

voice ▪ Stimme
She has a very pleasant voice.

wide ▪ groß
He looked at her with wide eyes.

ankle ▪ (Fuß-)Knöchel

The player had twisted his ankle and had to leave the field.

artery ▪ Arterie

Arteries transport blood away from the heart, veins transport it back.

bald ▪ glatzköpfig

His grandfather became bald very early in life.

bare ▪ nackt

You must not enter this church with bare shoulders. Put a scarf round them.

blond ▪ blond

All my family have had blond hair.

chest ▪ Brust, Brustkorb

Just look at his chest. He must have practised with weights a lot.

chin ▪ Kinn

The punch to his chin knocked him out on the spot.

curly ▪ lockig

The little girl had really curly hair.

delicate ['delɪkət] ▪ empfindlich, zerbrechlich

My grandmother is rather a delicate person.

to dress ▪ (sich) anziehen, sich kleiden

She dresses very elegantly.

feminine ['femənɪn] ▪ feminin, weiblich

She likes to stress her feminine appearance, which is why she often wears a skirt.

fingernail ▪ Fingernagel

She carefully paints her fingernails every day.

fingertip ▪ Fingerspitze

Can you balance a basketball on your fingertip?

giant ▪ riesig; Riese(-in)

He's got giant feet – size 52 in fact.

Some basketball players are real giants.

heel ■ Ferse, Hacke

The police were quickly on the criminal's heels.

height ■ Größe

Mary and Susan have about the same height.

hip ■ Hüfte

New hips are quite frequent among the elderly nowadays.

kidney ■ Niere

Kidneys clear your blood of dangerous substances.

knuckle ['nʌkəl] ■ (Finger-)Knöchel

Her knuckles became all white when she grabbed the chair.

lean ■ schlank

Jim always looks lean and fit.

left-handed ■ linkshändig

Two of my three children are left-handed.

limb [lɪm] ■ Glied

Human beings have four limbs – two legs and two arms.

lock ■ Locke

The little girl had beautiful black locks.

look ■ Aussehen; Blick

She was a woman of very good looks.

He had a very serious look on his face.

masculine ['mæskjəlɪn] ■ maskulin, männlich

She went so often to a gym that in the end she had a very masculine appearance.

mask ■ Maske

He wore a mask so that he would not be recognized.

mature [mə'tʃʊə] ■ reif; entwickelt, erwachsen

Considering that she's only twelve she's rather mature.

moustache [mə'stɑːʃ] ■ Schnurrbart

On old photographs you can see that many men had a moustache in those days.

neat ■ ordentlich, sauber
Everyone appreciated her neat appearance.

nerve ■ Nerv
Muscles only begin to work when nerves make them do so.

organ ■ Organ
All his major organs are in perfect order.

palm [pɑːm] ■ Handfläche
There are people who claim that they can see your future in your palm.

plump ■ rund, mollig
John loved his little, plump wife.

ponytail ■ Pferdeschwanz
Picasso painted a famous portrait of a girl with a ponytail.

prominent ■ ⚠ vorstehend
The little boy had rather prominent teeth.

rear ■ Hintern
He turned around furiously when someone kicked him in the rear.

to resemble ■ ähneln, sich gleichen
Mary and Liza are not twins but they resemble each other very much.

rib ■ Rippe
Human beings usually have twice twelve ribs, i.e. twenty-four.

sexy ■ sexy, attraktiv
She looks really sexy in that new dress of hers.

skinny ■ dünn, mager
Tom is so skinny! He ought to put on some weight.

smart ■ schick
He looks very smart in that suit.

stomach ■ Magen; Bauch
Food is primarily digested in the stomach.
Babies often have a big stomach.

thickness ▪ Dichte
The thickness of her hair is remarkable.

thumb [θʌm] ▪ Daumen
Most babies suck their thumb.

toenail ▪ Zehennagel
Elsie painted her toenails.

tough [tʌf] ▪ robust
Coalminers have to be very tough men.

trunk ▪ Rumpf
They discovered the trunk of a prehistoric human being in the forest.

to undress ▪ (sich) ausziehen
They all undressed before jumping into the lake.
Mary undressed the baby before bathing her.

vein ▪ Vene
Veins transport blood back to the heart.

waist ▪ Taille
The actress wore a scarf around her waist.

wrist ▪ Handgelenk
The singer had his expensive watch stolen from his wrist.

1.3 Bewegungen und physische Handlungen

to act ▪ handeln; sich verhalten
Act quickly if you want to make use of this special offer.
Sometimes he acts like a clown.

act ▪ Handlung
It would be an act of kindness to help me in this crisis.

action ▪ Handeln
He was a man of action rather than of thought.

active ▪ aktiv, lebendig
Cats are very active at night.

to appear ▪ erscheinen, auftreten
The driver who had caused the accident was asked to appear before court.

to approach ▪ sich nähern
He approached the dog quite carefully because he feared it might bite him.

to arise (arose, arisen) ▪ sich erheben
The guests arose when the President approached.

to arrange ▪ anordnen; vereinbaren
They arranged the chairs so that everybody could see the speaker.
They arranged another meeting to discuss the matter more fully.

to attach ▪ befestigen
He attached the tin opener to the wall.

to avoid ▪ aus dem Weg gehen, vermeiden
By stepping quickly aside he managed to avoid the oncoming car.

to bring (brought, brought) ▪ (mit)bringen
Can I bring you another cup of tea?

▸ **to bring up** ▪ großziehen, erziehen
After their parents' death the children were brought up by their grandparents.

to build (built, built) ▪ bauen
Building a house was their main ambition.

busy ['bɪzi] ▪ beschäftigt
Don't come in. Can't you see I'm busy?

to carry ▪ tragen
This bag is much too heavy for me. I can't carry it.

▸ **to carry on** ▪ weitermachen
You're doing nicely, John. Just carry on.

▸ **to carry out** ▪ ausführen, erfüllen
It's a very tricky task. I'm not sure whether I can carry it out.

to clear ▪ aufräumen, reinigen
Please clear your room before you go on holidays.

to climb [klaɪm] ▪ klettern, besteigen
Every year thousands of tourists climb Mont Blanc.

to close ▪ schließen
He closed the door carefully so that nobody could hear them.

to come [kʌm] (came, come) ▪ kommen
Could you come for a meal on Thursday?

▸ **to come up with s.th.** ▪ sich etwas ausdenken
She is such an interesting person. She keeps coming up with new ideas.

to copy ▪ kopieren; nachmachen
Children often copy the behaviour of adults.

to cover ['kʌvə] ▪ bedecken
It was so cold that he covered his head with a hat.

to cry (cries; crying) ▪ weinen; schreien
When her father died she cried all day.
He cried out in pain when the dog bit him.

to cut (cut, cut) ▪ schneiden
The cook cut the meat into small pieces.

to destroy ▪ zerstören
The gang destroyed a large number of cars – simply for the fun of it.

to disappear ▪ verschwinden
He just saw him disappear round the corner.

to divide ▪ verteilen
They divided the profit of the business among themselves.

to do (did, done) ▪ tun, machen
Dad, that's too difficult for you. Let me do it.

to drop ▪ fallen lassen
The rock was so heavy that I was forced to drop it.

to enter ▪ betreten, eintreten
The sign outside the building stated clearly: "Danger. Do not enter."

to escape ■ entkommen, fliehen
The prisoner found the door unlocked and managed to escape.

to fight (fought, fought) ■ kämpfen
Many people nowadays still have to fight for their rights.

to fill ■ füllen
He filled his glass with whisky.

to find (found, found) ■ finden; denken
After searching for hours I finally found our cat.
I find this rather difficult to do.

▸ **to find out** ■ herausfinden, herausbekommen
I hope the police will find out who stole my car.

to finish ■ beenden, abschließen
Next summer my daughter is going to finish school.

to fix ■ festmachen, reparieren
She fixed her new tin opener to the wall.
The door won't close properly. Can you fix it, please?

to fly (flew, flown; flies; flying) ■ fliegen
It's always been one of mankind's dreams to fly like birds.

to follow ■ folgen
I'll go ahead – just follow me.

to gather ■ aufsammeln
They gathered all the old newspapers and threw them away.

to get (got, got) ■ bekommen; werden
Mum, what are we getting for breakfast?
I hope the weather will get better soon.

▸ **to get in** ■ (ins Auto) einsteigen
You don't need to walk. Just get in the car.

▸ **to get off** ■ aussteigen; davonkommen
We'll have to get off the bus at the next stop.
Although John's crimes were very serious he got off lightly.

▸ **to get out** ■ (aus dem Auto) aussteigen
Stop telling me how to drive or get out!

▸ **to get up** ■ (aus dem Bett) aufstehen
School begins at 9 o'clock. So you must get up at 7.30 a.m.
"Get up, stand up, don't give up the fight" (Bob Marley).

to go (went, gone) ■ gehen, fahren
This year we're going to Italy for a holiday.

▸ **to go ahead** [ə'hed] ■ vorangehen; weitermachen
Don't wait for me. Just go ahead.
You're doing nicely. Just go ahead.

▸ **to go down** ■ sinken, fallen
After rising sharply for quite some time, prices at last began to go down.

▸ **to go on** ■ weitermachen, weitergehen
After a short break he went on washing his car.

▸ **to go out** ■ ausgehen
Although he couldn't really afford it he liked going out a lot.

▸ **to go up** ■ hinaufgehen, steigen
As a result of the high demand for petrol, prices went up.

to hand ■ geben, reichen
Can you please hand me the hammer?

to hang (hung, hung) ■ hängen; aufhängen; erhängen (in dieser Bedeutung: hanged, hanged)
A beautiful picture was hanging on the wall.
He hung up his coat when he came in.
They hanged Tom Dooley from a tree.

▸ **to hang around** (hung, hung) ■ rumhängen, herumlungern
Stop hanging around all day. Do something useful!

to harm ■ schädigen, verletzen
Don't harm innocent animals.

to hit (hit, hit) ■ schlagen, stoßen; treffen
Parents are not supposed to hit their children.
The bullet hit him in the back of his leg.

hit ■ Schlag, Stoß; Treffer
He received a hit on his head and fell down.

to hold (held, held) ■ halten
The title of a famous Beatles song is "I want to hold your hand."

to hop ■ hüpfen
Look at those little birds hopping around in the garden.

to hurry (hurries; hurrying) ■ sich beeilen
They saw the train coming. So they hurried to catch it.

▸ **hurry up** ■ beeil dich, beeilt euch

to join ■ verbinden, anfügen
Join the two broken pieces and tie them closely together. That may help.

to jump ■ springen
They jumped together into the swimming pool.

to keep (kept, kept) ■ behalten, aufheben
I always keep the receipts of what I've bought for some time.

▸ **to keep doing s.th.** ■ ständig etwas tun
He keeps telling stories.

▸ **Keep off!** ■ Nicht betreten!
Keep off the lawn!

to kneel [ni:l] (knelt, knelt) ■ knien
As a sign of his love he knelt before his fiancée.

to laugh [lɑ:f] ■ lachen
This type of joke doesn't really make me laugh.

to lay (laid, laid) ■ legen; (Tisch) decken
Hens do not usually lay more than one egg per day.
Could you please lay the table?

to lead (led, led) ■ führen, bringen
The nurse took the patient by the hand and led her to her bed.

to leave (left, left) ■ verlassen; zurücklassen; weggehen
He left the house at 8 p.m.
It didn't take him long to realize that he had left his umbrella in his office.
She was so annoyed by his remark that she simply left.

to lie (lay, lain; lying) ■ liegen
After a party I usually lie in bed until noon.

to lift ■ (hoch)heben
Can you help me lift this box?

to look ■ sehen, schauen, gucken; aussehen
Look what you've done. You've broken the cup.
You look beautiful.

▸ **to look at** ■ ansehen, betrachten
The student looked at the documents on his desk.

▸ **to look for** ■ suchen
I've been looking for this book for hours.

▸ **to look up** ■ nachschlagen
If only I didn't have to look up so many words in the dictionary.

to lose [luːz] (lost, lost) ■ verlieren
I'm afraid I've lost my keys.

to make (made, made) ■ machen; (veran)lassen
He made this chair all alone.
His boss made him do all the dirty work in the factory.

▸ **to make up s.th.** ■ sich etwas ausdenken, etwas erfinden
Some pupils make up strange stories to explain why they are late.

to manage ■ managen; zurechtkommen
My wife manages our financial affairs.
We don't have a lot of money, but we can manage.

to mark ■ markieren, kennzeichnen
Mark the bottles clearly if their content is dangerous.

motion ■ Bewegung
Do not get off the train when it is still in motion.

to move ▪ (sich) bewegen
Don't move or I'll shoot.

movement ▪ Bewegung
The night was so calm that there was not the slightest movement outside.

to nod ▪ nicken
She nodded to indicate that she agreed.

to note ▪ notieren
She briefly noted what she had seen so that she could report it to the police.

to observe ▪ beobachten
The police officer observed someone hitting an elderly person and arrested him.

to open ▪ öffnen
He opened his bag and took out a book.

to pass ▪ vorbeigehen, vorbeifahren; reichen
He passed his neighbour in the street without so much as saying "Hello".
A train passed.
Can you pass me the salt, please?

to point at ▪ hinweisen auf, zeigen auf
Little Max always points at the bread when he wants some more.

to prepare ▪ zubereiten
In preparing her dishes the cook only used fresh ingredients.

to present ▪ präsentieren; überreichen
She always tries to present herself in the best way.
Some restaurants present the bill in a little box.

to press ▪ drücken; bügeln; pressen
He pressed my hand to express his sympathy.
My son presses his shirts himself.
The company pressed thousands of records for its customers.

procedure [prə'siːdʒə] ▪ Verfahren, Vorgehen
This is the standard procedure in these cases.

to provide ■ bereitstellen; Vorsorge treffen
We'll provide whatever you need for this meeting.
We can easily provide for ourselves.

to pull ■ ziehen
They pulled the drowning man out of the water and saved him.

to push ■ drücken; drängen; schieben
Don't pull the door, push it.
Don't push ahead of me, please.
He pushed his bike because the hill was too steep.

to put (put, put) ■ (ver)setzen; stellen, tun; legen
Can't you put yourself in his position?
Just put your suitcase here. The porter will take care of it.
Could you put this book on top of the others?

▸ **to put up with** ■ sich abfinden mit
I am not going to put up with this kind of behaviour.

quick ■ schnell
The tennis player moved with quick and short steps.

to raise ■ heben; hochziehen
Raise your hands if you agree with this proposal.
When ships approach the bridge it is raised.

to reach ■ greifen
The little child reached for her mother's hand.

to realize ■ verwirklichen
At last we have been able to realize our plan.

to remove ■ entfernen; ausziehen
The doctor removed the thorn from my finger.
She removed her coat and hat because it was very warm in the room.

to replace ■ ersetzen, austauschen
She replaced her old necklace with a new one.

to rise (rose, risen) ▪ steigen; hochgehen; aufgehen; aufsteigen
At last the fog began to rise above the valley.
The lights went down and the curtain rose.
In summer the sun rises as early as 4 a. m.
His voice rose higher than that of the other singers.

to run (ran, run) ▪ laufen, rennen
The students were late so they had to run to catch the bus.

to save ▪ retten
He jumped into the river and was able to save the drowning girl.

to set (set, set) ▪ setzen, stellen, legen
Can you set the vase on the floor, please?

▸ **to set in** ▪ einsetzen
The rain set in just as we left the house to go for a walk.

▸ **to set off** ▪ aufbrechen
The party set off at six o'clock to reach the summit before midday.

▸ **to set up** ▪ aufschlagen
Let's set up our camp here.

to settle ▪ es sich bequem machen; (sich) beruhigen
I like to settle in front of my favourite TV comedy on Saturday nights.
When John had settled a little after the dispute, he went to bed.

to shake (shook, shaken) ▪ (sich) schütteln, zittern, beben
She was shaking with the cold.

to show (showed, shown) ▪ zeigen
Can I show you what I've written so far?

to shut (shut, shut) ▪ schließen
Could you please shut the door?

to sit (sat, sat) ▪ sitzen
The old lady was sitting in front of her TV all day doing nothing.

▸ **to sit down** ▪ sich (hin)setzen

to smile ▪ lächeln
Jennifer smiled when she heard Henry's compliment.

smile ▪ Lächeln
Estelle had a faint smile on her face when she saw Pip.

to spread [spred] (spread, spread) ▪ ausbreiten
Daddy spread his arms to welcome me.

to stand (stood, stood) ▪ stehen; (sich) stellen
Hundreds of people were standing at the ticket counter.
She stood the dripping umbrella in the bathtub.

▸ **to stand up** ▪ aufstehen
There was a time when gentlemen stood up when a lady entered or left the room.

to stare ▪ starren
Don't stare at me like that!

to stay ▪ bleiben
How long will you be staying in Britain?

to step ▪ treten
Don't step on my shoes.

▸ **to step aside** ▪ zur Seite treten, Platz machen
Could you please step aside so that the old lady can pass?

▸ **to step back** ▪ zurücktreten
If you do not wish to be be hurt you'd better step back a little.

▸ **to step forward** ▪ vortreten
Will any volunteers please step forward?

▸ **to step in** ▪ eintreten; einschreiten, intervenieren
There's room enough here. Just step in.
When I saw the two boys fighting I stepped in at once.

▸ **to step out** ▪ (kurz) weggehen
He stepped out to smoke a cigarette.

step ▪ Schritt
My toes hurt at every step.

to stop ▪ aufhören; hindern; stoppen
Stop kicking me, will you?
If you want to go for a walk, what's stopping you?
He is hopeless. He cannot even stop a ball properly.

to take (took, taken) ▪ nehmen; bringen
Can I have another lump of sugar? – Take as many as you like.
Can I take you home?

to throw (threw, thrown) ▪ werfen
Whenever he threw the ball his dog ran after it.

to touch ▪ berühren, anfassen
Don't touch that! It's hot.

to turn ▪ drehen; wenden; sich umdrehen; richten
He turned the key in the lock.
She turned her head to see who was entering the room.
When he heard John calling he turned.
Veronica turned the lamp on her brother.

▸ **to turn around** ▪ (sich) umdrehen
The old lady turned around to see who was coming.

turn ▪ Drehung
Give the screw another turn.

to undertake (-took, -taken) ▪ durchführen, unternehmen
He undertook an expedition to the South Pole.

to use ▪ benutzen
Please use your own toothbrush.

▸ **to be used to s.th.** ▪ an etwas gewöhnt sein
I'm used to going to bed very late.

▸ **used to** ▪ etwas gewöhnlich tun
I used to play tennis a lot, but now I can't.

use ▪ Nutzen; Gebrauch, Benutzung
This screwdriver is of no use. Do you have a better one?
Can you instruct me in the use of this machine?
The use of this car park is reserved for employees.

to walk ■ zu Fuß gehen
The school is only five minutes away. You can easily walk there.

walk ■ Spaziergang
The walk along the coast from Paignton to Brixham takes about two hours.

▸ **to take a walk** (took, taken) ■ einen Spaziergang machen
Granny likes to take a walk after lunch.

---

to bend (bent, bent) ■ biegen, krümmen, beugen
You cannot easily bend steel.

to bind (bound, bound) ■ binden
They discovered the victim bound hand and foot.

to bite (bit, bitten) ■ beißen
Mind that the snake doesn't bite you.

to bother ['bɒðə] ■ belästigen
Stop bothering me, will you?

to bound ■ springen
Little Marian bounded about in the garden.

to breathe [bri:ð] ■ atmen
He breathed a sigh of relief when he heard that his wife was safe.

to burst (burst, burst) ■ ausbrechen
On hearing of the accident she burst into tears.

to chew ■ kauen
Chew your food properly.

to clap ■ klatschen
The little girl clapped her hands for joy.

to clean ■ putzen; reinigen, säubern
Please clean your shoes before entering the gym.

to click ■ klicken
Some pupils will click their fingers when they put up their hands.

to copy ■ nachmachen, nachahmen
Children often copy the behaviour of adults.

to crawl ■ krabbeln, kriechen
Look, Mary. Baby can crawl now.

to crush ■ zerdrücken, zerquetschen
Could you crush some ice for me, please?

cry ■ Schrei; Geheul
He was so surprised that he gave a loud cry.

to decorate ■ schmücken
They decorated the dining room with balloons and candles.

to dig (dug, dug) ■ (um)graben
He does not like digging in the garden because of his bad back.

to drag ■ ziehen, schleifen, zerren
A monster came out of the wood and dragged him away.

to drift ■ treiben, sich treiben lassen
I didn't try to swim against the current. I just drifted along until I had reached the island ahead of me.

to dry (dries; drying) ■ trocknen, austrocknen
Mary was drying her hair with a towel.
Global warming is drying up the Colorado River.

to emerge ■ auftauchen, auftreten
He suddenly emerged from behind a tree.

to fetch ■ holen, bringen
Some dogs fetch their master's slippers.

to frown ■ die Stirne runzeln
The judge frowned to show how annoyed he was by what the witness had said.

to gaze ■ starren
My father gazed at me as if I was a ghost.

gesture ■ Geste, Handbewegung
The speaker reacted to the protest with an impatient gesture.

to glance ■ einen Blick werfen
After only glancing briefly at the exam paper the student gave up.

to grab ▪ (er)greifen, packen, zugreifen

Three police officers grabbed the suspect and took him to the station.

to grin ▪ grinsen, strahlen

The actor grinned with delight when he won the prize.

to imitate ▪ nachahmen, imitieren

The little girl kept imitating whatever her elder brother did.

to insert ▪ einwerfen, hineinstecken

You must insert a 50-pence coin before your ticket is printed.

to knit [nɪt] ▪ stricken

My grandma knitted a pair of socks for my birthday.

to knock [nɒk] ▪ klopfen

"Knocking On Heaven's Door" is a well-known song by Bob Dylan.

laughter ['lɑːftə] ▪ Gelächter

We couldn't sleep because of all the laughter in the street.

to lean [liːn] (leant [lent], leant; AE: leaned [liːnd], leaned) ▪ sich beugen, sich lehnen

She leant over so much that she almost fell out of her chair.

to leap [liːp] (leapt [lept], leapt; AE: leaped [liːpt], leaped) ▪ springen, einen Satz machen

When John saw the dog approach he leapt out of his chair and ran away.

to light ▪ beleuchten; anzünden

We'll need to buy some more lamps to light the room properly.

He went out on the balcony to light a cigarette.

to lock ▪ abschließen

Don't forget to lock the door when you go out.

to march ▪ marschieren

The soldiers marched all night to reach the front on time.

to mend ▪ flicken, reparieren

My grandmother always said that mending is better than ending.

to mix ■ (ver)mischen; mixen
She mixed the various ingredients to make a salad.
She mixed him a drink.

to moan ■ stöhnen
The hospital was full of moaning soldiers wounded in action.

to mount ■ besteigen
The soldiers mounted their horses and pursued the enemy.

occupation ■ Beschäftigung
Her mother's chief occupation was to look after her children.

to omit ■ auslassen; unterlassen
In a quotation in an essay you must not omit any word without indicating this.
Nor must you omit to mention your source.

pace ■ Tempo; Schritt
At last our yacht gathered pace.
Anne always walks at a fast pace.

to pack ■ packen
Whenever we start packing our bags our dog begins to bark.

to paste ■ kleben
Just take some glue and paste the pieces together.

to peel ■ schälen
I never peel the potatoes if I want to fry them.

to pinch ■ kneifen
Ouch, that hurts! Stop pinching me.

to polish ■ polieren, putzen
Polish your shoes before you go to the interview.

to pose ■ posieren, Modell sitzen
She posed as a model for a painting class.

to pour [pɔː] ■ einschenken
Would you like me to pour you some coffee?

to pretend ■ vortäuschen
She pretended to be asleep because she did not want to be disturbed.

to punch ▪ schlagen, boxen
Without any reason he got up and punched me in the face.

to quit (quit/quitted, quit/quitted) ▪ aufhören
He quitted smoking only after his father had died of cancer.

to race ▪ rennen; um die Wette laufen
The boys kept racing about the schoolyard.
I do like running but I don't like racing.

to risk ▪ riskieren, wagen
I know walking on ice is dangerous, but I'll risk it nevertheless.

to roll ▪ (sich) rollen
I don't like our dog to roll in the wet grass.
My golf ball rolled into the hole.

routine [ruː'tiːn] ▪ Routine
After their retirement my parents made it their routine to get up at eight o'clock.

to rub ▪ reiben
It was so cold that the explorers had to rub their hands to keep them warm.

to rush ▪ eilen; hetzen
They rushed to the box office to buy tickets before the show was sold out.
Don't rush me. I can't walk any faster.

to scratch ▪ kratzen
Don't tease the cat. It'll scratch you!

to seek (sought, sought) ▪ suchen
I've been seeking our dog for three hours.

to seize [siːz] ▪ ergreifen
When Kevin refused to stop his father seized him by the collar.

to separate ['sepəreɪt] ▪ trennen, auseinanderhalten
Separate the discs with classical music from those with pop songs.

to shift ▪ (weg)bewegen, verschieben
Before painting your walls you ought to shift all the furniture.

to shrug ▪ die Achseln zucken
Instead of answering the question Lynn simply shrugged and left.

to smash ▪ zerschlagen
The burglar smashed a window to get into the house.

to snap ▪ (ab)brechen
He snapped the twig in two pieces.

to sneeze ▪ niesen
Whenever my aunt had to sneeze she did it seven times.

to snore ▪ schnarchen
Jack's parents had separate bedrooms because his father snored a lot.

to sob ▪ schluchzen
At the news of her father's death she sobbed for several hours.

to spend (spent, spent) ▪ verbringen; investieren
We spent our vacation in Scotland.
He spends all his energy on preparing for his exam.

to spin (spun, spun) ▪ (sich) drehen
When he heard a noise behind him he spun round.

to spit (spat, spat) ▪ spucken
Don't spit on the floor, will you?

to split (split, split) ▪ spalten
The lightning split the tree in two parts.

▸ to split up ▪ aufteilen
The teacher split up the class into four groups.

to spoil (spoilt/spoiled, spoilt/spoiled) ▪ verderben; verwöhnen
She spoilt our evening by her strange behaviour.
Grandparents tend to spoil their grandchildren.

to spring (sprang, sprung; AE: sprung, sprung) ▪ springen
When he heard the alarm, he sprang out of bed immediately.

to squash ▪ quetschen
Don't squash the peaches.

to squeeze ■ ausquetschen; zwängen; drücken
Carol squeezed two oranges for a fruit cocktail.
Phil squeezed another suitcase into the trunk.
Margot squeezed Jack's hand.

to stir ■ sich bewegen
After his first marathon Matthew was so tired that he couldn't stir.

to stretch ■ sich recken
Whenever our dog wakes up he stretches.

to stroke ■ streicheln
Our dog likes being stroked.

to suck ■ saugen, lutschen
A lot of babies suck their thumbs.

to swim (swam, swum) ■ schwimmen
Justus learned to swim at the age of five.

to swing (swung, swung) ■ schwingen; schwanken; schaukeln
He swung his arms to regain his balance.
He had drunk so much alcohol that he swung in his walk.
The little girl swung in the garden.

swing ■ Schwingen, Schlag
He felled the tree with one swing of his axe.

to switch ■ schalten; wechseln
Could you switch on the light and switch the radio programme, please?

to tap ■ klopfen
When our teacher is nervous he taps his foot on the floor.

to tear [teə] (tore, torn) ■ (zer)reißen; rasen
Cindy tore a page out of the newspaper.
He tore down the street at an incredible speed.

to tie ■ binden, schnüren
Little Johnny is only four and he can already tie his shoelaces.

▸ to tie up ■ verschnüren, festbinden
Tie the parcel up properly before you take it to the post office.

to twist ■ drehen; auswringen

He twisted his head slightly to see who was coming.

She twisted the wet towel.

to vanish ■ verschwinden

Macbeth discovered that the witches had vanished into thin air.

to wake (woke, woken) ■ aufwachen; wecken

He woke up at exactly six o'clock in the morning.

The noise from the bar woke her at three o'clock in the morning.

to wander ■ schlendern; umherirren

They had so much time that they just wandered around the village.

The old lady wandered the streets because she had forgotten where she lived.

to whip ■ mit der Peitsche schlagen

You are not supposed to whip your horse.

to wind (wound, wound) ■ wickeln; aufziehen

He wound a scarf around his throat to keep warm.

She wound her watch.

▸ to wind up ■ aufziehen; hochziehen

Mr Shandy always wound up the clock on a Saturday.

He wound up the anchor.

to wipe ■ wischen

I spilt some wine and wiped it away.

to withdraw (-drew, -drawn) ■ sich zurückziehen; herausziehen

He withdrew behind the curtain because he was so shy.

He withdrew his hand from the machine so that it would not hurt him.

to yawn ■ gähnen

The party was so boring that Mark couldn't help yawning.

1.4 Psyche und Wahrnehmungen

to appear ▪ erscheinen, auftreten; scheinen
A sign appeared on the wall.
The company appeared to me to be very successful.

to assess ▪ einschätzen
We must assess our chances in the market before we start planning a new product.

attention ▪ Aufmerksamkeit
Lang Lang's playing attracted everybody's attention.

▸ **to pay attention to** ▪ beachten, achten auf
Charles did not pay much attention to what his brother was saying.

attitude ▪ Einstellung, Haltung
He has a very conservative attitude towards almost everything.

aware ▪ bewusst
Sorry, I wasn't aware that there is a speed limit here.

belief ▪ Überzeugung
It is my firm belief that democracy is the best political system.

to believe ▪ glauben
The train is delayed again! I don't believe it!

bright ▪ intelligent
Mike is a wonderful boy, bright and funny.

certain ▪ sicher, bestimmt
He was quite certain that he would be successful.

to choose (chose, chosen) ▪ wählen
Be careful what sports you choose.

to concentrate ▪ sich konzentrieren
She was so successful at school because she was able to concentrate on her tasks.

to conduct ▪ durchführen, leiten
The financial authorities conducted an enquiry into the company's financial affairs.

consideration ▪ Überlegung
My brother never takes an important step without a lot of consideration.

to contain ▪ zurückhalten
He had difficulties containing his anger.

to determine [dɪ'tɜːmɪn] ▪ entscheiden, beschließen
The workers determined to go on strike.

to discover ▪ entdecken
When they returned home, they discovered that their house had been broken into.

doubt ▪ Zweifel
The judge had serious doubts about Mr Mitchell's alibi.

▸ **no doubt** ▪ wahrscheinlich, sicher
What you say is no doubt true, but it is beside the point.

to encourage ▪ ermutigen, unterstützen
Her parents always encouraged her to take up a hobby.

to estimate ▪ (ein)schätzen
The architect estimated the cost of building our house at € 300,000.

fact ▪ Tatsache, Fakt(um)
The fact is that most people don't know more than two languages.

▸ **as a matter of fact** ▪ eigentlich
As a matter of fact, I wanted to talk about something quite different.

fame ▪ Ruhm
Her fame was based on her personal integrity and high intelligence.

to fear ▪ fürchten, sich Sorgen machen
I fear I've made a big mistake.

fear ▪ Angst
As a child Mr Scrooge always had a fear of getting poor.

to feel (felt, felt) ▪ fühlen, spüren
He felt a sharp pain in his arm.

▸ **to feel out of place** ▪ sich deplatziert fühlen
In the presence of all these important people Oliver felt completely out of place.

▸ **to feel sorry for s.o.** ▪ Mitgefühl mit jdm. empfinden
When she heard about the couple's separation she felt very sorry for them.

to focus ▪ sich konzentrieren
He had difficulties focusing on the speech because it was so boring.

foolish ▪ dumm, töricht
Foolish Tom keeps betting on hopeless horses.

to forget (-got, -gotten) ▪ vergessen
I shall never forget what you have done for me.

to form ▪ formen, bilden
After the discussion I was at last in a position to form my own opinion.

to hear [hɪə] (heard [hɜːd], heard [hɜːd]) ▪ hören
There's no need to shout. I can hear you perfectly well.

to imagine [ɪˈmædʒɪn] ▪ sich (etwas) vorstellen; sich einbilden
Just imagine you have become very rich. What would you do with your wealth?
None of this is true. You're just imagining things.

judgement ▪ Einschätzung; Urteilsvermögen
In my judgement the other driver is to blame for the accident.
Mr Myers was a man of very good judgement.

to know [nəʊ] (knew, known) ▪ wissen, kennen
She knows a lot about her husband because they've known each other for years.

knowledge [ˈnɒlɪdʒ] ▪ Wissen, Kenntnis
After his year in Italy Oliver had a very good knowledge of Roman history.

to learn [lɜːn] (learnt/learned, learnt/learned) ■ lernen; erfahren
Most young children learn to read and write a little before they go to school.
We learnt of her illness only after it was too late.

to listen ■ zuhören; horchen
Will you please listen to what I am telling you?
Listen! Do you hear the noise outside?

loud ■ laut
She spoke in a very loud voice.

memory ■ Erinnerung, Gedächtnis
Ruth has a very good memory. She never forgets any telephone number.

mental ■ geistig, mental
Pupils with mental problems require special help.

mind ■ Verstand; Geist
He has a beautiful mind.
An old proverb says, "Out of sight – out of mind".

narrow ■ beschränkt
He has rather narrow views.

noise ■ Lärm, Geräusch
We were woken up by some noise in the room next to ours.

noisy ■ laut
Our hotel room faced a very noisy street.

to note ■ wahrnehmen, bemerken; beachten
They noted something strange outside.
We beg to note that the front seats are reserved for special guests.

to notice ■ bemerken
They noticed at once that there was something wrong.

observation ■ Beobachtung
After the operation the patient was under strict observation for several days.

to occur (occurred, occurred) ▪ (jdm.) einfallen

It occurred to me just now that Marian rang to say she might come this afternoon.

to pick ▪ aussuchen

There are five books. Pick the one you like best.

▸ **to pick up** ▪ auf-, hochheben

Can I help you pick up the suitcase?

pressure ▪ Belastung

He was under a lot of pressure in his job.

probably ▪ wahrscheinlich

I'm not quite certain, but that's probably Mr Snyders over there.

project ▪ Projekt, Entwurf

The scientists were working on a new project to generate electricity.

quiet ['kwaɪət] ▪ leise; still; ruhig

We heard some quiet music in the background.

Please be quiet. I can't hear the news.

Marc is always very quiet at a party.

reaction ▪ Reaktion

His first reaction was to panic.

to read [riːd] (read [red], read [red]) ▪ lesen

Reading books was Juliet's hobby.

reader ▪ Leser(in)

The number of readers has declined in recent years.

to realize ▪ erkennen, wahrnehmen

Sorry, Officer, I didn't realize that this is a one-way street.

reason ▪ Grund, Anlass; Vernunft; Denkvermögen

There is a very good reason for me to stop smoking – my health.

The eighteenth century was called the Age of Reason.

A major difference between animals and man is man's power of reason.

reasonable ▪ vernünftig

Can you give me one reasonable argument why I should not study?

to recall ▪ sich erinnern
For some time he did not recall the day on which the accident happened.

recognition ▪ (Wieder-)Erkennung; Anerkennung
Tony's face showed no sign of recognition when he saw his old friend for the first time after twenty years.
He was given a medal in recognition of his services to the community.

to recognize ▪ (wieder)erkennen; anerkennen; erkennen
Even after twenty years Tony recognized his friend immediately.
The government recognized his services to the community and gave him a medal.

to refuse ▪ ablehnen, sich weigern
He refused to help his friend out of his financial difficulties.

to regard ▪ anschauen; betrachten
He regarded the stranger with some skepticism.
I cannot regard this as a serious proposal. It's simply nonsense.

relaxation ▪ Entspannung
You look as if you could do with some relaxation.

to remember ▪ sich erinnern; denken an; sich merken
I distinctly remember locking the door last night.
I must remember to lock the door tonight.
The actor was trying to remember his text.

to reveal ▪ zeigen, enthüllen, offenbaren
At last the result of the vote was revealed.

review ▪ Überprüfung
A careful review of his position made the director change his attitude.

scene ▪ Aussicht
The photographer was basically interested in mountain scenes.

to see (saw, seen) ▪ sehen; verstehen
Please stand in the light. I can hardly see you.
Oh yes, I see what you have in mind.

to seem ▪ scheinen
I'm not quite sure, but the weather seems to be getting better.

▸ **it seems** ▪ wie es scheint, anscheinend
It seems I made a mistake.

sense ▪ Verstand; Gefühl
No one with any sense will take his comments seriously.
I felt a great sense of relief after the operation had been successful.

to settle ▪ entscheiden; erledigen
After long talks it was settled where we would be going on holiday.
At last this problem was settled.

sight ▪ Sicht; Anblick
Get out of my sight.
In my sight, we do not have a solution yet.
It was love at first sight.

silence ▪ Stille, Schweigen
On the news of the president's death there was complete silence in the assembly.

to smell (smelt/smelled, smelt/smelled) ▪ riechen an; duften
I've smelt the roses. They smell lovely.

smell ▪ Geruch; Duft
There's a strange smell in this room.
That perfume has a lovely smell.

sound ▪ Laut; Ton; Geräusch
The cat made soft sounds.
The clarinet has a very pleasing sound.
There were strange sounds from the neighbouring flat.

sport ▪ ⚠ Vergnügen, Spaß
The party games were great sport.

to suppose ▪ annehmen, glauben
I suppose this is your house, isn't it?

sure ▪ sicher
Are you quite sure that this is their house?
Sure, I'll be back in ten minutes.

to surprise ▪ überraschen
We were quite surprised when he suddenly turned up out of the blue.

surprise ▪ Überraschung
Oh, it's you! What a pleasant surprise.

to take for granted (took, taken) ▪ für selbstverständlich halten
Don't take too much for granted, young man!

to tend ▪ tendieren; (zu etwas) neigen
I tend to think that Mary is cleverer than Jonathan.
My brother has always tended towards modern art.

to think (thought, thought) ▪ denken; glauben; meinen
Descartes said "I think therefore I am".
I think you are right.
What do you think about this plan?

thought ▪ Gedanke; Überlegung
My parents slowly accepted the thought that I would become a painter.

▸ **on second thoughts** ▪ wenn ich es mir genau überlege
On second thoughts I think you are right.

threat [θret] ▪ Drohung
In his fury he made wild threats against everyone.

to threaten ['θretn] ▪ drohen
The criminals threatened to kill the young boy they had kidnapped.

understanding ▪ Auffassungsgabe
Little Mary has a very keen understanding.

to undertake (-took, -taken) ▪ sich verpflichten zu
He undertook to deal with this difficult problem.

view ▪ Sicht; Anblick, Aussicht
It was a clear day and the view was perfect.
From the top of Ben Nevis you have a lovely view.

to watch ■ aufpassen; zuschauen
Hey, watch where you're going.
My grandchildren like watching TV – but only children's programmes.

▸ **Watch out!** ■ Pass auf!
Watch out! There's a car coming.

▸ **Watch your step** ■ Vorsicht, Stufe!

wise ■ weise, klug
Given your talent, choosing maths as your first subject was very wise.

to worry ■ sich Sorgen machen
Don't worry, be happy.

---

alien ■ ⚠ fremd; Fremde(r)
Cheating other people was alien to his character.
Some people believe that one day aliens from outer space will invade earth.

to anticipate ■ vorhersehen, vorwegnehmen
There is no way of anticipating what the future will bring.

to bore ■ langweilen
All this talk about politics bored me so much that I left the party.

to bother ■ sich sorgen
Don't bother about tomorrow.

to conceive ■ sich (etwas) vorstellen
When he was young he couldn't conceive that he would be a famous artist one day.

conception ■ Konzeption, Vorstellung
His sister had no clear conception of what she would like to do after school.

to confuse ■ verwechseln; verwirren
Unfortunately the cook confused the salt and the sugar.
I'm afraid Martin is not too clever. Don't confuse him by using difficult words.

confusion ■ Verwirrung
The lecture was so complex that many students shook their heads in confusion.

conscious ■ bewusst
All her life she was conscious of her faults and shortcomings.

content [kən'tent] ■ zufrieden
They lived in poverty all their lives, but they were still content.

conviction ■ Überzeugung
She was a woman of firm convictions.

crack ■ Schlag
We heard a loud crack of thunder just before midnight.

to dare ■ sich trauen, riskieren, wagen
It takes some courage to dare to jump from a bridge on the end of an elastic rope.

to distinguish ■ unterscheiden, erkennen
It was so foggy that we couldn't distinguish anything clearly.

to distract ■ ablenken
Mary can't concentrate properly. She is so easily distracted.

to doubt ■ bezweifeln, Zweifel haben
I doubt that what you say is really true.

echo ■ Echo
He heard the echo of his voice quite clearly.

fool ■ Dummkopf
A fool will ask foolish questions.

to frighten ■ ängstigen, erschrecken
Walking through a dark forest frightens many young children.

furious ■ wütend
Joan was furious when she lost the race by only half a second.

glance ■ (flüchtiger, erster) Blick
She realized at a glance that the situation was rather difficult.

to guess ■ raten, annehmen, schätzen
If you don't know the correct answer you can still guess.

ignorant ▪ unwissend, ungebildet

I'm afraid he's an ignorant fellow. He doesn't know the first thing about anything.

imaginary ▪ imaginär, frei erfunden

She was so lonely that she kept talking to imaginary persons.

impression ▪ Eindruck

I have the impression that you are lying to me.

insight ▪ Einsicht, Verständnis

If you wish to get insight into this novel you should read it.

to inspire ▪ inspirieren, anregen

Mary was inspired by her father's talent as a musician to pursue the same career.

intellectual ▪ intellektuell; Intellektuelle(r)

Her spectacles and the intellectual books she was always reading gave her the appearance of an intellectual.

intelligence ▪ Intelligenz

Despite her remarkable intelligence Agatha had difficulties getting a good job.

intelligent ▪ intelligent, klug

It became obvious very early that the girl was highly intelligent.

mystery ▪ Rätsel, Geheimnis

What the witches really told Macbeth remained a mystery to him until the end.

to neglect ▪ vernachlässigen

The boss neglected his employees' wishes.

noticeable ▪ spürbar, wahrnehmbar

There was a noticeable difference between morning and evening temperatures.

observer ▪ Beobachter(in)

It was clear to every observer that something illegal was going on.

odd ▪ seltsam

His behaviour strikes me as rather odd.

to opt ▪ sich entscheiden
They opted for Italy rather than Spain as a holiday destination.

option ▪ Wahl, Möglichkeit, Option
As they were given the opportunity to choose they chose the second option.

to outline ▪ umreißen, skizzieren
Let me briefly outline what I have in mind before going more into detail.

to overlook ▪ übersehen
My father never overlooked the slightest mistake we made.

panic ▪ Panik
Panic broke out when the tourist coach was suddenly attacked by rebels.

to perceive ▪ wahrnehmen; betrachten
He perceived a marked change in his wife's attitude towards him.
She was early perceived as a star among singers.

perception ▪ Wahrnehmung; Auffassung
Eyes and ears are two major organs of perception.
In my perception honesty is a very important virtue.

perspective ▪ Perspektive, Blickwinkel
Travelling to foreign countries can give you an entirely new perspective on life.

to please ▪ gefallen
However much you try you'll never please everybody.

preparation ▪ Vorbereitung
Building a house requires a lot of preparation.

presumably ▪ vermutlich
I'm not quite sure, but it's presumably the house we are looking for.

probability ▪ Wahrscheinlichkeit
There is a distinct probability that you are wrong.

probable ▪ wahrscheinlich
The most probable reason for the accident was the driver's carelessness.

proposition ▪ Vorschlag
She regarded his proposition as rather indecent.

to provoke ▪ provozieren
Kevin is easily provoked to fury.

to question ▪ bezweifeln, Zweifel haben
I question the truth of your statement.

rational ▪ rational, vernünftig
He is a very rational person. He hardly ever shows any emotions.

to react ▪ reagieren
Most mothers react immediately when their child cries.

realism ▪ Wirklichkeitssinn
It is true he did not have much of imagination, but he had a keen sense of realism.

realistic ▪ realistisch
It is not realistic to suppose that there will be a time without any wars.

reflection ▪ Reflexion, Spiegelbild; Überlegung
There was no wind and so Martha saw her own reflection in the water.
After serious reflection we decided to accept Mary's proposal.

refusal ▪ (Ver-)Weigerung
His refusal to co-operate annoyed all his friends.

to regret ▪ bedauern; bereuen
We regret to inform you that your application has been rejected.
I deeply regret offending you by my remark.

to relax ▪ (sich) entspannen, ausruhen
Stop worrying. Just relax, and you'll feel better.

to rely on ▪ sich verlassen auf
You can really rely on her. She has never disappointed me.

to review ▪ überprüfen, überdenken
After reviewing his position the director made a few changes before speaking to the board.

to rush ▪ überstürzen
He makes a lot of mistakes because he keeps rushing into things.

to scan ▪ absuchen; überfliegen
The soldiers scanned the horizon for fighter planes.
On scanning the draft of his lecture he found a number of mistakes.

secret ▪ Geheimnis
It will always be a secret to me why you don't like cats.

to sense ▪ wahrnehmen, spüren
Percy sensed that there was something wrong.

sensibility ▪ Empfindsamkeit
In Jane Austen's "Sense and Sensibility" Marianne represents sensibility and Elinor sense.

sensible ▪ vernünftig
Can't you be a little more sensible?

silent ▪ still; schweigsam
At last the audience was silent.
He was always a very silent person.

smart ▪ schlau, clever
He is a very smart little chap.

to solve ▪ lösen
She solved the difficult problem within minutes.

sophisticated ▪ kultiviert
She is a very sophisticated lady.

to speculate ▪ spekulieren
We can only speculate – we don't really know what happened.

to spot ▪ sehen, entdecken
At last they spotted their son in the crowd.

stupid ▪ dumm, blöd
That was a very stupid mistake, Bill.

to suspect ■ vermuten, verdächtigen
The teacher suspected one of his students of having cheated.

suspense ■ Spannung
The suspense created in this movie is terrible.

suspicion ■ Misstrauen
Full of suspicion he asked, "What are you hiding?"

taste ■ Geschmack
Ken was not very fond of the taste of beer.

terrified ■ erschrocken; verängstigt
Jack was terrified when he heard the explosion.

thinking ■ Denken, Überlegung
Most listeners did not agree with the speaker's thinking.

thrill ■ Erregung, Nervenkitzel
Watching a good football match always gives me a thrill.

tired ■ müde
After walking for five hours in the mountains Andrew felt rather tired.

tolerant ■ tolerant
Most people are primarily tolerant towards themselves.

torture ■ Qual, Tortur
Waiting for the test result was torture.

touch ■ Tasten; Berührung; Gespür
Blind people have to rely on their sense of touch.
The light will go on at the touch of this button.
The older he got the more he lost touch with reality.

unwilling ■ widerwillig
He thought the fine was unfair and was unwilling to pay it.

to view ■ ansehen; betrachten
There were quite a few people who wanted to view the new house.
I'm afraid you've got to view this from a different angle.

visible ■ sichtbar, deutlich
There is a visible improvement in the patient's health.

vision ■ Vorstellung, Vision; Weitblick
Seeing planes in the sky always gives me a vision of going on holiday.
Jonathan is really a man with a vision.

visual ■ visuell, Seh…, Sicht…
We established visual contact with the driver before crossing the road.

to vow ■ geloben
After his accident he vowed never to drink alcohol again before driving.

vow ■ Versprechen; Gelübde
The couple exchanged their marriage vows before the magistrate.

to wander ■ abschweifen
At first he talked to the point but after a while he began to wander.

to wonder ■ sich fragen; sich wundern, staunen
I wonder whether we have enough flour for the cake we want to bake.
I shouldn't wonder if she left him. He is a terrible fellow.

wonder ■ Wunder
It's a wonder he passed the test because he did not really work very hard.

worry ■ Sorge
May this be the least of your worries.

1.5 Hygiene, Körperpflege, Gesundheit, Leben und Tod

agent ■ Wirkstoff
Pencillin is the main agent in many antibiotics.

antibiotic ■ Antibiotikum
Don't use antibiotics if you have a simple cold.

blood ■ Blut
When the doctor arrived, there was blood all over the floor.

bloody ▪ blutig
Although he fell down the stairs he got away with a bloody nose.

to break (broke, broken) ▪ (sich etwas) brechen
He broke his arm when he fell off his bike.

care ▪ Sorge, Sorgfalt
When Henry's mother was 85 she required a lot of care.

▸ **to take care of** (took, taken) ▪ sich kümmern um
My brother and I took care of our parents for twelve years.
So far the boss has taken care of these problems herself.

clean ▪ sauber, rein
We always keep our bathroom completely clean.

cold ▪ Erkältung
Sorry I can't come to class today. I have a very bad cold.

dead ▪ tot
When the doctor arrived the patient was dead.

death ▪ Tod
She was very sad when she heard of her cousin's death.

to die (dies; dying) ▪ sterben
All creatures die at the end of their lives.

disease ▪ Krankheit
A cold is not a disease you usually die of.

drug ▪ Medikament; Droge
Aspirin is a very traditional drug.

examination ▪ Untersuchung
The doctor carried out a careful examination of the patient.

to examine [ɪg'zæmɪn] ▪ untersuchen
The school doctor examined all the students.

family doctor ▪ Hausarzt, -ärztin
Our family doctor is always very busy.

to feed (fed, fed) ▪ ernähren, füttern
Little babies need to be fed up to six times a day.

filling ▪ (Zahn-)Füllung
I'm afraid I need to see my dentist – one of my fillings has come out.

handicapped ▪ behindert
After his accident he was severely handicapped for some time.

handkerchief (hankie) ▪ Taschentuch
A handkerchief is often simply called a hankie or a tissue.

health [helθ] ▪ Gesundheit
The older you are the more important is it to look after your health.

healthy ['helθi] ▪ gesund
Smoking is not healthy.

hospital ▪ Krankenhaus
He had a broken leg. That's why he was in hospital.

to hurt (hurt, hurt) ▪ (sich) verletzen; weh tun
Don't hurt children.
Ouch, that hurts.

ill ▪ krank
My father was seriously ill. So he had to be taken to hospital.

illness ▪ Krankheit
An ordinary cold is not usually a serious illness.

injury ▪ Verletzung
He suffered so many injuries in the accident that he died eventually.

life (Pl.: lives) ▪ Leben
Grandma was healthy all her life.

low ▪ schwach
I don't know what's wrong with me. I feel rather low.

medical ▪ medizinisch, ärztlich
After the accident Felix had to ask for medical help.

mental ▪ psychisch; seelisch
People with mental problems require medical help or psychological aid.

mild ▪ leicht
There's nothing seriously wrong. I simply have a mild cold.

muscle ▪ Muskel
He often went to a gym to develop his muscles and to look better.

to nurse ▪ pflegen
They nursed their old parents for several years.

to operate ▪ operieren
Dr Baker operated on five patients without taking a break.

operation ▪ Operation
It took the patient only a couple of days to recover after his operation.

pain ▪ Schmerz
When he broke his leg he cried out with pain.

patient ▪ Patient(in)
In every room in the hospital there were no more than three patients.

period ▪ Periode
Mary couldn't take part in PE because she had her period.

physical ▪ körperlich, physisch
He lost the match because of his poor physical condition.

pool ▪ Lache
The victim lay in a pool of blood.

to pump ▪ pumpen
When the heart does not pump enough blood through the body the patient may die.

to recover ▪ sich erholen, gesund werden
At last the patient showed signs of recovering.

recovery ▪ Erholung, Genesung
After his recovery from his hip operation Father went on a long holiday.

to refer (referred, referred) ▪ überweisen
My doctor referred me to a specialist.

to rest ▪ (sich aus)ruhen
After playing tennis for two hours I like to rest for some time.

rest ▪ Pause, Erholung, Ruhe
After this long walk her friends needed some rest.

restless ▪ ruhelos, unruhig
The older Dad gets the more restless he becomes. He walks around for hours during the night.

sight ▪ Sehvermögen
I'm afraid my sight is not what it used to be.

to sleep (slept, slept) ▪ schlafen
After her operation Dorothy slept for 24 hours.

sleep ▪ Schlaf
Sleep is important if you want to remain healthy.

spot ▪ Pickel
When Arthur was fifteen his face was full of spots.

to suffer ▪ erleiden
He suffered a heart attack and was taken to hospital.

test ▪ Test, Untersuchung
We need to do a number of tests before we can give you a precise diagnosis.

toothache ▪ Zahnschmerzen
William went to the dentist because he had a very bad toothache.

toothbrush ▪ Zahnbürste
She bought an electric toothbrush last week.

toothpaste ▪ Zahnpasta
I don't like this toothpaste. It has a strange taste.

to treat ▪ medizinisch behandeln
The doctor knew how to treat a severe cold.

treatment ▪ medizinische Behandlung
The doctor's treatment of my mother proved effective in the end.

unit ▪ Abteilung
Most hospitals have an intensive care unit.

variation ▪ Abweichung
The doctor found a serious variation in the patient's blood pressure.

vital ▪ essenziell, unerlässlich, lebensnotwendig
The heart and lungs are vital organs.

to wash ▪ waschen
Wash your hands with soap – they are really dirty.

weak ▪ schwach
The patient was very weak after the operation.

well ▪ gut; gesund
He wasn't feeling well, but now he is well again.

---

abortion ▪ Abtreibung
Quite a few people think that abortion should not be allowed.

ache [eɪk] ▪ Schmerz
I couldn't sleep all night because I had a dull ache in my head.

acute ▪ akut, scharf
The patient experienced an acute crisis before recovering eventually.

addict ['ædɪkt] ▪ (Drogen-)Abhängige(r), Süchtige(r)
Our neighbour is a real television addict.

addicted [ə'dɪktɪd] ▪ abhängig, süchtig
Don't drink too much alcohol. You might easily get addicted.

addiction [ə'dɪkʃən] ▪ Abhängigkeit, Sucht
Some 19th century artists suffered from opium addiction.

AIDS ▪ Aids
There is no cure yet for AIDS, the acquired immune deficiency syndrome.

alcoholic ▪ alkoholisch; Alkoholiker(in)
Not everybody who drinks alcoholic drinks is an alcoholic.

alive ▪ lebendig
It's really astonishing. My grandpa is 100 – and still alive and kicking.

allergic ▪ allergisch
Mary is allergic to nuts.

allergy ■ Allergie
Many people suffer from allergies in spring.

ambulance ■ Krankenwagen
There's been an accident! I think we should call an amublance.

asleep ■ schlafend
After his operation he spent most of the day asleep.

awake ■ wach
He had such pains that he lay awake all night.

▸ wide-awake ■ hellwach
Because of the thunderstorm he was wide-awake until late after midnight.

bacterium (Pl.: bacteria) ■ Bakterie, Bakterien
The flu is not caused by bacteria but by viruses.

bandage ■ Bandage, Verband
After the accident he had to wear a bandage round his arm for two weeks.

to bleed (bled, bled) ■ bluten
They were bleeding from several wounds.

blind ■ blind
When the poet John Milton became blind he dictated all his poems to his daughter.

breakdown ■ Zusammenbruch
When he heard of his wife's death he suffered a nervous breakdown.

to brush ■ bürsten
My wife brushes her long hair carefully every morning.

to bury (buries; burying) ■ beerdigen, begraben
The dead should be buried soon after their death.

cancer ■ Krebs
Cancer is one of the worst diseases of our age.

cemetery ■ Friedhof
The dead are buried in a cemetery or a churchyard.

check-up ■ gründliche Untersuchung
Before going on an expedition you should see a doctor for a check-up.

clinic ■ Klinik
His doctor advised him to go to a clinic for a general check-up.

clinical ■ klinisch
New drugs must undergo a clinical trial before they can be sold.

to collapse ■ zusammenbrechen, kollabieren
It was intolerably hot, which is why a lot of people collapsed.

collapse ■ Zusammenbruch, Kollaps
Her father suffered a serious collapse so she had to call an ambulance.

conscious ■ wach, bei Bewusstsein
You can't talk to the patient. He isn't conscious yet.

consciousness ■ Bewusstsein
After his accident he never regained consciousness and died two days later.

to consult ■ konsultieren, zu Rate ziehen
My father had been feeling ill for some time and at last consulted a doctor.

cosmetics ■ Kosmetik
My sister spends a fortune on cosmetics.

to cough [kɒf] ■ husten
John's parents didn't sleep all night, because their baby kept coughing.

cough [kɒf] ■ Husten
Sorry I can't come to the concert. I've got a very bad cough.

cream ■ Creme
Have you got some cream for dry skin, please?

to cure ■ heilen
I wish something was found to cure cancer at last.

cut ■ Schnitt
He had a bad cut in his hand so he went to see a doctor.

deaf [def] ■ taub

Don't talk to him. He can't hear you. He's deaf.

deodorant ■ Deodorant

If you sweat too much, a deodorant might help.

to depress ■ bedrücken, deprimieren

The cold and dark spring this year has depressed quite a few people.

depression ■ Depression

If you suffer from depression you require professional help.

diagnosis ■ Diagnose

Fortunately, the GP's diagnosis was only a mild cold.

diet ['daɪət] ■ Ernährung, Diät

He never lost weight in any of his diets.

to digest ■ verdauen

Chew your food properly so that it can be digested more easily.

disability ■ Behinderung

Young people with a disability ought to go to the same school as everyone else.

disabled ■ behindert

Cars for the disabled may be parked near the entrance.

dizzy ■ schwindlig

I never walk up a steep hill because standing on top makes me dizzy.

DNA ■ DNS

A person's DNA (desoxyribonucleic acid) is their genetic fingerprint.

dose ■ Dosis

The patient was given three doses of penicillin a day.

to ease ■ erleichtern, lindern

These pills will ease your pain.

emergency ■ Notfall

In an emergency just call 999.

to extract ■ (heraus)ziehen

The dentist said, "I'm afraid I'll have to extract this tooth."

to faint ▪ ohnmächtig werden

She went to see a doctor because she fainted so often.

fatal ▪ tödlich, fatal

Unfortunately her heart attack proved fatal.

fever ▪ Fieber

My uncle was running a fever of 40 degrees Centigrade, so we called a doctor.

flesh ▪ Fleisch

As a result of the knife attack the young man suffered a severe flesh wound.

flu ▪ Grippe

Every autumn and winter a lot of people have the flu.

funeral ▪ Beerdigung, Bestattung

The funeral of Mr Myers will take place on Monday in Glasgow's Hill Cemetery.

gene ▪ Gen

Catherine's excellent drawing skills must be in her genes.

genetic ▪ genetisch

Unfortunately, this disease is passed down genetically.

GP (General Practitioner) ▪ Arzt/Ärztin für Allgemeinmedizin, praktische(r) Arzt/Ärztin

My GP gave me an appointment for Friday.

grave ▪ Grab

Mum used to go to dad's grave every week before she became too weak to do so.

harm ▪ Schaden

Smoking and drinking can cause serious harm to your health.

harmful ▪ schädlich

Overheating your flat can be harmful to your health.

headache ['hedeɪk] ▪ Kopfschmerzen

When he woke up after the party he had a terrible headache.

to heal ■ heilen
Love and care can heal even a serious disease.

hygiene ['haɪdʒiːn] ■ Hygiene
Personal hygiene is very important if you wish to stay healthy.

hygienic [haɪ'dʒiːnɪk] ■ hygienisch
Could you please clean the bathroom? It doesn't look particularly hygienic.

to infect ■ anstecken
A vast number of people became infected by the virus.

infection ■ Entzündung
As a result of a serious infection I had to cancel my holidays.

infectious ■ ansteckend
The flu is a highly infectious disease.

to injure ['ɪndʒə] ■ verletzen
He was severely injured in the car crash.

insane ■ wahnsinnig
King Lear went insane when he discovered the unnatural conduct of two of his daughters.

lifespan ■ Lebensdauer, Lebenserwartung
In recent years the average lifespan of human beings has increased.

lifestyle ■ Lebensstil
We must improve our lifestyle in order to remain healthy.

lifetime ■ Lebenszeit, Leben
That is an experience you only make once in a lifetime.

lipstick ■ Lippenstift
My grandmother never used lipstick.

live ■ lebend
There were live fish in the aquarium.

madness ■ Wahnsinn, Geisteskrankheit
As a result of his madness Schumann spent the last years of his life in hospital.

make-up ▪ Makeup

Some women spend a fortune on make-up.

measles ▪ Masern

The measles is still a widespread illness among children.

medicine ▪ Medizin

Keep this medicine out of the reach of children.

misuse ▪ Missbrauch

The misuse of medicine is a grave problem.

mobile ▪ mobil, beweglich

My father-in-law is quite mobile because he can still drive his car.

mortal ▪ sterblich

Every creature is mortal.

mortality ▪ Sterblichkeit

Infant mortality in nineteenth century Europe was very high.

mumps ▪ Mumps, Ziegenpeter

Most children have mumps at some time.

nail file ▪ Nagelfeile

She keeps her fingernails short by using a nailfile only.

nail polish ▪ Nagellack

She painted her fingernails in the national colours of Britain.

nappy ▪ Windel

Baby's nappy should be changed regularly.

nervous ▪ nervös, Nerven…

After her husband's death she suffered a nervous breakdown.

operating theatre ▪ Operationssaal

Our hospital has six operating theatres.

to overcome (-came, -come) ▪ überwältigen

After working all day I was overcome with tiredness.

painful ▪ schmerzhaft

Having a tooth extracted can be rather painful.

perfume ▪ Parfüm

Chanel No. 5 is an expensive perfume.

pharmacy ▪ Apotheke

Medicine is usually bought and sold in a pharmacy.

pill ▪ Tablette, Pille

Many elderly people take large numbers of pills.

▸ to be on the pill ▪ die (Antibaby-)Pille nehmen

She has five children already. That is why she is on the pill now.

plaster ▪ Pflaster

Let me put a plaster on that cut.

poison ▪ Gift

Shakespeare has Richard II say, "They love not poison who do poison need".

poisonous ▪ giftig

The bite of a poisonous snake can be very dangerous.

powder ▪ Puder

Mark's sister bought some powder to cover her spots.

to prescribe ▪ verschreiben, verordnen

My doctor doesn't like to prescribe sleeping pills.

psychological ⚠ [saɪkə'lɒdʒɪkəl] ▪ psychologisch; psychisch

Medical doctors should have good psychological training.

After the death of his wife John had severe psychological problems.

razor ▪ Rasierapparat

Many women use razors for their legs.

remedy ▪ Heilmittel

Aspirin™ is a very popular remedy for all sorts of minor illnesses.

to retire ▪ sich zurückziehen

After lunch Aunt Mary announced that she was going to retire for an hour.

salty ▪ salzig

Salty food is not really healthy.

sauna ▪ Sauna

In Britain and the USA you are not supposed to go into the sauna naked.

scar ▪ Narbe

The operation has left rather a large scar across her belly.

seasick ▪ seekrank

Going on a cruise is not something I would like to do. I become seasick easily.

sensitive ▪ empfindlich

I must go and see a dentist. One of my teeth is very sensitive to heat.

shampoo ▪ Shampoo

She's got very long hair, which means she needs a lot of shampoo.

to shave ▪ (sich) rasieren

Some men need to shave twice a day.

shock ▪ Schock

She had to be taken to hospital because she was suffering from shock.

shower ▪ Dusche

Many people think they need to have a shower every day.

sick ▪ krank

He is terrible. He always thinks he is sick with something and needs to see a doctor.

signal ▪ Anzeichen

A fever is a clear signal that you are ill.

to smoke ▪ rauchen

Smoking is banned from restaurants because it is bad for the smokers' and other guests' health.

soap ▪ Seife

Wash your hands please and do use some soap.

sober ▪ nüchtern

All her friends were drunk, but she managed to remain sober.

sore ▪ wund

My feet are sore from all the walking.

▸ a sore throat ▪ Halsschmerzen

Sorry, I can't sing today. I've got a sore throat.

sperm ▪ Sperma, Samenzelle

The couple did not have any children because he had a low sperm count.

spray ▪ Spray

Sprays must not contain any CFC gases.

to starve ▪ hungern, Hunger leiden, verhungern

Every year thousands of children starve because they haven't eaten for weeks.

to sting (stung, stung) ▪ brennen, schmerzen

Her skin was stinging from sunburn.

stitch ▪ Stich

The doctor gave his wound five stitches.

strain ▪ Belastung, Anstrengung

If you have a weak heart you should avoid any unnecessary strain.

stress ▪ Stress, Belastung

Stress can lead to a heart attack.

stroke ▪ Schlaganfall

Arthur suffered a stroke last week and is in hospital now.

suicide ▪ Selbstmord

After his wife's death the old man was so desperate that he committed suicide.

to sunbathe ▪ sonnenbaden

Sunbathing without proper protection can be very dangerous to your health.

sunburn ▪ Sonnenbrand

The sun was so hot that I got a sunburn.

surgery ▪ chirurgischer Eingriff, Operation; Arztpraxis

I need some surgery on my shoulder.

Our surgery will be closed for vacation until 25 August.

survival ▪ Überleben

After his operation the patient is still fighting for survival.

to survive ■ überleben

Fortunately all the victims of the terrorist attack survived.

survivor ■ Überlebende(r)

Robinson Crusoe was the only survivor when his ship sank.

to sustain ■ am Leben erhalten

The amount of water left was barely enough to sustain him.

to swallow ■ schlucken

Doctor, I can hardly swallow.

to sweat [swet] ■ schwitzen

Sweating in the sauna bath is supposed to be healthy.

sweat [swet] ■ Schweiß

He broke into a cold sweat.

symptom ■ Symptom

A fever is usually a symptom of an illness.

tablet ■ Tablette

Tablet is just another word for pill.

tender ■ empfindlich

You must look after your son very carefully. His has a very tender stomach.

therapy ■ Therapie

There is no therapy yet to cure AIDS.

throat ■ Kehle, Hals, Rachen

I've got a sore throat. I'd better see a doctor.

to twist ■ verdrehen

I think I've twisted my ankle.

unconscious ■ bewusstlos

When she entered the bedroom she found her husband unconscious in bed.

to undergo (-went, -gone) ■ durchmachen, sich unterziehen

James had to undergo three operations before recovering eventually.

vacancy ['veɪkənsi] ▪ freier Termin
The doctor has a vacancy next Friday at 11 a.m.

virus ▪ Virus
The flu is a virus infection.

ward ▪ (Krankenhaus-)Station
The emergency ward is on the ground floor.

weakness ▪ Schwäche
He went to see his doctor because he felt a sudden weakness in his left arm.

wheelchair ▪ Rollstuhl
He was so weak that he had to use a wheelchair.

wound ▪ Wunde
He went to hospital to have his wound looked after.

X-ray ▪ Röntgenuntersuchung
The doctor gave my arm an X-ray because he thought it might be broken.

1.6 Charaktereigenschaften, Temperament, Fähigkeiten, Erfolg

ability ▪ Fähigkeit
She was a woman of many abilities and talents.

able ▪ fähig
Without much effort he was able to beat his partner.

to achieve ▪ erreichen
It takes a lot of skills to achieve your goals.

authority ▪ Autorität
In his field of science Albert Einstein was a world authority.

to bear [beə] (bore, borne) ▪ ertragen
I've borne this stress for five years, but I can't bear it any longer.

behaviour ▪ Benehmen, Verhalten
She is well-known for her good behaviour.

bright ▪ fröhlich
She really is a bright little girl.

can (could, could) ▪ können
Of course I can swim.

▸ **cannot, can't** ▪ nicht dürfen; nicht sein können
You cannot walk on this lawn.
You cannot be serious.

capable ▪ fähig, kompetent
Mary is a very capable manager.

capacity ▪ Kapazität, Fähigkeit
Her boss told her that she certainly had the capacity to assume more responsibility.

careful ▪ sorgfältig, vorsichtig
You can trust him to do this tricky job. He is very careful and won't do any damage.

character ▪ Charakter
He's rather a difficult character. He easily starts a fight.

characteristic ▪ Kennzeichen, Merkmal
Honesty and loyalty are her chief characteristics.

concentration ▪ Konzentration
Reading a Shakespeare text requires a lot of concentration.

control ▪ Kontrolle, Gewalt, Macht
You really must try not to lose control of yourself.

to cope with ▪ zurechtkommen mit
Are you sure you'll be able to cope with this problem?

could ▪ könnte(st, n, t)
I could do this for you if you like.

dear ▪ lieb, reizend
When Dorothy was young she was really a dear little girl.
Dear customers, we will be closed for the holidays.

direct ■ direkt, gerade, offen
She is very direct. She never beats about the bush.

effort ['efət] ■ Mühe, Anstregung
She passed the test without making very much of an effort.

to enable ■ befähigen, ermöglichen
Many young people study because they believe that this will enable them to get a good job.

experience ■ Erfahrung
If you have a problem just ask Richard. He has a lot of experience.

to fail ■ scheitern, durchfallen
Shackleton's attempt to reach the South Pole failed tragically.
Martin was so lazy that he failed in all his exams.

failure ■ Scheitern, Versagen; Versager(in)
Her failure was due to her long illness, because she was anything but a failure.

fond ■ liebevoll, zärtlich
All his life he's been a very fond husband.

friendly ■ freundlich
Miss Havisham was not very friendly to Pip.

funny ■ lustig, witzig, komisch
Clowns are often not funny as private individuals.

gentle ■ sanft, mild
My grandparents were very gentle people.

happy ■ glücklich, froh
As a young girl she was a very happy child.

to help ■ helfen
I don't know how to do this. Can you help me?

help ■ Hilfe
Henry was a great help to his father.

helper ■ Helfer(in)
I could do with a helper to carry this heavy box.

honest ['ɒnɪst] ■ ehrlich
As children we were always told to be honest – never to tell lies.

hopeless ■ hoffnungslos
John was rather hopeless in maths. He never got anything better than a "C".

impossible ■ unmöglich
It appears to be impossible to ensure peace between the Israelis and the Arabs.

kind ■ freundlich, liebenswürdig, nett
My parents have always been kind to strangers.

liberal ■ liberal, aufgeschlossen, tolerant; großzügig
My uncle has always been a liberal person.
He was always very liberal when he bought us presents.

loser ['luːzə] ■ Versager
He is a born loser. He never achieves anything.

manners (Pl.) ■ Betragen, Verhalten
She has really very good manners.

nice ■ nett
Don't be afraid of him. He is a very nice person.

patience ■ Geduld
Patience was Griselda's characteristic virtue.

patient ■ geduldig
I've never been a patient person.

pattern ■ Verhaltensmuster
Her behaviour always follows the same pattern.

perfect ■ perfekt
Nobody is perfect.

positive ■ positiv
Mary has a very positive attitude. She never complains.

possible ■ möglich
It is clearly possible for me to do this job.

power ▪ Macht
This king used his power justly.

practical ▪ praktisch (veranlagt)
I'm afraid I can't repair your bike because I'm not a very practical person.

principle ▪ Prinzip, Grundsatz
Timothy was a man of principles.

problem ▪ Problem
I've always had problems writing properly.

responsible ▪ verantwortungsbewusst
Victoria is a very responsible person. You can really trust her.

rough [rʌf] ▪ grob
It's very difficult to like him. He's such a rough character.

self-confidence ▪ Selbstvertrauen
Considering she is only seven, Maggie has a lot of self-confidence.

self-consciousness ▪ Gehemmtheit, Verlegenheit, Befangenheit
Self-consciousness is almost the opposite of self-confidence.

severe ▪ streng
Fortunately we did not have a very severe teacher.

solution ▪ Lösung
The government cannot find a solution to every problem.

straight ▪ offen, ehrlich
She will always be straight with you.

to succeed ▪ erfolgreich sein; gelingen
Whenever she really tried she succeeded.
After failing twice he eventually succeeded in passing the test.

success ▪ Erfolg
The director's recent film met with quite some success.

successful ▪ erfolgreich
Charles Dickens was a very successful novelist.

technical ▪ fachlich

Christopher refused to read the book because it was too technical for him.

trouble ▪ Mühe

After some trouble at first we managed to do the job.

to try ▪ versuchen

If the door won't open, try turning the key the other way.

unable ▪ unfähig, außerstande

He was unable to solve the easiest mathematical problem.

understanding ▪ Verständnis; Kenntnis

Only after much effort did I arrive at an understanding of this subject.

Sorry I can't help you but I have no understanding of this matter.

---

achievement ▪ Leistung

Winning the world championship was her greatest achievement.

to adapt ▪ (sich) anpassen, adaptieren

He has no problem adapting to new circumstances.

adorable ▪ hinreißend, entzückend, bezaubernd

Kathy is an adorable little child.

adventurous ▪ abenteuerlustig

Roald Amundsen, who won the race to the South Pole, was an adventurous scientist.

aggressive ▪ aggressiv

He is difficult to deal with because he is so aggressive.

alert ▪ munter, hellwach

Little Jacob is an alert little chap.

ambition ▪ Ehrgeiz

In order to be promoted you will have to show at least some ambition.

anxious ▪ besorgt, bestrebt

As a young person Pip was always anxious to rise in society.

assurance ■ Selbstsicherheit
Sir Simon Rattle conducted the orchestra with his usual assurance.

bad-tempered ■ schlecht gelaunt
Don't talk to him in the morning. He's always bad-tempered when he wakes up.

to behave ■ sich benehmen, sich verhalten
You will have to behave better if you want to go on studying here.

brave ■ mutig, tapfer
Come on, be a brave boy. The doctor won't harm you.

bully ■ Rüpel, Rabauke
Everyone is afraid of him. He is a real bully.

calm ■ ruhig, gelassen, friedlich
Nothing will upset him. He is such a calm person.

capability ■ Fähigkeit, Potenzial
Emily is a singer of some capability.

careless ■ unvorsichtig, leichtsinnig
He is much too careless to bother about details.

charming ■ charmant, reizend, bezaubernd
Susan is really a very charming person.

cheerful ■ fröhlich, heiter
She was such a cheerful character that everybody liked her.

civilized ■ zivilisiert; kultiviert
He knows a lot about art, literature, music – he's so civilized!

clever ■ schlau, klug
She was clever enough to do all her homework carefully so she passed all her tests easily.

clumsy ■ unbeholfen, ungeschickt
She was so clumsy that she would drop something or other almost every day.

confidence ■ Vertrauen, Selbstvertrauen
He had a lot of confidence in his own abilities.

confident ■ zuversichtlich, selbstsicher
I am quite confident that we will achieve our aim.

conventional ■ konventionell, traditionsgebunden
He never does anything but what is conventional.

courage ■ Mut
It takes a lot of courage to apologize for serious mistakes.

coward ■ Feigling
He's a real coward. He's afraid of the slightest incident.

curiosity ■ Neugier
Curiosity is his defining weakness – he simply wants to know everything.

curious ■ neugierig
People who are too curious sometimes hear what they do not wish to hear.

decent ■ anständig, freundlich
We require decent applicants because they will be in contact with customers.

determination ■ Entschlossenheit, Entschiedenheit
He is full of determination. He never gives up.

discreet ■ diskret
She is so discreet that you can tell her any secret.

discretion ■ Diskretion, Klugheit
In writing about other people you should show discretion.

dishonest ■ unehrlich
King Lear did not realize that his two elder daughters were dishonest.

distant ■ unnahbar
He is a very distant character. It is difficult to get into contact with him.

efficient ■ leistungsfähig, wirksam, effizient
You will not pass your exam if you do not learn to work more efficiently.

emotional ▪ emotional, gefühlsbetont
Mary is so emotional that she never listens to reason.

faithful ▪ treu
Mark is a very faithful friend.

fault ▪ Schuld, Fehler
Don't blame me for the accident. It wasn't my fault.

fluent ▪ fließend
After a year in the USA her English was really fluent.

frank ▪ offen, ehrlich
The candidate is very frank. He always says exactly what he thinks.

generous ▪ großzügig, reichlich
My father is a very generous man. He supports deserving causes generously.

grip ▪ Griff, Kontrolle
You must get a grip on your temper if you want people to like you.

helpful ▪ hilfreich
As a girl she was very helpful. She was always willing to help.

humorous ▪ humorvoll
My grandfather was a humorous person. He used to tell us funny stories.

humour ▪ Humor
The British have a different sense of humour from the Germans.

impatient ▪ ungeduldig
Don't be so impatient. Wait until it is your turn.

impolite ▪ unhöflich
Not greeting your guests is regarded as impolite.

inability ▪ Unfähigkeit
His inability to look after his money led to his financial problems.

indifferent ▪ gleichgültig
He had so much self-confidence that he was indifferent to other people's opinion.

intellectual ■ intellektuell
She is known for her intellectual achievements.

intolerable ■ unerträglich
His behaviour is simply intolerable.

keen ■ scharf
She has very keen eyesight.

kindness ■ Freundlichkeit, Liebenswürdigkeit
Kindness is his chief characteristic.

lazy ■ faul
He never gets anything done. He is so lazy!

liar ■ Lügner(in)
Don't believe a word he says. He is a notorious liar.

mean ■ geizig; gemein, schäbig
Ebenezer Scrooge in Dickens' "A Christmas Carol" is very mean.
Giving away your best friend's secrets is mean.

modest ■ bescheiden, zurückhaltend
Though very talented, she's modest about her achievements.

negative ■ negativ, ablehnend
Christine had rather a negative attitude towards any type of physical activity.

optimism ■ Optimismus
Optimism is a positive characteristic.

optimistic ■ optimistisch
Little Juliet had a optimistic attitude.

ordinary ■ gewöhnlich, normal
There is nothing special about him. He is quite an ordinary character.

personality ■ Persönlichkeit
Dorothy has a very cheerful personality.

pessimism ■ Pessimismus
Pessismism is her chief characteristic.

pessimistic ■ pessimistisch
My brother has a very pessimistic attitude.

pleasant ['plezənt] ■ nett, freundlich
Harry's boss was a very pleasant person.

polite ■ höflich
She is a polite young lady. You'll never hear a rude word from her.

prejudice ■ Vorurteil
He had a lot of prejudices all his life.

pride ■ Stolz
Mr. Darcy's chief characteristic in "Pride and Prejudice" is his pride.

primitive ■ primitiv
I don't like him. He is so primitive.

prize ■ Preis
Anne won a prize in a lottery – a trip to Mexico.

proud ■ stolz
Her daughter was proud to have taken her degree so well.

reliable ■ zuverlässig; vertrauenswürdig
Ask Arthur to do this job. He is absolutely reliable.
Dorothy is very reliable. You can tell her everything.

reserve ■ Zurückhaltung
Her natural reserve makes it difficult to get into contact with her.

to resist ■ widerstehen
He simply can't resist having a glass of whisky before going to bed.

resolution ■ Entschlossenheit
Mrs Thatcher was a woman of resolution and determination.

savage ■ wild, brutal; Wilde(r)
The boxer was known to be a savage fighter.
The savage is one of the few positive characters in Huxley's "Brave New World".

scepticism (AE: skepticism) ■ Skepsis
He is so full of scepticism. He never believes anything.

selfish ▪ egoistisch
Little children are often very selfish.

sensitive ▪ verständnisvoll, sensibel
Mark's teacher was a very sensitive person.

shy ▪ schüchtern, scheu
It is difficult to make friends with her. She is so shy.

sincere ▪ ehrlich, aufrichtig
When he apologized, you never knew whether he was being sincere.

snob ▪ Snob
He's an awful snob, constantly talking about his noble friends.

sober ▪ sachlich
He is never carried away by emotions. He is so sober!

stable ▪ stabil, ausgeglichen
She has been a stable person all her life.

steady ▪ solide, verlässlich
She is a very steady girl. You can always rely on her.

stern ▪ ernst, streng
Mr Gradgrind was a stern father.

stiff ▪ förmlich
I don't know what to talk about with him. He is so stiff.

still ▪ bewegungslos, still
Can't you sit still while I cut your hair?

straightforward ▪ aufrichtig
Catherine is an entirely straightforward person.

stubborn ▪ stur, dickköpfig
He was so stubborn that you could never change his mind.

suspicious ▪ argwöhnisch
Christine is a very suspicious person.

swing ▪ Schwankung
Arthur is given to sudden mood swings.

sympathetic ▪ mitfühlend, verständnisvoll
Marianne is very sympathetic to all people in need.

sympathy ▪ Mitgefühl, Verständnis
Pip learned to have sympathy even for a criminal like Magwitch.

tactful ▪ taktvoll
Diplomats must be very tactful.

talent ▪ Talent, Begabung
Jennifer has a talent for abstract thinking.

timid ▪ ängstlich, schüchtern
Shirley is a timid little girl.

tricky ▪ verschlagen
Be careful. He is very tricky.

triumph ▪ Triumph
Winning a gold medal at the Olympic Games was a real triumph for Usain Bolt.

typical ▪ typisch, charakteristisch
Being late is really typical of George.

uncertainty ▪ Unsicherheit, Ungewissheit
His behaviour was characterized by uncertainty.
He was in some uncertainty concerning the result of his exam.

unfriendly ▪ unfreundlich
I can't stand him. He is so unfriendly!

unkind ▪ unfreundlich, gemein
That was a very unkind remark.

unpleasant [ʌn'plezənt] ▪ unfreundlich
Our new neighbours are very unpleasant people.

unsuccessful ▪ erfolglos, vergeblich
His efforts to deal with the problem were unsuccessful.

upright ▪ aufrichtig, redlich
She's been an upright person all her life.

utopia ▪ Utopie
To enjoy eternal peace we'd have to live in Utopia.

villain ■ Schurke, Schuft
Richard III is the villain in Shakespeare's play.

virgin ■ Jungfrau
She's never had sex. She is still a virgin.

vulgar ■ vulgär
I can't stand him. He is so vulgar!

weakness ■ Schwäche, schwacher Punkt
He always had a weakness for sweets.

weird ■ seltsam, eigentümlich, merkwürdig
I've never liked your friend. I think he is rather weird.

wicked ■ böse, gemein; raffiniert, verführerisch
The young people's attack on the old lady was really wicked.
She appealed to me with her wicked looks.

to yield ■ nachgeben
She never yields to pressure.

1.7 Gefühl, Wünsche, Bedürfnisse, Ethik und Moral

to adore ■ anbeten; vergöttern, aufrichtig bewundern; sehr gern tun
There are religions in which more than one god is adored.
The old couple have always adored each other.
I adore going to the gym.

afraid ■ verängstigt, ängstlich
When he saw the wolf he was so afraid that he did not move.

▸ **to be afraid** ■ (be)fürchten
I'm afraid I've lost my keys.

▸ **to be afraid** als Ausdruck höflichen Bedauerns: Leider …
I'm afraid you can't disturb him now.

aim ■ Ziel, Absicht
For a long time it was Marcus' aim to become a pilot.

to appeal ■ zusagen, reizen; bitten, flehen
Her looks and her charm appeal to me very much.
He appealed to me to help him.

desire ■ Wunsch, Verlangen
All his life he had the desire to become a scientist.

dream ■ Traum
It's been always my dream to have a house in Scotland.

duty ■ Pflicht
"It is my duty to do everything I can for our country," the prime minister said.

to expect ■ erwarten, annehmen
I expect you to be always honest with me.

feeling ■ Gefühl
Marianne in Jane Austen's "Sense and Sensibility" is ruled by feeling.

frustrating ■ frustrierend
It's so frustrating. However little I eat I never lose weight.

fun ■ Spaß
We had a lot of fun at Henry's party.

glad ■ froh
The student was glad when at last he had passed the exam.

goal ■ Ziel(vorstellung)
It has always been one of her goals in life to become a famous artist.

happy ■ glücklich, froh
As a young girl she was a very happy child.

to hate ■ hassen, nicht ausstehen können
Children often hate keeping their rooms tidy.

hate ■ Hass
He was full of hate when he found that his wife had left him for another man.

honour ['ɒnə] ■ Ehre
On my honour, I shall never do this to you.

to hope ■ hoffen
I hope I'll pass the exam.

hope ■ Hoffnung
My grandfather's main hope was to come home after the war.

to insist on ■ bestehen auf
Despite the icy roads he insisted on going to work by car.

to intend ■ beabsichtigen, vorhaben
My father intends to go to Torquay for a holiday this year.

intention ■ Absicht
It is definitely not my intention to hurt your feelings.

jolly ■ fröhlich, lustig
...for she is a jolly good fellow.

joy ■ Freude, Vergnügen
It was a real joy to see the little girl playing with her toys.

to lie (lies; lying) ■ lügen
Lying is a part of human nature.

lie ■ Lüge
Telling lies is not acceptable in politics.

to like ■ gern haben; mögen
She likes her cousin very much.
Jonathan likes swimming, but on cold days he likes to stay at home.

luck ■ Glück
With a lot of luck you can win in a lottery.

to mean (meant [ment], meant [ment]) ■ wollen, anstreben, vorhaben
His sister has always meant to become a doctor.

merry ■ fröhlich
We wish you a merry Christmas and a happy New Year.

moral ■ moralisch
It is your moral duty to report crimes to the police.

to need ■ brauchen, benötigen
What we need most in this situation is food.

need ■ Bedarf
There is an urgent need for hospitals in this area.

to plan ■ planen
We're planning to go to New Zealand next year.

pleasure ['pleʒə] ■ Freude, Vergnügen
It gives us great pleasure to announce the birth of our first child.

▸ **to take pleasure in** ■ sich erfreuen an, Vergnügen haben an
I've always taken pleasure in classical music.

positive ■ zuversichtlich
I am quite positive that we will win the match.

to prefer [prɪ'fɜː] ■ bevorzugen, vorziehen
Many men prefer beer to wine.

rather ■ lieber
Usually I like beer, but today I'd rather have a glass of wine.

▸ **rather than** ■ anstatt
Rather than eat meat I have decided to eat fish today.

relief ■ Erleichterung
Can you imagine my relief when I heard that Ken hadn't been injured in the accident?

sad ■ traurig
Liz was really sad when her dog died.

spirit ■ Stimmung, Geist; Einstellung
She was in the right spirit for a party.
You're in the right spirit to win the match.

▸ **in high spirits** ■ in gehobener Stimmung
After their victory the team were in high spirits.

to suffer ■ leiden
The children suffered a lot when their parents died.

truth ■ Wahrheit
She could always rely on their children speaking the truth.

to want s.th. ▪ etwas wünschen; etwas brauchen
She always gets what she wants.
Your hair wants cutting.

will ▪ Wille
Where there's a will there's a way.

to wish ▪ wünschen
I wish we had known this a little earlier.

wish ▪ Wunsch
Your wish is my command.

---

admiration ▪ Bewunderung
Many people still have a lot of admiration for their kings and queens.

alarm ▪ Besorgnis
When I heard there would be a hurricane I was filled with alarm.

to amaze ▪ erstaunen, verblüffen
King Richard II was amazed that his cousin did not kneel to him.

anger ▪ Ärger, Zorn, Wut
She was full of anger when she realized that her husband had deceived her.

angry ▪ verärgert, zornig, wütend
John Osborne wrote a play about angry young men.

to annoy ▪ ärgern, nerven
His impudent behaviour annoyed me very much.

anxiety ▪ Angst, Sorge
He was always full of anxiety that something might happen to his children.

ashamed: to be ashamed (was, been) ▪ sich schämen
You ought to be ashamed of yourself.

to astonish ▪ erstaunen, verblüffen
I was astonished to hear that I had failed the exam.

awkward ▪ unangenehm, peinlich
Oh dear, we'll miss the appointment. How awkward.

compassion ▪ Mitleid
Florence Nightingale felt compassion for the wounded soldiers in the Crimean War.

conscience ▪ Gewissen
It weighed heavily on Jim's conscience that he had caused an accident.

crazy ▪ verrückt, wahnsinnig
You're driving me crazy with your complaints.

delight ▪ Freude
Listening to classical music was my mother's chief delight.

delighted ▪ hocherfreut, vergnügt
She was delighted to hear that she had passed the exam.

desirable ▪ erstrebenswert, reizvoll
She always thought it desirable to become a medical doctor.

despair ▪ Verzweiflung
His son's notorious lying drove him to despair.

desperate ▪ verzweifelt
When I found that I had no money in my account I was really desperate.

to dream (dreamt [dremt] /dreamed, dreamt [dremt] / dreamed) ▪ träumen
Many young people dream of becoming superstars one day.

emotion ▪ Emotion, Gefühl
When Liz is in love she is so full of emotions that she cannot think clearly.

enthusiasm ▪ Begeisterung, Enthusiasmus
John was full of enthusiasm for all sorts of pop music.

enthusiastic ▪ begeistert, enthusiastisch
My friend Dieter is an enthusiastic supporter of Manchester City.

expectation ■ Erwartung
Her father's expectation was that Margaret should be happy all her life.

to fake ■ fälschen; vortäuschen
As he did not wish to go to school he faked a headache.

to fancy ■ gern tun, mögen
I don't fancy clearing all this rubbish.

to fascinate ■ faszinieren
Even as a young girl Florence Nightingale was fascinated by nursing.

fascinating ■ faszinierend
The music was really fascinating.

fascination ■ Faszination, Beigeisterung
He had a fascination for classical music.

to feel low ■ niedergeschlagen sein
After his defeat in the election the candidate felt quite low.

fury ■ Wut
She flies into a fury whenever she is contradicted.

grateful ■ dankbar
He is a very nice chap. He's even grateful for small mercies.

habit ■ (An-)Gewohnheit
It is a very nasty habit to keep contradicting people.

happiness ■ Glück, Zufriedenheit
What counts in life is happiness, not money.

homesick ■ heimwehkrank
Some boys had to leave the holiday camp because they were homesick.

hopeful ■ zuversichtlich
He had worked very hard so he was hopeful to pass the exam.

hopefully ■ hoffentlich
Our team has been rather poor lately. Hopefully they'll win the next match.

immoral ▪ unmoralisch
Many conservative people regard birth control as immoral.

to impress ▪ beeindrucken
The mere fact that someone has a lot of money does not impress me.

indecent ▪ unanständig
She regarded his behaviour as rather indecent.

intense ▪ intensiv, ernst
The divorce of his parents caused him intense stress.

laugh [lɑːf] ▪ Lachen
The comedy raised a lot of laughs in the audience.

to long ▪ sich sehnen
After so many months away he longed for his wife and children.

lucky ▪ glücklich; Glücks…
Ken was very lucky when he got the job.
Elinor was convinced that fifteen was her lucky number.

mad ▪ verrückt; wütend
Are you mad? You just frightened me to death.
My sister was mad at me when she discovered that I read her emails.

melancholy ▪ Melancholie
The foggy weather filled him with melancholy.

miserable ▪ elend, unglücklich
After his divorce John felt miserable for a long time.

to miss ▪ vermissen
Whenever Mary was away from home, she missed her family.

mood ▪ Stimmung, Laune
For several months after her father's death she was not in a mood for parties.

motivation ▪ Motivation
Jack felt no motivation to study during his holidays.

necessity ▪ Notwendigkeit, Lebensnotwendiges
Food is one of the basic necessities.

outburst ■ Ausbruch
There was an outburst of joy when the home team scored a goal.

particular ■ anspruchsvoll
With regard to food he is rather particular.

passion ■ Leidenschaft
All his life he had a passion for classical music.

pity ■ Mitleid
They felt a lot of pity for their aunt when they heard that her husband had died.

▸ what a pity / it's a pity ■ schade!
What a pity you can't come to our party.

pleased ■ froh; zufrieden
He was pleased to hear that he had won a prize.
The teacher was pleased with the students' performance.

preference ■ Vorliebe
I have a clear preference for wine.

rage ■ Wut
Henry gets into a rage quite easily – often without provocation.

reluctant ■ widerwillig
Mary was reluctant to follow her mother's advice.

resignation ■ Resignation
He sighed with resignation on receiving another letter of refusal.

respectable ■ anständig, ehrbar
Mr Smith was considered respectable by his neighbours.

sadness ■ Traurigkeit
It is with sadness that we advise you of the death of our senior partner.

satisfaction ■ Befriedigung, Zufriedenheit
Job satisfaction is more important to me than earning a lot of money.

to scare ■ erschrecken, Angst machen
The mere sound of a barking dog scares my brother.

scared ▪ verängstigt
When Mr Macomber saw the lion he was too scared to shoot.

scary ▪ unheimlich
Thomas Harris' "The Silence of the Lambs" is a rather scary movie.

to seek (sought, sought) ▪ anstreben; erbitten
After eight years as President Barack Obama could not seek re-election.
Henry sought permission to take part in the meeting.

sensation ▪ Gefühl, Empfindung
I had the strange sensation that I was being watched.

sentimental ▪ sentimental, gefühlvoll, empfindsam; Gefühls…
Joan's father was in a very sentimental mood on her wedding day.
He kept his wife's early letters for sentimental reasons.

shame ▪ Scham(gefühl)
How can you beat a child? Have you no shame?

shock ▪ Schreck
The unexpected explosion gave me a shock.

shocking ▪ schockierend
Mary and John have separated? – How shocking.

to sigh ▪ seufzen, aufatmen
Peter sighed with relief when he heard that he had passed the exam.

solemn ▪ ernst, fest
I give you my solemn promise that I will never leave you.

to stir ▪ (an)rühren, bewegen
The priest stirred his audience with his moving speech.

to suit [suːt, sjuːt] ▪ passen
Tomorrow morning? – That suits me fine.

to suppress ▪ unterdrücken
Can't you suppress your hatred just for once?

to sustain ▪ erleiden; aufrechterhalten
He sustained another serious loss.
It was the thought of travelling to the United States soon that sustained me.

taste ▪ Vorliebe
She has a taste for tall, blond men.

tear ▪ Träne
She wept tears of joy.

temper ▪ Laune, Stimmung; Wut
As a typical optimist he was always in a good temper.
He flew into a terrible temper.

tension ▪ Spannung, Anspannung
Physical exercise always helps me to reduce any tension.

terror ▪ schreckliche Angst
Charles, who is ninety, always lives in terror of burglars.

thirsty ▪ durstig
After climbing this steep hill I was very thirsty.

thoughtful ▪ nachdenklich
When she heard of her husband's illness she became rather thoughtful.

to tremble ▪ zittern, beben
When she heard of her boyfriend's betrayal she trembled with rage.

uncomfortable ▪ unbehaglich
George always felt uncomfortable at large parties.

uneasy ▪ unwohl, unsicher
Whenever he saw his mathematics teacher he felt uneasy.

unfortunate ▪ unglücklich, bedauerlich
It is rather unfortunate that nobody really likes him.

unhappiness ▪ Traurigkeit
After the death of his wife he was the very picture of unhappiness.

unhappy ■ unglücklich; unzufrieden
She was unhappy because her friend had left her.
He was rather unhappy with his poor performance.

upset ■ bestürzt; aufgebracht
They were upset when they heard of their father's accident.
Marian was really upset because her daughter had not remembered her birthday.

vice ■ Laster
Jealousy is a widespread vice ...

virtue ■ Tugend
... and justice is a virtue.

want ■ Mangel
We often suffered from a want of money when we were young.

to weep (wept, wept) ■ weinen
She wept for joy when she heard that her sister was well again.

willing ■ bereit, gewillt
I am always willing to listen to reasonable advice.

willingness ■ Bereitschaft, Bereitwilligkeit
The willingness of people to help the victims of the flood was impressive.

1.8 Religion und das Übernatürliche

belief ■ Glaube
Muslims, Jews and Christians share the belief in one god.

Bible ■ Bibel
The Old Testament of the Bible is the basis of the Jewish religion.

Christmas ■ Weihnachten
At Christmas Christians all over the world celebrate the birth of Christ.

church ■ Kirche
Churches tend to be full in times of crises.

to create [kri'eɪt] ▪ (er)schaffen
A lot of people believe that God created the world in seven days.

creation [kri'eɪʃən] ▪ Erschaffung
According to the Bible, the creation of the world took God only seven days.

faith ▪ Glaube, Vertrauen
I have complete faith in God's love.

to forbid (-bade, -bidden) ▪ verbieten
In the Hindu religion it is forbidden to kill cows.

god ▪ Gott
Especially in times of crises many people believe in a god.

hell ▪ Hölle
There are people who believe that everyone who is not a Christian will go to hell.

holy ▪ heilig
Saints are people who are believed to have lived holy lives.

Islam ▪ der Islam
Islam is a world religion.

Islamic ▪ Islamisch
Islamic art is different from Christian art.

Lord ▪ Herr, Gott
May the Lord be with you.

minister ▪ Geistliche(r)
A member of the Protestant clergy is often called a minister.

order ▪ Orden
The Benedictine order was established in 529.

religion ▪ Religion
Christianity, Buddhism and Islam are the world's most widely spread religions.

religious ▪ religiös
Many young people in western countries are not very religious.

sin ▪ Sünde
Lying and stealing are sins.

soul ▪ Seele
May his soul rest in peace.

spirit ▪ Geist; Gespenst; Seele
May the Father, the Son and the Holy Spirit bless you.
Nowadays many people do not believe in ghosts and spirits.
May your spirit find peace in heaven.

---

abbey ▪ Abtei
Westminster Abbey is London's best known church.

angel ▪ Engel
Many people believe that God has sent them an angel to protect them in their lives.

apostle ▪ Apostel
St. Peter was the apostle whom Christ made the first leader of his church.

archbishop ▪ Erzbischof
The Archbishop of Canterbury is the spiritual head of the Anglican Church.

being ▪ Existenz, Wesen, Sein
Whether we owe our being to God or to chance is hotly debated nowadays.

bell ▪ Glocke
The bells of our church can always be heard 15 minutes before mass begins.

to bend (bent, bent) ▪ beugen
When you are in front of the altar you are supposed to bend your knees.

bishop ▪ Bischof
The bishop of Rome is the Pope.

to bless ▪ segnen
God bless you.

Boxing Day ▪ Zweiter Weihnachtstag

On Boxing Day, i.e. on 26 December, employers used to give their staff boxes with Christmas presents.

cathedral ▪ Dom, Kathedrale, Münster

Cologne Cathedral is one of the most attractive sights in Germany.

Catholic ▪ katholisch; Katholik(in)

The number of Catholics and Protestants in Germany is almost identical.

chapel ▪ Kapelle

Our university has a chapel to serve both Protestants and Catholics.

charity ▪ Wohltätigkeit, Nächstenliebe

Faith, hope and charity are the main Christian virtues.

Christ ▪ Christus

Christ is said to have died on the cross to save mankind.

Christian ▪ Christ(in)

Christians believe that Christ saved the world.

Christianity ▪ Christentum

Christianity is supposed to be a peaceful religion.

clergy ▪ Geistlichkeit

For instance priests and preachers are members of the clergy.

clergyman ▪ Geistlicher

In the past many younger sons of earls and dukes became clergymen.

clergywoman ▪ Geistliche

In most Protestant churches there are also clergywomen.

cross ▪ Kreuz

The Cross is a symbol of Christianity.

curse ▪ Fluch

A curse is an appeal to God to do something bad to someone else.

devil ▪ Teufel

The devil's other name is Satan.

to devote ■ widmen, weihen
Saint Elisabeth of Thuringia devoted her life to helping the poor.

dignity ■ Würde
Priests' lives should be characterized by dignity and piety.

doctrine ■ Doktrin, Lehre
It is one of the key doctrines of Christianity that God knows everything.

Easter ■ Ostern
Easter is the festival celebrating Christ's rise from the dead.

essence ■ Wesen
Faith, hope and love are the essence of Christianity.

evil ■ böse, schlecht; das Böse, das Schlechte
By definition human beings can distinguish between good and evil.

fanatic ■ fanatisch, Fanatiker(in)
Fanatic followers of certain religions sometimes even commit suicide in order to show their faith.

fantasy ■ Hirngespinst
Most people regard the belief in ghosts as mere fantasy.

fate ■ Schicksal
My grandfather believes the fate of human beings is not in their own hands.

ghost ■ Geist, Gespenst
Strangely enough, some people do believe in ghosts.

heaven ■ Himmel
Most religious people hope to go to heaven after their death.

Lord's Prayer ■ Vaterunser
The Lord's Prayer begins with the words, "Our Father".

magic ■ Zauber(ei), Magie
The waters of the Red Sea parted as if by magic.

mass ■ (heilige) Messe
Catholics are supposed to go to mass on Sundays and holidays.

mercy ■ Gnade, Barmherzigkeit

Genghis Khan showed no mercy for his enemies.

miracle ■ Wunder

The Bible reports many miracles performed by Jesus.

mission ■ Mission

He became a priest because he wanted to work in a mission in Africa.

monastery ■ Kloster

Priests who live in a monastery are called monks.

monk ■ Mönch

Monks are priests who do not work in a parish but live in a monastery.

Muslim ■ Moslem(in)

Muslims, Jews and Christians share a belief in only one God.

myth ■ Mythos

Some people say that Christianity is no more than a myth.

mythology ■ Mythologie

Greek mythology with all its gods and heroes is rather difficult to follow.

nun ■ Nonne

Hildegard von Bingen was a well-known medieval nun.

paradise ■ Paradies

Some people live good lives because they hope to go to paradise after their deaths.

parish ■ Pfarrgemeinde

The number of parishes has been decreasing for some time.

pilgrim ■ Pilger(in)

Since 1400 pilgrims in England make a journey to Canterbury.

pious ['paɪəs] ■ fromm

Mary is a very pious lady. She goes to church every day and prays a lot.

Pope ■ Papst
After the resignation of Pope Benedict XVI, Pope Francis was elected in 2013.

to pray ■ beten
Let us pray for our new bishop.

prayer ■ Gebet
Every night I say a prayer before going to bed.

to preach ■ predigen
Our priest will preach far longer than necessary.

priest ■ Priester(in), Geistliche(r)
In almost all religions there are priests.

prophet ■ Prophet(in)
Muhammad is one of Allah's prophets.

Protestant ■ protestantisch; Protestant(in)
The number of Protestants and Catholics in Germany is roughly identical.
There are many Protestant churches in the world.

to repent ■ bereuen, Buße tun für
The sinner repented his sins.

Reverend ■ Pfarrer(in), Pastor(in)
The service will be taken by the Reverend Laurence Sterne.

saint ■ Heilige(r)
Saint George is a very popular saint in England.

sect ■ Sekte
Within the Christian Church there are many sects.

sermon ■ Predigt
John Knox was known for his very long sermons.

spell ■ Zauber, Bann
Even today some people believe in the power of spells.

spiritual ■ spirituell, geistig
Muhammad was the spiritual leader of Islam.

supernatural ▪ übernatürlich
Many people even nowadays believe in supernatural phenomena.

superstition ▪ Aberglaube
Crossing your fingers to avoid a misfortune is a sign of superstition.

to swear (swore, sworn) ▪ schwören
I swear by God that this is the truth.

synagogue ▪ Synagoge
Jews pray in a synagogue.

temple ▪ Tempel
Prambanan in Indonesia is one of the best known temples in the world.

to trust ▪ vertrauen
"In God we trust" is the motto of the USA.

veil ▪ Schleier
In many religious orders nuns wear a veil.

vicar ▪ Pfarrer(in)
"The Vicar of Wakefield" is a novel by Oliver Goldsmith.

Whitsun ▪ Pfingsten
Whitsun is celebrated seven weeks after Easter.

witch ▪ Hexe
A witch is a woman thought to have made a pact with the devil.

wizard ▪ Hexer, Zauberer
A wizard is the male equivalent of a witch.

worship ▪ Anbetung, Gottesdienst
This church is a place of worship and not a museum.

2. Gesellschaft

2.1 Familie

to adopt ▪ adoptieren
They had no children of their own so they adopted a little girl.

aunt ▪ Tante
My father's and my mother's sisters are my aunts.

background ▪ Herkunft
She had a very good family background.

brother ['brʌðə] ▪ Bruder
My brother is five years older than I am.

to call ▪ nennen
The Duchess of Cambridge and Prince William called their first son George.

child (Pl.: children) ▪ Kind
My children moved far away from the place of their birth.

Dad(dy) ▪ Papa
Most young children call their father Dad.

daughter ▪ Tochter
Henry VIII's daughter Elizabeth became one of the greatest queens of England.

to depend on ▪ abhängen von
As a student I depended on my parents because I didn't have any money of my own.

family ▪ Familie
In my family there are several twins.

father ▪ Vater
Mozart's father was also a famous musician.

father-in-law ▪ Schwiegervater
My wife's father, i.e. my father-in-law, was a teacher.

generation ▪ Generation
The younger generation have not experienced any war for more than seventy years.

Gran(ny) ▪ Oma
Most children call their grandmothers simply Gran.

grandchild ▪ Enkelkind
Uncle Albert has five grandchildren.

granddaughter ▪ Enkelin
Beatrice and Eugenie are two of Queen Elizabeth II's granddaughters.

grandfather ▪ Großvater
The Duke of Edinburgh is Prince William's grandfather.

grandmother ▪ Großmutter
In 2013 the Queen was the grandmother of eight grandchildren.

Grandpa ▪ Opa
As a boy I called my grandfather simply Grandpa.

grandparent ▪ Großelternteil
In the past, many grandparents used to live with their children.

grandson ▪ Enkel
Mary's grandson studied English, as did her father and grandfather.

husband ▪ Ehemann
When a man and a woman marry, they become husband and wife.

to maintain ▪ erhalten, pflegen
Our family have always maintained very close relationships.

marriage ▪ Ehe; Trauung
Their marriage ended only six weeks after their marriage at St. Peter's.

Mom (AE) ▪ Mama, Mutti
American children often call their mothers Mom.

mother ▪ Mutter
The mother of Queen Elizabeth II died at the age of 102.

mother-in-law ▪ Schwiegermutter
My mother-in-law still drives her car although she is almost ninety.

Mum(my) ▪ Mama, Mutti
She always addresses her mother as Mum.

parent ▪ Elternteil; Mutter…
The little girl was brought up by only one parent.
A parent company is a firm that owns or controls other firms.

parents ▪ Eltern
My parents always spend their holidays in Italy.

related ▪ verwandt
I'm related to Lizzy. She is my aunt's daughter. So we're cousins.

relation ▪ Verwandte(r)
We have quite a few relations in Britain.

sister ▪ Schwester
My sister went to London for a week.

son ▪ Sohn
My son now works as a lawyer.

trouble ▪ Ärger
I had a lot of trouble with my computer.

uncle ▪ Onkel
My father's and my mother's brothers are my uncles.

wife (Pl.: wives) ▪ Ehefrau
Henry VIII had six wives.

---

ancestor ▪ Vorfahre, Vorfahrin
My parents, grandparents etc. are my ancestors.

brother-in-law ▪ Schwager
Henry does not like his brother-in-law – because he married his sister.

childhood ▪ Kindheit
Parents should ensure that their children have a happy childhood.

cousin ▪ Cousin, Vetter, Cousine
My brother's children are my children's cousins.

daughter-in-law ▪ Schwiegertochter
When my son married I did not lose a son, I rather won a daughter-in-law.

dependent ▪ finanziell abhängig
Many young people live with their parents because they are dependent.

favourite ▪ Liebling, Lieblings…
Of all my grandchildren Luke is my favourite.
Of all holiday resorts Las Vegas is clearly my favourite destination.

fiancé [fiːɑːn'seɪ], fiancée ▪ Verlobter, Verlobte
In the past more couples were fiancés and fianceés before they married than today.

guardian ▪ Vormund
After the death of Eliza, her uncle was appointed her guardian.

to inherit ▪ erben
Agatha has inherited her mother's talent for mathematics.

nephew ▪ Neffe
My nephew, i.e. my sister's son, has moved to New Zealand.

niece ▪ Nichte
My brother's daughter Barbara, my niece, studied Philosophy at university.

to obey ▪ gehorchen
Children are supposed to obey their parents.

offspring ▪ Nachwuchs, Junge(s)
My brother is quite funny. He refers to my children as my offspring.

parents-in-law ▪ Schwiegereltern
Mary's parents-in-law lived in the same city all their lives.

to shape ▪ formen, prägen
Children's social behaviour is largely shaped by their parents.

sister-in-law ▪ Schwägerin
My sister-in-law was an English teacher.

son-in-law ▪ Schwiegersohn
Mr Stephens does not like his son-in-law simply because he married his daughter.

stepbrother ▪ Stiefbruder
Henry is my stepbrother, because he is the son of my mother's second husband.

stepfather ▪ Stiefvater
After my father's death my mother married Mark, my stepfather.

stepmother ▪ Stiefmutter
Prince Charles' second wife is Prince William's and Prince Harry's stepmother.

stepsister ▪ Stiefschwester
Mary, my stepmother's daughter, is my stepsister.

twin ▪ Zwilling
John and Mike are twins; Mike is ten minutes older.

union ▪ Union, Vereinigung
The traditional family begins with the union of husband and wife in marriage.

upbringing ▪ Erziehung
Her friends' children enjoyed a very good upbringing.

2.2 Persönliche Beziehungen

to accept ▪ akzeptieren
I cannot accept this behaviour.

affair ▪ Affäre
His wife left him because of his affairs with other women.

to affect ▪ beeinflussen, betreffen
Have you considered that what you do also affects other people?

alone ▪ allein
After her parents' death she was all alone.

anonymous [əˈnɒnɪməs] ▪ anonym
John never reads e-mails from anonymous senders.

to be attached to ▪ hängen an
They weren't really attached to each other very much.

to attract ▪ anziehen, Aufmerksamkeit erregen
Her appearance and her charm attracted all her friends.

attraction ▪ Anziehungskraft
From the start there was a lot of attraction between Peter and Anne.

to be concerned ▪ betroffen sein, besorgt sein
Fortunately we were not concerned by the strike.
They were very concerned when they heard about their friend's accident.

to boast ▪ prahlen, angeben
Stop boasting about your tennis skills.

boyfriend ▪ (fester) Freund
A girl's male friend is her boyfriend.

to break up (broke, broken) ▪ beenden
When Anne found that Mark had cheated her she broke up the relationship at once.

civil ▪ höflich
In a conversation with strangers one ought to be as civil as possible.

concern ▪ Angelegenheit; Besorgnis
What I do in my free time is no concern of yours, my friend.
The large number of accidents is a matter of considerable concern.

consideration ▪ Rücksicht
Young people should show some consideration for old people.

contact ▪ Kontakt, Verbindung
I'll get into contact with him immediately.

couple ▪ (Ehe-)Paar
The couple has been married for 25 years.

▸ **a couple of** ▪ ein paar, einige
What I like best for breakfast is a couple of eggs.

fellow ▪ Kerl, Freund, Typ
My friend is really a very good fellow.

to forgive (-gave, -given) ▪ vergeben
Whatever he did, she always forgave him.

girlfriend ▪ feste Freundin
Come on, Bob is only ten! Of course he doesn't have a girlfriend yet.

to give (gave, given) ▪ geben, schenken
What has your brother given you for your birthday?

▸ **to give away** ▪ verschenken, spenden; verraten
If you do not wear that coat any longer, give it away to people in need.
Don't give away what I've just told you. It's supposed to be a secret.

▸ **to give in** ▪ nachgeben
Henry is very stubborn. However much he may be in the wrong, he'll never give in.

▸ **to give out** ▪ austeilen, vergeben
The lecturer gave out the exam papers.

▸ **to give up** ▪ aufgeben
He only became such a well-known sportsman because he never gave up.

▸ **given ...** ▪ angenommen, in Anbetracht, angesichts der/des
Given the bad weather we shall have to cancel the excursion.
Given the difficult economic situation our company has done very well.

guy ▪ Typ, Kerl
John is a very nice guy.

guys (Pl.) ▪ Leute
"Guys" as a form of address is sometimes used for both men and women.

to ignore ▪ ignorieren, nicht beachten
Do you know why he keeps ignoring me?

individual ▪ einzeln; Individuum
He has his own individual style of writing.
Every individual ought to enjoy the same rights.

to influence ▪ beeinflussen
His mother kept trying to influence him even when he was forty.

influence ▪ Einfluss
Unfortunately his cousin had a very bad influence on him.

to introduce ▪ vorstellen
Let me first introduce you to my stepson.

to invite ▪ einladen
What a shame. I wasn't even invited to my brother's birthday party.

to joke ▪ spaßen, Witz(e) machen
Arthur was the soul of the party because he kept joking all night.

joke ▪ Spaß, Streich
Wilhelm Busch's Max and Moritz like playing jokes on other people.

to kiss ▪ küssen
Kissing people on the cheek is something different from kissing them on the mouth.

to love ▪ lieben
Ruth and Charles love each other very much.

love ▪ Liebe
The couple were deeply in love.

▸ **to fall in love** ▪ sich verlieben

to marry ▪ heiraten
After living together for six years they at last married.

master ▪ Herr; Meister(in)
The dog always obeyed his master.
Stephen King is a master of the horror novel.

to meet (met, met) ▪ (sich) treffen, begegnen
How about meeting for lunch on Monday?
I met an old friend on my way to school.

partner ▪ Partner(in)
Although Martin and Dorothy were partners for ten years they never married.

personal ▪ persönlich, privat
They entertained a very close personal relationship.

popular ▪ beliebt, populär
Queen Victoria was very popular.

to praise ▪ loben
If you never praise your child, you cannot expect it to love you.

present ▪ Geschenk
I was given a new camera as a birthday present.

to promise ['prɒmɪs] ▪ versprechen
Kenny promised that he would look after Isabel's cat when she was on holiday.

proposal ▪ Antrag
Arthur made a proposal of marriage to Evelyn.

to propose ▪ einen Heiratsantrag machen
Henry has proposed to Elizabeth. The wedding is to take place in June.

to quarrel ▪ streiten
William and Harry are always quarrelling.

quarrel (BE: quarrelled; quarrelling; AE: quarreled; quarreling) ▪ Streit
It took her some time to stop the quarrel among her children.

relationship ▪ Verhältnis
It is important to have a good relationship with your colleagues.

relative ■ Verwandte(r), Angehörige(r)
Joan and Ken are my relatives.

respect ■ Respekt; Rücksicht
You are supposed to show some respect to your boss.
Respect for the elderly is a common thing in East Asia.

round ■ Folge
For him, life often is simply a round of parties.

row ■ Streit, Krach
In this context "row" rhymes with "now".

to see (saw, seen) ■ sich treffen, besuchen
I'm afraid we can't come. We're seeing my parents at the weekend.

sex ■ Geschlechtsverkehr
We have sex several times a week.

sexual ■ sexuell; Sexual…
The scientific study of sexual behaviour started in the 1940s and 1950s.

sorry ■ tut mir leid; entschuldigen Sie …, Verzeihung …
Sorry, I can't come to your party.
Sorry but I can't help you.

to thank ■ danken, sich bedanken
Mary thanked her friend for helping her with her homework.

tool ■ Mittel
For Margaret, Jim was a mere tool to achieve her goals.

towards ■ gegenüber
The people in that country are usually friendly towards strangers.

to treat ■ behandeln
Pip was treated cruelly by Estella.

treatment ■ Behandlung
The children never forgave their father for their rough treatment.

trust ■ Vertrauen
He had complete trust in the honesty of his wife.

to accompany (-nies; -nying) ▪ begleiten
He never accompanies his wife when she goes shopping.

acquaintance ▪ Bekannte(r)
John is not my friend, he is just an acquaintance.

affection ▪ Zuneigung
Children must be brought up with a lot of affection.

alliance ▪ Bündnis, Allianz
The children formed a firm alliance against their new stepmother.

anniversary ▪ Hochzeitstag, Jahrestag
Jacqueline's parents celebrated their silver wedding anniversary in 2010.

to apologize ▪ sich entschuldigen
Mary apologized to Jack for causing him trouble.

apology ▪ Entschuldigung
Look at what you've done to my dress. The least I can expect is an apology.

authoritarian ▪ autoritär
In the past many parents brought up their children in a very authoritarian way.

bachelor ▪ Junggeselle
Henry's brother was a bachelor all his life. He never married.

to be bound (was, been) ▪ verpflichtet sein
He felt bound to keep his promise.

to be rid of (was, been) ▪ (jdn./etwas) los sein
Marian was glad that she was at last rid of her stepfather.

bitch ▪ Hexe, Miststück
Calling a woman a bitch is extremely insulting.

to blame ▪ verantwortlich machen
Don't blame me for the failure of our marriage.

bond ▪ Bindung
There was always a very firm bond between my mother and my father.

to bother ■ (sich) ärgern, stören
Her tendency to be late bothered me very much.

bouquet ■ (Blumen-)Strauß
My friends brought me a lovely bouquet when they came to visit me.

breach ■ Bruch
She accused her friend of a breach of confidence.

bride ■ Braut
On her wedding day the bride was dressed all in white.

bridegroom ■ Bräutigam
... and her bridegroom wore a tuxedo.

chap ■ Typ, Kerl
Mike is really a very nice chap.

childhood ■ Kindheit
We had a very happy childhood.

to comfort ['kʌmfət] ■ trösten
When Mary lost her job, her boyfriend tried to comfort her.

comfort ['kʌmfət] ■ Trost
The love of her children was Jennifer's only comfort after her husband's death.

companion ■ Begleiter(in), Kamerad(in)
Harriett is the best companion to her old aunt.

compliment ■ Kompliment
I got a lot of compliments for my new hairstyle.

co-operative ■ kooperativ, hilfsbereit
Elizabeth was very co-operative – she was always willing to help.

darling ■ Liebling, Schatz
June was her father's darling.

to date ■ (mit jdm.) ‚gehen'
When Julia was thirteen she dated a young boy from her neighbourhood.

date ■ Verabredung
Sorry, I can't come to your party. I have a date already.

to deceive ■ betrügen, täuschen
It took quite a while before he found that his wife had deceived him.

to disappoint ■ enttäuschen
He was very disappointed when he found that his friend had cheated him.

disappointment ■ Enttäuschung
The loss of his job was one of the big disappointments of his life.

disgrace ■ Schande, Schmach
Mary told her brother he was a disgrace to his family.

to disgust ■ ekeln, anwidern, empören
Mary was disgusted with her brother's cruel treatment of animals.

to dislike ■ nicht mögen, nicht leiden können
As a young man I always disliked living with my parents.

to divorce ■ sich scheiden lassen
They divorced after only three years.

divorce ■ Scheidung
Unfortunately, quite a number of marriages end in divorce.

enemy ■ Feind(in)
Jim has always been his own worst enemy.

to expose ■ aussetzen; bloßstellen
You mustn't expose babies to frost and rain.
Parents should not expose their children's weaknesses in public.

favour ■ Gefallen
Could you do me a favour and lend me your racket?

to fulfil (-filled, -filled) ■ erfüllen
She is not a very reliable person. Often she doesn't fulfil her promises.

gift ■ Geschenk
Mr Scrooge made his parish a gift of £10,000.

influential ■ einflussreich
Miss Havisham was highly influential in shaping Pip's character.

to insult ■ beleidigen
He insulted me by claiming that I had cheated him.

insult ■ Beleidigung
Calling someone a liar is an insult.

to integrate ■ (sich) eingliedern, (sich) integrieren
If you emigrate to a foreign country you should integrate as soon as possible.

integration ■ Eingliederung, Integration
The integration of handicapped people is very important.

to interact ■ aufeinander einwirken, interagieren
The sooner people learn to interact properly the better.

to interfere ■ sich einmischen, stören
Stop interfering. Your silly remarks don't really help.

interference ■ Einmischung
Interference in other people's problems can be very problematic.

invitation ■ Einladung
My mother sent invitations to her birthday party to twenty people.

jealous ■ eifersüchtig; neidisch
Their marriage did not work because he was so jealous.
She is always jealous of other people's success.

jealousy ■ Eifersucht
Othello's main vice was his jealousy.

lonely ■ einsam
Many people are lonely when they are old.

long-term ■ langfristig, Langzeit…
Some people don't marry because they don't like long-term relationships.

to look after ■ sich kümmern um, aufpassen auf
In the past it was only the women who had to look after their children.

lover ■ Liebhaber(in), Geliebte(r)
Casanova had a large number of lovers.

loyal ▪ loyal, treu
My father was always my most loyal friend.

loyalty ▪ Loyalität, Treue
She always felt a sense of loyalty to her friends.

mate ▪ Kumpel
Henry always went on holiday with his mates.

misunderstanding ▪ Missverständnis
It took them some days to clarify the misunderstanding between them.

mutual ▪ gegenseitig
What made them become friends was their mutual enthusiasm for golf.

neighbo(u)r ▪ Nachbar(in)
We've liked our neighbours ever since we moved in.

neighbo(u)rhood ▪ Nachbarschaft
We live in rather a strange neighbourhood.

to offend ▪ beleidigen
Mary doesn't like Martin because he keeps offending her.

outsider ▪ Außenseiter(in)
She is such an odd character that she has always been an outsider.

pair ▪ Paar
Kate and William are a lovely pair, aren't they?

to pardon ▪ verzeihen
Whatever her children did, she was always prepared to pardon them.

to pat ▪ tätscheln
Quite a few children do not like being patted on the head.

pregnancy ▪ Schwangerschaft
Liza's friend was delighted to hear of her pregnancy.

pregnant ▪ schwanger
Joan and Charles threw a party when they heard that she was pregnant.

promise ▪ Versprechen
Scarlett did not keep her promise to be faithful to her husband.

to punish ▪ bestrafen
In the past children would be punished for whatever wrong they did.

punishment ▪ Strafe
Physical punishment is definitely not the best strategy in educating children.

to repair ▪ wiedergutmachen
After their controversy it took Henry and Matthew several months to repair their relationship.

to respect ▪ respektieren, anerkennen
Henry is the most respected person in our club.

romantic ▪ romantisch
Sport is my husband's only topic. I wish he was a little more romantic.

rude ▪ unhöflich; unanständig
I do not like him at all. He is so rude!
He keeps making rude remarks.

scandal ▪ Skandal
Her indecent behaviour is really a scandal.

secret ▪ heimlich
He had long been her secret admirer but at last he declared his love for her.

to separate ['sepəreɪt] ▪ sich trennen; auseinander gehen
After only three years of living together Marion and Bert separated.

separation ▪ Trennung
The separation of their parents caused their children some problems.

stability ▪ Beständigkeit
My parents' marriage was characterized by stability.

stranger ▪ Fremde(r)
Young Goodman Brown did not realize that the stranger he met in the forest was the devil.

strict ▪ streng; strikt
In the past parents used to be stricter than today.
He had strict instructions to look after his younger brother.

tactic ▪ Taktik
Agreeing to everything is no good tactic in a negotiation.

to tease ▪ necken
He kept teasing his friends.

tender ▪ zärtlich
He is a very tender husband and father.

trick ▪ Streich
Don't play tricks on me, young lady.

wedding ▪ Hochzeit
The wedding will take place at Dunblane on Saturday at 11 a.m.

wedding anniversary ▪ Hochzeitstag
We celebrated our golden wedding anniversary in 2014.

wedding ring ▪ Ehering
Germans usually wear their wedding ring on their right-hand ring finger.

2.3 Soziales und soziale Dienste

aid ▪ Hilfe, Unterstützung
There are quite a few organizations supplying aid to those in need.

to appeal ▪ appellieren
After the earthquake the inhabitants appealed to the public to help them.

appeal ▪ Appell
The appeal for help met with huge success.

arrangement ▪ Abmachung, Vorbereitung, Plan
The arrangement was to meet on Friday.

to associate with ▪ verkehren mit
His sister was very shy. She did not easily associate with anybody.

association ▪ Vereinigung
The Red Cross is major aid association.

benefit ▪ Unterstützung
When you are out of a job you'll be paid unemployment benefit for a limited period.

to care for ▪ sich kümmern um, sorgen für
After his wife's death he had to care for his three children.

▸ **to care about** ▪ sich interessieren für, sich etwas machen aus
I don't care about your opinion.

circumstance ▪ Umstand, Tatsache
The family lived in rather difficult circumstances.

committee ▪ Komitee, Ausschuss
He was a busy person. He sat on a large number of committees.

community ▪ Gemeinschaft, Gemeinde
Our neighbourhood is a very close community. Everybody knows everybody else.

conflict ▪ Konflikt, Auseinandersetzung
William is a very peaceful boy. He always tries to avoid conflicts with others.

contribution ▪ Spende
She often makes a contribution to help people in need.

credit ▪ Ansehen, Verdienst
Our president enjoys a lot of credit.

to depend on ▪ sich verlassen auf
She is very reliable. You can always depend on her.

elderly ▪ ältere(r, s)
Politicians and families are equally responsible for looking after elderly people.

fair ▪ fair, gerecht
Our English teacher is always fair.

friend ▪ Freund(in)
Jane and Mary are good friends, so are Tom and Will.

friendship ▪ Freundschaft
Friendship is a very important element in society.

gang ▪ Bande, Gang
The police thought that a gang had caused the trouble at the match.

to gather ▪ sammeln, sich versammeln
Hundreds of people gathered at of the cinema to watch the film.

group ▪ Gruppe

member ▪ Mitglied
Many people in Germany are members of a club.

need ▪ Notlage
It is the state's responsibility to help those in need.

to offer ▪ anbieten
Can I offer you a drink?

organization ▪ Organisation, Verband
The OECD is the Organization for Economic Cooperation and Development.

to organize ▪ organisieren

party ▪ Party

people ▪ Menschen, Leute
A lot of people came to the funeral.

poor ▪ arm
Poor people ought to be helped by society.

population ▪ Bevölkerung; Bevölkerungszahl
In 2013 the average age of the population in Germany was 46 years.
Britain has a population of some 64 million.

provision ▪ Vorsorge; Versorgung, Bereitstellung; Vorkehrung
Most people make some provision for their old age.
The local authorities are responsible for the provision of cheap housing for the poor.
We have made provision to protect ourselves against the flood.

public ▪ öffentlich; Öffentlichkeit
There is a public telephone at the end of the park.
The theatre is now open to the public.

▸ **in public** ▪ in der Öffentlichkeit

purpose ▪ Grund, Zweck; Absicht; Ziel
The company made a collection for financial purposes.
Sorry, I didn't hit you on purpose.
The purpose of this collection is to help people in need.

relief ▪ Hilfe, Hilfs…
The Red Cross, a relief organization, provided relief to the victims of the war.

rich ▪ reich
Some professional football players are extremely rich.

to share ▪ (sich) teilen
Roger and Ken decided to share one car.

share ▪ Anteil
John paid a fifty-per-cent share of the rent for the apartment.

show ▪ Demonstration
Hundreds of people gathered in the square for a show of solidarity with the miners.

social ▪ gesellschaftlich, sozial
The large number of unemployed young people is a serious social problem.

society ▪ Gesellschaft
Children and old people are the weakest groups in society.

status ▪ Status, Stellung
Her promotion gave her an entirely new social status.

structure ▪ Struktur

to support ▪ unterstützen, sorgen für
One of the state's chief functions is to support the weak.

support ▪ Unterstützung
I could always rely on my parents' moral and financial support.

threat [θret] ▪ Bedrohung
Hooligans are a threat to peaceful citizens.

tradition ▪ Tradition

traditional ▪ traditionell

trouble ▪ Unruhe
There was a lot of trouble when the Sharks and the Jets met in New York.

unemployment benefit ▪ Arbeitslosengeld
In Britain, unemployment benefit was about £70 per week in 2014.

unfair ▪ ungerecht
It is unfair to pay men and women differently for the same job.

to visit ▪ besuchen
What about visiting Mary and Ken in Munich?

visitor ▪ Besucher(in)
At our party there were also visitors we hadn't invited.

working class ▪ Arbeiterklasse
Friedrich Engels wrote a book on the condition of the working class in England.

youngster ▪ Jugendliche(r)
A number of youngsters were celebrating the victory of their team.

---

to abandon ▪ im Stich lassen, verlassen, aufgeben
He did not know what to do when his parents abandoned him.

acceptable ▪ akzeptabel, annehmbar
Being late for a job interview without a proper excuse is not acceptable.

assistance ▪ Unterstützung, Hilfe
People in need require assistance.

to be involved in ▪ verwickelt sein in, beteiligt sein an
He is often involved in fights with his friends.

casual ▪ zufällig, gelegentlich
We like having casual parties with our friends.

to celebrate ■ feiern
Our friends invited fifty people to celebrate their silver wedding anniversary.

celebration ■ Feier
When the students had taken their exams, the university organized a celebration.

ceremony ■ Zeremonie, Feierlichkeit
There was a moving ceremony to mark the end of the war.

clash ■ Zusammenstoß, Konflikt
There were often clashes on whether to put meat or fish on the menu.

collective ■ kollektiv, gemeinsam
Coping with this crisis requires a lot of collective effort.

conduct ■ Verhalten, Benehmen
The group was so noisy that its members were arrested for their conduct.

to confront ■ konfrontieren, entgegentreten
You'd better not confront him when he is in a bad mood.

to congratulate ■ gratulieren
Grandpa was annoyed because his grandson didn't congratulate him on his birthday.

congratulation ■ Gratulation, Glückwunsch
The mayor wrote us a letter of congratulation on our golden wedding anniversary.

consensus ■ Übereinstimmung, Konsens
The club members reached a consensus that their chairman should resign.

consent ■ Zustimmung
You cannot do this without everybody's consent.

convention ■ Brauch, Konvention
My parents' life was governed by conventions and traditions.

custom ■ Brauch, Angewohnheit
It is a custom in Germany to shake hands when you meet someone.

to disturb ■ stören
No, I'm afraid you can't disturb him right now. He's having a meal.

division ■ Verteilung, Teilung
Under the traditional division of labour women had to do the housework.

dull ■ langweilig
The party was incredibly dull so we left early.

embarrassed ■ verlegen, peinlich berührt
She looked quite embarrassed when she was caught without a ticket.

embarrassing ■ unangenehm, peinlich
Being unable to pay your restaurant bill is rather embarrassing.

to encounter ■ treffen, stoßen auf
When Christine worked abroad she encountered a large number of nice people.

encouragement ■ Ermutigung
Without encouragement from her parents she would not have passed her exam.

fight ■ Kampf, Schlägerei
He's a very difficult character. He will get into fights on the slightest provocation.

folk ■ Leute
Country folk find living in big cities rather difficult.

for the sake of ■ um … willen
He will do everything for the sake of his friend's well-being.

to guide ■ leiten, lenken, führen
Parents ought to guide their children through the difficult phases of their youth.

hatred ■ Hass
The hatred of other people is a very dangerous thing.

hierarchy ['haɪrɑːki] ▪ Hierarchie
In the past, most societies had very clear hierarchies.

host ▪ Gastgeber(in), Wirt(in)
When we arrived at our B&B the host showed us our room.

ideology ▪ Ideologie, Weltanschauung
According to ideology, women did not have the right to vote in the 19th century.

involvement ▪ Beteiligung, Verwicklung
His involvement in politics cost him some his oldest friends.

to isolate ▪ isolieren
Children should not be isolated from their parents.

liability ▪ Belastung
Bringing up children can be quite a liability.

lively ▪ lebhaft, lebendig
The party was dull at first but became really lively later on.

luxury ▪ Luxus
His ambition was to be able to live a life of luxury.

melting pot ▪ Schmelztiegel
US-American society is sometimes described as a melting pot of peoples.

membership ▪ Mitgliedschaft
Membership in this club is free.

middle class ▪ Mittelklasse
The Conservatives have always been a party of the middle class.

millionaire ▪ Millionär(in)
There are too many millionaires and too many poor people in our country.

mob ▪ Mob, Menschenmenge
The demonstrators found themselves surrounded by a mob of radicals.

to participate ■ teilnehmen
I have never before participated in a demonstration but this time I will.

participation ■ Teilnahme, Beteiligung
At only 55 per cent, participation in the general election was disappointing.

pension ■ Pension, Rente
States often pay a pension to old people.

pensioner ■ Pensionär(in), Rentner(in)
Many elderly people look forward to being pensioners.

plain ■ einfach
Many people like plain food.

popularity ■ Popularität, Beliebtheit
Popularity is not always a positive achievement.

poverty ■ Armut
Poverty is still a serious problem – even in rich countries like Germany.

privilege ■ Privileg, Vorrecht
Today we have the privilege of welcoming a very prominent guest.

provocation ■ Provokation
He becomes furious at the least provocation.

racial ■ Rassen…, rassisch
There are some serious racial problems in this part of the city.
There is some evidence of racial discrimination.

racism ■ Rassismus
Racism is a widespread phenomenon in many countries.

racist ■ Rassist; rassistisch
He was known as a notorious racist.
She annoyed everyone with her racist remarks.

refugee ■ Flüchtling
Civilized societies ought to help refugees from other countries.

registration ▪ Anmeldung, Registrierung

Registration for this programme will begin tomorrow at 10 a.m.

to resolve ▪ lösen, beilegen

Unions and management found it difficult to resolve their conflict.

shame ▪ Schande

Our street is the shame of the town.

slave ▪ Sklave(-in)

There haven't been any slaves in Germany since the middle of the 19th century.

slavery ▪ Sklaverei

In the United Kingdom slavery was abolished in 1833.

social security ▪ Sozialhilfe

It's a scandal that so many people have to rely on social security.

social worker ▪ Sozialarbeiter(in)

Jennifer works as a social worker for Oxfam.

to sort out ▪ in Ordnung bringen, klären

She helped the family to sort out their financial problems.

sponsor ▪ Sponsor(in), Förderer(-in)

A variety of companies acted as sponsors of the aid programme.

to take part in (took, taken) ▪ sich beteiligen an

Tens of thousands of people took part in the demonstration against racism.

Thanksgiving Day ▪ etwa: Erntedankfest

In the USA, Thanksgiving Day is celebrated on the fourth Thursday in November.

unity ▪ Einigkeit; Einheit

My parents lived in perfect unity all their lives.

Families are supposed to form a real unity.

upper class ▪ Oberklasse

Earls and dukes are certainly members of the upper class.

to value s.th. ▪ auf etwas Wert legen

In our club we especially value good manners and honesty.

VIP (Very Important Person) ▪ VIP, Promi
Some people think they are VIPs only because they have money.

voluntary ▪ freiwillig
He helped the police with their enquiries on a voluntary basis.

volunteer ▪ Freiwillige(r)
Hundreds of people worked as volunteers to fight the crisis.

vulnerable ▪ verletzlich, verwundbar
Children and old people are the most vulnerable members of society.

welfare ▪ Wohlergehen; Sozialhilfe
She is rather concerned about the welfare of her parents.
She doesn't want them to have to rely on welfare.

welfare state ▪ Wohlfahrtsstaat
Britain became a welfare state in the first half of the twentieth century.

3. Wohn- und Lebensverhältnisse

3.1 Eigentum und Besitz

to acquire ▪ erwerben
In order to drive a car you must acquire a driving licence.

to belong ▪ gehören
No, this is not my car. It belongs to my wife.

holder ▪ Besitzer, Halter
You can only use this train if you are the holder of the correct ticket.

land ▪ Landbesitz
The Duke of Sutherland has a vast amount of land in Scotland.

owner ▪ Eigentümer(in)
The earl was the owner of a large number of houses.

property ▪ Eigentum; Grundbesitz
He left his heirs a lot of property – paintings, jewels, houses, shares.
He owned fifty acres of property.

to retain ▪ behalten
After his father's death Mark retained the right to his father's art collection.

site ▪ Platz, Ort; Grundstück; Baustelle
We have at last found a nice site for building a house.
Our site is near the forest and away from the road.
There was no worker on our site!

wealthy ['welθi] ▪ reich, wohlhabend, vermögend
Bill Gates is an extremely wealthy man.

---

domain ▪ Domäne, Bereich
My father-in-law regarded his workshop as his own domain.

fortune ■ Vermögen; Schicksal, Glück

She had inherited such a fortune that she could buy almost anything she liked.

It was her fortune to inherit a lot of money.

to own ■ besitzen

My brother owns a large collection of contemporary art.

ownership ■ Eigentum

Home ownership is much more widespread in Britain than in Germany.

to possess ■ besitzen

Both partners possessed their own bank accounts.

possession ■ Besitz

The car has been in my possession since 2010.

to secure ■ fest schließen, sichern

Before leaving the house please secure all doors and windows.

wealth [welθ] ■ Reichtum

What is the point of all your wealth if you do not enjoy it?

well-off ■ wohlhabend, reich

You must be rather well-off to be able to afford a house in Monterey.

3.2 Wohnort, Unterkunft, Gebäude

back ■ Rückseite

As children we always played in the garden at the back of our house.

basement ■ Kellergeschoss, Souterrain

Most houses in Britain do not have a basement.

block ■ Block

We'll move away from this ugly block of flats as soon as possible.

building ■ Gebäude

Our flat is in the last building on the right.

castle ■ Schloss, Burg
Hardly anybody lives in a castle nowadays.

cell ■ Zelle
Not only prisoners but also many members of religious communities live in cells.

cellar ■ Keller
Most houses in Britain do not have a cellar.

chimney ■ Kamin, Schornstein
The fire won't burn because the chimney is blocked.

entrance ■ Eingang
Our house has two entrances – a front door and a back door.

entry ■ Eintritt, Zugang
There was a sign at the gate: "Private. No entry."

estate ■ Grundbesitz; Siedlung
The Duke of Sutherland's estate is extremely large.
When my parents grew old they moved into a housing estate for the elderly.

flat ■ Wohnung
Most people in Germany live in flats rather than their own houses.

floor ■ Fußboden; Etage (AE: storey)
She likes to sit on the floor when watching TV.
They live on the twentieth floor and enjoy a beautiful sight.

gate ■ Tor
Don't forget to shut the gate when you come in.

ground ■ Boden; Grund
Our house is built on very even ground.
My decision is based on very solid grounds.

ground floor ■ Erdgeschoss
What is the ground floor in Britain is called first floor in the USA.

hall ■ Halle
The Royal Festival Hall is located on the south bank of the Thames.

house ▪ Haus
A lot of people in Britain live in their own houses.

landlady ▪ Vermieterin
The family had to move because their landlady did not tolerate dogs in her house.

landlord ▪ Vermieter
Our landlord is a very generous person so we do not think of moving.

to let (let, let) ▪ vermieten
There were a number of flats to let in this street.

to live [lɪv] ▪ leben; wohnen
I've been living in this city all my life.
For three years I have been living in this beautiful flat.

property ▪ Immobilie
They moved into quite a nice bit of property.

roof ▪ Dach
Our new house does not have a flat roof, because they can cause a lot of problems.

room ▪ Raum, Zimmer
Our flat has four rooms plus a kitchen and a bathroom.

sitting room ▪ Wohnzimmer
Our sitting room faces the garden.

step ▪ Stufe
533 steps will take you to the top of Cologne Cathedral.

storey (AE; BE: floor) ▪ Etage, Stockwerk
The Trump Tower has 58 storeys.

tall ▪ hoch
Currently Burj Khalifa in Dubai is the world's tallest building.

thick ▪ dick
The walls of this castle are very thick.

tower ▪ Turm
The Eiffel Tower is one of the major sights of Paris.

village ▪ Dorf
Cockington is a nice little village near Torquay.

wall ▪ Mauer; Wand
We had a wall built around our garden to keep animals out.
The wall in our living room needs painting.

wing ▪ (Gebäude-)Flügel
Our flat is in the west wing of the apartment block.

---

accommodation ▪ Unterkunft
At last we have found suitable accommodation.
We can offer five excellent accommodations in Hoboken.

apartment ▪ Wohnung, Appartement
In Britain a one-room flat is called an apartment. In the USA an apartment can have any number of rooms.

backyard ▪ Hinterhof; Garten hinter dem Haus
A British backyard can be something without any flowers and plants. The American backyard is a garden at the back of a house.

borough ▪ Verwaltungsbezirk
They've lived in this quiet borough all their lives.

brick ▪ Ziegel, Backstein
The Smiths live in that red brick building over there.

cave ▪ Höhle
People do not live in caves any longer as Neanderthal man did.

ceiling ▪ Zimmerdecke
In our old flat the ceilings were 2.6 metres high.

column ['kɒləm] ▪ Säule
The roof of the temple was supported by twelve columns.

complex ▪ Gebäudekomplex
The house is located in a new complex in the city centre.

to comprise ▪ umfassen
The house comprises a living-room, two bedrooms, a bathroom, a kitchen, and a dining-room.

to construct ■ bauen

Our house was constructed originally in 1850.

cottage ■ (Land-)Haus

Marian's parents liked to spend their weekends in their cottage in the Cotswolds.

elevator ■ Fahrstuhl, Lift

Our flat is on the eleventh floor. So we are glad there is an elevator.

fence ■ Zaun

"Good fences make good neighbours."

first floor ■ erste Etage

What is the first floor in Britain is the second floor in the USA.

garage ■ Garage

The roads were so icy that we didn't move our car out of the garage.

housing ■ Unterbringung, Unterkunft, Wohnung(en)

In some countries the government supplies the poor with cheap housing.

layout ■ Plan

The architect showed us the layout of our new house.

lease ■ Pachtvertrag; Mietvertrag

We've just signed the lease for two acres of land.

The lease on our flat expires on 6 June.

lift ■ Lift, Aufzug

We live on the fourth floor. So it's good we have a lift.

local ■ örtlich, hiesig

In the evenings we often go to our local pub.

to migrate [maɪ'greɪt] ■ wandern, umherziehen

Nomads do not have a fixed address. They migrate from one place to another.

migration ■ Migration, Wanderung

Some people dislike the migration of people from poor countries to the EU.

to occupy (occupies, occupying) ■ besetzen
They occupied the house for a number of years before they rented it.

outskirts ■ Außenbezirk, Stadtrand
They found accommodation in Wimbledon, i.e. in the outskirts of London.

palace ■ Palast
The Queen lives in Buckingham Palace when she is in London.

plaster ■ Putz
The building showed some cracks in the plaster.

real estate ■ Immobilien
At last they found a nice piece of real estate.

rear ■ hinterer Teil
A second door to the garage is at the rear of the house.

refuge ['refju:dʒ] ■ Zuflucht, Zufluchtsort
Our house had burnt down, so we had to seek refuge elsewhere.

removal ■ Umzug
Our removal from Berlin to Hamburg is due on Friday.

rent ■ Miete
The rent for our flat is not very high.

residence ■ Wohnhaus
There are really nice residences in this area.

residential ■ Wohn…
We live in a purely residential area.

restoration ■ Restaurierung
The restoration of the farmbuilding was quite expensive.

to restore ■ restaurieren
After we had restored the old building it really looked charming.

to ruin ■ ruinieren
The restoration of the house was a failure. It rather ruined the house completely.

ruin ■ Ruine
You don't expect us to pay so much for this ruin, do you?

semi-detached house ■ Doppelhaushälfte
We live in the semi-detached house just round the corner from here.

shelter ■ Schutz
Caves and tents were among the first types of shelter for human beings.

slum ■ Slum
Rio de Janeiro's favelas are a notorious slum.

stair ■ Treppenstufe
Nero, our dog, likes sitting on the bottom stair.

staircase ■ Treppenhaus, Treppenaufgang
The staircase from the ground floor to the first floor needs painting.

stairs ■ Treppe
To reach our flat just walk up the stairs to the second floor or use the lift.

strip ■ Streifen
They built their house on a small strip of land on the coast.

tenant ■ Mieter(in)
Mike has been a tenant in the same house for thirty-five years.

terraced house ■ Reihenhaus
When we were young we had a terraced house.

thickness ■ Dicke
The walls of the castle have a thickness of 2.5 metres.

to unlock ■ aufschließen
Mother unlocked the door for me beause I had forgotten my key.

vendor ■ (Immobilien-)Verkäufer(in)
He bought his property from a well-known vendor.

3.3 Wohnraum und Garten

bath ▪ Badewanne; Bad
In our bathroom we have a bath and a shower.

bathroom ▪ Badezimmer
... and also a toilet and a washbasin.

bathtub ▪ Badewanne
What's a bath in Britain is a bathtub in the USA.

bedroom ▪ Schlafzimmer
In this large house there are no fewer than four bedrooms.

bush ▪ Busch
They planted a number of bushes so that nobody could see them in their garden.

dining room ▪ Esszimmer
Our dining room faces the garden.

door ▪ Tür
Our living room has a large door providing access to the garden.

front ▪ Vorderseite, Fassade
After the long winter our neighbours had the front of their house painted.

▸ **front door** ▪ Haustür
Just come in by the back door. The front door is locked at night.

▸ **front garden** ▪ Vorgarten
Bill is proud of the roses in his front garden.

▸ **in front of** ▪ vor
We have a rose-garden in front of our house.

garden ▪ Garten, Gartenanlage
Our neighbours have a lovely garden.

hall ▪ Diele
Our flat comprises two bedrooms, a hall, a kitchen, a bathroom and a dining-room.

handle ▪ Griff, Klinke
Turn the handle if you want to open the door.

home ▪ Haus, Heim
"My home is my castle."

▸ **to go home** ▪ nach Hause gehen

hut ▪ Hütte
We have a garden hut to keep all our tools in.

kitchen ▪ Küche
Our flat has a lovely and large kitchen.

lawn ▪ Rasen
Good lawns must be mown regularly.

lawnmower ▪ Rasenmäher
We keep our lawnmower in the garage.

living room ▪ Wohnzimmer
I wish we had a larger living room.

pool ▪ Pool
Our friends have a pool in the garden, which they use in the summer for swimming.

post ▪ Pfosten, Pfahl
We have a post in our garden to tie our dog to so that he cannot run away.

seat ▪ Sitz(platz), Platz
We have enough seats in our house for some twenty guests.

study ▪ Arbeitszimmer
You can't disturb her. She is in her study writing an essay.

toilet ▪ Toilette
The Brooks have two bathrooms and three separate toilets.

window ▪ Fenster
Unfortunately we do not have a window in our bathroom.

yard ▪ Hof, Garten
We have a yard behind our house for our children to play in.

attic ■ Dachboden, Speicher
We do not have a cellar, but we have an attic for all the stuff we do not need.

chamber ■ Kammer
Small rooms are still occasionally called chambers.

corridor ■ Korridor
There's a long corridor between our bedroom and our bathroom.

to decorate ■ streichen, tapezieren, renovieren
Just look at our walls. It's about time we decorated our flat.

doorway ■ Eingang
When the door opened I was confronted by a barking Rottweiler in the doorway.

downstairs ■ im Erdgeschoss
Our living room and kitchen are downstairs. Bathrooms and bedrooms are upstairs.

to fasten ■ befestigen
Make sure you fasten the hose properly or it may come off.

hose ■ Wasserschlauch
If you want to water your garden properly, use a hose.

landing ■ Treppenabsatz
You'll find the toilet on the landing between the ground floor and the first floor.

lightning conductor ■ Blitzableiter
The first thing we installed in our new house was a lightning conductor.

lock ■ Schloss
If you wish to scare away burglars you must have good locks on your doors.

to mow (mowed, mowed/mown) ■ mähen
Our neighbours mow their lawn every week.

pole ■ Stange, Pfahl
We have a pole in our garden to fly our flag from.

pond ■ Teich
Our garden is not large enough for a pond, but there's a lovely pond near our house.

porch ■ Vordach; Veranda
Let's stand under the porch. It's raining.
Americans sit on their porch, the British sit on their veranda.

to reinforce ■ verstärken
The walls of our house are rather thin. We'd better reinforce them.

shed ■ Schuppen
Our neighbours have a shed in their garden for all their tools.

storage ■ Lagerung, Aufbewahrung
We have a cellar so we are not short of storage space.

sunbed ■ Sonnenliege
We have two sunbeds in our garden …

swimming pool ■ Schwimmbecken, Swimmingpool
… and a lovely swimming pool as well.

swing ■ Schaukel
We're going to buy a swing for our grandchildren and put it in the garden.

terrace ■ Terrasse
In the summer we like sitting on our terrace enjoying the sun.

tidy ■ ordentlich, sauber
Hannah always keeps her room tidy.

untidy ■ unordentlich
Evelyn's room was always untidy.

upstairs ■ oben; nach oben; im oberen Stockwerk
Father is upstairs in his study.
Can you carry this upstairs for me, please?
Our bedrooms are upstairs.

veranda(h) ■ Veranda
Fortunately we have a veranda so that we can sit outside even when it is raining.

wallpaper ▪ Tapete
They had wallpaper with red and blue stripes on it.

3.4 Einrichtung

bed ▪ Bett
This bed is large enough for two people to sleep in.

cabinet ▪ Schrank, Schränkchen
We keep our medicine in a cabinet in the bathroom.

chair ▪ Stuhl
Our dinner table is large enough for six chairs round it.

clock ▪ Wand-, Standuhr
Mr Shandy always wound up his clock on the same day of the month.

▸ **o'clock** ▪ ... Uhr
Let's watch the 7 o'clock news.

cupboard ▪ Schrank
A cupboard is used to store all sorts of things but not for instance clothes.

furnished ▪ eingerichtet, möbliert
When she took up her first job she moved into a furnished flat.

gas ▪ Gas
We have gas central heating in our flat.

heating ▪ Heizung
We have a new gas central heating in our house.

sofa ▪ Sofa
Our sofa in the living room is large enough for four people to sit on.

stuff ▪ Zeug, Sachen
Isabel's aunt had an awful lot of stuff in her flat.

table ▪ Tisch
Our dining table is large enough for eight people.

tablecloth ▪ Tischtuch
They bought a very expensive tablecloth for their dinner table.

television set ▪ Fernsehgerät
Almost all families in Germany have a television set today.

wardrobe ▪ Kleiderschrank
We have built-in wardrobes in our new house.

---

armchair ▪ Sessel
Grandfather used to sit in his armchair all day watching TV.

bookshelf (Pl.: -shelves) ▪ Buchregal
In the professor's study there are ten large bookshelves.

bureau ['bjʊərəʊ] ▪ Sekretär; Kommode
She has a beautiful Chippendale bureau in her room to work at.
My American friend says she puts all her socks and underwear in her bureau.

cardboard ▪ Pappe
When I moved I needed ten large cardboard boxes to put all my stuff in.

carpet ▪ Teppich, Teppichboden
We have carpets in all our rooms except the bathroom and the kitchen.

central heating ▪ Zentralheizung
Almost all new houses have central heating.

closet ▪ Abstellraum; (Wand-)Schrank
We store quite a number of things in the closet under the stairs.
Mary's aunt kept all her cosmetics in a closet in her bedroom.

comfort ▪ Komfort
These luxury flats offer every conceivable comfort.

comfortable ▪ bequem, gemütlich
This easy chair is really comfortable. I could sit in it for hours.

cooker ▪ Herd
What is a cooker in Britain is called a stove in the USA.

couch ▪ Couch, Sofa

Our neighbours have a huge couch in their living room.

curtain ▪ Vorhang, Gardine

The curtains in their living room have white and yellow stripes.

cushion ▪ Kissen, Polster

We need new cushions for our sofa.

desk ▪ Schreibtisch

He would sit for hours at his desk without doing anything.

drawer ▪ Schublade

You'll find the file in the top drawer.

furniture ▪ Möbel

Buying furniture was the first thing she did once she earned her own money.

lavatory ▪ Toilette

Modern houses often have a separate lavatory in addition to the bathroom.

light ▪ Lampe

He bought a new light for his desk.

loo ▪ Klo(sett)

You don't say "loo" in a restaurant but "toilet" or "lavatory".

mattress ▪ Matratze

In our bedroom we have a large double bed with a comfortable mattress.

mirror ▪ Spiegel

We have a large mirror in the bathroom.

radiator ▪ Heizkörper

One of the two radiators in our living room does not work properly.

shelf (Pl.: shelves) ▪ (Regal-)Brett, Bord, Regal

Her office is full of shelves for all the books she has.

stereo ▪ Stereoanlage

The first thing we bought when we had moved in was a stereo.

stool ▪ Hocker
We have four stools in the kitchen.

to store ▪ lagern
We store our potatoes in the cellar, where it is dark and cool.

stove ▪ Ofen; Herd
Before we had central heating we had an oil stove in every room.
What the British call a cooker is called a stove in the USA.

uncomfortable ▪ unbequem
We must buy a new sofa. The old one is so uncomfortable!

3.5 Haushalt, Haushaltsgegenstände und Werkzeuge

board ▪ Brett
Use the board for cutting bread, please.

bottle ▪ Flasche
Have you remembered to put the bottle out for the milkman?

cage ▪ Käfig
My daughter kept her rat in a cage.

chain ▪ Kette
Our dog is really dangerous. That is why it is to be kept on a chain.

comb ▪ Kamm
My hair is so short that I do not really need a comb.

cover ▪ Bettdecke
We have special covers for summer and winter.

cup ▪ Tasse
Some people use cups to drink coffee and tea, others collect them.

domestic ▪ häuslich
My wife has someone to help her with domestic duties such as cleaning.

doorbell ▪ Türklingel
Whenever our doorbell rings our dog begins to bark.

dustbin ▪ Mülleimer, Abfalleimer
What is called a dustbin in Britain is called a garbage can in the USA.

edge ▪ Schneide
Watch out. That knife has a very keen edge.

fork ▪ Gabel
It takes a couple of years before children learn to use a fork for eating.

fridge ▪ Kühlschrank
Meat, vegetables and milk are among the items to be stored in a fridge.

hammer ▪ Hammer
Be careful with that hammer. You might hit your fingers.

handle ▪ Griff
These goods break easily. Hold them by their handles if you want to be safe.

household ▪ Haushalt
My sister earns well, so her husband looks after the household.

jar ▪ Gefäß, Glas
My wife collects jars for her home-made jam.

to keep (kept, kept) ▪ aufbewahren
Where do you keep your tools?

key ▪ Schlüssel
We won't be at home tonight. So don't forget your key when you go out.

knife [naɪf] ▪ Messer
It takes some time before children learn how to use knives and forks properly.

lamp ▪ Lampe
We need more lamps to light our garage properly.

lid ▪ Deckel
Put the lid on the pot or the water will never boil.

line ▪ Leine
Could you help me hang the washing on the line?

mouth ▪ Öffnung
This bottle has a very narrow mouth.

nail ▪ Nagel
Harry fetched a hammer and some nails because he wanted to hang up a picture.

plate ▪ Teller, Platte
We have a large number of plates and cups and saucers in our cupboard.

sack ▪ Sack
We've got a sack of potatoes in the garage.

safety pin ▪ Sicherheitsnadel
If you do not want to hurt yourself use a safety pin to fasten your belt.

screw ▪ Schraube
Don't use a nail to hold those boards together. A screw is much safer.

screwdriver ▪ Schraubenzieher
Have you got a screwdriver for this type of screw?

set ▪ Set
Don't use a table cloth, just use six sets.

spoon ▪ Löffel
Mum, can you please bring me a spoon for the soup?

to stick (stuck, stuck) ▪ stecken
Just stick it in the fridge for a couple of minutes.

store ▪ Vorrat
We have a large store of wine in the garage.

tape ▪ (Maß-)Band; Klebeband
He used a tape to measure the distance from the kitchen to the living room.
Just stick the pieces together with tape.

tea towel ▪ Geschirrtuch

I'd like to to the dishes. Could I please have a tea towel?

teacup ▪ Teetasse

Could I please have a teacup? I don't like drinking tea from a glass.

teapot ▪ Teekanne

First put the tea into the teapot and then pour the hot water into it.

teaspoon ▪ Teelöffel

Could I have a teaspoon of sugar for my tea?

toaster ▪ Toaster

Veronica's aunt bought a new toaster yesterday.

tool ▪ Werkzeug

He needs a very large box for all his tools.

towel ▪ Handtuch

If you are looking for towels they are on the top shelf in the bathroom.

---

alarm ▪ Wecker

Of course we have an alarm in our bedroom because we tend to oversleep.

ashtray ▪ Aschenbecher

I'm sorry we don't have ashtrays in our flat.

axe ▪ Axt

You need an axe to chop wood.

ballpoint pen ▪ Kugelschreiber

The ballpoint pen was invented in the 19th century.

battery ▪ Batterie

Our flashlight doesn't work. I think we need new batteries.

bin ▪ Tonne, Mülltonne

Don't forget to place the bin on the pavement.

blade ▪ Schneide, Klinge

Watch out! The blade of this axe is very sharp.

box ▪ Schachtel, Kiste
I keep all my tools in a large box in the garage.

broom ▪ Besen
He took the broom and swept the terrace.

bucket ▪ Eimer
Can you get me a bucket of water, please? I'd like to clean the terrace.

candle ▪ Kerze
You should have some candles in your house just in case there is a power cut.

china ▪ ⚠ (Porzellan-)Geschirr
My boss is coming for dinner so we'd better lay the table with our best china.

collar ▪ Halsband
Mary, I'd like to walk the dog. Have you seen his collar?

container ▪ Behälter, Gefäß
You'll find a container for the rubbish in the garage.

cooker ▪ Herd
Mary and Gordon have a gas cooker in their new flat.

crockery ▪ Geschirr
Crockery is the collective name for cups, saucers, plates, etc.

cutlery ▪ Besteck
... and cutlery that for knives, forks, spoons, etc.

to disconnect ▪ trennen, abschalten
Since they had not paid their electricity bill they had their electricity disconnected.

dish ▪ Schale, Teller
Can you wash the dirty dishes, please?

fan ▪ Ventilator, Fächer
In many American houses without air conditioning there is at least a fan.

flashlight ■ Taschenlampe
In the event of a power cut a flashlight comes in quite useful.

freezer ■ Tiefkühler, Gefrierschrank
People often store meat in a freezer to consume it later.

frying pan ■ Bratpfanne
Don't allow the oil in the frying pan to get too hot. I might start burning.

garbage ■ Abfall, Müll
In our street the garbage collector always comes on a Thursday.

garbage can ■ Abfalleimer, Mülleimer
What is called a garbage can in the USA is called a dustbin in Britain.

glue ■ Klebstoff, Leim, Klebe
You've torn the documents? Just stick them together with glue.

hoover™ ■ Staubsauger
We have carpets everywhere. That's why we need a good hoover.

housework ■ Hausarbeit
If there is one thing I hate it is doing all the housework on my own.

iron ⚠ ['aɪən] ■ Bügeleisen
You often require an iron to make freshly washed textiles smooth.

kettle ■ (Wasser-)Kessel
Shall I put the kettle on for a cup of tea?

kit ■ Ausrüstung, Werkzeug
She got out her sewing kit and gave it to me so that I could sew the button on myself.

knot [nɒt] ■ Knoten
He couldn't get his shoes off because he had tied the shoelaces in a knot.

ladder ■ Leiter
Our ceilings are so high that we need a ladder if we want to exchange light bulbs.

laundry ■ Wäsche

My father used to bring my mother some chocolate on the day she did the laundry.

light bulb ■ Glühbirne

Could you please buy a new light bulb for our bathroom lamp?

lighter ■ Feuerzeug

Sorry, we don't have any matches, but we've got a lighter.

linen ■ Leinen; Wäsche

Linen is often used for making shirts and blouses.

In our hotel the bed linen is changed every day.

mat ■ Matte

However dirty his feet are he never uses the mat before coming in.

mug ■ Becher

I always drink my coffee from a mug.

needle ■ Nadel

He was looking for a needle because he wanted to sew on a button.

oven ■ Backofen

We have not only a cooker, but also an oven.

pan ■ Pfanne

If you want to fry a nice steak you need a large pan.

pillow ■ Kopfkissen

I can't sleep on pillows stuffed with feathers because I'm allergic to them.

pin ■ Stecknadel

You can use pins to hold pieces of cloth together.

plug ■ Stecker; Stöpsel

That toaster does not work. How about changing its plug?

How can I run myself a bath when its plug is nowhere to be seen?

pot ■ Topf; Kaffee-/Teekanne; Blumentopf

Mother made a large pot of soup.

Auntie poured the coffee from a nice china pot.

My uncle needed a lot of pots to plant flowers.

pram ■ Kinderwagen

You can have our pram for your little one. Our children don't need it any longer.

refrigerator ■ Kühlschrank

Of course we have a refrigerator to keep our food in.

rope ■ Seil, Strick

We have a rope so that the children can tie it to a branch and use it as a swing.

rubbish ■ Abfall

Can you put the rubbish out, please?

saucepan ■ Kochtopf

Heat the oil in a large saucepan, then add the vegetables.

saucer ■ Untertasse

We've got six saucers but only five cups because I broke one when doing the dishes.

scissors ■ Schere

Have you seen my scissors? I'd like to cut off this extra bit of cloth.

sewing machine ■ Nähmaschine

In the past there used to be a sewing machine in almost every household.

sheet ■ Bettlaken

It was so hot in the summer that we slept with only a sheet over us.

sieve ■ Sieb

Press the strawberries through a sieve, add sugar and eat it as a dessert.

socket ■ Steckdose

Matthew has a lot of sockets in his flat for all his electrical devices.

string ■ Schnur, Kordel

Do you have some string so that I can tie the parcel?

suitcase ['suːtkeɪs, 'sjuːtkeɪs] ■ Koffer

We only need a small suitcase for our weekend trip.

to sweep (swept, swept) ▪ fegen, kehren
A new broom sweeps clean.

switch ▪ Schalter
The switch is right beside the door.

tablespoon ▪ Esslöffel
Add one tablespoon of salt and bring the mixture to the boil.

tank ▪ (Flüssigkeits-)Behälter, Tank
In American houses there is often a water tank at the highest point of the house.

thread [θred] ▪ Faden
Get me some thread and a needle so that I can mend your coat.

torch ▪ Taschenlampe
It is useful to have a torch in one's house.

trash ▪ Abfall, Müll
Put the trash in the trash can, will you?

trash can ▪ Abfalleimer, Mülleimer
"Trash can" is another American term for "garbage can".

tray ▪ Tablett; Ablage
Mother brought Mike a tray with food.
Father kept the mail he received and the mail he sent in different trays.

tube ▪ Rohr; Tube
The tube of our hoover seems to be blocked.
We need a new tube of toothpaste.

umbrella ▪ Regenschirm
When you travel to the Irish west coast don't forget to take an umbrella.

vacuum cleaner ▪ Staubsauger
The official term for a hoover is "vacuum cleaner".

vessel ▪ Gefäß
Pour the remaining oil into a vessel holding at least a gallon.

wastepaper basket ▪ Papierkorb

Jean's wastepaper basket was always full.

wire ▪ Draht; Kabel

Have you some wire for me to tie these boards together?

Our telephone doesn't work because the wires have come loose.

3.6 Ernährung und Genussmittel

alcohol ▪ Alkohol

bacon ▪ Schinkenspeck

Many people in England like eating bacon and egg for breakfast.

to bake ▪ backen

bar ▪ Riegel, Stange

You shouldn't eat more than a bar of chocolate per day.

bean ▪ Bohne

beer ▪ Bier

breakfast ['brekfəst] ▪ Frühstück

Christine only ate cornflakes for breakfast.

▸ **to have breakfast** (had, had) ▪ frühstücken

Would you like to have breakfast at eight or later?

cereal ['sɪəriəl] ▪ Getreide, Frühstücksflocken

Wheat and rice are types of cereals.

Most people in Britain have cereals for breakfast.

chicken ▪ Hähnchen, Hühnchen

If you don't like pork or veal – why not eat chicken?

chocolate ['tʃɒklət] ▪ Schokolade

cigarette ▪ Zigarette

to cook ▪ kochen

course ▪ Gang (Speisen)

There will be a three-course dinner tonight.

delicious ■ köstlich, lecker
Do you still have those grapes I bought here yesterday – they were delicious.

dinner ■ Abendessen, Dinner
My parents insisted that we had our dinner at 6 p.m.

to drink (drank, drunk) ■ trinken

drink ■ Getränk
I'm so thirsty. Could I have a drink of water, please?

to eat (ate, eaten) ■ essen
I'm afraid we can't eat steaks tonight. The dog ate all the meat.

egg ■ Ei
My father likes eating eggs for breakfast – in any form.

fast food ■ Fertignahrung, Fast Food
If you eat only fast food you mustn't be surprised that you grow fat.

fat ■ fett, dick; Fett

food ■ Essen, Nahrung, Nahrungsmittel
Nowadays you can get all kinds of food all the year round.

fried eggs ■ Spiegeleier
O yes, I do like fried eggs for breakfast.

frozen food ■ Tiefkühlkost
Her brother is not very fond of frozen food. He prefers his food to be fresh.

fruit [fruːt] ■ Obst, Frucht; Früchte
His uncle liked all kinds of fruit, but the fruit he liked best was the apple.

to fry (fried; frying) ■ braten
What my grandfather liked most in the morning was fried bacon.

glass ■ Glas

ham ■ Schinken
I do like ham and eggs for breakfast.

hot ▪ scharf

Indian food tends to be very hot, so eat some rice with it.

hunger ▪ Hunger

hungry ▪ hungry

▸ **hungry for** ▪ hungrig nach

ice cream ▪ (Speise-)Eis

What I like best on a hot summer's day is an ice cream.

juice [dʒuːs] ▪ Saft

Could I have a glass of orange juice, please?

lunch ▪ Mittagessen

They never ate more than a yoghurt for lunch.

meal ▪ Essen, Mahlzeit, Mahl

They often invite their friends for a meal.

meat ▪ Fleisch

My daughter does not eat any meat. She prefers fish.

microwave ▪ Mikrowelle

I like my lunch fresh, not from a microwave.

nut ▪ Nuss

What I like best is chocolate with nuts.

provision ▪ Vorrat

We have enough provisions for the long winter.

pudding [ˈpʊdɪŋ] ▪ Pudding

rice ▪ Reis

rich ▪ gehaltvoll, schwer

I don't sleep well if I eat a rich meal before going to bed.

salad ▪ Salat

Potato salad is what I like best.

sandwich ▪ Sandwich

A sandwich is simply cold meat between two slices of bread.

scrambled eggs ▪ Rührei

Hannah likes scrambled eggs for breakfast.

snack ■ Snack, Imbiss

soup [suːp] ■ Suppe

to spread [spred] (spread, spread) ■ (be)streichen
She spread Marmite thinly on her slice of toast.

steak [steɪk] ■ Steak

straight ■ pur
Could I have my whisky straight please?

sugar ['ʃʊgə] ■ Zucker

sweet ■ Süßigkeit
She's stopped eating sweets in order to lose weight.

tea ■ Tee

tea bag ■ Teebeutel
Take the tea bag out after three minutes or the tea will be too strong.

toast ■ Toast

tobacco ■ Tabak
Some people chew tobacco, others smoke it.

to try ■ probieren
Do try our new orange marmalade.

veal ■ Kalbfleisch
In order to prepare a Wiener Schnitzel you need veal.

vegetable ■ Gemüse
My wife buys vegetables at a Turkish greengrocer's.

vegetarian ■ Vegetarier(in)

vitamin ■ Vitamin

weak ■ dünn
Unfortunately the coffee was very weak.

whisky (AE: whiskey) ■ Whisky
I prefer Scotch whisky to Irish or American whiskey.

wine ■ Wein

yoghurt ['jɒgət] ■ Joghurt

ale ▪ Ale (obergäriges Bier)
English ales are entirely different from German "Bier".

biscuit ▪ Keks
After dinner we were served cheese and biscuits.

to boil ▪ kochen
Please boil my eggs for four minutes.

bowl ▪ Schüssel, Schale
Mix all the ingredients for the soup in a bowl.

bubble gum ▪ Kaugummi, Bubble Gum
He blew big bubbles with his bubble gum.

candy ▪ Süßigkeit
Eating too much candy makes you fat and damages your teeth.

champagne [ʃæm'peɪn] ▪ Champagner

chewing gum ▪ Kaugummi
It is not regarded as polite to talk with chewing gum in your mouth.

chips (Pl.) ▪ Pommes frites
Fish and chips are very popular in Britain.

to chop ▪ hacken, schneiden
Chop the carrots into little pieces before adding them to the pot.

cigar [sɪ'gɑː] ▪ Zigarre

to consume ▪ verbrauchen, konsumieren
Germans consume more than a hundred litres of beer per head in a year.

cookie (AE) ▪ Keks
What's called a cookie in the USA is a biscuit in the UK.

cream ▪ Sahne
Would you like some cream with your coffee?

crisp ▪ knusprig
The bacon we had for breakfast was nicely crisp.

cuisine ▪ Küche, Art zu kochen
French cuisine is popular throughout the world.

dessert [dɪ'zɜːt] ■ Dessert
Ice cream is a very popular dessert with children.

dish ■ Gericht
In 2001 I ate haggis, a Scottish national dish, for the first time in my life.

to dissolve ■ auflösen
Dissolve the sugar in hot water.

draught [drɑːft] ■ vom Fass, Fass…
My brother never drank beer from a bottle. He preferred draught beer.

flavour ■ Geschmack, Aroma
This coffee has rather a strange flavour.

flour [flaʊə] ■ Mehl
In order to bake bread you need flour as the main ingredient.

fluid ■ Flüssigkeit
Often old people do not drink enough fluids.

french fries ■ Pommes frites

ginger ■ Ingwer
Ginger is used a lot in Britain.

grape ■ Weintraube
Wine is made from grapes.

gravy ■ Bratensoße
Ruth likes her leg of lamb with lovely gravy.

ingredient ■ Zutat, Bestandteil
Stir the ingredients slowly.
Potatoes and onions are key ingredients of a potao salad.

jelly ■ Gelee, Götterspeise
What Charles likes best as a dessert is jelly.

junk food ■ (ungesunde) Schnellgerichte, Fraß
You wouldn't be so fat if you didn't eat so much junk food.

lactose ['læktəʊs] ■ Laktose

lager ■ Lagerbier (untergäriges Bier)
Harry liked drinking two or three pints of lager after work.

lemon ■ Zitrone

lemonade ■ Limonade

lobster ■ Hummer
Not everybody can afford to eat lobster.

mashed potatoes ■ Kartoffelbrei
My dad liked eating mashed potatoes with liver and onions.
I like my boiled eggs with a bit of mayonnaise.

mince ■ Hackfleisch
A shepherd's pie consists primarily of mashed potatoes and mince.

mustard ■ Senf
I like my grilled sausages with mustard.

orange ■ Orange, Apfelsine

pack ■ Packung
He smoked two packs of cigarettes every day.

pancake ■ Pfannkuchen
Pancakes with syrup are Anne's favourite dish.

paste ■ Teig
Mix the powder with enough water to make a smooth paste.

pie ■ Pastete
One of Karen's favourite dishes is steak pie with chips.

pipe ■ Pfeife

plum pudding ■ Plumpudding
Strangely enough, a plum pudding or Christmas pudding does not contain any plums.

porridge ■ Porridge, Haferbrei
If there is one thing I can't stand it's porridge for breakfast.

to preserve ■ einmachen, konservieren
Mary's grandmother preserved all the fruit she harvested in the garden.

to process ■ bearbeiten

I like my food fresh from the farmer, not processed and stored in a freezer.

protein ■ Eiweiß

Fish, meat, and of course eggs are rich in protein.

raw ■ roh

The Japanese are quite fond of raw fish.

recipe ■ (Koch-, Back-)Rezept

Granny has a nice recipe for plum pudding.

roll ■ Brötchen

He's putting on weight because he keeps eating three rolls with butter for breakfast.

sauce ■ Soße

sausage ■ Wurst

In Germany you can buy a large number of different types of sausage.

Scotch ■ Scotch (Whisky)

Scotch is made from barley.

sherry ■ Sherry

slice ■ Stück, Scheibe

Could I have another slice of bread, please?

soft drink ■ alkoholfreies Getränk

I don't drink alcohol, I prefer soft drinks.

soya bean ■ Sojabohne

Vegetarians eat a lot of food made from soya beans.

spice ■ Gewürz

Pepper and ginger are spices.

spicy ■ würzig

Indian dishes can be quite spicy.

spirits ■ Spirituosen

John does drink wine and beer, but no spirits.

spread [spred] ▪ Brotaufstrich
Marmite is a popular spread in Britain.

squash ▪ Erfrischungsgetränk aus Konzentrat
Could I have some orange squash, please?

to stir ▪ rühren
Stir the rice so that it does not stick.

straw ▪ Strohhalm
Soft drinks are often drunk through a straw.

supper ▪ Abendessen; später Imbiss
Supper is often another word for dinner.
We had a piece of cake for supper just before we went to bed.

syrup ▪ Sirup

tender ▪ zart
Charles wanted his steak to be quite tender.

tin ▪ Büchse, Dose
She opened a tin of baked beans for her breakfast.

vanilla ▪ Vanille

variety [və'raɪəti] ▪ Vielfalt, Auswahl; Sorte
I have a large variety of whiskies in my drinks cabinet. The variety I like most is Laphroaig.

vinegar ▪ Essig
Most people in Britain put vinegar on their chips.

whipped cream ▪ Schlagsahne
Heather always eats her cheese cake with whipped cream.

4. Ausbildung und Beruf

4.1 Vorschule, Schule, Universität

assembly ■ Versammlung
Many schools in England start their day with an assembly.

to attend ■ besuchen, teilnehmen
Students must attend classes regularly.

bachelor ■ 1. akademischer Abschluss
In Britain, students usually take their bachelor's degree after three years.

biology ■ Biologie
Biology was not a very popular subject at my school.

board ■ Schwarzes Brett, Schild; Tafel; Behörde
You can use the board for notices.
Come to the board and write down the following words.
Examinations are managed by the examination board.

campus ■ Universitätsgelände, Campus
The Stirling University campus has excellent sports facilities.

candidate ■ Kandidat(in)
Next Wednesday we have to examine ten candidates.

chalk ■ Kreide
There are still good teachers who prefer chalk to all those modern devices.

challenge ■ Herausforderung
Studying three subjects for a degree is rather a challenge.

chemistry ■ Chemie
Chemistry is not the easiest subject to study.

class ■ Klasse; Jahrgang
My class are going to the Cotswolds for a couple of days.

classmate ▪ Klassenkamerad(in)
Ten of my classmates have become medical doctors.

classroom ▪ Klassenzimmer
We were supposed to stand up when the teacher entered the classroom.

college ▪ (Fach-)Hochschule
After graduating my sister went to the Royal College of Art to study.

combination ▪ Kombination
The subject English is a combination of many fields – for instance Linguistics, Literature, and Cultural Studies.

correct ▪ korrekt, richtig
Yes, John, that's correct. The battle of Hastings took place in 1066.

to count ▪ zählen
One of the first things children learn at school is to count properly.

degree ▪ Abschluss
After studying for three years at university she took her degree.

department ▪ Institut, Abteilung
When she had taken her degree she became secretary in the German department.

development ▪ Entwicklung, Wachstum
It is the main job of teachers to help pupils in their personal development.

dictionary ▪ Wörterbuch
Even the best translators have to look up some words in a dictionary.

difficulty ▪ Schwierigkeit
Stephanie never had any difficulty doing her maths exercises, but at languages she was lost.

discipline ▪ Disziplin
Maintaining discipline in a class of fourteen-year-olds is not easy.

to divide ▪ dividieren, verteilen
It took a while before Jason learnt to divide properly.

to educate ■ bilden, ausbilden, erziehen
Children are educated by their parents and their teachers.

education ■ Bildung; Pädagogik
The children were well known for their excellent education.
When she had finished school she studied education at Stirling University.

educational ■ Bildungs..., pädagogisch
There are too often new educational theories – practically every year.

error ■ Fehler, Irrtum
Charlotte's essay was full of careless errors so she only got a C for it.

essay ■ Essay, Aufsatz
William's essay was very good.

examination ■ Prüfung, Examen
In English schools there is usually an examination at the end of each year.

to examine [ɪg'zæmɪn] ■ prüfen
All the candidates were examined carefully.

explanation ■ Erklärung
One of a teacher's main jobs is to give good explanations.

fee ■ Gebühr
After many protests college fees were abolished.

final ■ letzte(r, s), endgültig
Margaret is to take her final exam on Wednesday.

form ■ Schulklasse
She finished school after the sixth form with four A levels.

foundation ■ Stiftung
Many young people can only study because they are supported by a foundation.

geography ■ Geographie, Erdkunde
Mary's favourite subject at school was Geography.

grammar ■ Grammatik
If there was one subject at school I hated it was grammar.

higher education ■ Hochschulbildung
Students at university enjoy higher education.

hint ■ Hinweis
Let me give you a hint so that you can answer this question more easily.

holiday ■ Urlaub, Ferien
We're going to spend our summer holiday in Italy this year.

homework ■ Hausaufgaben
If you only come home from school at 4 p.m. you cannot do a lot of homework.

learning ■ Lernen, Bildung
Alexander Pope said, "A little learning is a dangerous thing."

lesson ■ Unterrichten; (Unterrichts-)Stunde
A teacher's job involves more than just lessons.
Lessons in Germany usually last 45 minutes.

to mark ■ korrigieren, benoten
I've been marking essays for five hours now.

mark ■ Note
The best mark you can achieve is an A+.

master (BE) ■ Lehrer(in); 2. akademischer Abschluss
Ms Bicknell is our singing master.
At some British universities students take their master's degree two years after their first degree.

mistake ■ Fehler, Irrtum
I'm afraid you've made too many careless mistakes.

module ■ Kurseinheit
This module consists of three classes on similar subjects.

to obtain ■ bekommen, erhalten
Ian obtained his degree from Oxford University.

page ▪ Seite
Open your books on page 10, please.

paper ▪ (schriftliche) Arbeit, Klausur; Referat
Universities students are required to write a number of papers.

to pass ▪ bestehen
90 per cent of all students passed their exam this time.

performance ▪ Leistung
Mary, your performance in the test was really excellent.

period ▪ Stunde
We've got English in the fourth period.

physics ▪ Physik
Regrettably few women study physics.

to prepare ▪ (sich) vorbereiten
In order to pass this test you must prepare yourselves carefully.

psychology ⚠ [saɪˈkɒlədʒi] ▪ Psychologie
She studied psychology at Aberdeen University.

pupil [ˈpjuːpəl] ▪ Schüler(in)
At our school we have ten times as many pupils as teachers.

RE ▪ (Religions-)Unterricht
RE (Religious Education) is a subject also taught at school.

result ▪ Ergebnis, Resultat; Folge
The results of his tests were so poor that as a result he failed his exam.

to return ▪ zurückgeben
You must return the book to the library. Others want to read it as well.

RI ▪ (Religions-)Unterricht
Religious Instruction (RI) is not compulsory at British state schools.

school ▪ Schule; Universität
Children in Britain attend school from age 5.
The term can also refer to a university, such as in London School of Economics.

schoolboy ▪ Schüler
At Eton you will only find schoolboys.

schoolgirl ▪ Schülerin
As a schoolgirl you cannot apply to be admitted at Eton.

seat ▪ Sitzgelegenheit
Our classroom has forty seats.

sociology ▪ Soziologie
She was always interested in the problems of society so she studied sociology.

staff ▪ Lehrkörper
The English Department at Stirling University has a staff of 22.

to stick (stuck, stuck) ▪ kleben
Just stick the two pages together.

student ▪ Student(in); Schüler(in)
In Britain a student is someone who studies at university.
In the USA a student is someone who goes to school or university.

to study ▪ studieren; lernen
Henry studied German and philosophy at Harvard.
I can't disturb him. He is studying.

subject ▪ Fach
Chemistry is a demanding subject.

to teach (taught, taught) ▪ lehren; unterrichten
Leopold Mozart taught his son Wolfgang to compose.
Barbara teaches German and art at a secondary school.

teacher ▪ Lehrer(in)
Being a teacher is not as easy as it appears to some people.

test ▪ Prüfung; Klassenarbeit
At the end of term there is going to be a test.
In Germany pupils take a large number of tests each year.

▸ **to take a test** ▪ eine Prüfung machen

to tick ▪ abhaken
Tick the items on the list of tasks as you do them.

to tick off (AE) ■ abhaken
In the USA you would tick those items off.

university ■ Universität
Oxford and Cambridge are very old universities.

---

academic ■ akademisch, Universitäts...
Boris was very good at sports but less so in academic subjects.

academy ■ Akademie
Joan started her career at the Academy of Traditional Chinese Medicine.

A level ■ (etwa) Abitur
She finished school with A levels in mathematics, physics, and chemistry.

attendance ■ Anwesenheit
Regular attendance in this class is compulsory.

bachelor's degree ■ BA
British students often take their BA after three years.

bell ■ Klingel
The lesson is over when the bell rings.

blank ■ leer, unbeschrieben
Write your essay on a blank sheet of paper.

boarding school ■ Internat
Boarding schools are less popular in Germany than in Britain.

calculator ■ (Taschen-)Rechner
When I was young we were not supposed to use a calculator at school.

certificate ■ Zeugnis, Zertifikat, Urkunde
The pupils were glad when they received their school-leaving certificate.

to compose ■ verfassen
At university you are supposed to compose quite a few essays.

composition ■ Aufsatz
This is an excellent composition and deserves an A+.

comprehension ■ Verständnis
In a listening comprehension test students hear a text once and must then answer questions on it.

comprehensive school ■ Gesamtschule
A comprehensive school teaches pupils of all abilities.

consistent ■ folgerichtig
Make sure that in an essay all your arguments are consistent.

to correct ■ korrigieren
Our teachers always corrected our mistakes.

curriculum ■ Lehrplan
English and mathematics are important elements of every school's curriculum.

economics ■ Wirtschaftswissenschaften
He studied economics at a very good university.

encouraging ■ ermutigend
Without his teacher's encouraging attitude he would have failed his exam.

fountain pen ■ Füllfederhalter
Fountain pens are increasingly being replaced by ballpoint pens.

go ■ Versuch
If you can't solve the problem the first time round just give it another go.

grade ■ Note; (AE) Klasse
I'm afraid I can't give you a good grade for this exam.
He's an eighth grade high school student.

to graduate ■ einen Abschluss machen
In the USA you graduate from high school, in the UK from university.

graduate ▪ Hochschulabsolvent(in); Absolvent(in) (einer Sekundarschule in den USA)

In "The Graduate" Dustin Hoffman plays someone who has just finished high school.

grant ▪ Stipendium

Students whose parents do not earn a lot of money often get a grant.

handwriting ▪ Handschrift

After he had started using the computer his handwriting became worse and worse.

headmaster [hed'mɑːstə] ▪ (Schul-)Direktor

Our headmaster may be an excellent organizer but he is not a very good teacher.

headmistress [hed'mɪstrɪs] ▪ (Schul-)Direktorin

Our headmistress is both a top organizer and a good teacher.

high school ▪ höhere Schule

After primary school young people in the USA go to a high school.

inspector ▪ Inspektor(in), Untersuchungsbeamte(r)

The headmaster was not looking forward to the arrival of the school inspector.

to instruct ▪ beibringen, belehren, unterrichten

The teacher instructed his students on how to proceed in a case of emergency.

to interpret ▪ interpretieren

I have no idea how to interpret this story.

junior high school (AE) ▪ Aufbauschule

A junior high school is attended by students between 11 and 14 or 12 and 15.

kindergarten ▪ Kindergarten

A kindergarten is also sometimes called a play group.

Latin ▪ Latein; lateinisch

Latin used to be a world language like English today.

Many languages use the Latin alphabet.

lecture ■ Vorlesung, Vortrag
The professor's lecture on Shakespeare was very interesting.

linguistic ■ sprachlich
A child's linguistic development should be fairly advanced before it goes to school.

margin ■ Rand, Spielraum
The students were asked to leave a wide margin for the professor's remarks.

master's degree ■ Magister
After her BA she studied for a master's degree.

mathematics ■ Mathematik
After taking her degree she became a professor of mathematics.

middle school ■ Übergangsschule
In Britain there are some middle schools for 8- or 9-year-old pupils. In the USA the pupils are between 10 and 13 or 14 years old.

nursery ■ Kindergarten, Vorschule
Max went to a nursery every day because he was too young to go to school.

optional ■ wahlfrei, optional
This course is optional.

overhead projector [əʊvə'hed] ■ Overheadprojektor
In my classrooms there were overhead projectors but certainly no video projectors.

to paraphrase ■ paraphrasieren, umschreiben
The students were asked to paraphrase the short story.

pass ■ Bestehen
She only received a "Pass" in the exam although she had hoped to get a B.

to paste ■ einfügen
As you have relied too much on copy-and-paste your essay cannot be accepted.

PE (Physical Education) ▪ Sportunterricht

PE is an important subject at school.

PhD ▪ Doktortitel

Angela Merkel, the German Chancellor, has a PhD in physics.

polytechnic ▪ Fachhochschule

In Britain, polytechnics were converted into universities in 1993.

presentation ▪ Präsentation

The teacher gave a convincing presentation of the new electronic blackboard.

primary school ▪ Grundschule

In Britain children usually go to primary school from age 5 to age 11.

principal ▪ Direktor(in), Schulleiter(in); (Universitäts-)Rektor(in)

She was appointed principal of a research institute and of Stirling University.

public school ▪ private Sekundarschule

In England a public school is a private secondary school for children of well-to-do parents. In Scotland and the USA a public school is a state school for everybody.

quotation ▪ Zitat

Make sure that all your quotations are correct in every detail.

replacement ▪ Vertretung

Our English teacher was ill so Ms McKinley taught us as a replacement.

report ▪ Zeugnis

When the report arrived Kevin was nervous because he knew it would not be good.

riddle ▪ Rätsel

Algebra remained a riddle to Percy all his life.

rubber ▪ Radiergummi

If you write with a pencil you can delete a word by using a rubber.

ruler ▪ Lineal

Use a ruler if you wish to draw a straight line.

satisfactory ▪ zufriedenstellend, befriedigend

Your essay was not good but certainly satisfactory.

scholar ▪ Stipendiat(in)

She studied as a scholar at King's College, Cambridge.

scholarship ▪ Stipendium

She won a scholarship to Harvard University.

school report ▪ Zeugnis

Matthew never liked the day he received his school report.

schoolchildren ▪ Schüler(innen)

All schoolchildren in Britain have to wear uniform.

secondary school ▪ Sekundarschule, weiterführende Schule

In England pupils go to a secondary school from age 11.

seminar ▪ Seminar

A seminar is a class in which students present papers, which are discussed afterwards.

senior high school (AE) ▪ weiterführende Schule für die Jahrgangsstufen 10 bis 12 in den USA

Once you graduate from senior high school you can study at a university.

to spell ▪ buchstabieren, schreiben

One of the first things children learn at school is to spell.

state school ▪ staatliche/öffentliche Schule

More than ninety per cent of all pupils in GB go to a state school.

to summarize ▪ zusammenfassen

Read the text and summarize it in 150 words.

summary ▪ Zusammenfassung

Read the following text and write a short summary of it.

supervisor ▪ Betreuer(in)

Professor Elliott was my supervisor when I wrote my thesis.

term ▪ Semester, Trimester
Ken spent the summer term at Stirling University.

textbook ▪ Lehrbuch
Textbooks in mathematics tend to be very expensive.

thesis ▪ wissenschaftliche Arbeit; Dissertation
At the end of their studies students usually write a thesis.
He received his PhD as a result of his thesis and his oral exam.

thoughtful ▪ wohl überlegt
That was a very thoughtful analysis, Emma.

timetable ▪ Stundenplan; Zeitplan; Fahrplan, Flugplan
Bo has a very good timetable this year.
Our CEO has a very tight timetable.
Our timetable will be published on 1 October.

tutor ▪ Tutor(in); Privatlehrer(in)
After taking her degree she was offered a job as a tutor at her college.
He would never have passed the test if he hadn't had the help of a tutor.

undergraduate ▪ Student(in)
Before they take their final exams students are called undergraduate.

vacation (AE) ▪ Ferien
As a student I did not have enough money to go on vacation.

video projector ▪ Beamer
Video projectors have long replaced overhead projectors at school.

workbook ▪ Arbeitsbuch
The students had an excellent workbook for their English course.

4.2 Berufsausbildung und Berufe

accountant ▪ Buchhalter(in)
As an accountant you are responsible for the bookkeeping in your business.

agent ▪ Vertreter(in); Agent(in)
She is an agent for artists and her husband is a travel agent.

baker ▪ Bäcker(in)
As she liked baking cakes as a young girl she wanted to become a baker.

captain ▪ Kapitän; Hauptmann
The person supposed to leave a sinking ship last is its captain.
He had the rank of captain in the army.

career ▪ Karriere, Laufbahn
If you take up a job in this promising company you'll be sure to make a career.

course ▪ Kurs, Unterricht, Lehrgang
She attended an evening course in typing.

doctor ▪ Arzt/Ärztin
If you need to see a specialist in the UK, you must go to your family doctor first.

education ▪ Ausbildung
This job requires an excellent education.

farmer ▪ Bauer, Bäuerin, Farmer(in)
Farmers in the UK tend to be rather well-to-do because their farms are large.

to fill in (AE: to fill out) ▪ ausfüllen
Would you please fill in this form before you hand in your application?

to fill out (AE) ▪ ausfüllen
I'm afraid you haven't filled out this form properly.

fisher ■ Fischer(in), Angler(in)
Ten fishers – five men and five women – took part in the competition.

▸ **fisherman** ■ Fischer, Angler

▸ **fisherwoman** ■ Fischerin, Anglerin

gardener ■ Gärtner(in)
If you have a very large garden you may wish to employ a gardener to look after it.

general ■ General(in)
A general has a very high position in the armed forces.

greengrocer ■ Obst- und Gemüsehändler(in)
A greengrocer sells fruit and vegetables.

housewife ■ Hausfrau
In the past most married women did not have paid jobs, they were housewives.

instructor ■ Lehrer(in)
School teachers are not called instructors like for instance driving instructors.

manager ■ Manager(in), Geschäftsführer(in)
She started her career as a secretary and left the company as a manager.

mechanic ■ Mechaniker(in)
After finishing school she trained to become a mechanic.

officer ■ Offizier(in); Beamte(r); Polizist(in)
She is an officer in the army.
My father was an officer in the Foreign Office.
The officers checked the city centre for suspicious persons.

official ■ Amtsperson, Beamte(r)
He served as an official for the examination board.

police ■ Polizei
The police have done a very good job.
The police is a very important institution.

policeman (Pl.: -men) ▪ Polizist
Monica's husband is a policeman.

police officer ▪ Polizist(in)
"Police officer" is a politically more correct term than "policeman".

policewoman (Pl.: -women) ▪ Polizistin
Robert's wife is a policewoman.

practical ▪ Praktikum
Students are advised to do a practical before deciding what career to pursue.

professor ▪ Professor(in)
Woodrow Wilson was a law professor before he became President of the USA.

representative ▪ Vertreter(in)
The politician had begun his career as a representative of an automobile producer.

sales manager ▪ Verkaufsleiter(in)
Mary was appointed sales manager for Germany.

salesperson ▪ Verkäufer(in)
Salespersons do not as a rule earn a lot money.

secretary ▪ Sekretär(in)
She started her career as a secretary and retired as her company's CEO.

senior ▪ Chef..., vorgesetzt
She was appointed senior secretary.

soldier ▪ Soldat(in)
After school she joined the army to become a soldier.

solicitor ▪ Rechtsanwalt/Rechtsanwältin
If you want to go to court or buy property you should see a solicitor first.

tailor ▪ Schneider(in)
Jack's father always had his suits made by a tailor.

to train ▪ ausbilden
Ron was trained in electrical engineering.

training ▪ Schulung, Ausbildung
She received her training at her employer's academy.

worker ▪ Arbeiter(in)
He's been a worker all his life.

---

air hostess ▪ Stewardess
Up to 24 air hostesses work on an Airbus A380.

analyst ▪ Analytiker(in)
She works as an analyst in a chemical factory.

apprentice ▪ Auszubildende(r)
He served as an apprentice to a butcher.

architect ▪ Architekt(in)
Renzo Piano is the famous Italian architect who built Malta's opera and parliament.

assistant ▪ Assistent(in); Verkäufer(in)
Most executives have a PA, i.e. a personal assistant.
After school he trained as an assistant because he wanted to work in a supermarket.

attorney ▪ Anwalt/Anwältin
The American attorney is a barrister or a solicitor in the UK.

barrister ▪ plädierende(r) Rechtsanwalt/-anwältin
A solicitor does not represent you in court, but a barrister does.

bricklayer ▪ Maurer(in)
A bricklayer is also sometimes called a brickie.

builder ▪ Bauarbeiter(in)
Fifteen builders worked on the construction site.

bus driver ▪ Busfahrer(in)
Bus drivers have a very responsible job.

businessman (Pl.: -men) ▪ Geschäftsmann
He was a very successful businessman employing fifty people …

businesswoman (Pl.: -women) ▪ Geschäftsfrau
... and his wife was also a very successful businesswoman.

butcher ['bʊtʃə] ▪ Metzger(in)
Mary and John worked as butchers in their own shop cutting up and selling meat.

carpenter ▪ Zimmermann, Schreiner(in)
Maria's fiancé Jonathan was a carpenter.

chef ▪ Küchenchef
Jamie Oliver is one of the best known chefs in Britain.

chemist ▪ Chemiker(in); Apotheker(in)
We are looking for a chemist for our research department.
What is a chemist in the UK is a pharmacist in the USA.

chief ▪ Leiter(in) einer Organisation
"Chief" is short for chief executive officer, i.e. a company's highest-ranking officer.

clerk ▪ Büroangestellte(r)
After school she decided to become a clerk because she likes working in an office.

colonel ['kɜːnəl] ▪ Oberst
A colonel is usually the chief officer of a regiment.

consultant ▪ Facharzt/Fachärztin
In Britain consultants usually work in a hospital.

cook ▪ Koch/Köchin
The restaurant was looking for a third cook.

correspondent ▪ Korrespondent(in)
He was promoted USA correspondent for his newspaper.

dentist ▪ Zahnarzt/Zahnärztin
If you have a toothache, you'd better see a dentist.

designer ▪ Designer(in), Konstrukteur(in)
Colani is a top designer of furniture and other household equipment.

diplomat ▪ Diplomat(in)
Diplomats are the official link between their country and another country.

dressmaker ▪ (Damen-)Schneider(in)
Sorry, sir, I don't make suits for gentlemen. I'm a dressmaker.

engineer ▪ Ingenieur(in), Techniker(in)
The mechanic had trouble with my car so he had to ask an engineer for help.

entertainer ▪ Entertainer(in)
Frank Sinatra is still regarded as one of the world's greatest entertainers.

firefighter ▪ Feuerwehrfrau/-mann
Hundreds of firefighters tried in vain to prevent the fire from spreading.

fireman ▪ Feuerwehrmann
Firemen often rescue people from burning houses.

firewoman ▪ Feuerwehrfrau
Mark's sister was one of the first firewomen in her town.

flight attendant ▪ Flugbegleiter(in)
On an A 340-600 there are 12 flight attendants and two pilots.

foreman ▪ Vorarbeiter
The foreman told the bricklayer to clear all the bricks from the fourteenth floor.

forewoman ▪ Vorarbeiterin
After working only three months for her company she was already made forewoman.

further education ▪ Weiterbildung
If you wish to make a career you should go to a college for further education.

guidance ▪ Führung, Beratung, Anleitung
After school young people usually require some guidance concerning their future careers.

hairdresser ■ Friseur(in)
Hairdressers do much more than just cut your hair.

historian ■ Historiker(in)
Many historians have written about the Roman Empire.

interpreter ■ Dolmetscher(in)
When her boss travelled to Portugal she accompanied him as an interpreter.

joiner ■ Tischler(in), Schreiner(in)
We had our new cupboard made by a joiner.

junior ■ untergeordnet
Although she is fifty she still works as a junior secretary.

lawyer ■ Rechtsanwalt/Rechtsanwältin
After taking her degree she became a lawyer.

librarian ■ Bibliothekar(in)
She became chief librarian in our local library.

manual ■ manuell, Hand…
He was a manual worker all his life.

MD (AE) ■ Arzt/Ärztin, Dr. med.
The letters MD after your name indicate that you may practise as a medical doctor.

meteorologist ■ Meteorologe(-in)
Meteorologists are becoming better and better at forecasting the weather.

miner ■ Bergarbeiter(in)
The number of miners in Germany has been decreasing considerably.

model ■ Modell
In her youth she worked as a model in the fashion industry.

nurse ■ Krankenschwester, Krankenpfleger
She became a nurse and so did her brother.

painter ■ Anstreicher(in)
We need to call a painter to paint the doors in our flat.

peasant ■ (Klein-)Bauer

Many people in poor countries earn their living as peasants.

pharmacist ■ Apotheker(in)

An American pharmacist would be a chemist in the UK.

photographer ■ Fotograf(in)

He turned his hobby into a job and became a professional photographer.

pilot ■ Pilot(in); Lotse, Lotsin

She worked as a pilot for British Airways.

Mark Twain worked as a pilot on the Mississippi.

plumber ['plʌmə] ■ Klempner(in)

Plumbers instal and repair water pipes etc.

practitioner ■ Arzt/Ärztin; Anwalt/Anwältin

If you need to see a specialist, you must go to your general practitioner first.

She worked in a legal firm as a practitioner.

printer ■ Drucker(in)

The traditional job of the printer is dying out.

professional ■ professionell

My grandson wants to become a professional football player.

qualification ■ Abschluss

GCE A levels are the highest school-leaving qualifications in England.

questionnaire ■ Fragebogen

Before starting their training the trainees had to fill in a questionnaire.

reporter ■ Reporter(in)

After taking her degree she became a reporter for the Times.

sailor ■ Seemann, Matrose(-in), Segler(in)

Working as a sailor can be very hard.

self-employed ▪ selbstständig
If you are self-employed you must provide for your old age yourself.

sergeant ▪ Sergeant, Feldwebel(in); Polizeimeister(in)
Mary has joined the Air Force. She is a sergeant now.
Her friend is a sergeant with the police.

servant ▪ Diener(in); Dienstbote(-in); Angestellte(r)
Lord Ashville has twenty servants.
Timothy works as a servant for the Cumbernauld Hotel.
My father used to be a public servant. He worked for the government.

shepherd ['ʃepəd] ▪ Hirte(-in), Schäfer(in)
Looking after their sheep is the job of shepherds.

shop assistant ▪ Verkäufer(in)
The shop assistant showed the customer the goods she wanted to buy.

skilled worker ▪ Facharbeiter(in)
For this complex job we only employ skilled workers.

steward ▪ Flug-, Schiffsbegleiter, Steward
He worked as a steward on an ocean liner.

stewardess ▪ Flug-, Schiffsbegleiterin, Stewardess
Being a stewardess used to be the dream of many young girls.

storekeeper ▪ Lagerist(in); Geschäftsinhaber(in)
He worked as a storekeeper for his boss, before he set up as storekeeper himself.

supervisor ▪ Aufsichtsbeamte(r); Vorarbeiter(in)
She works as a supervisor in the town council.
Her husband is a supervisor in a coal mine.

surgeon ▪ Chirurg(in)
She works as a heart surgeon in St. Thomas' Hospital.

tax consultant ▪ Steuerberater(in)
If you have various types of income you may need the help of a tax consultant.

technician ▪ Techniker(in)
I can't do this for you. You'd better ask a technician to help you.

trainee ▪ Auszubildende(r)
After school he was offered a job as a trainee in the retail trade.

trainer ▪ Trainer(in)
He had a trainer to teach him how to make speeches.

travel agent ▪ Reisebürokaufmann/-frau
Phil is being trained to become a travel agent.

trick ▪ Trick
Jack knows all the tricks of his trade.

unskilled worker ▪ ungelernter Arbeiter
As an unskilled worker you will not earn much money.

waiter ▪ Kellner
He began his career as a waiter and later became the manager of a restaurant.

waitress ▪ Kellnerin
She began her career as a waitress and later became the manager of a restaurant.

4.3 Berufsbezogene Ausdrücke

absence ▪ Abwesenheit, Fehlen
The boss asked his secretary to explain his absence.

application ▪ Bewerbung
If you wish to be invited for an interview you'll have to write a good application.

to apply ▪ sich bewerben
The company had fifty people applying for this fascinating job.

to appoint ▪ berufen, ernennen
Ms Yellen was appointed boss of the Fed, the US central bank.

appointment ■ Ernennung
The appointment of Mr Myers as president caused some problems.

assessment ■ Einschätzung, Prüfung
It was decided to send some of those looking for a job to an assessment centre.

to assume ■ übernehmen
In my new job I had to assume a lot of responsibility.

authority ■ Weisungsbefugnis
Every boss has authority over his or her staff.

award ■ Belohnung, Auszeichnung, Preis
She won the award for employee of the month for her excellent suggestions.

benefit ■ Nutzen, Vorteil
It is a clear benefit that my new company is not far from our house.

boss ■ Chef(in)
She is the best boss I ever had.

to check ■ prüfen, kontrollieren
The customer checked the goods to see whether they were damaged.

chief ■ oberste(r, s)
He was appointed chief secretary.

colleague ['kɒliːg] ■ Kollege(-in)
He told his boss that his colleagues treated him unfairly.

to consider ■ erwägen, betrachten
After considering the list carefully we have decided to employ Shirley Myers.

criterion (Pl.: criteria) ■ Kriterium
If you want to employ someone, his or her qualification and experience should be your main criteria.

to earn ■ verdienen
A medical doctor earns more money than a nurse.

to entitle ■ berechtigen
After working all my life I think I am entitled to a decent pension.

expert ▪ Experte(-in)
If you have problems doing this job ask Mary. She's an expert.

face-to-face ▪ persönlich
At last he was granted a face-to-face conversation with his boss.

fellow worker ▪ Arbeitskollege(-in)
One of my fellow workers is not very nice.

file ▪ Akte, Datei
Could you please pass me the file of the Smith case?

to fill ▪ Position besetzen
All the candidates are good. So I think we won't have any problems filling this new position.

to fire ▪ entlassen; feuern
In the USA it is quite easy for employers to fire workers.

flexibility ▪ Flexibilität
If you show some flexibility you will surely find a job.

folder ▪ Ordner
Put the bill into the folder on my desk.

formal ▪ formell, formal
If you apply for a job you must usually write a formal letter of application.

function ▪ Funktion, Aufgabe
What is the function of a foreman, I wonder?

to handle ▪ anfassen umgehen mit
Handle with care.

to hire ▪ einstellen
Hiring and firing people used to be a widespread practice in the USA.

holiday ▪ Feiertag; Urlaub (AE: vacation)
Fortunately there are quite a number of holidays this month.
Mr. Larsen is on holiday and will be back next week.

income ▪ Einkommen
Some football players have a very high income.

instruction ▪ Unterricht
New employees receive regular instruction by our experts.

to interview ▪ Einstellungsgespräch führen
The boss interviews the applicants herself.

interview ▪ Einstellungsgespräch
The applicant's answers in the interview were so good that he got the job.

job ▪ Arbeit, Anstellung; Aufgabe
In contrast to English the German term "Job" does not usually refer to a permanent position.

key ▪ wichtigste, Schlüssel...
The finance minister holds a key position in every government.

labor union ▪ Gewerkschaft
The American labor unions are not quite as important as the British trade unions.

to maintain ▪ warten
It is John's job to maintain all the machines in our company.

to manage ▪ leiten
John managed the High Street branch of the "Shopper" supermarket chain.

management ▪ Management, Leitung; Verwaltung
The management was sorry for the trouble caused to customers.
The management of this large property is rather difficult.

meeting ▪ Besprechung, Treffen
You can't talk to the boss because he is at a meeting.

office ▪ Büro
She works in an office.

to operate ▪ betreiben
He operated his father's building business for thirty years.

place ▪ Stellung
She was very lucky to have so many friends in high places.

post ■ Posten, Stelle
After only a few years in the company she was already given a very well paid post.

to present ■ vorlegen
He presented his proposal for a reorganization to his boss.

private ['praɪvət] ■ persönlich
He asked for a private conversation with his boss.

to promote ■ befördern; werben für
Jennifer was promoted section leader after only six months in the company because she had so successfully promoted the company's products.

rate ■ Maß, Menge
The rate of people who do not come to work on a Monday is intolerable.

to record [rɪ'kɔːd] ■ aufzeichnen, protokollieren
It is the secretary's job to record the conversation between her boss and his business partner.

record ['rekɔːd] ■ Aufzeichnung, Protokoll
Could I see the record of yesterday's meeting, please?

reference ■ Referenz
Before taking up another job Kenneth asked his employer for a reference.

to remove ■ entlassen
After almost ruining the company the CEO was removed from his post.

responsibility ■ Verantwortung
Elinor applied for a job with more responsibility.

to serve ■ dienen
After school I served in the army for two years.

skill ■ Geschick, Fähigkeit
Jamie is very useful for his boss because of his many skills.

specialist ▪ Spezialist(in)
In order to solve this problem we need to hire a specialist.

to strike (struck, struck) ▪ streiken
The transport workers' union has decided to strike.

strike ▪ Streik
All the workers in our factory were on strike.

task ▪ Aufgabe, Pflicht
It was her task to maintain contact with all the new customers.

unemployment ▪ Arbeitslosigkeit
Unemployment is both a major economic and psychological problem.

upper ▪ höhere(r, s)
He works in the upper ranks of his company's management.

vacation (AE) ▪ Urlaub
Many Americans have only fourteen days of vacation per year.

wage ▪ Lohn
The minimum wage to be paid employees in Germany is €8.50 per hour.

to work ▪ arbeiten; funktionieren
Father had worked for 45 years before he retired at 65.
We had our clock repaired because it did not work any longer.

work ▪ Arbeit
You can't see Mike. He is at work.

working hours ▪ Arbeitszeit
Our working hours are 38.5 hours a week.

work permit ▪ Arbeitserlaubnis
I'm afraid you cannot work here without a work permit.

works ▪ Arbeiten
Danger. Road works ahead.

workshop ▪ Werkstatt
My boss has a very well equipped workshop.

absent ▪ abwesend
Quite a few workers were absent on Monday morning.

to adjust ▪ angleichen, regulieren, ändern
Those items are not precise enough. Try adjusting your tool.

administrative ▪ Verwaltungs…
Elizabeth was not happy with her purely administrative job.

advance ▪ Vorschuss
Sir, do you think you could possibly give me an advance?

to advertise ▪ werben für, inserieren
The company advertised a new job in a trade journal.

adviser ▪ Berater(in)
Ms Frances Page works as a personnel adviser in our company.

agenda ▪ Tagesordnung, Agenda
Let us proceed to the next item on the agenda.

applicant ▪ Bewerber(in)
There were no fewer than ten applicants for this job.

to assign ▪ zuweisen, übertragen
After working in the company for only six months she was already assigned a job with more responsibility.

to assist ▪ unterstützen, helfen
She assisted her boss in personnel affairs.

assurance ▪ Zusicherung
The staff were given an assurance that nobody would have to leave firm.

to award ▪ (Preis) verleihen
A prize of fifty pounds will be awarded for the best suggestion.

bonus ▪ Prämie, Bonus
Many employees get a Christmas bonus on top of their salary.

break ▪ Pause
There is a thirty-minute lunch break.

▸ to take a break (took, taken) ▪ eine Pause machen
Coach drivers must take a break regularly.

burden ▪ Last, Belastung
Doing this job is quite a burden. It is almost too much for me.

cafeteria ▪ Kantine
We have an excellent – though rather expensive – cafeteria in our company.

canteen ▪ (Werks-)Kantine
Our canteen offers basic food at very reasonable prices.

chief ▪ Leiter(in) einer Organisation
Not every boss is a chief – only the highest ranking boss of an organization is sometimes referred to as chief.

to co-operate ▪ zusammenarbeiten, kooperieren
We'll only be able to deal with this tricky problem if we co-operate.

co-operation ▪ Zusammenarbeit, Kooperation
A talent for co-operation is essential for this position.

counsellor ▪ Berater(in)
When she lost her job, Ruth went to see a job counsellor.

craft ▪ Handwerk, Gewerbe
The number of people employed in a craft has been decreasing steadily over the years.

curriculum vitae ▪ Lebenslauf
Every application must be accompanied by the applicant's curriculum vitae.

CV ▪ Lebenslauf
CV is the abbreviation of curriculum vitae.

diary ▪ Tagebuch, Terminkalender
I've got so many appointments that I'd be completely lost without a diary.

to dictate ▪ diktieren
My boss dictates all her letters to her personal assistant.

discrimination ▪ Diskriminierung
Even today women often experience discrimination in their jobs.

to dismiss ■ entlassen

The boss dismissed one of his employees for unprofessional conduct.

disorder ■ Durcheinander, Unordnung

The boss was annoyed when he saw the disorder in his secretary's office.

dispute ■ Auseinandersetzung

Management and unions were engaged in a long dispute about working conditions.

division ■ Abteilung

The company is organized into several divisions.

dominant ■ beherrschend, tonangebend

In his team of architects he was definitely the dominant character.

to dominate ■ beherrschen

Our company dominated our competitors for a long time.

expense ■ Ausgabe, Aufwendung

As he travelled on business he had his expenses paid back by his company.

fax ■ Fax(nachricht)

My brother stopped writing faxes long ago. He prefers emails.

to file ■ ablegen

Please, file this document under the heading "Expenses".

flexible ■ flexibel, beweglich

American workers are much more flexible than Germans when it comes to changing their jobs.

flexitime ■ gleitende Arbeitszeit

Parents can profit from flexitime in their jobs because one parent can look after the children in the morning and the other in the evening.

full-time ■ ganztags, Vollzeit...

As a single parent you cannot really be a full-time worker.

hourly rate ■ Stundenlohn

Workers who are paid by the hour work for an hourly rate.

hourly wage ▪ Stundenlohn

He was paid an hourly wage of only £5.

labour (AE: labor) ▪ (harte physische) Arbeit; Arbeitskräfte

He was exhausted from the labour of digging the garden.

There is a distinct labour shortage in this country.

living ▪ Lebensunterhalt

He earned his living as a journalist.

to load ▪ verladen, beladen; aufladen

It is my job to see to it that all tools are loaded into the cars.

My boss keeps loading me with new responsibilites.

maintenance ▪ Instandhaltung, Wartung

The proper maintenance of our expensive machines is extremely important.

to make up for s.th. ▪ für etwas entschädigen

We hope this bonus will make up for the trouble you have had to put up with.

mediation ▪ Schlichtung

Let's see what mediation can do to resolve the conflict between the workers and the management.

monthly ▪ monatlich

Salaries in Britain are quoted on an annual basis but paid on a monthly basis.

to negotiate ▪ verhandeln

The unions negotiated with the employers about a pay rise.

negotiation ▪ Verhandlung

The negotiations between management and staff were concluded successfully.

noticeboard ▪ Aushang, schwarzes Brett

The management displays important messages on the noticeboard in the canteen.

occupation ▪ Beruf

What is your occupation? – I am a carpenter.

operator ■ Bediener(in)
She works as a computer operator.

out of work ■ arbeitslos
After so many years of working he found it hard to be suddenly out of work.

overtime ■ Überstunden, Mehrarbeit
In times of very heavy demand you must expect to work overtime.

to paint ■ streichen
We had our house painted.

part-time ■ Teilzeit…
After the birth of their son both parents decided to work part-time for a number of years.

pay ■ Bezahlung, Lohn, Gehalt
The management promised to grant their staff a pay rise.

PDS ■ tabellarischer Lebenslauf
Most CVs today are written in the form of a PDS (personal data sheet).

to practice (AE) ■ üben; praktizieren
Americans practice on the violin, people in Britain practise on it.
She practiced as a dentist in Milwaukee for twenty years.

practice ■ Übung; Praxis
Playing the violin well requires talent and a lot of practice.
The young lawyer opened a legal practice as a solicitor in his home town.

to practise (AE: to practice) ■ üben; praktizieren
He practised on his violin several hours a day.
She practised as a GP in London for several years.

premium ■ Bonus
The company paid its staff a premium for good suggestions.

proceeding ■ Vorgehen, Verfahrensweise
The personnel manager explained the proceeding of the test session.

processing ■ Bearbeitung
The processing of your application will only take some days.

profession ■ Beruf
The traditional professions were those of the lawyer, the clergyman, and the medical doctor. Now they include basically every job.

professional ■ beruflich; akademisch; fachmännisch
Would you like to talk to me in your professional function?
As a university professor he has excellent professional qualifications.
The electrician did a very professional job fixing my problems.

promotion ■ Beförderung; Werbekampagne
Thomas was promised a promotion for his successful promotion of the company's products.

qualification ■ Qualifikation
For a successful application the candidate will have to have the following qualifications.

to quit (quit/quitted, quit/quitted) ■ kündigen
She quit her job after only three months.

rank ■ Position, Stellung
He was promoted to the rank of chief supervisor.

to recruit [rɪ'kruːt] ■ einstellen; rekrutieren
British Rail recruited 150 technicians.
The army recruited a large number of young people.

remuneration ■ Vergütung
The directors' remuneration included their salaries, company cars and share portfolios.

to repair ■ reparieren
We must repair one of our machines before we can carry out your order.

repair ■ Reparatur
I'm afraid the watch is beyond repair. You'll have to buy another one.

to reproduce ■ reproduzieren
Can you please reproduce the report for all the members of the board.

to resign ■ kündigen
Since his wife found a well paid job in another part of the country he resigned from his job to follow her.

resignation ■ Kündigung
She handed her letter of resignation to her boss.

to resume ■ wieder aufnehmen
After the lunch break the secretary resumed writing the report for his boss.

résumé ['rezjʊmeɪ] ■ Lebenslauf
An American writes his or her résumé, someone in the UK writes his or her curriculum vitae (CV).

to retire ■ in den Ruhestand treten
I decided to retire at the age of sixty although it did mean a loss of income.

retirement ■ Ruhestand
Some people look forward to their retirement, others don't.

to reward ■ belohnen
Arthur was rewarded by his company for making good suggestions.

reward ■ Belohnung
The reward he received was three days extra holiday.

salary ■ Gehalt
In Britain your salary is calculated on an annual basis.

schedule ■ Terminplan
Attached please find the schedule for our meeting on Thursday.

scheme [skiːm] ■ Plan
Our company offers its employees a generous pension scheme.

shift ■ Schicht(arbeit)
Mike hated night shifts.

shortlist ■ Auswahlliste, engere Wahl
Invitations for an interview have been sent to all the applicants on our shortlist.

sick note ■ Krankenschein
You are required to send a sick note to your employer on the second day of absence from work.

skilful ■ geschickt
She is a very skilful dressmaker.

skilled ■ ausgebildet, qualifiziert
He is a skilled carpenter.

specification ■ genaue Angabe, Spezifizierung
What we require is a specification of your professional career.

sphere ■ Sphäre
His particular sphere of responsibility is the protection of the environment.

spokesman ■ Sprecher
He was appointed spokesman for the company.

spokeswoman ■ Sprecherin
She was appointed spokeswoman for the company.

to tackle s.th. ■ etwas in Angriff nehmen
Do you think you can tackle this job alone or would you like some help?

term ■ Laufzeit
The term of this contract begins on 1 July 2015.

to type ■ Maschine schreiben, tippen
The CEO's secretary types at an incredible speed.

typewriter ■ Schreibmaschine
In the past CVs used to be written by hand and not by typewriter or computer.

typist ■ Schreibkraft
She began her career as a typist.

unemployed ▪ arbeitslos

Most people find it difficult to put up with being unemployed.

union ▪ Gewerkschaft

The more employees there are in a union the stronger it is.

union official ▪ Gewerkschaftsfunktionär

A union official is a paid employee of a trade union.

union member ▪ Gewerkschaftsmitglied

Some companies don't like their employees to be union members.

unprofessional ▪ unfachmännisch; berufswidrig

The plumber did a very unprofessional job. The pipe still leaks.

She was fired for unprofessional conduct.

vacancy ['veɪkənsi] ▪ freie Stelle

As a result of lively business we have a few vacancies to fill.

wildcat strike ▪ wilder Streik

Without any warning the workers began a wildcat strike.

working ▪ berufstätig

Life as a working mother is rather exhausting.

to xerox™ s.th. ▪ etwas kopieren

Could you please xerox this for me?

5. Freizeit

5.1 Hobbys

activity ■ Tätigkeit, Beschäftigung
Playing the guitar is his favourite activity.

ball ■ Ball, Tanzveranstaltung
What I like best of all is going to balls to dance with my girlfriend.

block ■ Klotz
As a little child Marian liked playing with building blocks.

camp ■ Lager
When I was young I spent all my summer holidays in a camp with my friends.

camping ■ Zelten, Campen
Camping in all types of weather was Henry's favourite hobby.

card ■ Karte
Bridge is a difficult card game.

to collect ■ sammeln
My father collected stamps from all over the world.

doll ■ Puppe
Whatever I tried – Mary would only play with her dolls.

to draw (drew, drawn) ■ zeichnen
She was so good at drawing portraits that eventually she turned her hobby into a job.

to enjoy ■ genießen, gern tun, gern haben
My wife and I have always enjoyed playing Scrabble.

▸ **Enjoy your meal!** ■ Guten Appetit!

hobby ■ Hobby, Freizeitbeschäftigung
People need a hobby in order not to be bored in their old age.

interest ▪ Interesse
My youngest son has always had a very keen interest in photography.

painting ▪ Gemälde; Malerei
Da Vinci's "Mona Lisa" is one of the most famous paintings in the world.
Bernard told me that his hobby was painting.

picnic ▪ Picknick
Every weekend my landlord has a picnic in the country even if the weather is bad.

to play ▪ spielen
The boys liked playing football in the park.

play ▪ Spiel
Don't disturb the girls. They're at play.

to ride (rode, ridden) ▪ reiten
I like riding my horse on a weekend.

to shoot (shot, shot) ▪ schießen, feuern
He shot at the bull but missed it.

show ▪ Ausstellung, Schau
Going to dog shows is her favourite hobby.

to ski ▪ Ski laufen
Louis is very good at skiing.

toy ▪ Spielzeug
After doing his homework Jacob likes playing with his toys.

trip ▪ Ausflug, Reise
Going on trips is their main hobby.

---

to amuse ▪ belustigen, amüsieren
This novel amused me so much that I read it twice.

to balance ▪ balancieren
Her main hobby is balancing on a rope.

balloon ■ Ballon
I like riding a hot-air balloon.

bubble ■ Blase
What he likes best is blowing bubbles with his bubble gum.

to dance ■ tanzen
Running about and dancing to music were Joan's favourite hobbies.

descent ■ Abstieg
The tourists began their descent from the mountain at 6 a.m.

to dive ■ tauchen, einen Kopfsprung machen
Diving from bridges into rivers is a rather dangerous hobby.

drum ■ Trommel
Do practise on your drum, but don't do it between one and three in the afternoon.

enjoyment ■ Vergnügen
Reading a good book was my grandmother's chief enjoyment.

entertainment ■ Unterhaltung
My grandpa's chief entertainment was classical music.

to favour s.th. ■ etwas bevorzugen, etwas lieber tun
I certainly favour classical music over rock music.

fireworks ■ Feuerwerk
On 31 December many people enjoy watching the fireworks.

to gamble ■ um Geld spielen
It is not a good idea to gamble in order to make money.

to hide (hid, hidden) ■ (sich) verstecken
The burglar hid in a dustbin, but the police discovered him.

▸ to play hide-and-seek ■ Verstecken spielen

to hunt ■ jagen
Ken loves hunting deer.

hunter ■ Jäger(in)
My uncle is a keen hunter.

hunting ■ Jagen, Jagd
Hunting was my grandfather's favourite hobby.

to jog ■ einen Dauerlauf machen, joggen
Ever since I was young I have liked jogging several times a week.

to kick ■ treten, (Ball) schießen
From her early youth she liked kicking a ball in her parents' garden.

leisure ['leʒə] ■ Freizeit
Many people's favourite leisure activity is watching TV.

to occupy ■ ausfüllen
His hobbies occupy much of his time.

puzzle ■ Rätsel
Doing puzzles on the weekend is one of my favourite hobbies.

recreation ■ Entspannung, Freizeitbeschäftigung, Hobby
After five days of working most people use the weekend for recreation.

ride ■ Ritt
We often go for a ride in Hyde Park.

rod ■ Angel
The fish was so strong that it broke my fishing rod.

saddle ■ Sattel
Marion spends up to three hours in the saddle every day.

to sail ■ segeln
We like sailing in the Mediterranean.

sail ■ Segel
We're going to set sail at 6 o'clock tomorrow morning.

scout ■ Pfadfinder(in)
Nowadays both boys and girls can be scouts.

stroll ■ Spaziergang
Every day she goes for a stroll in the park.

to take up s.th. ■ etwas anfangen
She took up playing the recorder when she was young.

trick ■ Stich
Gerd is good at all card games. He usually takes most tricks.

5.2 Sport

to aim ▪ zielen
Margot aimed at the target but missed it.

to attack ▪ angreifen
In the fifth round the boxer started to really attack his opponent.

attempt ▪ Versuch
He managed to clear the height of 2.30 metres at his third attempt.

ball ▪ Ball
Lampard passed the ball to Rooney.

to be behind (was, been) ▪ hinten liegen, im Rückstand sein
At half time, our team was three goals behind.

to beat (beat, beaten) ▪ schlagen, besiegen
In 2014 Germany beat Argentina to win the Football World Cup.

biathlon ▪ Biathlon
The biathlon is a combination of long-distance skiing and shooting.

to catch (caught, caught) ▪ fangen
The defender caught the ball with his hand and was shown the yellow card.

to challenge ▪ herausfordern, auffordern
When my wife had defeated me at tennis I challenged her to another match.

chance ▪ Möglichkeit, Chance
I don't think you've got a chance of defeating him.

to cheat ▪ betrügen
If you are caught cheating you'll be disqualified.

club ▪ Club, Verein
There are some sports which are best done in a club.

competition ▪ Konkurrenz, Wettbewerb
There used to be a lot of competition between Glasgow Rangers and Celtic Glasgow.

condition ▪ Zustand
Despite his injury the player was in excellent condition.

court [kɔːt] ▪ (Sport-)Platz
The final will take place on court no 1.

cricket ▪ Kricket
Cricket is very popular in England, less so in Scotland.

eleven ▪ Elf
He joined a different club because he wanted to play in the first eleven.

to face ▪ sich stellen, sich gegenübersehen
In our last match this season we'll be facing the champion's team.

fast ▪ schnell
Formula One cars are very fast.

final ▪ Endspiel, Finale
Argentina and Germany reached the final of the 2014 Football World Cup.

finish ▪ Schluss, Ziel
After a disappointing first half the team put in a brilliant finish.
He reached the finish of his first marathon after 3 hours and eight minutes.

fit ▪ fit, gesund, in Form
He runs five miles every day to keep fit.

football ▪ Fußball
Spain won the Football World Cup in 2010. Mind you, it's called "soccer" in the USA.

form ▪ Form, Kondition
Our team were in splendid form so we easily defeated our rivals.

forward ▪ Stürmer(in)
Our forwards were very good last year. They scored plenty of goals.

game ▪ Spiel
Football is a very popular game.

goal ■ Tor
He is in splendid form. He keeps scoring goals in every match.

golf ■ Golf
In Germany, golf is still regarded as a sport for the rich.

league ■ Liga, Verband
Manchester City are currently leading the Premier League.

opposition ■ Widerstand
I'm afraid our team could not offer any serious opposition to our opponents.

player ■ Spieler(in)
Steffi Graf is still regarded as one of the greatest tennis players of all times.

position ■ Platz
He never achieved more than the third position in a contest.

to pull ■ zerren
In kicking the ball the player pulled a muscle and had to leave the field.

race ■ Wettlauf; Rennen
Usain Bolt won the race for gold at the Olympic Games.
In 2013 Sebastian Vettel came first in 13 Formula One races.

ring ■ (Box-)Ring
They had to carry the fighter out of the ring.

rough ■ hart, rau
The defender was warned for rough play.

round ■ Runde
Our team were defeated in the third round of this competition.
The team bought their guests several rounds.

rowing ■ Rudern
Every year there is a rowing match between Oxford and Cambridge.

rule ■ Regel
The football rules say that you must not handle the ball.

▸ **as a rule** ▪ in der Regel, im Allgemeinen, normalerweise
As a rule, I go to bed at 10 p.m.

to serve ▪ servieren, den Aufschlag haben
Game Miss Halep. Miss Kvitova to serve.

set ▪ Satz
Herbert had won the first set and was up 3 to 1 in the second and still lost the match.

shot ▪ Schlag
Angelique Kerber finished the match with an incredible shot.

sport (AE: sports) ▪ Sport, Sportart
Rugby is a popular sport in Britain.
Americans say "sports", the English say "sport".

start ▪ Start
The start of the race is at 4 p.m.

to strike (struck, struck) ▪ schlagen, treffen
In baseball it is important that the ball is struck properly.

target ▪ Ziel
In the biathlon it is important to ski fast and to hit the target as often as possible.

team ▪ Mannschaft, Team
At last my team managed to win yesterday.

training ▪ Training
Little wonder I lost this match. I'm entirely out of training.

volleyball ▪ Volleyball
Poland is the current volleyball world champion.

to warn ▪ verwarnen
The player was warned for foul play.

to win (won, won) ▪ gewinnen
The team won its last five matches.

winner ▪ Gewinner(in)
The winner of Wimbledon in 2014 was Petra Kvitova.

ace ▪ Ass

In the 1980s Boris Becker was a real ace at tennis and he also hit quite a few aces.

athletics ▪ Leichtathletik

"Athletics" is a British term for "track and field".

away team ▪ Gastmannschaft

The away team won the match 3 to 1.

to back ▪ unterstützen

Although the home team failed to score a goal the crowd backed them.

to bet (bet, bet) ▪ wetten

He lost all his money by betting on horses.

blow ▪ Schlag

Boxing is a dangerous sport because of all the blows fighters receive to their heads.

bookmaker ▪ Buchmacher

My brother often went to a bookmaker to bet on the horses.

champion ▪ Meister, Meisterin, Champion

After trying for several years our team at last became national champion.

championship ▪ Meisterschaft

At last Andy Murray won the Wimbledon Championship.

circuit ▪ Rennstrecke

The horses ran the circuit in 5 minutes.

coach ▪ Trainer(in)

Otto Rehhagel used to be the coach of the Greek national football team.

to compete ▪ konkurrieren, (im Sport) antreten

Matthew was thirty-five when he first competed in a marathon.

competitive ▪ ehrgeizig, konkurrenzorientiert

He is rather too competitive to be fun to play with.

competitor ▪ Konkurrent(in)
Manchester United and Manchester City are fierce competitors.

contest ▪ Wettbewerb, Wettkampf
Yesterday's boxing contest was one of the most thrilling ever.

crowd ▪ Menschenmenge, Masse
A large crowd watched the Liverpool – Manchester United match.

to cycle ▪ Fahrrad fahren
The Tour de France is the greatest cycling event in the world.

defeat ▪ Niederlage
If there was one thing the champion hated it was defeat.

defender ▪ Verteidiger(in)
Nobby Stiles was an excellent defender in the English football team.

dramatic (⚠ Adv.: dramatically) ▪ dramatisch
This year's Cup Final was highly dramatic.

draw ▪ Unentschieden
Both teams managed to score one goal. So the match ended in a draw.

to eliminate ▪ ausschalten
Murray eliminated his opponent in the fourth round of the tournament.

to exceed ▪ übersteigen, überschreiten
Her sprinting skill exceeded that of all her competitors.

favourite ▪ Lieblings…
Jogging is my favourite sport.

fencing ▪ Fechten
Fencing is one of the oldest sports in the world.

to foul ▪ ein Foul begehen
The defender fouled the forward and was sent off.

gymnasium, gym ▪ Turnhalle, Fitnessstudio
I often go to a gymnasium in order to keep fit.

home team ▪ Heimmannschaft
The home team managed only to achieve draw.

hooliganRandalierer(in)
Hooligans are the most serious problem in football.

junior ■ Junior…, Jugend…
He is only fifteen. So he plays in the junior league.

jury ■ Kampf-, Preisgericht, Jury
The jury decided by a clear majority that Russia's boxer had won the match.

lead ■ Führung
Although he had been in the lead for most of the time he did not win the race.

locker ■ Schließfach, Spind
Put your purse and your mobile into a locker before you start playing tennis.

match ■ Match, (Wett-)Spiel
Arsenal won the last three matches and are now top of the league.

to miss ■ verfehlen
He missed the goal by several yards.

nil ■ Null
Chelsea three – Tottenham Hotspurs nil.

offside ■ Abseits
The referee blew the whistle because the forward was offside.

opponent ■ Gegner(in)
I simply wasn't good enough for my opponent and lost the match in two sets.

partial ■ parteiisch
The Chelsea supporters thought the referee was partial to Arsenal.

participant ■ Teilnehmer(in)
Would all participants in the race please register with the club at 1 p.m.?

pass ■ Pass
That was a first class pass to Rooney.

penalty ■ Elfmeter
The club was awarded penalty.

penalty area ■ Strafraum
Bob handled the ball in the penalty area and was sent off.

pitch ■ Platz; Wurf
He ran almost the whole length of the pitch and scored a marvellous goal.
The player's pitch was so good that his team won the match.

preliminary ■ einleitend, vorbereitend
Unfortunately our team did not get beyond the preliminary stages of the tournament.

racket ■ Racket, Schläger
She never goes on court to play tennis without two rackets.

referee, ref ■ Schiedsrichter(in), Schiri
The referee was unpopular among the players because of his strictness.

reserve ■ Reservespieler(in)
After playing in the first team for ten years he finished his career as a reserve.

rider ■ Reiter(in)
Princess Anne used to be a good rider.

rival ■ Rivale(-in)
Borussia Dortmund and Schalke 04 have long been rivals.

rugby ■ Rugby
Rugby is popular in all parts of the United Kingdom.

run ■ Lauf
Matthew goes for a five-kilometre run every other day.

runner ■ Läufer(in)
In 2013 more than 40,000 runners ran the Berlin marathon.

running ■ Laufen
Road running is not good for my knees.

to score ▪ erzielen, Punkt(e) machen

Celtic scored the only goal of the match in the 90th minute.

score ▪ Punktestand, Ergebnis

The final score was Real Madrid 3, Atletico Madrid 1.

shuttle(cock) ▪ Federball

Badminton players need a racket and a lot of shuttlecocks.

to smash ▪ schmettern

Federer reached the high ball and smashed it into the other side of the court.

soccer ▪ Fußball

Soccer is another word for football.

spectacular ▪ sensationell, atemberaubend

Germany's 7 to 1 defeat of Brazil in 2014 was really spectacular.

spectator ▪ Zuschauer(in)

15,000 spectators at Wimbledon witnessed the victory of Novak Djokovic.

sportsman (Pl.: -men) ▪ Sportler

Jesse Owens was a great sportsman.

sportswoman (Pl.: -women) ▪ Sportlerin

Steffi Graf was a great sportswoman.

squad ▪ Mannschaft

The German football squad for the World Cup consisted of 23 players.

squash ▪ Squash

Squash is a very tough game.

stadium (Pl.: stadiums/stadia) ▪ Stadion

The new Wembley stadium was opened in 2007.

stake ▪ Einsatz

For the stake of one pound you can win fifty pounds if you are lucky.

stand ■ Tribüne

At Liverpool's home match against Manchester United the stand was packed.

substitute ■ Ersatzspieler(in)

One of Germany's substitutes scored the decisive goal in the World Cup final.

supporter ■ Fan, Anhänger(in)

In England you cannot be a supporter of both Arsenal and Chelsea.

to surf ■ windsurfen

Surfing is not just a hobby, it is a real sport.

table tennis ■ Tischtennis

Many excellent table tennis players come from China.

to tackle s.b. ■ jdn. angreifen

The defender tackled the forward just in time.

tennis ■ Tennis

The biggest tennis tournaments are in Melbourne, Paris, Wimbledon, and New York.

torch ■ Fackel

The Olympic torch was carried into the stadium by a former sports star.

tournament ■ Turnier

In 2014 Novak Djokovic won the tournament at Wimbledon.

track and field ■ Leichtathletik

Track and field is often simply called athletics in British English.

trainer ■ Sportschuh

There is a hole in my left trainer. I'd better have it repaired.

unfair ■ unfair

The defender was known to be unfair, which is why he was often sent off.

whip ■ Peitsche

Never use a whip to hit your horse.

whistle ■ Pfeife

The ref blew his whistle.

win ■ Sieg

After seven defeats the team at last achieved a win.

windsurfing ■ Windsurfen

Windsurfing has been an Olympic sport since 1984.

wrestling ■ Ringen

Since 2004 wrestling has also been an Olympic sport for women.

6. Kaufen und Verkaufen

6.1 Allgemeines

to afford s.th. ▪ sich etwas leisten (können)
Our parents could afford one holiday per year, but not two or three.

article ▪ Artikel
I'm sorry, but this article is not available at present.

available ▪ verfügbar
We regret to inform you that the article ordered is not available any longer.

bag ▪ Tasche, Tüte; Sack
I brought my own bag so that I didn't have to buy a plastic bag.
Yesterday I bought a 50 kilo-bag of potatoes.

balance ▪ Waage
The balance showed that the apples bought weighed exatly 5 lbs.

to be subject to (was, been) ▪ etwas ausgesetzt sein, etwas unterliegen
All our products are subject to discounts of up to twenty per cent.

to buy (bought, bought) ▪ kaufen
Marge buys things because she likes buying, not because she needs something.

can ▪ Dose, Büchse, Kanister
We always have several cans of beer in the fridge.

case ▪ Kiste
I've still got ten cases full of books to unpack.

checkout ▪ Kasse
British supermarkets usually have a large number of checkouts.

consumer ▪ Verbraucher(in), Konsument(in)
As a result of the crisis consumers are not spending a lot of money.

customer ▪ Kunde(-in)
The managers had many customers complaining about the quality of their service.

to deliver ▪ liefern, zustellen
For a small additional charge we also deliver the goods to your home.

distribution ▪ Verteilung, Verbreitung
Mark's department organizes the distribution of goods to shops.

drugstore (AE) ▪ Drogerie
In a drugstore you can buy all sorts of products – from shampoo to health products.

expenditure ▪ Ausgabe
You always ought to make sure that your expenditure is never higher than your income.

for sale ▪ zu verkaufen
Quite a few houses in our neighbourhood are for sale.

free ▪ kostenlos
Notice in a shop: Buy one – get one free.

fund ▪ Geldmittel, Fonds
I'm afraid I can't buy this dress. I'm out of funds.

item ▪ Gegenstand
I went to the store to buy a few items for my tool box.

open ▪ offen, geöffnet
A note in the shop window said "We are open from 9 to 5".

opening ▪ Öffnung; Öffnungs…
Our opening hours are from nine to five.

quality ▪ Qualität
Our store sells only goods of superior quality.

range ▪ Reihe, Spektrum
The store had a wide range of products on offer.

reasonable ▪ angemessen
Prices in this shop are quite reasonable.

sale ▪ Schlussverkauf
Buying in a sale can save you a lot of money.

to save ▪ sparen
Don't spend all your money – save some of it against a rainy day.

to sell (sold, sold) ▪ verkaufen
Goods that are not easily sold are sometimes called shelf warmers.

to serve ▪ bedienen
Are you being served, Sir?

to settle ▪ bezahlen
I'll settle the invoice immediately after receiving the goods.

shop ▪ Laden, Geschäft
I wouldn't buy anything in that shop. It's rather expensive.

shopping ▪ Einkaufen
Shopping is Timothy's favourite hobby.

shopping centre ▪ Einkaufszentrum
Mall of America is a large shopping centre in Minnesota.

special ▪ speziell, Sonder…
The coat she bought was a special offer.

stock ▪ Vorrat
We do not have this article in stock any longer.

store ▪ Geschäft; Lager
Our store is open twenty-four hours a day and seven days a week.
We have a large store of household goods.

sum ▪ Betrag
If you buy here you are likely to save a nice sum of money.

supermarket ▪ Supermarkt
Our local supermarket has twelve checkouts.

to use ▪ verbrauchen
We need some eggs because we have used them all.

value ▪ Wert, Nutzen
This shop offers very good value for money.

waste ■ Verschwendung
Buying this device is a complete waste of money.

---

acquisition ■ Erwerb, Anschaffung
His shop became successful after the acquisition of modern machines.

availability ■ Verfügbarkeit
This offer is subject to availability.

to balance ■ im Gleichgewicht halten
When you do your shopping you must balance your income and your expenses.

bargain ■ Schnäppchen, Gelegenheit
At this low price the shoes are really a bargain.

basket ■ Korb
My wife prefers a basket for her shopping rather than a plastic bag.

buyer ■ Käufer(in)
We had a large number of buyers on Saturday.

consumption ■ Konsum, Verzehr, Verbrauch
The consumption of alcohol in public is illegal for under-sixteens.

counter ■ (Laden-)Theke
Fish and meat are usually sold at separate counters.

delivery ■ Auslieferung, Zustellung
Delivery within the city is free.

department store ■ Warenhaus, Kaufhaus
Harrods is one of the best-known department stores in England.

discount ■ Diskont, Rabatt
During the summer sale all our purchases are subject to a twenty per cent discount.

display ■ Auslage
The shop is known for its excellent display of books.

to distribute ■ verteilen, vertreiben
Wholesalers distribute goods to retailers.

DIY (Do It Yourself) ▪ Heimwerker…
In a DIY store you can get everything you need in order to do it yourself.

to equip (equipped; equipping) ▪ ausstatten, (aus)rüsten
We can equip you with everything you need for a modern kitchen.

equipment ▪ Ausstattung, Ausrüstung
We only sell top-quality kitchen equipment.

expense ▪ Ausgabe(n)
If you wish to avoid financial trouble, cut down your expenses.

hardware ▪ Geräte, Haushaltswaren
Fridges are best bought in a hardware store.

High Street (AE: Main Street) ▪ Hauptgeschäftsstraße
Most expensive brands are bought in High Street stores.

Jiffy bag™ ▪ Jiffybag, gepolsterte Versandtasche
We'll put the CDs in a jiffy bag and send them to you.

Main Street (AE) ▪ Hauptgeschäftsstraße
What is the High Street in Britain is the Main Street in the USA.

mall ▪ Einkaufszentrum
Mall of America is one of the world's largest covered shopping centres.

net ▪ netto, Netto…
The net price of this product is £55.

packet ▪ Paket, Schachtel
Cereals and cigarettes are sold in packets.

purchase ▪ Kauf; Anschaffung; Einkaufs…
The purchase of oil has become considerably less expensive.
The purchase of a car requires a lot of money.
Our purchase department has a new manager.

purchaser ▪ Käufer(in)
At a price of $500,000 for this house you will hardly find a purchaser.

receipt [rɪ'siːt] ■ Quittung, Beleg
Please keep the receipt in case you wish to return the book within seven days.

replacement ■ Ersatz
The shop owner gave her customer a replacement for her broken cellphone.

saving ■ Einsparung
You can make a lot of savings by buying special offers.

seller ■ Verkäufer(in)
Caryl is the best seller in our store.

shopping bag ■ Einkaufstasche
Don't use plastic shopping bags. They are not environment-friendly.

shopping list ■ Einkaufsliste
Mother always uses a shopping list for her weekend shopping.

shopping mall ■ Einkaufszentrum
Most major cities have their own shopping malls.

to spend (spent, spent) ■ ausgeben
He spends all his money on his car.

spending ■ Ausgaben
Families ought to make sure that their spending does not exceed their income.

stationery ■ Schreibwaren
Nowadays most supermarkets also sell stationery.

to swap ■ tauschen
Before the introduction of money, people simply swapped things.

to unload ■ entladen, ausladen
Can you help me unload all my shopping, please?

to value s.th. ■ etwas schätzen
John valued the old car at £5,000.

vendor ■ (Straßen-)Verkäufer(in)
He worked as a vendor selling icecream in the streets of New York.

warehouse ▪ Lagerhaus
We have a huge warehouse in the north of the city.

to waste ▪ verschwenden, vergeuden
Don't waste all your money on sweets.

to wrap ▪ einwickeln, verpacken
Would you like me to wrap this in paper or would you like a bag?

6.2 Lebensmittel

apple ▪ Apfel

banana ▪ Banane

beef ▪ Rindfleisch
Beef is traditionally very popular in Britain.

bread ▪ Brot

butter ▪ Butter

cake ▪ Kuchen

cheese ▪ Käse

cherry ▪ Kirsche

coffee ▪ Kaffee

honey ▪ Honig

loaf (Pl.: loaves) ▪ Laib (Brot)
We need two loaves of bread.

margarine [mɑːdʒəˈriːn] ▪ Margarine

marmalade ▪ Marmelade (aus Zitrusfrüchten)
Marmalade is made with citrus fruit, jam is made with all other types of fruit.

milk ▪ Milch

pepper ▪ Pfeffer; Paprika
Salt and pepper are used a lot in cooking.
Peppers are either green or yellow or red.

pork ▪ Schweinefleisch
Muslims do not eat pork and Hindus don't eat beef.

potato (Pl.: potatoes) ▪ Kartoffel
Her brother likes peeled potatoes best.

salt ▪ Salz
Salt can be produced from a mine or by processing it from sea water.

tomato (Pl.: tomatoes) ▪ Tomate

---

apricot ▪ Aprikose

berry ▪ Beere

blackberry ▪ Brombeere
My landlady made a lovely blackberry pie.

cabbage ▪ Kohl, Kraut
Many Germans like to eat cabbage – even in the form of "Sauerkraut".

carrot ▪ Möhre, Karotte

cauliflower ▪ Blumenkohl
You only eat the white centre of a cauliflower, not its green leaves.

cucumber ['kjuːkʌmbə] ▪ Schlangengurke
Slices of cucumber are often eaten raw in a salad.

currant ▪ Johannisbeere
I like black currants better than red.

dairy ['daɪəri] product ▪ Molkereiprodukt
Cheese, butter and milk are typical dairy products.

date ▪ Dattel
Dates grow on palm trees.

garlic ▪ Knoblauch
Garlic is usually crushed before it is put into a dish.

grocer's (AE: grocery) ▪ Lebensmittelgeschäft
Sally stopped at the grocer's to buy some cheese.

groceries (Pl.) ▪ Lebensmittel
Most people buy their groceries in a supermarket.

grocery (AE) ▪ Lebensmittelgeschäft
In an American grocery you buy for instance vegetables, dairy products and bread.

jam ▪ Konfitüre, Marmelade
Jam is made on the basis of fruit other than oranges or lemons.

mutton ▪ Lammfleisch
My Dad doesn't eat mutton.

onion ▪ Zwiebel
For this dish we need two onions.

pea ▪ Erbse
Peas and carrots are often eaten with chicken.

peach ▪ Pfirsich
Peaches grow best in warm countries.

peanut ▪ Erdnuss
Peanuts are eaten a lot in the USA.

pear ▪ Birne
My favourite types of fruit are apples and pears.

pineapple ▪ Ananas
My mother sometimes prepares pork with pineapple.

plum ▪ Pflaume

raspberry ▪ Himbeere
What Camilla likes best on her toast is raspberry jam.

spinach ▪ Spinat

strawberry ▪ Erdbeere
Anne likes strawberry jam.

6.3 Kleidung, Accessoires und Schmuck

clothes (Pl.) ■ Kleidung
If there was one thing Mr Stingy hated it was buying new clothes.

coat ■ Mantel
Last winter it was so cold that I very often wore a coat to keep warm.

dress ■ Kleid
She bought a beautiful new dress for the reception.

elegant ■ elegant

fabric ■ Stoff, Gewebe
I don't like synthetic fabrics.

fashion ■ Mode
The fashion industry is very important.

fashionable ■ modern
High heels have always been very fashionable.

to fold ■ zusammenlegen, -falten
Joan's mother always folds her daughter's clothes before putting them away.

gear ■ Ausrüstung, Sachen
Just wait a minute. I've got to get my gear together.

handbag ■ Handtasche
Most ladies do not go out without their handbag.

hat ■ Hut

jacket ■ Jacke, Jackett
He looked rather funny. He wore a yellow jacket and a blue tie.

jeans (Pl.) ■ Jeans

jewel ■ Edelstein, Kostbarkeit, Kleinod
Jewels and "diamonds are a girl's best friend".

large ■ groß
Could I have this jacket in "large", please?

leather ■ Leder

pattern ■ Muster
This sweater has a very nice pattern.

pocket ■ Hosentasche
Most men in Britain carry their change in their pockets.

pullover ■ Pullover
A pullover is also called a sweater.

ring ■ (Finger-)Ring

shirt ■ Hemd
It's hot outside. You'd better wear a shirt with short sleeves or a T-shirt.

shoe ■ Schuh

size ■ (Schuh-, Kleider-)Größe
My sizes are 10 for shoes and large for clothes.

skirt ■ Rock
I like that new skirt of yours.

sock ■ Socke

stocking ■ (Damen-)Strumpf
In the past women wore stockings, nowadays most women wear tights.

suit [suːt, sjuːt] ■ Anzug
He took his black suit to the cleaner's.

to take off (took, taken) ■ ausziehen
When she came in out of the rain she took off her wet coat.

tights (Pl.) ■ Strumpfhose
I need a new pair of tights.

T-shirt ■ T-Shirt

trousers (Pl.) ■ Hose
Sir Alfred went to Savile Row to have a new pair of trousers made.

watch ■ Armbanduhr
She had her expensive watch stolen.

to wear [weə] (wore, worn) ■ tragen; abnutzen, abtragen
Soldiers are supposed to wear uniform when they are on duty.
You need a new pair of trousers. These ones are beginning to wear out.

wool ■ Wolle

amber ■ Bernstein, bernsteinfarben
Jack's grandmother had a very old amber necklace.

belt ■ Gürtel
She bought a nice belt for her new jeans.

blouse ■ Bluse

boot ■ Stiefel
There was so much snow outside that I decided to put on my boots.

bra ■ BH
Bra is the short form of the French word "brassière".

briefs (Pl.) ■ Unterhose
Many young men wear boxer shorts as briefs.

button ■ Knopf
There are no buttons on this blouse.

cap ■ Mütze, Kappe
In rain or cold weather you should wear a cap.

casual ■ lässig
Michael was not supposed to wear casual clothes in his job.

cloth ■ Stoff, Tuch
Silk is a very expensive type of cloth.

clothing ■ Kleidung
When going mountain-climbing you should wear appropriate clothing.

collar ■ Kragen
Henry likes wearing shirts with a collar.

dinner jacket (AE: tuxedo) ■ Smoking
What the British call a dinner jacket is called a tuxedo in the USA.

discreet ▪ dezent
She impressed everyone by her discreet clothes.

fibre ▪ Faden, Faser
Silk is a very expensive fibre.

glove ▪ Handschuh
For a polar expedition you definitely need very warm gloves.

heel ▪ Absatz
Shoes with high heels are very fashionable.

jewellery ▪ Schmuck
My wife keeps all her jewellery in a box in the wardrobe.

knickers (Pl.) ▪ (Damen-)Schlüpfer
The term "knickers" refers only to ladies' underwear.

label ▪ Etikett, (Kleider-)Schildchen; Marke
The label contains information about size and washing instructions.
Armani is a very expensive label.

lace ▪ Spitze; (Schnür-)Band
Her blouse had a very nice lace collar.
He just couldn't manage to untie the knot in his laces.

necklace ['neklɪs] ▪ (Hals-)Kette
He bought his wife an expensive necklace.

nightdress ▪ Nachthemd
He bought his wife a silk nightdress for her birthday.

old-fashioned ▪ altmodisch
I don't like this tie. It's old-fashioned.

outfit ▪ Aufmachung
She appeared in rather a strange outfit.

panties (Pl.) ▪ (Damen-)Slip
She had a habit of buying very expensive panties.

pants (Pl.) ▪ Unterhose; Hose
In Britain pants are a piece of male underwear, in the USA the word has the same meaning as trousers.

patch ▪ Flicken

My dad liked to have sweaters with patches on the elbows.

pearl ▪ Perle

precious ▪ kostbar

She wore a very precious necklace.

purse ▪ Portemonnaie, Geldbörse; Handtasche

Patrick bought his wife a purse for her money.

American ladies have a purse, not a handbag.

to put on (put, put) ▪ anziehen, aufsetzen

Oh dear. It's cold outside. You'd better put on a jacket and a cap.

pyjamas (Pl.) ▪ Schlafanzug, Pyjama

Professor Higgins only wore silk pyjamas in bed.

to range ▪ reichen

Sizes generally range from XXS to XXXL.

to reverse ▪ umdrehen, wenden

You can also wear this jacket if you reverse it.

roll ▪ Rolle

I like that cloth. Could I buy a roll of it, please?

scarf (Pl.: scarfs/scarves) ▪ Schal

It was so cold outside that Jeremy wore a scarf.

to sew (sewed, sewn/sewed) ▪ nähen

Sorry, Sir. There's a button missing on this jacket. Let me sew one on for you.

shabby ▪ abgetragen, schäbig

Harry, your coat's rather shabby. I think we ought to buy you a new one.

shoelace ▪ Schnürsenkel

I don't like tying my shoelaces. That's why I prefer slip-ons.

shorts (Pl.) ▪ Shorts, kurze Hose

My father wore shorts only when he was on holiday.

silk ▪ Seide

Silk is a very expensive material.

sleeve ■ Ärmel
I can't wear this shirt. Its sleeves are too tight.

slip ■ Unterrock
Women often wear a slip under their skirts.

to slip on ■ überstreifen
She slipped on a coat because it was cold outside.

slip-on ■ Slipper
I don't like tying my shoelaces. I prefer slip-ons.

slipper ■ Hausschuh
Our dog always brings me my slippers.

stain ■ Fleck, Verfärbung
Susan did not buy the blouse because there was a stain on it.

string ■ Kette
Grandfather bought Grandmother a string of pearls.

stripe ■ Streifen
He liked to wear sweaters with blue and yellow stripes.

sunglasses (Pl.) ■ Sonnenbrille
My wife likes wearing sunglasses even if the sun isn't shining.

sweater ['swetə] ■ Pullover
A sweater is basically the same thing as a pullover.

sweatshirt ['swet-ʃɜːt] ■ Sweatshirt
Sweatshirts are usually worn for jogging.

swimming costume (AE: swimsuit) ■ Badeanzug
I would like to buy a swimming costume for myself, …

swimming trunks (Pl.) ■ Badehose
… and swimming trunks for my sons.

swimsuit ['swɪmsuːt, 'swɪmsjuːt] (AE) ■ Badeanzug
The American swimsuit is a swimming costume in Britain.

synthetic fibre ■ Kunstfaser
Many inexpensive textiles today are made of synthethic fibre.

tank ■ Pullunder
When it gets cool I like to wear a tank over my shirt.

tank top ▪ Pullunder

Tank top is just a synonym for tank.

textile ▪ Stoff, Gewebe

Silk is a very expensive textile.

tie ▪ Krawatte

Jack was glad that in his job he did not have to wear a tie.

tight ▪ fest; eng

Don't tie your shoelaces too tight.

My shirt is rather tight. I'd better lose some weight.

tissue ▪ Taschentuch; Gewebe

I've got a bad cold. Have you got a tissue for me?

Silk is a very expensive tissue.

tuxedo (AE; BE: dinner jacket) ▪ Smoking

He wore a tuxedo at his son's wedding.

undershirt (AE) ▪ Unterhemd

The English call an undershirt a vest.

underwear ▪ Unterwäsche

When I go on my skiing holiday I always remember to take very warm underwear.

to undo (-did, -done) ▪ aufmachen

Can you undo this button for me, please? I'm too weak to do it.

uniform ▪ Uniform

vest (AE: undershirt) ▪ Unterhemd; (AE) Weste

In winter I like to wear a vest under my shirt.

The Americans call a waistcoat a vest.

waistcoat (AE: vest) ▪ Weste

My father liked to wear a waistcoat under his jacket.

wallet ▪ Brieftasche

English men have only banknotes and documents in their wallets.

woollen ▪ wollen, aus Wolle

Grandpa only wore woollen socks.

zip ■ Reißverschluss
My coat has a zip, which is more convenient than buttons.

6.4 Geldverkehr und Preise

to advance ■ anziehen, steigen
Prices have not advanced very much in recent years.

bank ■ Bank
Without banks the economy would collapse.

banknote ■ Geldschein
In the past there was only a one-pound banknote in England, no one-pound coin.

cash ■ Bargeld, Barzahlung
Could I possibly pay by card? I haven't got any cash on me.

cashpoint ■ Geldautomat
If you need cash just go to the nearest cashpoint.

change ■ Wechselgeld
Just keep the change.

cheap ■ billig
This is a special offer. It's really cheap.

check (AE) ■ Scheck
American checks are not usually paid cash.

cheque [tʃek] ■ Scheck
I'm afraid we do not accept cheques any longer.

to cost (cost, cost) ■ kosten
I won't buy this. It costs far too much.

cost ■ Kosten
The cost of living has remained relatively constant in recent years.

credit ■ Kredit; Gutschrift
Many people buy expensive goods on credit.
A credit is an amount of money transferred to someone's account.

▸ **on credit** ▪ auf Kredit

credit card ▪ Kreditkarte
If you have a credit card, you can go shopping without any cash.

to deal (dealt [delt], dealt [delt]) ▪ sich befassen
Banks deal with the financial situation of their customers.

dear ▪ teuer
I'm afraid we can't afford this car. It's much too dear.

debt [det] ▪ Schuld
He bought so many expensive presents for his girlfriend that he ran up a heavy debt.

demand [dɪˈmɑːnd] ▪ Nachfrage
Supply and demand determine prices.

dollar ▪ Dollar
In the USA you pay with the dollar.

due ▪ fällig
Payment is due within fourteen days of receiving the goods.

euro ▪ Euro
You can pay with the euro in the currently 19 countries of the euro-zone.

expensive ▪ teuer, kostspielig
I'm not going to buy this article. It's much too expensive.

to include ▪ beinhalten
The price includes VAT.

interest ▪ Zinsen
If you buy this item on credit we charge an interest of only 5 per cent.

to lend (lent, lent) ▪ (ver)leihen
Banks make a profit for instance by lending money to their customers.

loan ▪ Kredit, Darlehen
Your bank will usually grant you a loan if you have a regular income.

money ■ Geld
If we had more money, we'd go on holiday more often.

to pay (paid, paid) ■ (be)zahlen
You have to pay the bill within a week.
If you want a luxury car, you have to pay the price.

pound ■ Pfund (Sterling)
In the UK you use the pound for payments, in Ireland the euro.

price ■ (Kauf-)Preis
We offer this suit at a special price of £300.

rate ■ Zinssatz
We herewith advise an increase in the interest rate on your loan.

safe ■ Tresor
Grandma doesn't trust banks. She keeps her money in a safe.

savings account ■ Sparkonto
Many old people still have a savings account.

statement ■ Auszug, Abrechnung
If you have an account with a bank you receive regular statements of account.

transfer ['trænsfɜː] ■ Überweisung
The transfer of the amount due will be made tomorrow.

---

to amount to ■ sich belaufen auf
Your credit amounts to $450.

ATM (Automatic Teller Machine) ■ Geldautomat
If you need cash there is an ATM outside our shop.

bank transfer ■ Überweisung
You don't need to pay cash. You can also pay by bank transfer or by credit card.

cent ■ Cent
A cent is the basis of the currency in the eurozone and some other countries.

coin ■ Münze

Paying with coins is becoming increasingly less common.

currency ■ Währung

You'll have to convert your euros into dollars.

deposit ■ Einzahlung, Anzahlung

We require a deposit of 10 per cent.

gross ■ brutto

Gross prices are always higher than net prices.

in advance ■ im Voraus

I do not like to pay bills in advance.

invoice ■ Rechnung

The internet shop sent me an invoice for the goods they had sent me.

payment ■ Bezahlung

We expect payment to be made by credit card.

pence (Pl. von: penny) ■ Pence

There are 100 pence in a pound.

penny ■ Penny

A penny is the hundredth part of a pound.

PIN (Personal Identification Number) ■ PIN, Pin-Nummer

If you pay by bank card you must tap in your PIN.

to price ■ Preis festsetzen

The computer is cheaply priced at $ 450.00.

price tag ■ Preisschild

7. Reise und Verkehr, Gastronomie

7.1 Verkehr allgemein

access ■ Zugang, Zugangs...
Because of an accident the access road to the airport was closed.

accident ■ Unfall
He broke his leg in an accident and had to be taken to hospital.

aircraft ■ Luftfahrzeug
Aeroplanes, balloons and zeppelins are types of aircraft.

airport ■ Flughafen
Heathrow is Britain's largest airport.

automobile (AE) ■ Kfz, Kraftfahrzeug, Auto
What the English call a car is sometimes called an automobile in the USA.

bicycle ■ Fahrrad
When the trains aren't running I ride to work on my bicycle.

bike ■ Fahrrad; Motorrad
All my family have bikes.
A motorcycle is often simply called a bike.

boat ■ Boot, Schiff

bridge ■ Brücke

bus ■ Omnibus

car (AE: automobile, auto) ■ Auto
Don't park your car on double yellow lines. They mean "No parking at any time".

car park (BE) ■ Parkplatz
There is a car park right around the corner from us.

to cross ■ überqueren, kreuzen
You must not cross the street when the lights are red.

dead end (street) ▪ Sackgasse
There's no exit from this street. It's a dead end.

to drive (drove, driven) ▪ fahren
After driving for hours we at last arrived at our hotel.

drive ▪ Fahrt; Einfahrt
We arrived after a four hours' drive.
The drive was just wide enough for a car to pass.

driver ▪ Fahrer(in)
After three hours of driving our driver was so tired that he had to take a break.

engine ▪ Motor, Triebwerk
Diesel engines are very economical if you drive long distances.

gas (AE; BE: petrol) ▪ Benzin
My car runs on gas, not on diesel.

gas station (AE; BE: petrol station) ▪ Tankstelle
The nearest gas station is just round the corner from here.

gate ▪ Schranke; Flugsteig
Don't cross the rails when the gates are closing.
Last call: Will passengers please proceed to gate no. 5?

gear ▪ Gang (Kfz)
When you drive up a steep hill, you may need to change into a lower gear.

lane ▪ Gasse, enge Straße; Spur
The Wallaces live in a beautiful lane near the lake.
Lorries must not use the right-hand lane on a British motorway with three lanes.

late ▪ verspätet
The train was late – as usual.

limit ▪ Begrenzung, Beschränkung
Watch it! There's a speed limit here.

main road ▪ Hauptstraße
It's rather noisy here because our house is on a main road.

motorbike ■ Motorrad
Every year dozens of motorbikers die on this mountain road.

motorcycle ■ Motorrad
The term "motorcycle" is not very often used by young people.

motorway ■ Autobahn
British motorways usually have three lanes in both directions.

to park ■ parken
At last we found a space to park our car in.

parking lot (AE; BE: park) ■ (großer) Parkplatz
There are hardly any parking lots in Manhattan, so you'd better use the bus or the subway.

passage ■ Durchgang, Gang; Überfahrt
Just walk through the narrow passage between the two houses ahead of you.
The passage from Hull to Rotterdam takes some ten hours.

petrol ■ Benzin
What is called petrol in Britain is called gas in the USA.

petrol station ■ Tankstelle
What the British call a petrol station is a gas station in the USA.

plane ■ Flugzeug
As a result of a strike almost all planes to Chicago were delayed.

platform ■ Bahnsteig, Gleis
The intercity to Glasgow departs from platform 7.

port ■ Hafen; Backbord
The old admiral would sit for hours at the window watching the ships enter the port.
Sailing south, they saw a ship approaching from their port side, i.e. from the east.

quay ■ Kai

railroad (AE; BE: railway) ■ Eisenbahn
In the USA the railroad is mainly used for transporting goods.

railway (AE: railroad) ▪ Eisenbahn
The first railway in Britain operated on the Stockton-Darlington line in 1825.

to release ▪ lösen
Don't forget to release the brakes after starting your car.

to ride (rode, ridden) ▪ fahren
You ride a bike but you drive a car.

right-hand ▪ Rechts…
Sweden introduced right-hand traffic in 1967.

road ▪ Straße
Before crossing the road look right and then left – at least in Britain.

roundabout (AE: traffic circle) ▪ Kreisverkehr
Roundabouts are often more useful than traffic lights.

route ▪ Strecke, Route
The quickest driving route from London to Glasgow is via Scotch Corner.

ship ▪ Schiff

side ▪ Rand
Just park your car at the side of the road.

sign ▪ (Verkehrs-)Schild
The driver did not see the stop sign and just carried on.

to slow ▪ langsamer werden
She saw that the lights were red and slowed.

slow ▪ langsam
The cars moved at a slow speed.

speed ▪ Geschwindigkeit
My car has a top speed of 100 mph.

to stop ▪ anhalten
You are supposed to stop when the lights are red.

stop ▪ Halt
Watch it! There's a stop sign.

street ■ Straße

▸ **in the street** ■ auf der Straße

to take off (took, taken) ■ abheben, starten

The plane took off exactly on time.

tour ■ Tournee

The band are going on another tour next month.

track ■ Schiene

High voltage. Keep off the tracks.

traffic ■ Verkehr

Traffic in London can be very dense.

traffic circle (AE) ■ Kreisverkehr

What is a traffic circle in the USA is a roundabout in Britain.

train ■ Zug

Transporting goods by train is better for the environment than doing it by road.

transport ['trænspɔːt] ■ Transport; Beförderungsmittel

We need to improve our transport system in order to remain competitive.

Fortunately we had our own means of transport.

transportation ■ Transport, Beförderung; Beförderungsmittel

Our company is concerned with the transportation of goods.

"Do you have your own means of transportation?", my US-American host asked me.

turn ■ Kurve

He took a turn to the left.

vehicle ■ Fahrzeug

Strictly private! No parking of vehicles at any time.

wheel ■ Rad

Ken had to buy a new wheel for his bike.

accelerator ▪ Gaspedal
The accelerator is the pedal right next to the brake.

bend ▪ Kurve
Watch out. There is a sharp bend right ahead.

to block ▪ blockieren, im Weg stehen
The road was blocked by fallen trees.

to brake ▪ bremsen
I would also brake for animals to avoid a collision.

brake ▪ Bremse
When she saw the approaching lorry she stepped on the brakes.

breakdown ▪ Panne
Our car was so old that it had breakdowns quite regularly.

bypass ▪ Umgehungsstraße
The M25 was planned as a bypass round London to keep traffic away from the city.

carriage ▪ Wagen; Kutsche
We had first-class tickets. So we went to the first-class carriage.
Before the introduction of the railway, carriages were drawn by horses.

carrier ▪ Flug-; Transportgesellschaft
Lufthansa is Germany's biggest carrier.
National Carriers is a large British transport company.

clutch ▪ Kupplung
Make sure that you let out the clutch slowly or you may damage the engine.

coach ▪ Reisebus
Jack prefers to travel to his holiday destination by coach rather than by train or plane.

collision ▪ Zusammenstoß, Kollision
There was a serious collision on the M40, when two lorries crashed into each other.

crew ▪ Besatzung, Mannschaft
The Airbus 380 has a crew of up to thirty members.

curve ▪ Kurve, Rundung, Biegung
Roads in the mountains have a lot of curves.

to fasten ▪ schließen, zumachen
For take-off and landing fasten your seatbelt.

fast lane ▪ Überholspur
Heavy goods vehicles must not use the fast lane on the motorway.

ferry ▪ Fähre
You can go to England by ferry or by train, through the Channel Tunnel.

flat ▪ Reifenpanne
We couldn't continue our trip because our automobile had a flat.

freight car (AE) ▪ Güterwagen
What the Americans call a freight car is called a truck or goods truck in Britain.

fuel ▪ Treibstoff, Brennstoff
Most buses use diesel as fuel.

garage ['gærɪdʒ, gə'rɑːʒ] ▪ Tankstelle; Kfz-Werkstatt
We've run out of petrol. We'd better go to a garage.
I'm having trouble with the brakes of my car. I'd better take it to the garage.

headlight ['hedlaɪt] ▪ (Auto-)Scheinwerfer
The car crashed into a tree and broke its left headlight.

hold ▪ Halt
Passengers are advised to keep a firm hold on the boat.

horn ▪ Hupe
When he saw the oncoming vehicle he sounded his horn.

ignition ▪ Zündung
Turn the key in the ignition lock to start the engine.

indicator ▪ Blinker, Anzeiger
Before turning you must use your indicator.

internal flight ▪ Inlandsflug
Karen flew from London to Las Vegas, then took an internal flight to Florida.

jet ■ Jet, Düsenflugzeug
Most modern passenger planes are jets.

junction ■ Kreuzung
Don't enter the junction if your exit is blocked.

landing ■ Landung
Despite the bad weather the pilot managed a very smooth landing.

launch ■ Stapellauf
Thousands of people watched the launch of the new cruise ship.

licence plate ■ Nummernschild
He bought a licence plate for his new car – VIP 010.

light(s) ■ Ampel
When the lights show red you must stop.

lorry ■ LKW, Laster
In order to remove all this rubbish we need a lorry.

maximum ■ Höchst…, maximal
The maximum speed allowed in this street is 30 mph.

to merge ■ zusammenlaufen
My friend lives exactly where West End Avenue and Broadway merge.

motorist ■ Kraftfahrer(in)
Strangely enough, the term "motorist" refers only to car drivers.

mph (miles per hour) ■ Meilen pro Stunde
The speed limit in Britain is 70 mph, i.e. 112 km/h.

number plate ■ Nummernschild
In Britain you can buy a number plate of your own choice.

one-way street ■ Einbahnstraße
You can't drive your car in this direction. It's a one-way street.

to overtake (-took, -taken) ■ überholen
The road is so narrow that it is difficult to overtake.

passenger ■ Passagier(in)
The passengers enjoyed a comfortable crossing.

pavement (AE: sidewalk) ▪ Bürgersteig

Cars must not use the pavement. It is for pedestrians only.

pedestrian ▪ Fußgänger(in)

Pedestrians should make eye contact with drivers before crossing the street.

rail ▪ Bahn; Schiene

Don't go from London to Manchester by plane. Go by rail.
The train went off the rails but nobody was hurt.

to reverse ▪ zurücksetzen

If you reverse in a one-way street be very careful.

ride ▪ Fahrt

Daddy, can you please give me a ride to school? I'm a bit late.

right of way ▪ Vorfahrt

You'd better stop. The other cars have the right of way.

road tax ▪ Kraftfahrzeugsteuer

If you haven't paid your road tax you are not allowed to use your car.

run ▪ Strecke

By car the run to the coast does not take more than thirty minutes.

runway ▪ Startbahn, Landebahn

The pilot broke off the touch-down routine because a plane was blocking the runway.

rush hour ▪ Stoßzeit

Don't ever try driving on Oxford Road during the rush hour.

to shift ▪ schalten

Shift into a lower gear when you're driving up a steep hill.

sidewalk (AE) ▪ Bürgersteig

What is the pavement in Britain is the sidewalk in the USA.

signal ▪ Signal; Ampel

The train driver realized that the signal showed that he had to stop.
The driver saw that the signal showed red so he stopped his car.

to sink (sank, sunk) ▪ untergehen, sinken
The Titanic sank in 1912 when it hit an iceberg.

slippery ▪ rutschig
After all this rain the roads are slippery.

to speed (speeded/sped, speeded/sped) ▪ sausen, flitzen; zu schnell fahren
He sped along the motorway at 80 mph until the police stopped him for speeding.

speed limit ▪ Geschwindigkeitsbegrenzung
Don't drive so fast. There's a speed limit here.

speedometer ▪ Tachometer
After the accident the speedometer of the car still showed a speed of 100 mph.

starboard ▪ Steuerbord
Sailing north, we saw ships approaching from our starboard side, i.e. from the east.

steamer ▪ Dampfer
The first steamer, i.e. a ship driven by a steam engine, was built in France in 1783.

to steer ▪ steuern, lenken
It is very difficult to steer a lorry through the old town because the roads are so narrow.

steering wheel ▪ Lenkrad
Mike often has only one hand on the steering wheel.

stem ▪ Bug
If you stand at the stem of a moving ship you'll face the wind.

stern ▪ Heck
From stem to stern the ferry is 234 metres long.

through road ▪ Durchgangsstraße
Sorry, you can't use this street. It's not a through road.

toll ▪ (Straßen-)Zoll, Maut
Until recently drivers had to pay a toll of £1 for using the Forth Road Bridge.

toll bridge ▪ gebührenpflichtige Brücke
The Golden Gate Bridge in San Francisco is a toll bridge.

to tow ▪ (ab)schleppen
He had his car towed to the nearest garage.

traffic light ▪ Ampel
My Sicilian friend tends to ignore traffic lights.

traffic warden ▪ Polizist(in) (zur Überwachung des ruhenden Verkehrs), Politesse
Traffic wardens are not popular among car drivers.

trailer ▪ Anhänger
If you want to transport all this stuff, you'll need a trailer.

transporter ▪ (Schwer-)Transporter
Yesterday we saw a transporter on the motorway carrying eight new Ferraris.

truck ▪ LKW, Laster, Lastwagen; Güterwagen
Many goods are nowadays transported by truck on the roads.
The goods train we saw in California had more than 150 trucks or freight cars.

trunk ▪ Kofferraum
My American cousin's Chevrolet has a huge trunk.

tunnel ▪ Tunnel
Crossing from France to England by tunnel takes only 35 minutes.

tyre ▪ Reifen
When winter is coming, you have to change your tyres.

underground car park ▪ Tiefgarage
You'll find the underground car park right behind the cathedral.

unleaded ▪ unverbleit
We always fill up with unleaded fuel.

van ▪ Transporter, Lieferwagen
We had so much luggage that we had to hire a van to transport it to our hotel.

vessel ▪ Schiff
The term "vessel" can refer to all sorts of large boats or ships.

warning ▪ Verwarnung
The police gave the driver a warning for his speeding offense.

windscreen (AE: windshield) ▪ Windschutzscheibe
What the Americans call a windshield is a windscreen in Britain.

windshield (AE) ▪ Windschutzscheibe
What the British call a windscreen is a windshield in the USA.

to wind up (wound, wound) ▪ hochkurbeln
Can you wind up the window please. It's getting cold.

zebra crossing ▪ Zebrastreifen
We told our children to use zebra crossings for crossing streets.

7.2 Personenbeförderung

to arrive ▪ ankommen
In the past trains used to arrive on time.

cab (AE; BE: taxi) ▪ Taxi
We took a cab from Central Station to the Lincoln Center.

departure ▪ Abfahrt, Abflug
Our departure was delayed because of a strike by air traffic controllers.

fare ▪ Fahrpreis
The fare for a return ticket is twice the price for a single ticket.

fast train ▪ Schnellzug
The fast train from London to Glasgow takes less than five hours.

flight ▪ Flug
The flight had to be cancelled because the pilots were on strike.

journey ■ Reise, Fahrt
The journey from Glasgow to London takes 4.5 hours by train and 7 hours by car.

queue [kjuː] ■ (Warte-)Schlange
Because of the holiday there are likely to be long queues at the bus stop.

safety ■ Sicherheit(s)…
Safety belt is another word for seat belt.

season ticket ■ Dauerkarte
A season ticket is useful for frequent travellers.

seat belt ■ Sicherheitsgurt
Fasten your seat belts, please.

station ■ Bahnhof
This train stops at all stations between Chorley and Manchester.

taxi (AE: cab) ■ Taxi
We missed the train so we had to take a taxi.

ticket ■ Fahrschein
The price for a return ticket is twice the price of a single ticket.

tram (AE: streetcar) ■ Straßenbahn
In 1992 trams were introduced again in Manchester.

---

aeroplane ■ Flugzeug
If you wish to travel long distances you might consider travelling by aeroplane.

airline ■ Fluggesellschaft
Lufthansa is Germany's largest airline.

announcement ■ Bekanntgabe, Mitteilung, Durchsage
Every airport has a public announcement system.

arrival ■ Ankunft
The arrival of Flight 246 will be delayed by thirty minutes.

to commute ▪ pendeln
Every morning hundreds of thousands of people commute to and from London.

compartment ▪ (Zug-)Abteil
The passenger occupied a seat in a first-class compartment.

conductor ▪ Schaffner(in)
It is the conductor's job to check tickets.

crossing ▪ Überfahrt
The captain told us that we would have a rather rough crossing.

delay ▪ Verzögerung, Verspätung
Bad weather and accidents often lead to delays on the motorways.

descent ▪ (Lande-)Anflug
We have begun our descent. Please fasten your seatbelts.

highway ▪ Fernverkehrsstraße, Highway
To go from Manchester to Birmingham by car you can take the A34 highway.

liner ▪ Passagierschiff
Crossing the Atlantic on a liner was the dream of my youth.

to navigate ▪ navigieren; befahren
The captain navigated the ferry safely into the port.
Only very narrow boats can navigate the Leeds & Liverpool Canal.

one-way ticket ▪ Einzelfahrschein
A one-way ticket usually costs half the price of a return ticket.

public transport ▪ öffentliche Verkehrsmittel
Well organized public transport is a major concern in large cities.

rank ▪ Reihe
There is often a long taxi rank at the railway station.

to sail ▪ segeln; auslaufen
The ferry from Europoort to Hull sails at 6 p.m.

schedule ▪ Fahrplan
We are pleased to advise that all flights will be on schedule today.

shuttle ■ Pendelzug

The airport shuttle goes every twenty minutes.

single ticket ■ Einzelfahrschein

The price of a single ticket is half that of a return ticket.

sleeper ■ Schlafwagen(platz)

I've booked a sleeper for our trip to Rome.

streetcar (AE; BE: tram) ■ Straßenbahn

In New Orleans there is a streetcar whose final destination is the suburb of Desire.

tube ■ U-Bahn

The tube is the London Underground.

valid ■ gültig

I'm afraid, Sir, your ticket isn't valid any longer.

van ■ Kleinbus

Our American friends have five children, so they need a van.

7.3 Tourismus

attraction ■ Attraktion

The Tower is one of London's chief attractions.

B&B (Bed and Breakfast) ■ Übernachtung mit Frühstück

B&B offered by many families in Britain is a very popular type of accommodation.

bag ■ Reisetasche

Your bags must not be heavier than 20 kilos if you don't wish to pay an extra charge.

campground (AE) ■ Campingplatz, Zeltplatz

There is a brilliantly equipped campground in Yosemite National Park.

camping site (AE: campground) ■ Campingplatz, Zeltplatz

At last we found a camping site with adequate facilities in the Lake District.

charge ▪ Gebühr

Is there a charge for children under three or are they free?

to collect ▪ abholen

Our plane arrives at ten. Can you collect us at the airport?

connection ▪ Verbindung

Unfortunately we did not manage to catch our connection to Penzance.

day trip ▪ Tagesausflug

If you live in Hamburg Munich is too far away for a day trip.

to declare ▪ angeben

After landing we met under the sign "Goods to declare".

documents ▪ (Reise-)Papiere

Passport and driving licence are important personal documents.

guide ▪ Reiseleiter(in)

The guide showed us all the fascinating sights of Luxor.

holiday ▪ Urlaub

We're going to spend our summer holiday in Italy this year.

to inquire ▪ sich erkundigen

You can also inquire about accommodation at the local tourist office.

to issue ▪ ausstellen, ausfertigen

My passport was issued on 5 April 2010.

to land ▪ landen; an Land gehen

You must remain seated until the plane has landed and stopped completely.

Some passengers couldn't wait to land after their rough crossing.

map ▪ Landkarte

Before we went to Lake Garda we bought a good map of the area.

party ▪ Gruppe

A party of fifteen people went to see the sights of Valletta.

passport ▪ Reisepass
If you wish to travel to the USA you require a passport – and possibly a visa.

path ▪ Weg, Pfad
A steep path will take you to the mountain top in two hours.

ready ['redi] ▪ fertig, bereit
Please be seated. The train is ready to depart.

to return ▪ zurückkehren
Passengers are requested to return to the ship by 6 p.m.

sightseeing ▪ Besichtigungen, Sightseeing
Holidays are always a problem because my wife likes sightseeing and I don't.

to stay ▪ (vorübergehend) wohnen
Where will you be staying when you're in London?

stop ▪ Pause; Zwischenlandung; Haltestelle; Anlegestelle
We usually make a stop every two hours when we go on holiday by car.
When you fly to Sydney there will be a stop at Dubai.
There's a bus stop right round the corner.
There's a stop for your boat quite near our hotel.

subject ▪ Untertan(in), Staatsbürger(in)
Polish born author Joseph Conrad became a British subject.

terminal ▪ Terminal
Heathrow Airport in London has five terminals.

tour ▪ Tour, Reise, Rundfahrt
In 2010 we did a five-week tour of New Zealand.

tourist ▪ Tourist(in)

track ▪ Weg, Pfad
Follow the track along the fence until you reach a bridge over the river Dart.

to travel (BE: travelled; travelling; AE: traveled; travelling) ▪ reisen
Anne and Herbert like travelling a lot.

traveller ▪ Reisende(r)
In recent years we've been frequent travellers to Malta.

villa ▪ Ferienhaus
We usually spend our summer holidays in a villa in a Mediterranean country.

way ▪ Weg; Richtung
This is the quickest way to the cathedral.
This way is North.

▸ **by the way** ▪ übrigens, nebenbei gesagt

---

adventure ▪ Abenteuer, Abenteuer…
Since we like adventure holidays we have decided to book a trip on the Amazon.

backpack (AE) ▪ Rucksack
What's called a backpack in the USA is a rucksack in Britain.

baggage ▪ Gepäck
You can leave your baggage in our store room once you've checked out.

bench ▪ Bank
There are many benches for tourists to relax on.

brochure ▪ Broschüre, Prospekt
The Devon Tourist Board has sent me lovely brochures on their area.

to cancel (BE: cancelled; cancelling; AE: canceled; canceling) ▪ absagen, rückgängig machen, löschen
We're afraid that as the result of an accident we are forced to cancel our reservation.

caravan (AE: trailer) ▪ Wohnwagen, Caravan
What people in the UK call a caravan is called a trailer in the USA.

charter ▪ Charter
There are a number of charter airlines to take you to your holiday destination.

to check out ▪ auschecken
Tourists are kindly asked to check out before 2 p.m.

confirmation ▪ Bestätigung
Herewith we send you your booking confirmation for your flight to Malta.

conversion ▪ Umrechnung
The conversion of currencies is not too difficult.

to convert ▪ konvertieren, umrechnen
One of the advantages of the euro is that you do not always have to convert national currencies when you go abroad.

cruise ▪ Kreuzfahrt
They celebrated their golden wedding anniversary by going on a cruise.

customs ▪ Zoll
Will travellers who have goods to declare please proceed to customs?

customs officer ▪ Zollbeamte(r)
The customs officer found some cannabis in the tourist's suitcase.

destination ▪ Reiseziel
Spain and Italy are still popular destinations for German tourists.

dock ▪ Dock, Pier, Kai
The ferry to Staten Island sails from a dock at South Ferry.

fleet ▪ Flotte
Some shipowners operate fleets of ships for cruises.

to hire ▪ mieten
For a tour around the national parks in California tourists are advised to hire a car.

jet lag ▪ Jetlag
After flying from Germany to California we suffered from jet lag for a couple of days.

monument ■ Monument, Denkmal
Monument Valley is a famous National Park in Utah.

off-peak ■ außerhalb der Hauptbedarfszeit
Our off-peak fares apply from 10 a.m. to 4 p.m.

off-season ■ Nebensaison…
Our off-season rates apply from December through February.

overcrowded ■ überfüllt
When we arrived on the beach it was completely overcrowded.

package tour ■ Pauschalreise
Many young people like package tours because they are usually not expensive.

rail ■ Geländer, Reling
Please do not lean against the ship's rails.

refreshment ■ Erfrischung(sgetränk)
During the trip refreshments and snacks will be served.

reservation ■ Reservat
We'll also make a trip to the Canyon de Chelly in the Navajo reservation in Utah.

resort [rɪˈzɔːt] ■ Urlaubsort
There are beautiful resorts on Lake Garda like Sirmione and Riva.

rucksack (AE: backpack) ■ Rucksack
If you go for long walks in the Highlands don't forget your rucksack.

season ■ Saison
Summer is definitely not a good season for taking holidays in Florida.

self-catering ■ Selbstverpflegung
I've booked a lovely self-catering cottage in the Cotswolds.

souvenir ■ Souvenir, Andenken
Maggie's flat is full of souvenirs she brought home from other countries.

standby ▪ Standby

My friends managed to get standby tickets for their flight to Alicante.

stay ▪ Aufenthalt

During my four weeks' stay in New York I saw a large number of sights.

stopover ▪ Zwischenlandung, Zwischenstation

On our flight to Auckland we made a stopover in Sydney.

swimming ▪ Schwimmen; Schwimm…

Swimming is what I like best when I'm on holiday.

Our hotel has a nice swimming pool.

to take one's time (took, taken) ▪ sich Zeit nehmen

When I am on holiday I like to take my time.

tent ▪ Zelt

When I was young I liked to go on a tent holiday.

tour guide ▪ Reiseführer(in), Fremdenführer(in)

I prefer sightseeing on my own – without a tour guide.

tour operator ▪ Reiseveranstalter

TUI is a large tour operator.

trailer (BE: caravan) ▪ (AE) Wohnwagen

When Marcus and Juliet were young their parents spent their holidays in a trailer.

travel ▪ Reisen

I wish air travel was a little cheaper.

travel agency ▪ Reisebüro

Travel agencies help their clients with the preparation of their holidays.

visa ⚠ ▪ Visum

Travellers from many countries require a visa if they want to travel to the USA.

voyage ▪ Seereise; Reise

The Smiths have gone on a voyage to Iceland.

Voyages into space do not any longer begin at Cape Canaveral.

yacht ■ Yacht

At St. Tropez you can see large numbers of expensive yachts.

youth hostel ■ Jugendherberge

Occasionally even adults can stay at youth hostels.

7.4 Gaststätten und Hotellerie

to accept ■ annehmen

Most restaurants accept cash and credit cards nowadays.

bar ■ Bar, Kneipe

The bar in this building does not only serve drinks but also snacks.

bill ■ Rechnung

Could I have the bill, please?

café ■ Cafeteria

There's a café round the corner – mind you, not one of your German "Cafés".

Cheers! ■ Prost!

The all raised their glasses and said "Cheers!"

choice ■ Wahl, Auswahl

The restaurant in our hotel offered a wide choice of dishes.

double bed ■ Doppelbett

Could we have a double bed in our room, please – not twin beds?

double room ■ Doppelzimmer

What we need is a double room and a single room.

facility ■ Anlage, Einrichtung

Our hotel features all the facilities to guarantee a fascinating holiday.

guest ■ Gast

We're pleased to welcome you as a guest in our hotel.

hotel ■ Hotel

inn ▪ Gasthaus
We found a lovely inn in the Lake District so we spent a couple of days there.

landlady ▪ Wirtin
The landlady in our local pub does not sell alcohol to people under eighteen.

landlord ▪ Wirt
... nor does the landlord.

luggage ▪ Gepäck
You can leave your luggage with us before you check in.

medium ▪ medium, halb durch
Could I have my steak medium, please?

menu ▪ ⚠ Speisekarte
Waiter, could you bring me the menu, please?

motel ▪ Motel

pub ▪ Kneipe
Many pubs nowadays also offer simple types of food.

rare ▪ nicht durch(gebraten)
Would you like your steak rare, medium, or well-done, sir?

reception ▪ Empfang, Rezeption
Our reception is open twenty-four hours a day.

reservation ▪ Reservierung, Buchung
Herewith we confirm your reservation of two double rooms from 26 July to 5 August.

to reserve ▪ reservieren, buchen
John reserved two double rooms with breakfast in the Hilton for the weekend.

restaurant ▪ Restaurant

round ▪ Runde
Thanks for the drink, mate, but the next round is on me.

self-service ▪ Selbstbedienung
It goes without saying that a self-service restaurant is usually not expensive.

to serve ▪ servieren
Breakfast is now being served in the restaurant on Blue Deck.

service ▪ Service, Bedienung
The service charge is included in our prices.

to set (set, set) ▪ (Tisch) decken
Can you set the table for six people, please?

snack bar ▪ Imbiss(stube)
Oh dear, we've nothing to eat in the house. Let's get something from a snack bar.

tip ▪ Trinkgeld
In the USA the tip should be at least 10%, up to about 20% if you have had exceptional service.

well-done ▪ gut durch(gebraten)
Could I have my steak well-done, please?

---

to accommodate ▪ unterbringen
Our banqueting hall accommodates up to 200 people.

blanket ▪ (Bett-)Decke
You will find spare blankets on the top shelf of the wardrobe.

to book ▪ buchen, bestellen
Can we please book a table for tonight?

check (AE) ▪ Rechnung
Let me pick up the check for you.

to check in ▪ einchecken
Could we possibly check in a little earlier than usual?

to check out ▪ auschecken
Would our guests please check out no later than 11 a.m.?

full board ▪ Vollpension

If you book full board, you'll get breakfast, lunch and an evening meal.

guesthouse ▪ Gasthof, Pension

A guesthouse is usually less expensive than a hotel because it offers fewer facilities.

half board ▪ Halbpension

Oliver preferred half board because he planned to be out most of the day.

king-size bed ▪ extragroßes Bett

In American hotels you often find king-size beds large enough for three people to sleep in.

night porter ▪ Nachtportier

No matter when you arrive at night there will always be a night porter to help you.

to overlook ▪ überblicken, einen Blick bieten auf

Could we possibly book a room overlooking the beach?

porter ▪ Gepäckträger

When we entered our hotel room the porter had already delivered our luggage.

preparation ▪ Zubereitung

The preparation of all the dishes for the reception takes quite some time.

queen-size bed ▪ (Einzel-)Bett mit Übergröße

A queen-size bed measures about 150 × 200 cm.

receptionist ▪ Portier(in), Empfangschef(in)

Please advise our receptionist if you require help with your luggage.

restroom (AE) ▪ Toilette (in öffentlicher Einrichtung)

Lavatories in American restaurants or cinemas, etc. are called restrooms.

single bed ▪ Einzelbett

I'm afraid we have no rooms with single beds.

single room ■ Einzelzimmer

We have only three single rooms.

takeaway (AE: takeout) ■ Imbissbude, Restaurant mit Straßenverkauf

Young people often buy fish and chips at a takeaway.

take-out ['teɪkaʊt] (AE) ■ Imbissbude, Restaurant mit Straßenverkauf

... and young Americans often buy their burgers at a take-out.

tariff ■ Preisliste; Tarif

You'll find our tariffs in the folder on your desk.

The tariff for your suite is € 200 per night.

to tip ■ Trinkgeld geben

John tends to tip waiters generously.

twin-bedded room ■ Doppelzimmer mit Einzelbetten

We'd like to book a twin-bedded room for our two children.

vacancy ['veɪkənsi] ■ Zimmer frei

During the high season the hotel hardly ever has any vacancies.

8. Medien

8.1 Sachbücher, Zeitschriften, Zeitungen

article ▪ Aufsatz
F. R. Leavis wrote a vast number of articles on nineteenth century literature.

book ▪ Buch
This book on twentieth century history has more than six hundred pages.
Many novels have subdivisions such as books and chapters.

chapter ▪ Kapitel
This book has twenty chapters.

cover ▪ Einband, Deckel
This book has a beautiful cover.

feature ▪ Reportage
This week's issue contains a feature on Afghanistan.

issue ▪ Ausgabe
I refer to your article on Greece published in your issue of 6 June.

magazine ▪ Zeitschrift, Magazin
"Time", "Life" and "Newsweek" are political magazines.

newspaper ▪ Zeitung
We always have our newspaper delivered to our home.

paper ▪ Zeitung
"The Guardian" is a very good British paper.

press ▪ Presse
The freedom of the press is a very important good.

to publish ▪ veröffentlichen; herausgeben
"Time" publishes political and cultural essays on national and international subjects.
Penguin publishes a very large number of literary texts at low prices.

reader ▪ Textsammlung
Reclam has published readers on France and America.

reading ▪ Lektüre
Dorothy's favourite reading was history books.

section ▪ Abschnitt
I'll finish reading this section, and then we can go for a walk.

volume ▪ Band
Many novels in the nineteenth century were published in three volumes.

---

ad ▪ Anzeige, Inserat, Werbespot
Without ads, newspapers and TV would hardly survive.

advert ▪ Anzeige, Inserat
Adverts are a major source of revenue for newspapers and magazines.

appendix ▪ Anhang
All the sources for this book are listed in the appendix.

catalogue ▪ Katalog
This catalogue lists all available titles of Longman publishers.

column ▪ Kolumne
Adrian Searle is responsible for the art column in the "Guardian".

critic ▪ Kritiker(in)
He was a very harsh critic of Günter Grass's most recent novel.

edition ▪ Ausgabe, Auflage
Her book on English history has just come out in a new edition.

editor ▪ Redakteur(in), Herausgeber(in), Lektor(in)
The editor is the middleman between the author and the publisher.

et al. (Lat.: et alii) ▪ und andere
This book was written by Henry Smithers et al., that means there are some more authors.

fake news ▪ Fake News, Falschmeldung
The whole story was revealed to be fake news.

to feature ▪ bringen; vorkommen

This week's issue features a report on Guatemala.

Sports does not feature prominently in this newspaper.

freelance ▪ freiberuflich

Nowadays many newspapers rely on freelance journalists.

hardback ▪ gebundenes Buch

My uncle has one of the very early "Ulysses" hardbacks.

heading ['hedıŋ] ▪ Überschrift

Nobody will read a newspaper article with a boring heading.

headline ['hedlaın] ▪ Überschrift, Schlagzeile

Catastrophes make good headlines.

journal ▪ Zeitschrift

"Time" and "Life" are political journals.

journalism ▪ Journalismus

Journalism is sometimes called the fourth power.

journalist ▪ Journalist(in)

Journalists have a very important social and political function.

paperback ▪ Taschenbuch

A paperback is less expensive than a hardback.

to print ▪ drucken; veröffentlichen

The report is not on time because printing was delayed.

The book is also printed in paperback.

print ▪ Druck

This book, I'm afraid, is out of print.

profile ▪ Porträt

The journalist wrote a short profile of the recently elected prime minister.

publisher ▪ Verlag; Verleger(in)

Reclam is the publisher of many important literary and cultural texts.

It was established by the publisher Anton Philipp Reclam in 1828.

report ■ Bericht
The "Guardian" published a long report on the situation in Mali.
weekly ■ Wochenzeitschrift
"Die Zeit" is a leading German weekly.

8.2 Radio, Fernsehen, Ton- und Bildaufzeichnung

camera ■ Kamera
CD (Compact Disc) ■ CD
channel ■ (Sende-)Kanal
There's a very interesting programme on Channel Four tonight.
disc ■ Scheibe, (Schall-)Platte
The LP has long been replaced by compact discs.
hi-fi (high fidelity) ■ Hi-Fi, Hi-Fi-Anlage
I've bought a new hi-fi so that I can enjoy my CDs of classical music.
news ■ Nachrichten(sendung)
It is nine o'clock. Here is the news.
photo(graph) ■ Fotografie, Foto
▸ **to take a photo** ■ ein Foto machen
photocopy ■ Fotokopie
programme (AE: program) ■ Sendung
There's a TV programme on Shakespeare tonight.
radio ■ Radio(gerät), Rundfunk
record ■ Schallplatte
All the composer's music is available on record or CD.
remote control ■ Fernbedienung
John's main activity is playing with the remote control of his TV.
series ■ Serie
"East Enders" is a popular TV series.

speaker ■ Lautsprecher
We had to buy new speakers for our radio.

station ■ Sender
BBC Radio 2 is the most popular radio station in the UK.

television ■ Fernsehen

TV ■ Fernseher; Fernsehen

video ■ Video
Since the introduction of DVDs most people do not watch videos any longer.

to videotape s.th. ■ etwas auf Video aufnehmen
My parents still occasionally videotape birthday parties.

Wi-Fi™ ■ Wi-Fi (Bezeichnung für die Vernetzung von Geräten mittels Funkschnittstellen)

---

blu-ray™ ■ Blu-Ray
Blu-rays are increasingly replacing DVDs – not to mention videos.

to broadcast (-cast, -cast) ■ senden
Yesterday the BBC broadcast a programme on the euro crisis.

cable ■ Kabel

coverage ■ Berichterstattung
Newspaper coverage of minor events is sometimes excessives.

current ■ aktuell, laufend
The radio news reports all the important current events.

DVD (Digital Versatile Disc) ■ DVD

episode ■ Episode, Folge
I hate those afternoon series on TV with their countless episodes.

interference ■ Interferenz, Störung
I'm afraid I can't watch this TV station. There's too much interference.

live [laɪv] ■ live, direkt
The match was broadcast live from the stadium.

loudspeaker ▪ Lautsprecher
The voice over the loudspeaker warned us not to use electricity from 2 to 4 p.m.

microphone ▪ Mikrophon

MP3-player ▪ MP3-Player

podcast (iPod + Broadcasting) ▪ Podcast

print ▪ Abzug
I collect prints of old photographs of my home town.

receiver ▪ Empfänger
We need to buy a new radio receiver. Our old one doesn't work any longer.

report ▪ Meldung
There was a report of a severe flood in Italy on the radio.

satellite dish ▪ Satellitenschüssel
Many people today have a satellite dish on their roof.

selfie ▪ Selfie

serial ▪ Serie, Sendereihe
"Steptoe and Son" used to be a famous TV serial.

snap ▪ Schnappschuss
His favourite hobby was taking snaps of people.

tape ▪ Tonband
Tapes and LPs are very much out of fashion nowadays.

to turn off ▪ abstellen
Don't forget to turn off the TV when you go.

to turn on ▪ anstellen, einschalten
Peter will turn on the TV whenever he enters the room.

8.3 Telefon, elektronische Medien

app (application software) ▪ App, Zusatzprogramm

attachment ▪ Attachment, (Mail-)Anhang

backup ■ Backup, Sicherungskopie

blog ■ Blog, Internettagebuch

busy ['bɪzi] ■ besetzt

The secretary couldn't talk to the customer because his line was busy all day.

to call ■ anrufen

Someone called while we were away. I'll just call them back.

call ■ Anruf

If you'd like to talk to my husband just give him a call. He'll be at home all evening.

to chat ■ plaudern, chatten

Our grandparents chatted when they were having a cup of tea, we chat online.

computer ■ Computer

to copy ■ kopieren

I'll copy this document and email it to you.

copy ■ Kopie, Exemplar

Can you mail me a copy of this document?

device ■ Gerät, Vorrichtung

Mobiles and the internet are very important devices nowadays.

to dial (BE: dialled; dialling; AE: dialed; dialing) ■ wählen

If something serious has happened and you need help dial 999.

digital ['dɪdʒətl] ■ digital

to download ■ downloaden, herunterladen

e-book ■ E-Book, elektronisches Buch

e-book reader ■ E-Book-Reader, elektronisches Lesegerät

to email ■ Emailen

email ■ E-Mail

GB (Gigabyte) ■ Gigabyte

GPS (Global Positioning System) ■ GPS, Navi, Navigationssystem

homepage ▪ Homepage

icon ▪ Icon, Bildsymbol

interactive ▪ interaktiv

IT (Information Technology) ▪ IT (Informationstechnologie)

key ▪ Taste

Her secretary always hit the wrong keys when she got tired.

keyboard ▪ Tastatur

Without a keyboard a computer is useless.

laptop ▪ Laptop

laser (Light Amplification by Stimulated Emission of Radiation) ▪ Laser

line ▪ Leitung

Whenever I rang, the line was always engaged.

to log in ▪ sich einloggen, sich anmelden

mailbox ▪ Mailbox

MB (Megabyte) ▪ Megabyte

message ▪ Botschaft, Mitteilung, Nachricht

Please leave a message after the tone.

mobile (phone) ▪ Handy, Mobiltelefon

mouse pad ▪ Mauspad

net (internet) ▪ Internet

network ▪ Netzwerk, Netz

notebook ▪ Notebook

offline, off-line ▪ offline

online, on-line ▪ online

operating system ▪ Betriebssystem

Windows™ is a popular operating system.

PC (Personal Computer) ▪ PC, Personalcomputer

to phone (to telephone) ▪ telefonieren, anrufen

phone (telephone) ▪ Telefon

printer ▪ Printer, Drucker
A computer is almost useless if it is not connected to a printer.

processor ▪ Prozessor

to ring (rang, rung) ▪ läuten, klingeln; anrufen
The phone is ringing – or is it the doorbell?
My aunt rang me this morning.

ring ▪ Klingeln, Läuten
The telephone's ring is rather loud.

to save ▪ speichern
You ought to save your files regularly.

to scan ▪ scannen, einlesen

scanner ▪ Scanner, optisches Lesegerät

server ▪ Server

smartphone ▪ Smartphone

sms (Short Message Service) ▪ SMS, Kurznachricht

spam (SPiced hAM) ▪ Spam

to stream ▪ streamen

to surf ▪ (im Internet) surfen
Surfing the internet can be quite helpful when you write a paper.

tablet ▪ Tablet-Computer

telecommunications ▪ Telekommunikation
Telecommunications has become increasingly important in recent years.

telephone ▪ Telefon

telephone number ▪ Telefonnummer

tone ▪ Signalton
You can leave a message after the tone.

touch screen ▪ Touchscreen, berührungsempfindlicher Bildschirm

transfer ▪ Übertragung
Data transfer on our computer is rather slow.

to tweet ▪ tweeten

to twitter ▪ twittern

to update ▪ updaten, aktualisieren, auf den neuesten Stand bringen

to upload ▪ uploaden, (hoch)laden

USB stick (Universal Serial Bus) ▪ USB-Stick

user ▪ User, Benutzer(in)

Web (World Wide Web) ▪ Web

web browser ▪ Webbrowser, Internetbrowser

website ▪ Website, Webseite

---

answering machine ▪ Anrufbeantworter
The answering machine has widely been replaced by the mailbox.

area code ▪ Vorwahlnummer
The area code of Glasgow is 0141.

augmented reality ▪ (durch Computer) erweiterte Realität

cellphone ▪ ⚠ Handy, Mobiltelefon
Early cellphones were as long and heavy as a brick.

to connect ▪ verbinden, anschließen
To transfer photographs, connect your mobile with a USB-port of your computer.

country code ▪ Ländervorwahlnummer
The country code for Germany is 0049.

dialling code ▪ Vorwahlnummer
For calls within the UK, 0131 is the dialling code for Edinburgh.

directory ▪ Telefonbuch, Verzeichnis
The London directory lists all telephone numbers in London.

disk ▪ Diskette
What is a disk in your computer is a disc in your CD-player.

dot ▪ Punkt
Email addresses in Germany often end with ".de", read as "dot de".

to hang on (hung, hung) ▪ kurz warten, dranbleiben
My boss isn't here right now. Hang on, I'll go and get him.

to install ▪ anschließen, einrichten, installieren
An expert had to help me install my computer properly.

installation ▪ Einrichtung, Anlage
The installation of a computer is rather something for experts.

IoT (Internet of Things) ▪ Internet der Dinge

jet ▪ Strahl
An ink-jet printer can be expensive because the required ink is not cheap.

junk mail ▪ Post für den Papierkorb; Spam
It often takes me hours to delete all my junk mail.

keyword ▪ Schlüsselwort
No one gets access to my computer without the correct keyword.

LAN (Local Area Network) ▪ lokales Netzwerk

like ▪ Like (positive Rückmeldung zu einer Nachricht im Internet)

long-distance call ▪ Ferngespräch
Long-distance calls can be quite expensive.

manual ▪ Handbuch, Bedienungsanleitung
For further instructions on how to install the software please refer to the manual.

menu ▪ Menü (Computer)
The menu on the screen will tell you how to proceed.

mode ▪ Modus
Your computer is now in a stand-by mode.

phone booth (AE: phone box) ▪ Telefonzelle
In Britain, the nice red phone booths are becoming increasingly rare.

phone box (AE) ▪ Telefonzelle
There's a phone box right round the corner.

receiver ▪ Hörer
He held the receiver close to his ear so that he could hear better.

to route a call ▪ (Telefongespräch) verbinden

The secretary routes incoming calls to her boss.

shortcut ▪ Shortcut, Tastenkombination

storage ▪ Speicherung, Speicher…

My computer has a storage capacity of more than 300 GB.

to store ▪ speichern

Don't forget to store your data before turning off your computer.

switchboard ▪ Vermittlung

Operating the switchboard of a large company can be quite exhausting.

to tap ▪ tippen

Don't forget to tap in your password.

telephone book ▪ Telefonbuch

If you don't know their telephone number you can look it up in the telephone book.

telephone directory ▪ Telefonbuch

If you do not have a telephone directory look up telephone numbers in your computer.

user-friendly ▪ benutzerfreundlich

I wish computer programs were more user-friendly.

wearable ['weərəbəl] ▪ Wearable (am Körper getragenes oder in die Kleidung integriertes elektronisches Gerät wie Fitness Tracker, Smartwatch usw.)

world wide web ▪ das Internet

The world wide web is very useful but also very dangerous.

8.4 Post

letter ▪ Brief

People nowadays do not write many letters, they write emails instead.

package ▪ Paket
A package is a small parcel usually sent by post.

post ▪ Post(sendung)
Has there been any post for me today?

post office ▪ Postamt
Can you tell me where the nearest post office is?

postage ▪ Porto
What, please, is the postage for postcards to Britain?

postcard ▪ Postkarte
Whenever they are on holiday Martha and Henry write dozens of postcards.

postman ▪ Postbote
Our postman comes every day at 11 a.m.

postwoman ▪ Postbotin
Sometimes our postwoman comes as early as 9 a.m.

to send (sent, sent) ▪ schicken, senden
Anne likes sending postcards to her friends when she is on holiday.

side ▪ Seite
This side up.

stamp ▪ Briefmarke
You can buy stamps in the post office.

---

airmail ▪ Luftpost
Letters from Britain to New Zealand are usually sent by airmail.

envelope ▪ Briefumschlag
Mary couldn't post the letter because she didn't have an envelope to put it in.

junk mail ▪ Wurfsendung
Most of the mail the postman brings is junk mail.

letter box (AE: mailbox) ▪ Briefkasten
The nearest letterbox is just on the corner.

mail ▪ Post(sendung)
Hasn't there been any mail today?

mailbox ▪ Briefkasten, Postkasten
What is a letter box in Britain is a mailbox in the USA.

parcel ▪ Paket
The TV set was delivered by post in a large parcel.

postcode (AE: zip code) ▪ Postleitzahl
FK9 5RD was my postcode when I lived at Stirling near Falkirk (FK).

to send off (sent, sent) ▪ abschicken
Can you send off this parcel for me, please?

sender ▪ Absender(in)
The letter was returned with the message, "Return to sender, address unknown".

to sort ▪ sortieren
Letters are sorted automatically in the post office.

sort code ▪ Postleitzahl
The sort code of the University of Stirling in Scotland is FK9 4LA.

surface mail ▪ Standardsendung
We'll send the letter by surface mail because airmail is too expensive.

telegram ⚠ ▪ Telegramm
Telegrams are not used a lot any longer.

to trace ▪ zurückverfolgen
You can trace your parcel by clicking on the following link.

zip code (AE) ▪ Postleitzahl
Americans have their zip code, i.e. zone improvement plan.

9. Kunst und Kultur

9.1 Allgemeines

art ▪ Kunst
Most major cities have a museum of art – such as the Louvre or the Prado.

audience ▪ Publikum, Zuschauer
Freddy Mercury had his audience on their feet right away.

cultural ▪ kulturell
Her main hobby was going to cultural events, for instance concerts and plays.

culture ▪ Kultur
Many people go to exhibitions because they are interested in culture.

event ▪ Ereignis, Veranstaltung
The Salzburg Festival is one of the year's major cultural events.

image ▪ Image
Anna Netrebko has a very good image.

performance ▪ Vorführung, Auftritt
Unfortunately tonight's performance must be cancelled.

show ▪ Show
Granny likes quiz shows on TV best.

star ▪ Star
Marilyn Monroe was a famous film star in the 1950s.

ticket ▪ Eintrittskarte
Tickets for the Rolling Stones' concert were quite expensive.

writer ▪ Schriftsteller(in)
Ernest Hemingway and Doris Lessing were famous writers.

writing ▪ Schreiben, Schriftstellerei
The author gave up writing when he was eighty.

to applaud ▪ applaudieren, Beifall spenden
The audience applauded frenetically at the end of the performance.

artistic ▪ künstlerisch, kreativ
I have no artistic talent but I am a pretty good scientist.

Art Nouveau ▪ Jugendstil
Art Nouveau began in the late nineteenth century.

Baroque ▪ Barock
The famous Baroque church, the "Wieskirche", was completed in 1754.

Classicism ▪ Klassik, Klassizismus
The period of art called Classicism followed after the Baroque period.

fan ▪ Bewunder(er, in), Fan
George's father was a fan of the Beatles all his life.

Gothic ▪ Gotik, gotisch
Salisbury Cathedral is a beautiful example of an early Gothic cathedral.

manuscript ▪ Manuskript
The museum purchased a large number of manuscripts from the Middle Ages.

performer ▪ Künstler(in), Darsteller(in)
He was an excellent composer but only a poor performer.

proverb ▪ Sprichwort
Many proverbs go back to classical Greece or Rome.

Renaissance [rɪˈneɪsəns] ▪ Renaissance
The Renaissance is a fifteenth- and sixteenth-century movement.

Romanticism ▪ Romantik
Romanticism is a 19th century movement in Europe and America affecting all art.

to stage ▪ aufführen, veranstalten
In the summer the city staged a rock concert, an opera, and a play.

stereotype ▪ Stereotyp, Klischee
Mr Bounderby in Dickens' "Hard Times" is the stereotype of a capitalist.

treasure ▪ Schatz
Professor Kerry owned a huge treasure of valuable books.

9.2 Theater, Drama, Spielfilm

to act ▪ eine Rolle spielen
Kenneth Branagh acted brilliantly in his role as Benedict.

act ▪ Akt
Romeo kills Tybalt in the third act of "Romeo and Juliet".

action ▪ Handlung
The action in "Romeo and Juliet" gathers pace after the death of Tybalt.

actor ▪ Schauspieler
In English 16th century theatre there were only actors and no actresses.

actress ▪ Schauspielerin
Sarah Bernhardt was one of the most famous French actresses.

appearance ▪ Erscheinen, Auftritt
The actress made her first appearance as Juliet when she was only sixteen.

character ▪ Charakter, Figur
Rosalind is a central character in Shakespeare's "As You Like It".

cinema (AE: movie theater) ▪ Kino
There are not too many cinemas around because so many people prefer DVDs.

director ▪ Regisseur(in)
Peter Brook, the famous director of plays by Shakespeare, was born in 1925.

film ▪ Film
Hollywood is the capital of the American film industry.

part ▪ Rolle
My father was surprised to see Mel Gibson play the part of Hamlet.

to perform ▪ aufführen, vorführen, spielen
Every year the students of this university perform in a play produced by themselves.

play ▪ Schauspiel
Harold Pinter wrote a large number of plays …

role ▪ Rolle
… and played a number of roles on the stage.

scene ▪ Szene; Schauplatz
Originally Shakespeare's plays had only scenes, not acts.
The scene of "Hamlet" is Denmark.

screen ▪ Leinwand, Bildschirm
Films can be seen on a screen in the cinema or on TV.

set ▪ Bühnenbild
The production was praised for its attractive set.

stage ▪ Bühne
In recent years quite a few novels have been adapted for the stage.

theatre ▪ Theater
Mike travelled to London only to see a Shakespeare play in the Globe Theatre.

western ▪ Western
"High Noon" was a typical western dealing with the lives of cowboys.

---

box office ▪ Kasse (Theater, Kino)
Our box office opens two hours before every performance.

chorus ▪ Chor
In some of Shakespeare's plays there is a chorus, e.g. in "Romeo and Juliet" and "Henry V".

classic ▪ klassisch

"Twelfth Night" is a classic example of a Shakespearean comedy.

comedy ▪ Komödie

Not all comedies are funny.

comic ▪ komisch

In some tragedies there are scenes of comic relief, e.g in "Macbeth".

counterpart ▪ Gegenspieler, Gegenstück

Tybalt is Romeo's counterpart in "Romeo and Juliet".

drama ▪ Drama, Schauspiel

Comedy and tragedy are important forms of drama.

to engage ▪ anstellen, engagieren

The director engaged a very prominent actor for this demanding role.

feature ▪ Hauptfilm

This week's feature is Antonioni's "Blow Up".

film-script ▪ Drehbuch

The film-script for this film was written by Harold Pinter, the famous author.

flashback ▪ Rückblende

In films, flashbacks often show events that took place before the main action.

fool ▪ Narr

In a tragedy the fool is very often an intelligent observer of events.

hero ['hɪroʊ] ▪ Held

Romeo is the hero in Shakespeare's "Romeo and Juliet"...

heroine ['heroʊɪn] ▪ Heldin

... and Juliet is its heroine.

interval ▪ Pause

Champagne was served during the interval after the third act.

monologue ▪ Monolog

Nobody on stage listened to the actor's monologue.

movie ▪ Film (Kino)

Hollywood is a major centre of the movie industry.

movie theater (AE) ▪ Kino

In Britain a movie theater is called a cinema.

orchestra (AE) ▪ Parkett

A seat in the orchestra, called the stalls in Britain, will cost you as much as $ 100.

prologue ▪ Prolog, Vorrede

Classical plays like those of Seneca often begin with a prologue spoken by a chorus.

rehearsal ▪ (Theater-, Konzert-)Probe

Quiet please. Rehearsal in progress.

Restoration ▪ Restauration

The Restoration set in with Charles II's return from exile in 1660.

to resume ▪ wieder einnehmen

Please resume your seats. The performance is about to continue.

run ▪ Laufzeit

Agatha Christie's "The Mousetrap" has had a run of sixty years so far.

scenery ▪ Bühnenbild

On the Elizabethan stage there was hardly any scenery.

script ▪ Drehbuch

Harold Pinter wrote a large number of plays and scripts.

soliloquy ▪ Monolog

When actors speak a soliloquy they are alone on stage.

stage direction ▪ Bühnenanweisung

Bernard Shaw's stage directions are often very long.

stalls (Pl.) ▪ Parkett

A seat in the stalls, called the orchestra in the USA, will cost you as much as £50.

tragedy ▪ Tragödie

Tragedy and comedy are major types of drama.

trilogy ▪ Trilogie

The three parts of Shakespeare's "Henry VI" form a trilogy.

9.3 Bildende Kunst

artist ▪ Künstler(in)
Van Gogh did not live to see his fame as an artist.

background ▪ Hintergrund
In the background of the painting you can see a castle and a park.

creation [kri'eɪʃən] ▪ Schöpfung, Kreation
Leonardo da Vinci's "Mona Lisa" is one of the greatest creations in the world of art.

exhibition [eksə'bɪʃən] ▪ Ausstellung
We went to see the Dürer exhibition in Frankfurt.

frame ▪ Rahmen
The gallery owner ordered a very expensive frame for his new painting.

gallery ▪ Galerie, Ausstellungsraum
Painters usually show their paintings in a gallery.

museum ▪ Museum
The Metropolitan Museum of Art in New York has one of the most impressive art collections in the world.

painting ▪ Gemälde
Leonardo da Vinci's "Mona Lisa" is one of the world's most famous paintings.

picture ▪ Bild
The National Gallery in London exhibits a lot of beautiful pictures.

to represent ▪ darstellen
What is this painting supposed to represent?

representation ▪ Darstellung
Da Vinci's "Mona Lisa" is probably the representation of a lady from Florence.

studio ▪ Studio; Atelier
They recorded their new CD in a new studio.
The painter Paul Cézanne had a lovely studio in Aix-en-Provence.

abstract ▪ abstrakt
Most modern paintings are abstract.

architecture ▪ Architektur
Rome is one of the major centres of classical architecture.

caricature ▪ Karikatur
William Hogarth was famous for his caricatures.

collection ▪ Sammlung
The Tate Britain has a marvellous collection of British paintings.

collector ▪ Sammler, Sammlerin
The Glaswegian William Burrell was a collector of virtually everything he liked.

drawing ▪ Zeichnung
Dürer's drawings are deservedly famous.

fake ▪ Fälschung
The experts found that the painting was only a fake.

foreground ▪ Vordergrund
In the foreground of the painting you can see a large crowd of observers.

initials ▪ Anfangsbuchstaben, Initialen
Albrecht Dürer signed his picture with his initials AD.

landscape ▪ Landschaftsgemälde
John Constable was a famous landscape painter.

life-size ▪ lebensgroß
Henry Moore made some life-size sculptures.

to paint ▪ malen
Constable painted lovely landscapes.

painter ▪ Maler(in)
Claude Monet was one of the major nineteenth-century painters.

photography ▪ Fotografie
Photography can be an art like painting.

portfolio ▪ Mappe
Sybil brought her portfolio of drawings when she arrived for the interview at the Glasgow School of Art.

portrait ▪ Porträt
Velázquez was a major 17th-century painter of portraits at the Spanish court.

poster ▪ Poster, Plakat
The posters for the Manet exhibition were brilliant.

profile ▪ Profil
The artist likes to paint his models in profile.

sculptor ▪ Bildhauer(in)
Michelangelo is one of the most famous sculptors of the Renaissance.

sculpture ▪ Skulptur, Plastik
In Rome's Villa Borghese you can also see some marvellous sculptures by Bernini.

to shape ▪ gestalten
The architect Capability Brown shaped a large number of gardens in England.

sketch ▪ Skizze
The painter always makes a sketch of a painting before painting it.

statue ▪ Statue
When we were in Paris we went to see the statue of the Venus of Milo.

symbol ▪ Symbol
The rose is a symbol of love.

treasury ▪ Schatzkammer
The cathedral has a marvellous treasury.

9.4 Musik

band ▪ Band, Gruppe
The Rolling Stones were a famous rock band in the late twentieth century.

to blow (blew, blown) ▪ blasen
Louis Armstrong blew the trumpet very well.

concert ['kɒnsət] ▪ Konzert
The New York Philharmonic gave a brilliant concert in the Avery Fisher Hall.

to conduct ▪ dirigieren
Tonight's concert will be conducted by Sir Simon Rattle.

festival ▪ Festival, Festspiele
Every summer there is a famous opera festival in Glyndebourne.

guitar ▪ Gitarre
I like playing the guitar for fun, but my brother plays guitar in a band.

hit ▪ Schlager
There are people who never listen to anything but hits on the radio.

melody ▪ Melodie
Dvořák's music is full of beautiful melodies.

movement ▪ Satz (Musik)
The fourth movement of Beethoven's ninth symphony is well known.

music ▪ Musik
I listen to classical music all day when I am at home.

to record ▪ aufnehmen
The orchestra plans to record its next concert.

recorder ▪ Blockflöte
Antonio Vivaldi wrote a lot of music for the recorder.

to release ▪ herausbringen
The Beatles released a vast number of records.

to sing (sang, sung) ■ singen
Maria Callas was known for her excellent singing.

singer ■ Sänger(in)
Placido Domingo used to be a brilliant singer.

song ■ Lied
I like the songs of the Beatles better than those of the Rolling Stones.

theme ■ Thema; Melodie
Katherine knows all the major themes in Mozart's "Magic Flute".
In Dvořák's music there are many beautiful themes.

tone ■ Ton
C sharp is half a tone higher than C.

variation ■ Variation
Brahms composed variations on a theme which he thought was composed by Haydn.

---

adaptation ■ Adaptation, Bearbeitung
Verdi's opera "Macbeth" is an adaptation of Shakespeare's play.

album ■ Album
Jonathan has a complete collection of the albums released by the Beatles.

big band ■ Bigband
Glenn Miller's band was a typical big band.

choir ['kwaɪə] ■ Chor
The Monteverdi Choir is regarded as one of the best choirs in Britain.

clarinet ■ Klarinette
Mozart wrote his first work for clarinet in 1771.

classical ■ klassisch
What I like most is classical music – you know: Haydn, Mozart, and Beethoven.

to compose ■ komponieren
Mozart composed no fewer than 41 symphonies.

composer ■ Komponist(in)
Edward Elgar was a famous 20th century composer.

composition ■ Komposition
Beethoven's ninth symphony is definitely one of the best known classical compositions.

conductor ■ Dirigent(in)
Sir Neville Marriner, the conductor, died in 2016.

creative ■ schöpferisch, kreativ
Haydn was very creative. He composed 104 symphonies.

to dance ■ tanzen
Dancing in a professional ballet is the dream of some young people.

dance ■ Tanz
The gigue and the sarabande are very old classical dances.

flute ■ Flöte
Mozart was not very fond of flutes but he wrote beautiful music for them.

folk ■ Folk-Musik
Thousands of people came to the folk festival.

interval ■ Intervall
The interval between a C and a B, i.e. what Germans call an H, is rather large.

lyrics ■ Liedtext
I like his music but some of his lyrics are rather banal.

major ■ Dur
Mozart's 41st symphony is in C major, his Requiem is in D minor.

minor ■ Moll
Beethoven's ninth symphony is in D minor.

musical ■ musikalisch; Musical
She was very musical and started playing an instrument early in life.
Andrew Lloyd Webber composed a number of popular musicals.

musician ▪ Musiker(in)
She became a musician and played in the first violins in an orchestra later on.

opera ▪ Oper
"Don Giovanni" is probably Mozart's most famous opera.

orchestra ▪ Orchester
The New York Philharmonic is one of the world's best orchestras.

organ ▪ Orgel
Handel also composed some music for the organ.

piano ▪ Klavier
Chopin wrote famous pieces for piano.

prologue ▪ Vorspiel
"Rheingold" is the prologue to Wagner's "Ring".

recording ▪ Aufnahme, Aufzeichnung
I have three different recordings of Beethoven's fifth symphony.

to rehearse [rɪ'hɜːs] ▪ proben
Tomorrow we shall rehearse the second movement of Mozart's 41st symphony.

to render ▪ wiedergeben
Joyce di Donato rendered the song brilliantly.

rhythm ▪ Rhythmus
You need a good feeling for rhythm to play drums.

spiritual ▪ Spiritual
Spirituals are religious songs originally sung by black slaves in America.

string ▪ Saite
The concert had to be interrupted because the soloist's D-string broke.

tune ▪ Melodie
Verdi's operas are full of beautiful tunes.

violin ▪ Violine, Geige
Listening to a beginner practising on a violin can be a painful experience.

9.5 Fiktionale Literatur und Dichtung

author ▪ Autor(in)
Joanne K. Rowling is the author of the Harry Potter books.

block ▪ Hemmung, Blockierung
Ernest Hemingway is said to have suffered from writer's block.

commentary ▪ Kommentar, Erläuterung
The professor wrote an excellent commentary on the novel.

device ▪ (Stil-)Mittel
Among the devices used by poets are rhyme, rhythm, and metre.

figure ▪ Gestalt
Dickens is one of the most important figures in 19th-century literature.

literature ▪ Literatur
Even trivial literary texts are literature.

metre ▪ Metrum
Most lines in English poetry employ a metre with five stresses.

opening ▪ Anfang
The opening of the novel was rather disappointing.

point ▪ Pointe
The point is that Joseph Andrews is in reality Mr Wilson's son and can thus marry Fanny, who is Mr Andrews' daughter.

reading ▪ Lesung
Many people came to T. C. Boyle's reading of his most recent novel.

short story ▪ Kurzgeschichte
Short stories can also be very long like Melville's "Bartleby".

story ■ Geschichte, Handlung; Erzählung
The story in this novel can be summarized in a few sentences.
Alice Munro has written a large number of stories.

style ■ Stil
Ernest Hemingway wrote in a very clear style.

version ■ Version
William Butler Yeats often wrote many versions of his poems before publishing them.

---

chorus ■ Refrain
Every stanza of this poem ends in a chorus.

to construct ■ entwickeln
James Joyce's novels are very carefully constructed.

to entertain ■ unterhalten
The main functions of literature are to teach and to entertain.

epic ■ episch; Epos
Epic poetry usually deals with heroes and gods.
Homer's "Odyssey" is one of the finest epics ever written.

fable ■ Fabel
A fable is a story whose protagonists are animals.

fantasy ■ Fantasie
"Lord of the Rings" is a typical fantasy novel.

fiction ■ Erzählliteratur; Erfindung
Most things that are told in fiction did not really happen – they are fiction.

fictional ■ erfunden, fiktiv
The plot and character in a novel are usually fictional.

figurative ■ bildlich
In poetry many expressions are not literal but figurative.

Gothic ■ Schauer…
Many Gothic novels were written in early nineteenth century England.

imagery ▪ Metaphorik
The poet employed a rather strange imagery.

imagination ▪ Fantasie, Vorstellungskraft
Charles Dickens had an usually rich imagination.

imaginative ▪ einfallsreich
Laurence Sterne was a highly imaginative writer.

introduction ▪ Einführung
The new edition of "Tristram Shandy" begins with a long introduction by the editor.

legend ▪ Legende, Sage
Legend has it that King Arthur was a king of Britain in the fifth century.

literal ▪ wörtlich
A literal translation of a text is usually nonsense.

literary ▪ literarisch
Studying a language often also means studying literary works in that language.

lyric ▪ lyrisches Gedicht
A lyric is usually defined as a short poem expressing the speaker's personal feelings.

metaphor ▪ Metapher
John Donne's poetry is full of unusual metaphors.

mystery ▪ Krimi
Sir Arthur Conan Doyle wrote a large number of mysteries.

narrative ▪ Erzählung
Novels and short stories are types of narrative.

narrator ▪ Erzähler(in)
Lockwood is the narrator in Emily Brontë's "Wuthering Heights".

novel ▪ Roman
James Joyce's "Ulysses" is one of the most important 20th century novels.

novelist ■ Romancier, Romanschriftsteller(in)
John Steinbeck, whose family came from Germany, was a major American novelist.

ode ■ Ode
Keats wrote an "Ode to a Nightingale".

omniscience [ɒm'nɪsiəns] ■ Allwissenheit
Omniscience allows the narrator to tell the reader the thoughts of his characters.

omniscient [ɒm'nɪsiənt] ■ allwissend
Fielding's narrator is almost as omniscient as God.

outline ■ Übersicht
Some novelists supply outlines of their chapters for the reader's benefit.

parody ■ Parodie
Fielding made fun of epic poetry by using the art form of parody, i.e. by writing in its serious style about trivial subjects.

plot ■ Handlung, Handlungsgerüst, Plot
The novel's story is clear, but the way it is turned into a plot makes it difficult to follow.

poem ■ Gedicht
A poem differs from a story in that it has clearly defined lines.

poet ■ Dichter(in)
In the past poets usually wrote their poems in rhymes.

poetry ■ Dichtung, Lyrik
Wordsworth and Coleridge published the first collection of Romantic poetry.

point of view ■ Perspektive
"The Catcher in the Rye" is written from a first-person point of view.

prose ■ Prosa
Novels are written in prose, poems in verse.

pun ■ Pun, Wortspiel
"Seven days without water make one weak" is a pun because it plays on the identical pronunciation of "week" and "weak".

realism ■ Realismus
Realism in literature is a difficult concept and not easy to define.

rhetorical ■ rhetorisch
In traditional poetry a lot of rhetorical devices are used.

to rhyme ■ (sich) reimen
"Steak" and "teak" do not rhyme in English.

rhyme ■ Reim
In English "sweat" and "bet" are a rhyme, "steak" and "sweet" are not.

satire ['sætaɪə] ■ Satire
Jonathan Swift wrote a lot of satires in which he criticized his contemporaries.

science fiction ■ Science Fiction
H. G. Wells was one of the first authors to write science fiction novels.

simile ['sɪməli] ■ Gleichnis
A simile is a comparison of two items which belong to different categories.

sonnet ■ Sonett
In addition to his plays and other works, Shakespeare wrote 154 sonnets.

sophisticated ■ anspruchsvoll
John Donne's poetry is highly sophisticated.

stanza ■ Strophe
A sonnet is a poem in one stanza with fourteen lines.

tale ■ Geschichte, Erzählung
In the nineteenth century the Grimm brothers collected a large number of tales.

thriller ▪ Thriller, Reißer, Krimi
Stephen King has written a large number of thrillers.

verse ▪ Dichtung, Poesie, Lyrik; Strophe
I can't find my Oxford Book of Eighteenth Century Verse.
What in literary analysis is called a stanza is colloquially also called a verse.

10. Wissenschaft und Technik

10.1 Allgemeines

to adopt ■ übernehmen, verwenden
As they didn't find a solution they adopted a different approach.

A.I. (Artifical Intelligence) ■ KI (Künstliche Intelligenz)

approach ■ Ansatz
In order to solve this problem we need an entirely new approach.

assumption ■ Annahme, Voraussetzung
They started the project on the assumption that it would be finished within weeks.

basis (⚠ Pl.: bases) ■ Basis, Grundlage
Mathematics is the basis of many sciences.

concept ■ Idee, Begriff, Konzept
Before you start working you must have a clear concept in mind.

experiment ■ Experiment

instruction ■ Belehrung, Anweisung
Follow the instructions carefully or the experiment will fail.

logic ■ Logik

opinion ■ Gutachten
If you wish to set up a business you should seek an expert's opinion first.

publication ■ Veröffentlichung
The young scholar was made a professor because of his excellent publications.

reference ■ Verweis
His list of references included 550 quotations from other books and essays.

source ■ Quelle
In an essay you must indicate all the sources you have used.

structure ▪ Aufbau

Scientific essays ought to have a clear structure.

study ▪ Studie

According to a recent study our climate will change considerably.

systematic ▪ systematisch

theory ▪ Theorie

---

to calculate ▪ ausrechnen, kalkulieren

Before running a series of tests you must calculate the costs of the project.

calculation ▪ Berechnung

A thorough calculation of the costs of this scientific project is essential.

classification ▪ Klassifizierung, Einordnung

What is particularly important in science is the correct classification of phenomena.

expertise ▪ Fachkenntnis, Sachverstand, Expertise

Solving this technical problem requires a lot of expertise.

footnote ▪ Fußnote

For each quotation – whether direct or indirect – you must supply a footnote.

graphics ▪ Graphik(en), graphische Darstellung(en)

You should illustrate your paper with graphics to make it easier to understand.

hypothesis ▪ Hypothese, Annahme

Make sure you base your thesis on a sound hypothesis.

to quote ▪ zitieren

If you quote other people's texts make sure that you quote correctly and supply the source.

résumé ['rezjʊmeɪ] ▪ Resümee, Zusammenfassung

He was asked to write a résumé of the conference.

sophisticated ■ raffiniert, ausgeklügelt
This is a highly sophisticated approach.

theoretical ■ theoretisch
He has a keen interest in anything theoretical.

thesis ■ These
Aristotle's thesis that knowledge is power is still widely accepted.

10.2 Geisteswissenschaften

factor ■ Faktor
It is difficult to find a solution because of the many factors involved in the problem.

focus ■ Mittelpunkt, Brennpunkt
The scholar's focus is on the relationship between France and England.

historical ■ historisch
Everything that has ever happened is a historical event, even if it was trivial.

history ■ Geschichte
Joan studied history at Cambridge University.

index ■ Verzeichnis, Index
Most books on demanding subjects have an index.

interpretation ■ Interpretation, Deutung
There have been quite a number of different interpretations of this complex work.

library ■ Bibliothek, Bücherei
We have one of the very early editions of Joyce's "Ulysses" in our library.

philosophy ■ Philosophie
John has always been interested in philosophy.

review ▪ Rezension, Kritik
All reviews of Edward Bond's new play were favourable.

---

civilization ▪ Kultur, Zivilisation
Among the major civilizations of America were those of the Aztecs and the Incas.

discovery ▪ Entdeckung
1492 is the year of the discovery of America by Christopher Columbus.

equation ▪ Gleichung
Solving equations is one of the key activities of mathematicians.

historic ▪ historisch bedeutsam
The fall of the Berlin Wall was a historic event for Germany.

linguistic ▪ sprachlich, linguistisch
Dialects and accents are very interesting linguistic phenomena.

mankind ▪ Menschheit
History is also concerned with the early development of mankind.

philosopher ▪ Philosoph(in)
Aristotle was one of the most important philosophers of ancient Greece.

to restore ▪ wiedereinführen; wiedereinsetzen
The monarchy in Britain was restored in 1660.
Charles II was restored as King in 1660.

to review ▪ besprechen
Unfortunately Marianne's book was not reviewed favourably.

to revise ▪ überarbeiten; revidieren
The scholar had a revised edition of his work on the Romans published.
However, he did not revise his major theses and arguments.

revision ▪ Überarbeitung
He carried out major revisions to his book.

scholar ■ Gelehrte(r)
Erasmus of Rotterdam was a famous sixteenth-century scholar.

scholarship ■ Gelehrsamkeit
The new book on Wagner is a brilliant piece of scholarship.

statistics ■ Statistik
Statistics is a branch of mathematics.

variable ■ Variable
There are too many variables in this equation for me to solve it.

10.3 Naturwissenschaften

acid ■ Säure
I can't drink this wine. It has too much acid.

to base ■ gründen, stützen
She based her experiment on the assumption that all the available data were correct.

condition ■ Bedingung
Water is a necessary condition for the existence of life on earth.

data (Pl.) ■ Daten
Collecting all the important data was a very tough job.

to define ■ definieren, festlegen, bestimmen
In science it is important that everything is defined quite clearly.

definition ■ Definition, Erklärung
Every term in science requires a clear definition.

to demonstrate ■ beweisen
All the available data demonstrate that our thesis is correct.

detail ■ Detail, Einzelheit
Before we inform the public of this important finding we must check all the details once again.

detailed ■ ausführlich, detailliert
A detailed examination of all the available facts proved that our thesis was incorrect.

to develop ▪ (sich) entwickeln
It would be wonderful if scientists at last developed a therapy to cure Alzheimer's disease.

to display ▪ anzeigen, zeigen
All the important data were displayed on a screen.

element ▪ Element, Bestandteil
This material contains a large number of elements.

to explore ▪ erforschen
Columbus wished to explore a route to India but he discovered America instead.

to generate ▪ hervorrufen
Good luck often generates scientific progress.

to illustrate ▪ veranschaulichen, illustrieren
The scientist illustrated his theory by brilliant experiments.

laboratory ▪ Laboratorium
In science you cannot achieve good results if you do not have a good laboratory.

magnet ▪ Magnet
A magnet attracts iron.

to perform ▪ ausführen
To prove our thesis we'll have to perform a number of tests.

physical ▪ physikalisch
The physical laws of electricity have always interested me very much.

research ▪ Forschung, Untersuchung
Benjamin Franklin did a lot of research – e.g. he invented the lightning conductor.

science ▪ Naturwisssenschaft
Physics and Chemistry are examples of sciences.

scientific ▪ wissenschaftlich
Stephen Hawking's "A Brief History of Time" is a major scientific work.

scientist ▪ Wissenschaftler(in)
Marie and Pierre Curie were major scientists working on radioactivity.

species ['spiːʃiːz] ▪ Spezies, Art
Darwin wrote his book "On the Origin of Species" in 1859.

specific ▪ spezifisch
The specific weight of water is approximately 1 kg/dm³.

standard ▪ Standard, Richtlinie, Maßstab
Celsius is a major standard for measuring temperature.

table ▪ Tabelle
The table shows all the relevant data.

---

advance ▪ Fortschritt
There has been quite some advance in the development of alternative energies.

to analyse ▪ analysieren, untersuchen
Before publishing your results you ought to analyse your tests thoroughly.

analysis ▪ Analyse
The results of the analysis of our tests are very satisfying.

angle ▪ Winkel
There are only right angles in a square.

atom ▪ Atom
Scientists once thought that an atom could not be divided into smaller components.

biological ▪ biologisch
Sweating is the result of a biological process in stress situations.

chart ▪ Tabelle, Diagramm
The chart illustrates the result of the test quite clearly.

circuit ▪ Schaltsystem
Before you start the test make sure that the circuit works properly.

composition ▪ Zusammensetzung
The composition of this chemical agent is highly complex.

to consist of ▪ bestehen aus
Air consists basically of 80 per cent nitrogen and 20 per cent oxygen.

cycle ▪ Zyklus, Kreislauf
Spring, summer, autumn, and winter are repeated in an eternal cycle.

database ▪ Datenbank
A database needs to be reliable to be useful.

demonstration ▪ Vorführung
The scientists' demonstration showed that their thesis was correct.

to detect ▪ entdecken, bemerken
What we require is software which can detect any attack on our computers.

diagram ▪ Schaubild, Diagramm, Grafik
It is very helpful to illustrate all your data by a diagram.

display ▪ Anzeige, Display
An error message appeared on the display.

distinction ▪ Unterschied; Ehre, Auszeichnung
There is a clear distinction between Indian and African elephants. They have entirely different ears.
The scientist was awarded a distinction for his invention.

evolution ▪ Evolution, Entwicklung
Charles Darwin developed the theory of evolution.

to evolve ▪ sich entwickeln
Most scientists are convinced that the world evolved gradually.

experimental ▪ Versuchs…
After a lot of experimental research the hypothesis at last proved correct.

extensive ▪ umfassend, umfangreich
Extensive tests showed that the theory was wrong.

finding ■ Entdeckung, Ergebnis

After the expedition the scientists published their findings in a scientific journal.

formula ■ Rezept(ur)

The chemical formula for this type of medicine is highly complex.

interaction ■ Wechselwirkung, Interaktion

The interaction of these chemical agents can lead to an explosion.

liquid ■ Flüssigkeit

Water, milk and oil are types of liquids.

matter ■ Materie

An atom is an important part of the matter of the universe.

molecule ■ Molekül

The name of the water molecule is H_2O.

origin ■ Ursprung, Herkunft

Charles Darwin wrote a famous book on the origin of human beings.

phenomenon (Pl.: phenomena) ■ Phänomen

Meteors have always been fascinating phenomena.

prize ■ Preis

Marie Curie was the first woman to win a Nobel prize in Chemistry.

to prove ■ beweisen

It is still debated whether man is responsible for the drastic climate change.

radiation ■ Strahlung

Not all radiation is harmful, but radioactive radiation is.

radioactive ■ radioaktiv

After the destruction of the reactor there was a huge radioactive cloud above the site.

radioactivity ■ Radioaktivität

Radioactivity can both harm and heal human beings.

to research ■ (er)forschen

Marie and Pierre Curie researched uranium and discovered radioactivity.

researcher ■ Forscher(in)
After taking her degree she started working as a researcher for ICI.

scope ■ Rahmen
Let us widen the scope of our research to include possible side effects.

spectrum ■ Spektrum; Skala
In the rainbow you can see all the colours of the spectrum.
The spectrum of agents in this compound is remarkable.

statistical ■ statistisch
Statistical evidence shows that there is a relationship between smoking and cancer.

steam ■ (Wasser-)Dampf
Water turns to steam at a temperature of 100 degrees Celsius.

survey ■ Untersuchung
The architects carried out a careful survey of the building before offering it for sale.

vacuum ■ Vakuum
A vacuum is a space without any gas in it.

variable ■ variabel
The oxygen content in this atmosphere is variable.

10.4 Technik

to advance ■ Fortschritte machen
IT has advanced dramatically in recent years.

automatic ■ automatisch

dam ■ Staudamm
Dams across rivers are often built to generate electricity.

electric ■ elektrisch
Many people in Britain have an electric kettle to boil water in.

electrical ▪ elektrisch; Elektro…
We have a lot of electrical appliances in our workshop.
My brother studied electrical engineering.

electricity ▪ Elektrizität, Strom

electronic ▪ elektronisch

engineering ▪ Technik; Maschinenbau, Ingenieurwesen
This F1-car is a beautiful piece of engineering.
She studied engineering at Hanover.

to invent ▪ erfinden
The steam engine was not invented by James Watt, but he improved it a lot.

invention ▪ Erfindung
The invention of the steam engine was a major step in the development of industry.

motor ▪ Motor

to operate ▪ funktionieren
The engine operated smoothly even after fifty hours of continuous driving.

operation ▪ Funktionsweise; Betrieb
The operation of a computer is difficult to explain.
The machine has been in operation for several hours.

support ▪ Stütze
The bridge had to be closed because one of its supports was in danger of collapsing.

technical ▪ technisch

technique [tek'niːk] ▪ Verfahren, Technik, Methode
There are various techniques for dealing with pollution.

technology ▪ Technologie
In the past fifty years there has been a rapid development in technologies.

appliance ▪ Gerät, Instrument

In our field of research we require a lot of highly precise appliances.

boot ▪ Kofferraum

Just put the suitcases into the boot of the car.

disposal ▪ Entsorgung, Beseitigung

The safe disposal of nuclear waste is a major problem.

functional ▪ funktionell, funktionstüchtig

It took some time before the machine was functional again.

hardware ▪ Hardware (die Geräte im Gegensatz zur Software, den Anwendungsprogrammen)

to incorporate ▪ einfügen, eingliedern

A large number of new components have been incorporated in this new device.

innovation ▪ Neuerung

It is said that the Industrial Revolution was the result of technical innovations.

inventor ▪ Erfinder(in)

Benjamin Franklin was a very important inventor.

mechanism ▪ Mechanismus

microscope ▪ Mikroskop

patent ▪ Patent

Every year thousands of people apply for patents for their inventions.

radiator ▪ Kühler

Make sure that there is enough water in your radiator or the engine might get too hot.

scope ▪ Möglichkeit, Spielraum

I wonder if there is still some scope for improving this device.

software ▪ Software, Anwendungsprogramme

spaceship ▪ Raumschiff

The Russian spaceship Sojus has been in operation since 1966.

spare ■ Ersatz...
We can fix your car because we've got the necessary spare parts.

specification ■ genauer Entwurf
The car was produced according to the customer's specifications.

stability ■ Stabilität

steam engine ■ Dampfmaschine
The invention of the steam engine led to a revolution in the manufacturing industries.

strain ■ Druck
The strain on the structure was so strong that it collapsed.

to survey ■ begutachten
The engineer surveyed the building.

survey ■ Untersuchung
The architects carried out a careful survey of the building before offering it for sale.

to transform ■ transformieren
Electric current must be transformed to a lower voltage before households can use it.

transformation ■ Transformation
After transformation to a low voltage electric current can be used by households.

voltage ■ (Strom-)Spannung
The voltage in the USA (120 volts) is different from that in Europe (240 volts).

working ■ Arbeits...
I have no idea about the working mode of this clock.

11. Natur, Umwelt

11.1 Allgemeines

bottle bank ▪ Altglascontainer
More and more bottle banks have been introduced in Britain.

to burn (burnt/burned, burnt/burned) ▪ (ver)brennen
We should stop burning so much coal and oil.

earth ▪ Erde, Land
As a result of the heat wave the earth was entirely dry.

environment ▪ Umwelt, Umgebung
Burning coal and oil is not good for the environment.

environmental ▪ Umwelt…
Simply throwing rubbish away leads to major environmental problems.

moon ▪ Mond
The time from one full moon to the next is nearly thirty days.

natural ▪ natürlich, Natur…
Water is a very important natural resource.

nature ▪ Natur
There is little one can do against the forces of nature.

object ▪ Gegenstand, Objekt
After the storm we found quite a number of objects on our lawn.

reality ▪ Realität, Wirklichkeit
Reality includes everything around us so that we cannot really escape it.

resource ▪ Ressource
We must do whatever we can to preserve our natural resources.

space ▪ Weltraum
There are quite a few satellites in space.

star ▪ Stern
It was a beautiful night and the sky was full of stars.

sun ■ Sonne
The sun is not the centre of the universe.

thing ■ Ding, Gegenstand, Sache
Scientists believe that there are still many things to discover in nature.

▸ **things** (Pl.) ■ die Dinge, die Lage
Things are getting better.

waste ■ Abfall
Waste is collected in New York five times a week.

CFC (Chlorofluorocarbon) ■ FCKW (Fluorchlorkohlenwasserstoff)
CFC destroys the ozone layer, which is bad for people's health.

conservation ■ Schutz, Erhaltung
The conservation of our energy resources is of vital importance.

emission ■ Emission, Ausstoß
Cutting down on our use of cars will reduce polluting emissions.

environment-friendly ■ umweltfreundlich
Coal-fired power stations are not environment-friendly.

filter ■ Filter
In some parts of the world it is advisable to use filters before you drink water.

high tide ■ Flut
You cannot walk across to the island at high tide.

litter ■ Abfall (Papier, Verpackung)
Everywhere in the forest there were vast amounts of litter left by tourists.

low tide ■ Ebbe
You can walk across to Mont Saint-Michel at low tide.

marine ■ Meeres…
The Alfred Wegener Institut does a lot of research in marine biology.

Milky Way ▪ Milchstraße
The Milky Way is a strip of light consisting of many stars across the sky.

national park ▪ Nationalpark
Bryce Canyon in Utah is the national park I like best.

new moon ▪ Neumond
It was very dark outside and the new moon did not help much either.

organism ▪ Organismus
Every living plant and animal is an organism.

planet ▪ Planet
Earth, Venus, Mars, and Jupiter are major planets.

to pollute ▪ verschmutzen
The beaches on that island were so polluted that the water was not fit for swimming.

pollution ▪ Umweltverschmutzung
The pollution of our environment is a very serious problem.

to preserve ▪ bewahren
A lot of efforts are made to preserve our environment.

to recycle ▪ recyceln, wiederverwenden
It is better to recycle material than to just throw it away.

satellite ▪ Satellit
The moon is the earth's satellite, as are all those artificial objects moving around the earth.

season ▪ Jahreszeit
The four seasons are spring, summer, autumn, and winter.

soil ▪ Boden, Erde
The soil is very good. So you can even grow wheat here.

solar system ▪ Sonnensystem
Earth is only a very small element of the solar system.

sustainable development ▪ nachhaltige Entwicklung
Short-term progress is not enough. What we need is a sustainable development.

universe ■ Universum
Our world is only a tiny part of the universe.

wax ■ Wachs
We always have real wax candles on our Christmas tree.

11.2 Rohstoffe, Elemente

coal ■ Kohle
There are hardly any coal mines left in the Ruhr area.

gold ■ Gold
Some people prefer buying gold to saving their money in a savings account.

iron ⚠ ['aɪən] ■ Eisen
Iron is required for the production of steel.

oil ■ Öl
In the 1970s it was thought that in 2000 the world's oil reserves would have come to an end.

rock ■ Stein; Fels; Felsbrocken
He picked up a rock and used it to smash the window.
The mountain side consisted of sheer rock.
With a lot of effort he managed to lift the rock.

silver ■ Silber
A lot of silver is produced in Taxco, Mexico.

stone ■ Stein
Stone steps last longer than wooden steps.

---

carbon ■ Kohlenstoff
Plants convert carbon into oxygen.

copper ■ Kupfer
Copper is a rather expensive mineral.

diamond ■ Diamant
Diamonds, among the world's most precious metals, are also found in South Africa.

hydrogen ■ Wasserstoff
Water is a combination of one part oxygen and two parts hydrogen.

lead [led] ■ Blei
Lead is a heavy metal with a low melting point.

marble ■ Marmor
A lot of marble is imported from Carrara in Italy.

natural gas ■ Erdgas
Russia is a major supplier of natural gas.

nitrogen ■ Stickstoff
Nitrogen is the main component of air.

oxygen ■ Sauerstoff
Water is a combination of one part oxygen and two parts hydrogen.

ozone ■ Ozon
Ozone is a colourless gas, which can be harmful.

ozone layer ■ Ozonschicht
The ozone layer high above the earth is recovering gradually.

petroleum ■ Erdöl, Petroleum
Saudi Arabia is one of the most important producers of petroleum.

rust ■ Rost
Rust forms on iron if it comes into contact with water.

sand ■ Sand
Sand is a very useful building material.

substance ■ Substanz, Materie, Stoff
Lead is a very heavy substance.

tin ■ Zinn
Tin used to be produced in Cornwall and Devon.

uranium ■ Uran
Uranium is a very useful but also potentially dangerous element.

11.3 Pflanzen und Anbau

branch ▪ Zweig
There was so much snow on the branches that they broke off.

corn ▪ Korn; Mais
In the USA corn is maize, in Britain "corn" can also refer to wheat for instance.

flower ▪ Blume
In spring our garden is full of flowers.

to grow (grew, grown) ▪ wachsen, anbauen, züchten
The soil in this area is good enough for farmers to grow wheat.

growth ▪ Wachstum
Without water there can't be any growth.

leaf (Pl.: leaves) ▪ Blatt
All the oaks in our garden have lost their leaves.

maize ▪ Mais
In the USA people usually call maize corn.

to pick ▪ pflücken
We picked some apples for an apple pie.

to plant ▪ pflanzen
My uncle planted apple trees in his garden.

plant ▪ Pflanze
Make sure that you do not have too many plants in your garden.

top ▪ (Baum-)Krone
The top of the tallest tree in the USA is 115 m high.

tree ▪ Baum
In Sequoia National Park you can see trees which are up to 84 metres high.

wheat ▪ Weizen
The EU is the world's largest producer of wheat.

wood ▪ Holz; Wäldchen
The chair is made of wood.
There is a wood at the back of our house.

---

barley ▪ Gerste
Barley is used for making beer and whisky.

beech ▪ Buche
There is a large forest of beeches and oaks in our area.

birch ▪ Birke
Birches grow primarily in the northern zones of the world.

to bloom ▪ blühen
Our tulips began to bloom last week.

bud ▪ Knospe
In early spring you can see the first buds everywhere.

core ▪ Kern
If you put the core of a pear into the ground a pear tree may grow from it.

cotton ▪ Baumwolle
The USA is a large-scale producer of cotton, which grows primarily in its southern states.

fertile ▪ fruchtbar
The soil in our area is so fertile that we can even grow wheat.

fir ▪ Tanne
Christmas trees are usually firs.

harvest ▪ Ernte
During the harvest period many people work on farms to help.

hedge ▪ Hecke
A well-planted hedge can shelter plants from the wind.

lettuce ▪ (Kopf-)Salat
Lettuce is a key ingredient in many salads.

maple ▪ Ahorn
Canada's flag shows a maple leaf.

mushroom ■ Pilz
Not all mushrooms can be eaten safely.

oak ■ Eiche
Oaks are widespread in some parts of Germany.

oats (Pl.) ■ Hafer
Without oats there wouldn't be any porridge.

organic ■ Bio…
More and more people are buying organic products nowadays.

palm ■ Palme
Palms require a hot climate. They grow in deserts and on beaches.

pine ■ Kiefer
Pines have very long needles – much longer than those of firs.

poppy ■ Mohnblume, Mohn
In Britain, the First-World-War battle fields of Flanders are associated with poppies.

ripe ■ reif
The apples are ripe. Let's pick them.

rod ■ Stange, Stab
Harry's uncle reinforced his roof with steel rods.

root ■ Wurzel
Firs tend to have very long roots.

rose ■ Rose
Unfortunately, even red roses have thorns.

rubber ■ Gummi
Rubber is either harvested from rubber trees or it is a synthetic fibre.

rye ■ Roggen
The British prefer wheat bread to rye bread.

seed ■ Samen, Keim, Saat
Do not sow the seeds too deep in the earth.

shell ■ Schale, Hülse
You cannot eat the shells of peanuts.

stem ■ Stiel, Stängel

These red roses have very long stems.

stick ■ Stock, Zweig

We need some dry sticks to get the fire burning properly.

straw ■ Stroh

The old lady wore a straw hat.

trunk ■ Stamm

The trunk of a Sequoia tree can be up to eight metres thick.

tulip ■ Tulpe

Every year millions of people travel to Holland to see all the fields of blooming tulips.

twig ■ Zweig

Cut off the brown twigs.

vegetation ■ Vegetation, Pflanzen

There is very little vegetation in Death Valley.

violet ■ Veilchen

In one of his poems Wordsworth describes a girl as a "violet by a mossy stone".

to wither ■ welken

In autumn flowers wither and trees shed their leaves.

wooden ■ Holz…, hölzern

Jack kept all his toys in a large wooden box.

11.4 Tiere und Tierpflege

animal ■ Tier

Birds, cats, and dogs are only three examples of animals.

bear [beə] ■ Bär

bee ■ Biene

If there were no bees, we would not have honey.

bird ■ Vogel

Chickens are birds which can't fly properly.

bull ▪ Bulle, Stier

cat ▪ Katze

chicken ▪ Huhn
What comes first – chicken or egg?

cow ▪ Kuh

dog ▪ Hund
Many people say that a dog is man's best friend.

▸**to walk the dog** ▪ den Hund ausführen
Whatever the weather is like we walk the dog three times a day.

feeding ▪ Fütterung
Notice in a zoo: The next feeding of the lions takes place at 4 p.m.

fish ▪ Fisch

fly ▪ Fliege
Most flies can do you no harm, but they can get on your nerves.

hen ▪ Henne
Our best hen lays one egg per day.

horse ▪ Pferd
My daughter is interested in only one thing – riding her horse.

lamb ▪ Lamm

lion ▪ Löwe
The lion is often called the king of animals.

lioness ▪ Löwin
A lioness is particularly dangerous when she is a mother.

monkey ▪ Affe
Little Johnny always wanted to see the monkeys in the zoo.

mouse (Pl.: mice) ▪ Maus

pig ▪ Schwein
The farmer had ten pigs and twenty cows.

rat ▪ Ratte

tail ▪ Schwanz
There are people who will cut off their dog's tail.

tiger ■ Tiger

wild ■ wild

Wild lions can be very dangerous.

wing ■ Flügel

Chickens have wings but they can hardly fly.

wolf (Pl.: wolves) ■ Wolf

---

ant ■ Ameise

The ant is a very busy little animal.

to bark ■ bellen

Whenever somebody enters our flat our dog begins to bark furiously.

beak ■ Schnabel

The flamingo has a very long beak.

bitch ■ Hündin

A female dog is a bitch.

blackbird ■ Amsel

The blackbird is a common bird in Europe.

breeding ■ Zucht

Sir Peter's hobby is dog breeding.

buffalo (Pl.: buffalo(e)s) ■ Büffel

On the Great Plains in the USA there used to be vast numbers of buffalos.

butterfly ■ Schmetterling

A butterfly is an insect with a slim body and often beautiful wings.

calf (Pl.: calves) ■ Kalb

A young cow is a calf, but its meat is called veal – after French "veau".

cattle ■ Vieh, Rinder

Cattle supply meat and milk.

creature ■ Kreatur, Geschöpf, Lebewesen

Animals are also God's creatures.

cricket ■ Grille
The noise of the crickets in the nearby trees kept us awake all night.

crow ■ Krähe
Crows are large black birds and make a harsh noise.

cuckoo ■ Kuckuck
The cuckoo's cry, which sounds like its name, is often heard in June.

deer ■ Hirsch
Hunting deer is popular in Scotland.

duck ■ Ente
Donald Duck is the uncle of Huey, Dewey, and Louie.

eagle ■ Adler
We saw an eagle soaring high above the mountain top.

feather ['feðə] ■ Feder
The lark has brown feathers.

fox ■ Fuchs

fur ■ Fell, Pelz
Bears and foxes are among the animals which have fur.

hare ■ Hase
Hares are larger than rabbits, have longer ears and don't live in holes in the earth.

horn ■ Horn, Geweih
Cows and deer have horns.

kangaroo ■ Känguru

lark ■ Lerche
The lark sings early in the morning.

mosquito (Pl.: mosquito(e)s) ■ Stechmücke
Some mosquitoes like the tsetse fly are very dangerous.

nest ■ Nest

nightingale ■ Nachtigall
The nightingale does not look very pretty but it sings beautifully.

penguin ['peŋgwɪn] ■ Pinguin

pet ▪ Haustier
Before I met my wife I never had a pet and now we have three cats.

pigeon ▪ Taube
Pigeons are a symbol of peace.

pony ▪ Pony

rabbit ▪ Kaninchen
Rabbits look almost like hares but they live in holes in the ground.

rattlesnake ▪ Klapperschlange
If you hear a rattlesnake, it means that it might bite you.

to reproduce ▪ sich vermehren
Penguins always return to the same place to reproduce.

to roar ▪ brüllen
While he was having breakfast Francis Macomber heard a lion roar.

roe deer ▪ Reh
Roe deer are smaller than other deer.

salmon ▪ Lachs
We had breakfast with salmon, scrambled eggs and bacon.

seal ▪ Seehund
Many fishermen dislike seals because they eat a lot of fish.

shark ▪ Hai
Every year sharks kill people.

sheep (⚠ Pl.: sheep) ▪ Schaf
The farmer had fifty sheep.

shell ▪ Muschel
You can find marvellous shells on Sanibel Island in Florida.

snake ▪ Schlange
Cleopatra was killed by a poisonous snake.

sow ▪ Sau
The word for the female pig rhymes with "cow".

sparrow ▪ Spatz, Sperling
Sparrows are very common in Germany and Britain.

spider ▪ Spinne

Spiders make webs to catch flies in.

stable ▪ (Pferde-)Stall

The family had ten horses in their stable.

stag ▪ Hirsch

Grandma has the picture of a stag with 14 ends to his horns above her sofa.

to sting (stung, stung) ▪ stechen

Make sure you're not stung by bees.

stork ▪ Storch

swallow ▪ Schwalbe

One swallow doesn't make a summer.

tame ▪ zahm

Don't be afraid. Our dog is quite tame.

to trap ▪ (ein Tier) fangen

The vet trapped the animal so that he could treat it.

trunk ▪ Rüssel

Elephants use their trunks for drinking.

turkey ▪ Truthahn, Truthenne, Pute(r)

Many people in the USA and Great Britain eat turkey for Christmas.

vet ▪ Tierarzt/-ärztin

Our dog doesn't feel well. We'd better see a vet.

veterinary surgeon ▪ Tierarzt/-ärztin

Mary likes animals so much that she would like to be a veterinary surgeon.

whale ▪ Wal

wildlife ▪ Tierwelt

The wildlife in Namibia is very impressive.

zoo ▪ Zoo, Tierpark

11.5 Klima

air ▪ Luft
At last the air has become a little warmer.

atmosphere ▪ Atmosphäre
The earth's atmosphere is influenced by a lot of heavy traffic.

to blow (blew, blown) ▪ pusten, wehen
A cold wind began to blow.

Celsius ▪ Grad Celsius
In Great Britain temperatures have been measured officially in Celsius since 1962.

clear ▪ klar, unbewölkt
The night sky was completely clear so that they could see a lot of stars.
It is clear that we will not go to Hamburg tomorrow.

cloud ▪ Wolke
Look at that cloud over there. It's going to rain in a minute.

fog ▪ Nebel
The tourists couldn't see the Golden Gate Bridge because it was hidden in fog.

foggy ▪ neblig
It's very often foggy on the Californian coast.

frost ▪ Frost
In the severe frost last winter most lakes were covered in ice.

heat ▪ Hitze
The heat in Death Valley was extreme – the temperature went up to 50 ° Celsius.

ice ▪ Eis
In winter there's often ice on the roads.

icy ▪ eisig
Yesterday's icy roads caused many accidents.

to melt ▪ schmelzen

As a result of rising temperatures the ice at the poles has been melting for some time.

mild ▪ mild

Where we live temperatures this winter have been very mild.

pressure ▪ Druck

High pressure over the Atlantic will make our weather warm and dry all week.

rain ▪ Regen

Last winter we had very little rain and no snow at all.

to settle ▪ beständiger werden

After three days of rain the weather settled at last.

to shine (shone [ʃɒn], shone [ʃɒn]) ▪ scheinen, leuchten

The sun shone brightly from a clear blue sky.

sky ▪ Himmel

The sky was deep blue and the moon was shining bright.

sunny ▪ sonnig

Let's hope the weather tomorrow is nice and sunny.

temperature ▪ Temperatur

Temperatures in Siberia can be as low as –60 °Celsius.

thermometer ▪ Thermometer

The thermometer showed that it was very cold outside.

thunder ▪ Donner

She heard the first thunder just after midnight.

thunderstorm ▪ Gewitter

Last summer there were many thunderstorms in our region.

wave ▪ Welle

In a tsunami the waves can be up to thirty metres high.

weather ['weðə] ▪ Wetter

The weather was surprisingly good when we were in Scotland.

wind ▪ Wind
There is often a lot of wind on the coast.

to absorb ▪ aufsaugen, absorbieren
Plants absorb carbon dioxide.

carbon dioxide ▪ Kohlendioxyd, Kohlensäure
Carbon dioxide is converted into oxygen by plants.

climate ▪ Klima
The climate in Germany has been changing for quite some time.

damp ▪ feucht, klamm
After the heavy rain the air was very damp.

drizzle ▪ Nieselregen
In November we don't usually have heavy rain but a lot of drizzle.

drop ▪ Tropfen
In Death Valley there are months in which not a single drop of rain falls.

dull ▪ trüb
Last Monday was a very dull day without any sun and with a steady drizzle.

forecast ▪ Vorhersage
The weather forecast said it would be bright and warm today.

to freeze ▪ (ge)frieren
It's been freezing so long that you can skate on the ponds.

global warming ▪ Erderwärmung
The current global warming appears to be at least partly man-made.

greenhouse effect ▪ Treibhauseffekt
Burning fossil fuels is a major factor contributing to the greenhouse effect.

hail ▪ Hagel
Hail can cause serious damage to cars.

hurricane ■ Hurrikan, Orkan, tropischer Wirbelsturm
In America hurricanes often occur in September, less often in May.

lightning ■ Blitz
The tree was struck by lightning and started burning.

mist ■ Dunst, (leichter) Nebel
The valley was covered by a beautiful morning mist.

misty ■ dunstig, (leicht) neblig
It was impossible to see the mountains in the background because it was so misty.

patch ■ Flecken
In the morning there are going to be some patches of fog.

to pour ■ gießen, schütten
It was pouring with rain from morning to night.

rainbow ■ Regenbogen
There is said to be a pot of gold at the foot of a rainbow.

shade ■ Schatten
Jack, come into the shade. The sun is too strong for you.

shadow ■ Schatten
The runners were relaxing in the shadow.

shower ■ Schauer
The weather will be bright and fine with occasional showers in the afternoon.

smog ■ Smog
Smog is a mixture of fog, smoke and gases.

snow ■ Schnee
Alberto from Malta had never seen snow in his life when he visited us in winter.

storm ■ Gewitter; Unwetter
Lightning can also strike you if you hide under a tree during a storm.
Last June our area was struck by a storm which killed several people.

tornado (Pl.: tornado(e)s) ▪ Tornado
Every year up to 1,200 tornado(e)s are registered in the USA.

tropical ▪ tropisch
Surprisingly enough, Inverewe Gardens in the north of Scotland is a tropical garden.

warmth ▪ Wärme
After the long winter everyone enjoyed the warmth of the sun in April.

weather forecast ▪ Wetterbericht
I once heard the following weather forecast: "It's going to rain – everywhere."

to whip ▪ peitschen
The wind whipped the rain against the windows.

windy ▪ windig
According to the weather forecast it is going to be very windy tomorrow.

11.6 Landschaften und Landschaftsformen

area ▪ Fläche, Gebiet; Bereich
The UK covers an area of 243,000 square kilometres.
Chemistry was the professor's main area of competence.

bank ▪ Ufer, Böschung
The river bank is very steep. Mind you don't slip.

beach ▪ Strand
There are brilliant sandy beaches in Portugal.

chalk ▪ Kalkstein
The highest chalk cliff in Britain is Beachy Head near Brighton and Eastbourne.

channel ▪ Kanal
The English Channel separates France from Britain.

field ■ Wiese, Weide; Feld, Acker
Chris had a large number of fields – for his cows to graze on and for growing corn.

forest ■ Wald
The Black Forest is one of the largest forests in Germany.

harbour ■ Hafen
There are quite a few beautiful harbours on the British south coast.

hill ■ Berg, Hügel
There are hills in the Lake District, but not many real mountains.

hole ■ Loch
To plant a tree, you first dig a hole.

horizon ■ Horizont
Slowly the sun rose above the horizon promising a beautiful day.

island ['aılənd] ■ Insel
Great Britain is an island, so is Ireland.

lake ■ See
We are going to spend our next holidays in the Lake District.

land ■ Land, Boden
The land in the Sahara is almost completely dry.

mountain ■ Berg
Ben Nevis in Scotland is Britain's highest mountain.

mouth ■ Mündung
Newcastle is quite near the mouth of the river Tyne.

North Sea ■ Nordsee
A lot of oil is produced in the North Sea.

pool ■ Tümpel
The area is full of little pools, especially after a lot of rain.

rain forest ■ Regenwald
The rainforest in Brazil has been declinig in recent years.

range ▪ Bergkette; Weideland
The Sierra Nevada, a major mountain range in the USA, is up to 4421 metres high.
5,000 horses grazed on the range near Kansas City.

region ▪ Region, Gegend
Scotland is one of the regions of Britain which demand more independence.

regional ▪ regional
The regional council of the West Midlands is in Birmingham.

river ▪ Fluss
The longest German rivers are the Rhine and the Danube.

rural ▪ ländlich
The Lake District is very rural. There are no cities but a lot of hills and lakes.

sea ▪ Meer
Britain is entirely surrounded by the sea.

spring ▪ Quelle
There are a lot of hot springs in Rotorua.

surface ▪ Oberfläche
71 per cent of the earth's surface consists of water.

top ▪ (Berg-)Gipfel
It took the tourists several days to reach the top of Mount Kilimanjaro.

valley ▪ Tal
Scotland has a lot of beautiful valleys and mountains.

water ▪ Wasser
Water covers 71 per cent of the earth's surface.

---

bay ▪ Bucht
The coast of Cornwall has plenty of beautiful bays with sandy beaches.

canal ▪ Kanal
The Leeds & Liverpool Canal is not used for commercial shipping any longer.

cliff ▪ Klippe
Some of the cliffs on the English sea coast are up to 150 metres high.

coast ▪ Küste
On the English west coast it can be rather wet, while the east coast is much drier.

countryside ▪ Landschaft, Gegend
The countryside in large parts of New Zealand is marvellous.

crack ▪ Riss, Krachen
As a result of the very dry weather there were cracks in the soil everywhere.

desert ▪ Wüste
The Sahara is the world's largest desert.

farmland ▪ Ackerland
Most of the area was converted into farmland hundreds of years ago.

flat ▪ flach, eben
The countryside was entirely flat. You could see for miles on end.

iceberg ▪ Eisberg
The Titanic sank when it hit an iceberg near Greenland.

isle ▪ Insel
The Isle of Man lies between England and Ireland.

landscape ▪ Landschaft
The landscape in Yosemite National Park is really wonderful.

meadow ▪ Wiese
The meadow was full of lovely flowers.

mud ▪ Schlamm
After three days of rain all the roads in the valley were full of mud.

ocean ▪ Ozean, (Welt-)Meer
Last year my friend crossed the Atlantic Ocean on his yacht.

Pacific Ocean ▪ Pazifischer Ozean
Hawaii is an island right in the middle of the Pacific Ocean.

pass ▪ Pass
At 2715 m, the Col de la Bonette is the highest pass in the French Alps.

peak ▪ Gipfel, Bergspitze
The highest peak in Scotland is Ben Nevis, which is 1344 metres high.

pit ▪ Grube
It was dangerous to walk in the forest because it was full of pits.

pole ▪ Pol
The ice caps at the North Pole have been melting for some time.

reservoir ▪ Stausee
Lake Powell in Utah and Arizona is one of the largest reservoirs in the world.

sandy ▪ sandig, Sand…
In Scotland you find a lot of sandy beaches.

scenery ▪ Landschaft
The Milford Sound scenery was absolutely stunning.

shore ▪ Küste; Ufer; Strand
Only few people survived the shipwreck and managed to reach the shore.
After rowing for two hours on the Rhine he at last dragged the boat on shore.
In this area the shore is full of rocks and not suitable for swimming.

slope ▪ Hang
The slope is very steep. So use a low gear.

stream ▪ Bach; Flut, Schwall
The Scottish Highlands are full of clear streams and a few rivers like the Torridon.
In the past couple of weeks we've had to deal with a stream of complaints.

summit ▪ (Berg-)Gipfel
From their base camp the climbers reached the summit of Mount Everest in only three days.

surf ▪ Brandung
You could hear the sound of the surf from the coastal road.

tide ▪ Gezeiten
When the tide is low you can walk to St. Michael's Mount in Cornwall.

tip ▪ Spitze
What you see of an iceberg is only its tip.

urban ▪ städtisch
New York and its neighbouring towns are a very densely populated urban area.

volcano ▪ Vulkan
Mount Etna on Sicily is Europe's highest active volcano.

wilderness ▪ Wildnis
Much of the Everglades National Park is wilderness.

11.7 Siedlungsformen, Gebäude und Infrastruktur

capital ▪ Hauptstadt
Ottawa is Canada's capital.

city ▪ (Groß-)Stadt
In the past a city had to have a cathedral, nowadays a city is just larger than a town.

county ▪ Bezirk, Grafschaft
A county is a region in the UK which has its own regional government.

inhabitant ▪ Bewohner(in)
Manchester has some 500,000 inhabitants.

park ▪ Park
The largest park in Manhattan is Central Park.

settlement ▪ Siedlung

What was a tiny Dutch settlement became one of the world's famous cities – New York.

suburb ▪ Vorort

I'd rather live in a suburb than in the city centre.

subway ▪ U-Bahn; Unterführung

What is the Underground in Britain is a subway in the USA.

In Britain a subway is a tunnel under a road for use by pedestrians.

town ▪ Stadt

In everyday British English, a town is usually not as large as a city, so you would not call London or Glasgow towns. They are cities.

---

alley ▪ Gasse, Weg

There is a narrow alley behind our back garden.

avenue ▪ Avenue, Allee, Boulevard

A wide, straight road, often with trees on either side, is called an avenue.

city centre ▪ Innenstadt, Stadtzentrum

What is called the city centre in Britain is called downtown in the USA.

district ▪ Bezirk, Stadtviertel

Our district is a purely residential area.

downtown (AE) ▪ Innenstadt, Stadtzentrum

What is called downtown in the USA is the city centre in Britain.

intersection ▪ Schnittpunkt, Kreuzung

Our headquarters is at the intersection of Great Castle Street and Oxford Street.

office block ▪ Bürogebäude

In the city centre you find mainly shops and office blocks.

port ▪ Hafenstadt

Savannah is a major American port.

settler ▪ Siedler(in)

The first European settlers of Manhattan were Dutch.

skyscraper ▪ Wolkenkratzer

From Hoboken you have a marvellous view of the skyscrapers in Manhattan.

town hall ▪ Rathaus

The Mayor's office is the Town Hall.

11.8 Kontinente, Länder, Völker und Sprachen

Africa ▪ Afrika

Large areas of Africa suffer from a very hot climate.

African ▪ afrikanisch; Afrikaner(in)

Barack Obama is of partly African descent.

Africans in the north of Africa and those in the centre look different.

America ▪ Amerika

Columbus discovered America in 1492.

American ▪ (US-)amerikanisch; Amerikaner(in)

"Casablanca" is No. 1 on the list of best American movies of all times.

Most Americans in the USA speak English and quite a few speak Spanish.

Asia ▪ Asien

The Bosporus and the Urals mark the border between Europe and Asia.

Asian ▪ asiatisch; Asiate(-in)

Asian cultures are entirely different from European ones.

There is a large Asian community in San Francisco.

Australia ▪ Australien

Australia is the smallest continent.

Australian ▪ australisch; Australier(in)
Australian football is different from our type of football.
A lot of Australians have European roots.

Austria ▪ Österreich
Austria's capital is Vienna.

Austrian ▪ österreichisch; Österreicher(in)
Mozart and Bruckner are two of the most important Austrian composers.
More than 1.8 million Austrians live in Vienna.

Belgian ▪ belgisch; Belgier(in)
The Belgian football team is very good.
Most Belgians speak at least two of the three languages French, Dutch and German.

Belgium ▪ Belgien
Belgium borders on the Netherlands, France, Luxembourg and Germany.

Britain ▪ Großbritannien
Britain consists of England, Scotland and Wales.

British ▪ britisch; (die) Briten
The British type of humour is not liked by everybody.
The British have a special type of humour.

Briton ▪ Brite(-in)
On holiday I met three Britons from Preston.

Bulgaria ▪ Bulgarien
Bulgaria has lovely beaches on the Black Sea.

Bulgarian ▪ bulgarisch; Bulgare(-in); Bulgarisch
Bulgarian and Russian art are closely related.
The 7 million Bulgarians speak Bulgarian.

Canada ▪ Kanada
In Canada, French and English are the official languages.

Canadian ▪ kanadisch; Kanadier(in)
Alice Munro is a major Canadian writer.
Not everybody who lives in Canada is a native Canadian.

China ▪ China
China's role in the world is increasing dramatically.

Chinese ▪ chinesisch; Chinese(-in); Chinesisch
Chinese culture is entirely different from that of other countries.
1.42 billion Chinese live in the People's Republic of China.
Not many people in the West speak Chinese.

continent ▪ Erdteil, Kontinent
The American continent was discovered by Columbus in 1492.

country ['kʌntri] ▪ Land
Canada is one of the largest countries in the world.

Croatia ▪ Kroatien
In 2013 Croatia became the 27th member of the EU.

Croatian ▪ kroatisch; Kroate(-in); Kroatisch
Dubrovnik is one of the most beautiful Croatian cities.
Some 80 per cent of Croatia's inhabitants are Croatians. They speak Croatian, which is similar to Serbian.

Czech ▪ tschechisch; Tscheche(-in); Tschechisch
The Czech ice hockey team is excellent.
Some ten million Czechs live in the Czech Republic.
Czech is a difficult language.

Czech Republic ▪ Tschechische Republik, Tschechien
The Czech Republic has existed since 1992.

Dane ▪ Däne(-in)
The Danes are very liberal people.

Danish ▪ dänisch; Dänisch
Danish dairy products are known worldwide.
People in Denmark speak Danish.

Denmark ▪ Dänemark
Copenhagen is Denmark's capital.

Dutch ▪ holländisch; (die) Holländer; Holländisch
Dutch cheese is known worldwide.
The Dutch are very good at football.
Many people in the Netherlands speak Dutch and one or two other languages.

England ▪ England
Great Britain consists of England, Scotland and Wales.

English ▪ englisch; (die) Engländer; Englisch
My uncle reads only English novels.
The English are very proud of their history.
English has become a world language.

Englishman (Pl.: -men) ▪ Engländer
William Shakespeare is one of the best-known Englishmen of all times.

Englishwoman (Pl.: -women) ▪ Engländerin
The writer George Eliot was a nineteenth-century Englishwoman.

Europe ▪ Europa
Europe stretches from Portugal in the west to the Ural Mountains in Russia.

European ▪ europäisch; Europäer(in)
The European Union was founded as the European Economic Community in 1957.
Some 700 million Europeans live in the EU.

Far East ▪ Ferner Osten
China is the most important country in the Far East.

Federal Republic of Germany ▪ Bundesrepublik Deutschland
The Federal Republic of Germany has existed since 1949.

Finland ▪ Finnland
Finland has borders with Norway, Sweden and Russia.

Finn ▪ Finne(-in)
The Finns are said to have a good education system.

Finnish ▪ finnisch; Finnisch
Jean Sibelius is a major Finnish composer.
Most people in Finland speak Finnish but quite a few also speak Swedish.

foreign ▪ ausländisch, Fremd…
Travelling to foreign countries and learning foreign languages is what I like doing best.

France ▪ Frankreich
The area of France is much larger than that of Germany.

French ▪ französisch; (die) Franzosen; Französisch
French fashion may be very much in demand, but French as a language isn't.
The French are very proud of their nation.

Frenchman (Pl.: -men) ▪ Franzose
We have invited three Frenchmen and five Italians to our party.

Frenchwoman (Pl.: -women) ▪ Französin
In addition to six Englishmen five Frenchwomen took part in our expedition to Canada.

German ▪ deutsch; Deutsche(r); Deutsch
Dürer was a German painter.
Not everybody who lives in Germany is a German and speaks German.

Germany ▪ Deutschland
Not everybody who lives in Germany was also born in Germany.

Great Britain ▪ Großbritannien
Great Britain consists of England, Scotland and Wales.

Greece ▪ Griechenland
Greece is a very old democracy.

Greek ▪ griechisch; Grieche(-in); Griechisch
Ancient Greek civilization has had a major influence on European culture.
The Greeks had serious economic problems at a certain moment.
There are even areas in Italy where people speak Greek.

Greenland ▪ Grönland
Greenland has only 56,000 inhabitants.

Holland ▪ Holland, Niederlande
Holland has beautiful beaches and nice towns and villages.

Iceland ▪ Island
Iceland is a country and an island north-west of Britain.

Icelander ▪ Isländer(in)
Many Icelanders profit from the hot springs in Iceland.

Icelandic ▪ isländisch; Isländisch
The Icelandic countryside is rather rough.
Icelandic is an independent language only remotely related to Danish.

India ▪ Indien
India achieved its independence in 1947.

Indian ▪ indisch; Inder(in)
I've always been fascinated by Indian culture.
The inhabitants of India are called Indians.

Ireland ▪ Irland
The Republic of Ireland and Northern Ireland, which is part of the UK, share the island of Ireland.

Irish ▪ irisch; (die) Iren; Irisch
The Irish economy recovered in the early 21st century.
The Irish speak English or Irish, but most Irishmen and Irishwomen speak English.
Irish has nothing in common with English.

Irishman (Pl.: -men) ▪ Ire
When I was in Dublin I met quite a few Irishmen …

Irishwoman (Pl.: -women) ▪ Irin
… and also quite a few Irishwomen.

Italian ▪ italienisch; Italienier(in); Italienisch
Early Italian art was much influenced by Greece.
Many young Italians like living with their parents even when they are adults.
Many Italians near the border with Austria speak both Italian and German.

Italy ▪ Italien
Italy is very rich in cultural sights.

Japan ▪ Japan
Tokyo is Japan's capital.

Japanese ▪ japanisch; Japaner(in); Japanisch
Japanese art is entirely different from western art.
We often see Japanese travelling in large groups.
Japanese is a very difficult language.

Latin America ▪ Lateinamerika
Brazil is the largest country in Latin America.

Luxembourg ▪ Luxemburg
Luxembourg is one of the founding members of the EU.

Luxembourger ▪ Luxemburger(in)
Most Luxembourgers speak at least two languages.

Luxembourgian ▪ luxemburgisch
Luxembourgian banks offer favourable conditions.

Luxembourgish ▪ Luxemburgisch
Luxembourgish is closely related to German.

nation ▪ Nation, Land, Volk
Britain used to be one of the leading industrial nations in the world.

national ▪ national, National…
The British and the French have different national characters.

Netherlands (Pl.) ▪ Niederlande
The Netherlands borders on Belgium, France and Germany.

Northern Ireland ▪ Nordirland
UK is the abbreviation for United Kingdom of Great Britain and Northern Ireland.

Norway ▪ Norwegen
Oslo is Norway's capital.

Norwegian ▪ norwegisch; Norweger(in); Norwegisch
The Norwegian economy profits very much from North Sea oil.
The Norwegians speak Norwegian, a language close to Danish and Swedish.

people ▪ Volk
The UN tries to achieve peace among the peoples in the world.

Poland ▪ Polen
Poland and Germany share a very long border.

Pole ▪ Pole(-in)
Frédéric Chopin is one of the best known Poles.

Polish ▪ polnisch; Polnisch
Roman Polanski has contributed very much to the success of Polish films.
Polish is difficult to learn.

Portugal ▪ Portugal
Lisbon, Portugal's capital, was partly destroyed by an earthquake in 1755.

Portuguese ▪ portugiesisch; Portugiese(-in); Portugiesisch
The Portuguese economy profits from tourism.
Many Portuguese understand Spanish, and many Spaniards understand Portuguese.

Romania ▪ Rumänien
Romania became a member of the EU in 2007.

Romanian ▪ rumänisch; Rumäne(-in); Rumänisch
Romanian culture is influenced very much by its many neighbours.
Romanian is spoken by most of the 21 million Romanians.

Russia ▪ Russland
Russia is the world's largest country, which explains some of its problems.

Russian ▪ russisch; Russe(-in); Russisch
Russian literature experienced its climax in the nineteenth century.
Russian is spoken by most Russians.

Scotland ▪ Schottland
Scotland was independent until 1707.

Scot ▪ Schotte(-in)
Kenny Dalglish was a popular Scot, playing for Scottish and English clubs.

Scotsman (Pl.: -men) ▪ Schotte
Sir Walter Scott was one of the most famous Scotsmen, so is Rod Stewart.

Scotswoman (Pl.: -women) ▪ Schottin
J. K. Rowling, the author of the Harry Potter novels, is one of the best-known Scotswomen.

Scottish ▪ schottisch; Schottisch
Scottish industry used to be famous for its shipbuilding industry.
Most Scottish literature is written in English, not in Scottish.

South America ▪ Südamerika
Brazil and Argentina are South America's largest countries.

Soviet ▪ sowjetisch, Sowjet…
There is no Soviet sector of Berlin nor does the Soviet Union still exist.

Spain ▪ Spanien
Spain is the favourite holiday country of many Germans and British.

Spaniard ▪ Spanier(in)
An individual who is a Spanish citizen is called a Spaniard.

Spanish ▪ spanisch; Spanisch
Velázquez was a famous Spanish painter.
Spanish is spoken in Spain, and also in South America with the exception of Brazil.

Swede ▪ Schwede(-in)
Some 10 million Swedes live in Sweden.

Sweden ▪ Schweden
Sweden is a member of the EU but not of NATO.

Swedish ▪ schwedisch; Schwedisch
Famous Swedish authors are August Strindberg and Astrid Lindgren.
In addition to Swedish many Swedes also speak English.

Swiss ▪ schweizerisch, Schweizer…; Schweizer(in)
Friedrich Dürrenmatt was a Swiss author.
The cheese I like best is Swiss cheese, the one with the holes in it.
Martina Hingis is Swiss, so is Roger Federer.

Switzerland ▪ Schweiz
The capital of Switzerland is Bern.

Turk ▪ Türke(-in)
There are almost as many Turks as Germans.

Turkey ▪ Türkei
Only a small part of Turkey is in Europe.

Turkish ▪ türkisch; Türkisch
Turkish culture is basically an Islamic culture.
Turkish is a difficult language.

UK ▪ Vereinigtes Königreich von Großbritannien und Nordirland
The UK consists of England, Scotland, Wales and Northern Ireland.

United Kingdom ▪ Vereinigtes Königreich von Großbritannien und Nordirland
The United Kingdom was founded in 1707.

United States of America ▪ Vereinigte Staaten von Amerika
The United States of America consists of 50 federal states and the District of Columbia (Washington).

USA ▪ USA
The USA is a world power.

Wales ▪ Wales
Wales has been part of Great Britain since the sixteenth century.

Welsh ▪ walisisch; Walisisch
Dylan Thomas was a well-known Welsh poet.
Welsh and English are entirely different languages.

Welshman (Pl. -men) ▪ Waliser
The author Ken Follett is a Welshman.

Welsh woman (Pl. -women) ▪ Waliserin
The actress Catherine Zeta-Jones is a Welsh woman.

world ▪ Welt
The USA is one of the most powerful countries in the world.

---

abroad ▪ im Ausland
Living abroad can be very interesting but also is quite difficult.

Arab ▪ arabisch; Araber(in)
Most of the Arab countries border on the Mediterranean or the Gulf of Persia.
Arabs live in many Mediterranean countries.

Arabic ▪ Arabisch
Arabic is widely spoken in countries around the Mediterranean.

Argentina ▪ Argentinien
Most people in Argentina speak Spanish.

Argentine ▪ argentinisch; Argentinier(in)
Argentine beef is known throughout the world.
Many Argentines are immigrants from Italy.

Brazil [brəˈzɪl] ▪ Brasilien
The 2014 Football World Cup took place in Brazil.

Brazilian ▪ brasilianisch; Brasilianer(in)
Brazilian coffee is drunk throughout the world.
Some 200 million Brazilians live in Brazil.

California ▪ Kalifornien
Calfornia has always been my favourite holiday destination.

Egypt ■ Ägypten
Egypt is one of the oldest civilized nations in the world.

Egyptian ■ ägyptisch; Ägypter(in); Ägyptisch
Egyptian cotton is exported a lot.
Some 80 million Egyptians live in Egypt. Most of them speak Egyptian-Arabic.

Estonia ■ Estland
Estonia's capital is Tallinn.

Estonian ■ estnisch; Este(-in); Estnisch
Some 1.3 million Estonians live in Estonia.
Over a third of the Estonian territory is covered by forest.
Estonian is a language closely related to Finnish.

Hebrew ■ Hebräisch
Hebrew is the official language of Israel.

Hindu ■ Hindu
Most inhabitants of India are Hindus.

Hungarian ■ ungarisch; Ungar(in); Ungarisch
Johannes Brahms wrote six Hungarian dances.
Some 10 million Hungarians live in Hungary.
Hungarian is rather a difficult language to learn.

Hungary ■ Ungarn
The capital of Hungary is Budapest.

Iran ■ Iran
Iran's old name was Persia.

Iranian ■ iranisch; Iraner(in)
Iranian culture is an Islamic culture.
Some 75 million Iranians live in Iran.

Iraq ■ Irak
Iraq's capital Bagdhad has 17 million inhabitants.

Iraqi ■ irakisch; Iraker(in)
Iraqi art has suffered a lot from the wars of the recent past.
29 million Iraqis live in Iraq. Most of them speak a form of Arabic.

Israel ■ Israel
Israel was founded in 1948 in Palestine.

Israeli ■ israelisch; Israeli
Israeli culture is basically a Jewish culture.
Israelis come from all over the world.

Jew ■ Jude, Jüdin
Israel was founded to give the Jews a country of their own.

Jewish ■ jüdisch
The Rothschilds are a Jewish family.

Korea ■ Korea
Korea has been a divided country since 1948.

Korean ■ koreanisch; Koreaner(in); Koreanisch
The South Korean economy is pretty strong.
Korean is spoken by Koreans in both North and South Korea.

Latvia ■ Lettland
Latvia introduced the euro on 1 January 2014.

Latvian ■ lettisch; Lette(-in); Lettisch
Latvian choirs enjoy a worldwide reputation.
Latvian is the language spoken by most Latvians.

Lithuania ■ Litauen
In 2004 Lithuania became a member of the European Union.

Lithuanian ■ litauisch; Litauer(in); Litauisch
I know hardly anything about Lithuanian art.
Lithuanian is the language spoken by Lithuanians.

Malta ■ Malta
Malta is a small island in the Mediterranean and a member of the EU.

Maltese ■ maltesisch; Malteser(in); Maltesisch
Maltese history is highly interesting.
Most Maltese speak two languages – Maltese and English.

Mediterranean ■ Mittelmeer
Many countries on the Mediterranean are popular among tourists.

Middle East ▪ Naher Osten

The Middle East comprises Iran and all the Asian countries to the west and south-west of Iran.

multicultural ▪ multikulturell

We live in a multicultural society.

nationality ▪ Nationalität, Staatsangehörigkeit

The flight attendants on the plane were of six different nationalities.

Native American ▪ amerikanische(r) Ureinwohner(in)

The original inhabitants of North America are called Native Americans.

New Zealand ▪ neuseeländisch; Neuseeland

I like New Zealand wines.

Wellington is New Zealand's capital.

New Zealander ▪ Neuseeländer(in)

All the New Zealanders we met were very friendly.

North America ▪ Nordamerika

North America consists of the USA and Canada.

overseas ▪ Ausland, Übersee…; im Ausland, in Übersee

Every visitor to Britain comes from overseas, even if from nearby France.

Matthew has been living overseas for three years now.

Pakistan ▪ Pakistan

English and Urdu are the official languages in Pakistan.

Pakistani ▪ pakistanisch; Pakistaner(in)

There are many Pakistani corner shops in Britain.

Some 127 million Pakistani live in Pakistan.

Roman ▪ römisch; Römer(in)

Roman and Greek culture have a lot in common.

In Rome do as the Romans do.

Serbia ▪ Serbien

Serbia used to be part of former Yugoslavia.

Serbian ▪ serbisch; Serbe(-in); Serbisch
Novi Sad is a major Serbian city.
Serbian, which is similar to Croatian, is spoken by Serbians.

Slovakia ▪ Slowakei
The capital of Slovakia is Bratislava.

Slovakian ▪ slowakisch; Slowake(-in); Slowakisch
Bratislava, the Slovakian capital is close to the Austrian border.
Some five million Slovakians live in Slovakia.
Slovakian is an independent language, related to Czech.

tribe ▪ (Volks-)Stamm
The Navajo are a major native American tribe.

Ukraine ▪ Ukraine
The Ukraine is almost twice as large as Germany.

Ukrainian ▪ ukrainisch; Ukrainer(in); Ukrainisch
The Ukrainian economy depends mainly on agriculture.
Ukrainian is spoken by most Ukrainians, but quite a few also speak Russian.

Vietnam ▪ Vietnam
Hanoi is the capital of Vietnam.

Vietnamese ▪ vietnamesisch; Vietnamese(-in); Vietnamesisch
Vietnamese culture is influenced by the Chinese culture.
Vietnamese is spoken by some 90 million Vietnamese.

12. Wirtschaft

12.1 Allgemeines

administration ■ Verwaltung
The company was looking for someone with good skills in administration.

balance ■ Gleichgewicht
If supply and demand are in balance, prices are not likely to rise.

business ['bɪznəs] ■ Geschäft, Handel, Unternehmen
They had only a small business.

campaign ■ Kampagne, Aktion
The company launched an advertising campaign in order to improve sales.

capital ■ Kapital
If you wish to set up an enterprise make sure that you have enough capital.

client ■ Klient(in)
Ms Barrow discussed the business with her client.

company ■ Gesellschaft, Unternehmen
A company is a business which is owned by shareholders.

contract ■ Vertrag
The contract with the builder was signed on 24 June.

crisis ■ Krise
The euro crisis was the result of the weak economic performance of a number of EU-member states.

design ■ Entwurf, Design, Muster
An attractive design certainly helps producers to sell their products.

director ■ Leiter(in), Direktor(in); Vorstandsmitglied
She was the director of the Glyndebourne festival.
She was the finance director in her company.

domestic ▪ inländisch
Domestic trade is concerned with trade within a country.

economic ▪ wirtschaftlich
Our country has at last recovered from its economic problems.

economy ▪ Wirtschaft
It is about time the economy in our area showed signs of improving.

to employ ▪ beschäftigen, einstellen
Germany's largest company employs some 400,000 staff worldwide.

employee ▪ Arbeitnehmer(in), Angestellte(r)
Our business is doing so well that we are looking for new employees.

employer ▪ Arbeitgeber(in)
My employer is a large bank.

employment ▪ Beschäftigung; Anstellung, Einstellung
One of the most important things in life is a good and steady employment.
In his company he was responsible for the employment of new staff.

enquiry ▪ Anfrage
We have received your enquiry of 25 May concerning kitchen equipment.

enterprise ▪ Unternehmen
Sole traders, partnerships and companies are forms of enterprises.

to extend ▪ erweitern
They decided to extend their business considerably.

financial ▪ finanziell
Our company's financial situation has improved very much.

firm ▪ Firma, Personengesellschaft
If lawyers set up a business, it is often called a law firm.

to gain ▪ erlangen, erwerben; gewinnen, zunehmen
If you have a business, you will want to gain a profit.
Fortunately we have considerably gained in profits in recent months.

to import ▪ einführen, importieren
Despite its strong agricultural sector Britain needs to import a lot of fruit.

to indicate ▪ hinweisen, andeuten, zeigen
The recent development indicates an improvement of our economic situation.

industrial ▪ industriell, gewerblich
Agriculture is one element of the primary industrial sector.

industry ▪ Gewerbe, Branche, Industrie
The service sector has become the most important industry.

interest ▪ Beteiligung
The company had a fifty per cent interest in its rival.

internal ▪ intern
The company set up an internal investigation of the incident.

to introduce ▪ einführen
We've introduced an entirely new product in the market.

location ▪ Lage, Position
We have at last found a suitable location for our new plant.

market ▪ Markt
The introduction of markets was a major step in the development of the economy.

objective ▪ Zielsetzung
The main objective of every business is to make a profit.

to order ▪ bestellen
We would like to order twenty bottles of wine.

output ▪ Ausstoß, Produktion
One way of increasing our profit may be to increase our output.

partner ▪ Teilhaber(in)
As partners in the business they shared in its success and in its failure.

plan ▪ Plan, Vorhaben
We're currently studying plans to expand our business.

planning ■ Planung; Planungs…
Building a motorway junction requires some planning.
Finding a site for our new factory is the job of our planning department.

policy ■ Programm, Strategie; …politik
Our company pursues a policy of employing experienced candidates only.
Making a profit is the business policy of all enterprises.

profit ■ Gewinn, Profit
Last year our company made a handsome profit of £155m.

rate ■ Geschwindigkeit
The economy is developing at a moderate rate.

reduction ■ Reduzierung, Abnahme
The economy was helped very much by a reduction of interest rates.

to reject ■ zurückweisen
The goods are of inferior quality, which is why we reject them.

relation ■ Beziehung
Labour relations are a tricky subject.

resource ■ Mittel
The CEO announced that the company did not have the required resources to expand.

revenue ['revənjuː] ■ Erträge, Einkünfte
We will have to generate more revenue if we wish to become profitable again.

sample ■ Muster, Probe
Please send us some samples so that we can examine the quality of your products.

to satisfy (-fies; -fying) ■ befriedigen, zufriedenstellen
We shall always try to satisfy our customers' wishes.

section ■ Abteilung
John works in the finance section of our enterprise.

settlement ■ Vereinbarung, Vergleich; (Geschäfts-)Abwicklung
The two parties at last reached a settlement of their conflict.
They celebrated the settlement of their business transaction.

share ■ Aktie
Many more people in Britain than in Germany have shares.

shareholder ■ Aktionär(in)
As a shareholder you can attend the annual general meeting of shareholders.

to shut (shut, shut) ■ zumachen, schließen
The management announced that they would shut the plant.

staff ■ Belegschaft, Personal
Our company has a staff of 2,500 employees.

start ■ Gründung
2012 was a very successful year. It saw the start of fifty new businesses in our city.

stock ■ (AE) Aktie
Stocks in the USA are called shares in the UK.

strategy ■ Strategie, Taktik
The retailer has developed an entirely new sales strategy.

target ■ Zielvorgabe
The chairman was pleased to announce that the company had achieved its targets.

tax ■ Steuer
There is a very high tax on fuel.

---

to accommodate ■ entgegenkommen
The company accommodated the customer by giving him a twenty per cent discount.

to acknowledge ■ anerkennen, bestätigen
We acknowledge herewith receipt of your letter of 15 July.

advertisement ▪ Werbung, Reklame
The new shop placed an advertisement in the local newspaper to attract customers.

AFL/CIO ▪ Amerikanischer Gewerkschaftsbund
AFL/CIO is short for American Federation of Labor / Congress of Industrial Organizations.

bankrupt ▪ bankrott
After struggling for several years the company eventually went bankrupt.

bankruptcy ▪ Bankrott
After the firm's bankruptcy all its employees were out of a job.

bid ▪ Gebot, Angebot
We have made a bid for our rival company.

brand ▪ Marke
Electrolux is a famous brand of electrical equipment.

capitalism ▪ Kapitalismus
In capitalism prices are determined by supply and demand.

capitalist ▪ kapitalistisch
Many people are convinced that a purely capitalist society is unjust.

cargo ▪ Ladung, Fracht
The ship had a cargo of bananas on board.

CEO ▪ Vorstandsvorsitzende(r)
The Chief Executive Officer (CEO) is the most important person in a plc.

chairman (Pl.: -men) ▪ (Vorstands-)Vorsitzender
At the shareholders' meeting Henry Ferguson was elected chairman of the board, which comprises both executive and non-executive directors.

chairperson ▪ (Vorstands-)Vorsitzende(r)
The term "chairperson" is politically more acceptable than "chairman".

chairwoman (Pl.: -women) ▪ (Vorstands-)Vorsitzende
It's a pity that there are not more chairwomen in companies.

commercial ▪ geschäftlich, gewerbsmäßig
The object of every commercial enterprise is to make a profit.

commission ▪ Provision
A sales representative usually receives a commission for every item he sells.

to comply with ▪ entsprechen, erfüllen
Once you have complied with all the requirements we shall deal with your application.

consultant ▪ Berater(in), Experte(-in)
In difficult situations some companies hire a consultant to deal with their problems.

container ▪ Container
A standard container measures eight by eight by twenty feet.

corporate ▪ Unternehmens..., Firmen...
Corporate identity is an important concept nowadays.

corporation ▪ Kapitalgesellschaft; Körperschaft
A US corporation is a company in Britain, i.e. owned by shareholders.
The BBC is a corporation. So are German radio stations like the WDR and the BR.

creditor ▪ Gläubiger(in)
The shopkeeper was not able to pay his creditors and had to go out of business.

deadline ▪ Termin, Frist
It is essential that you meet the deadline if you wish us to honour the contract.

decline ▪ Rückgang, Verschlechterung
The secondary sector in the UK has been in continuous decline for quite some time.

deficit ▪ Defizit
Britain's balance of payments often shows a deficit.

delay ■ Verzug

We regret to inform you that there is a delay in the delivery of your goods.

to dispatch/despatch ■ versenden, absenden

We'll dispatch the goods immediately on receipt of the order.

dividend ■ Dividende

A dividend is paid on the nominal value of a share.

drop ■ Rückgang

In the past three months we have experienced a sharp drop in employment.

earnings ■ Verdienst, Ertrag

In the past financial year our company improved its earnings.

economical ■ sparsam, wirtschaftlich

Producing our goods in low-wage countries is more economical than doing it here.

entity ■ Einheit

A public limited company is a distinct legal entity.

estimate ■ Schätzung; Kostenvoranschlag

According to recent estimates production costs are not likely to rise any further.

He insisted on an estimate before placing the order to repair his car.

executive ■ leitende(r) Angestellte(r); geschäftsführend

The financial director is one of the most important executives of a company.

On the board of a plc there are both executive and non-executive directors.

to expand ■ expandieren, (sich) erweitern

If we wish to remain successful we must consider expanding our product range.

expansion ■ Erweiterung, Expansion

The expansion of our company in recent years has been very successful.

export ■ Export, Ausfuhr
Germany profits a lot from its strong exports.

to finance ■ finanzieren
Since their economic situation was weak, they had difficulties financing their ambitious project.

foreign trade ■ Außenhandel
All countries depend to a large extent on foreign trade.

formation ■ Bildung, Gründung
The formation of a company is a difficult process.

to fund ■ finanzieren
It's one of the main functions of a bank to fund commercial investments.

gain ■ Gewinn
In a capitalist society it is the aim of most enterprises to achieve a net gain.

to guarantee ■ garantieren
Of course we cannot guarantee that the suggested programme will be successful.

guarantee ■ Garantie
Our guarantee on this product expires in twelve months.

headquarters ['hedkwɔːtəz] (Pl.) ■ Hauptquartier
Our company's headquarters is in Stuttgart.

holding ■ Anteil; Holdinggesellschaft
The family had a holding of 25 per cent of the shares of the company.
Google is part of a holding company named Alphabet.

incentive ■ Anreiz, Ansporn
The company offered its best employees a company car as an incentive.

indication ■ Anzeichen, Hinweis
There are hardly any indications that the situation of our company will improve.

industrial action ■ Arbeitskampf
The union threatened to initiate industrial action.

industrial union ■ Gewerkschaft
In England industrial unions were established in 1871.

input ■ Beitrag
Many companies reward their employees for any valuable input.

to invest ■ investieren, Geld anlegen
In order to make a profit we must invest in new machinery.

investment ■ Investition, (Geld-)Anlage
Last year's investment in machinery has proved very useful.

investor ■ Kapitalanleger(in), Investor(in)
At last we have found an investor so that we can expand our business.

to launch ■ beginnen; einführen
They launched an advertising campaign in order to improve their economic situation.
We shall soon launch an entirely new product on the market.

launch ■ (Markt-)Einführung; Gründung
Our recent market launch of a new car has been very successful.
The launch of a new business is always a risky matter.

liable ■ haftbar, verantwortlich
In a partnership at least one partner is fully liable.

liability ■ Haftung
Both a plc and an Ltd are limited liability companies.

limited ■ beschränkte(r, s) (Haftung)
An Ltd is a private limited liability company.

Ltd ■ GmbH
In Britain many family businesses are Ltds.

margin ■ Spanne
A profit margin of 6 per cent will hardly be enough for the product to be successful.

means ■ Geldmittel, Gelder
At last the company found the means to expand its business.

to merge ■ fusionieren
The two companies saw their only hope in merging.

merger ■ Fusion, Zusammenschluss
The merger of Daimler and Chrysler was not very successful.

monopoly ■ Monopol
The government took steps to prevent a monopoly in the power industry.

non-executive ■ nicht geschäftsführend
On the board of a British plc there are both executive and non-executive directors.

obligation ■ Verpflichtung; Verbindlichkeit
You are under no obligation to pay if the goods are damaged.
Unfortunately our obligations exceed our financial capacity.

offer ■ Angebot
ICI made its rival a very favourable offer.

organic ■ organisch
Organic growth is the objective of our policy, not short-term success.

partnership ■ Partnerschaft, Teilhaberschaft
A partnership involves all its partners in some degree of liability.

payroll ■ Gehaltsliste
We have 500 employees on our payroll.

peak ■ Höchstwert
Prices usually reach their peak when demand is strong.

personnel ■ Personal
Our economic situation is so good that we have decided to take on more personnel.

plc ■ AG
The shares of a public limited company (plc) are dealt on the stock exchange.

potential ▪ Potential; potenziell, möglich
In the view of experts the company has some potential for development.
There are potential dangers in the approach you have chosen.

productivity ▪ Produktivität
In order to remain successful we must increase our productivity.

receiver ▪ Konkursverwalter(in)
The business is now in the hands of the receiver.

recession ▪ Rezession, Konjunkturrückgang
At last the economy is recovering after five years of recession.

reminder ▪ Mahnung
This is a reminder that you have failed to remit the amount of £564.50 due on 1 May.

remittance ▪ Überweisung
Of course you can also settle our invoice by remittance.

rent ▪ Miete, Pacht
The rent for farmland has risen again.

rival ▪ Konkurrent(in), Konkurrenz
Airbus is still Boeing's most serious rival.

roll ▪ Liste
I can't find Harry Wycombe on the roll of our employees.

running ▪ Leitung
The CEO is responsible for the everyday running of the company.

shortage ▪ Knappheit, Mangel
They built a factory in Norway because there was no shortage of skilled labour there.

sole trader ▪ Einzelhändler(in)
Sole traders reap the profits of their businesses but they are also liable for losses.

stake ▪ Anteil
A Spanish investor acquired a large stake in our company.

to stimulate ▪ stimulieren, anregen

The central bank lowered interest rates to stimulate growth.

stimulus ['stɪmjʊləs] (Pl.: stimuli ['stɪmjulaɪ]) ▪ Anreiz, Ansporn

Low interest rates serve as a stimulus for the economy.

stock exchange ▪ Börse

Shares are bought and sold on the stock exchange.

strategic ▪ strategisch

For strategic reasons the company decided to close one of its plants.

structural ▪ strukturell, Struktur…

By introducing structural changes we have managed to become profitable again.

to take over (took, taken) ▪ übernehmen

A company that has been taken over loses its independence.

takeover ▪ Übernahme

In Britain takeovers of a company by another company occur fairly frequently.

tough ▪ zäh, schwierig

Wage negotiations between the management and the trade unions were rather tough.

turnover ▪ Umsatz

Our turnover has improved a lot in the past four weeks.

union ▪ Verband

The CBI (Confederation of British Industry) is the union of British employers.

venture ▪ Unternehmen, Wagnis

Setting up a new business in this difficult economic climate is quite a venture.

12.2 Primärindustrie

barrel ▪ Fass
A barrel of oil, i.e 159 litres, cost as little as $ 28 in 1980.

farm ▪ Bauernhof, Farm
All the farmer's family worked on his farm.

fishing ▪ Fischfang
On the coast fishing is still an important economic factor.

material ▪ Material, Stoff
Bricks are a very important building material.

sector ▪ Sektor
Farming is part of the primary sector.

---

agricultural ▪ landwirtschaftlich
In Britain only about 2 per cent of the population work in the agricultural sector.

agriculture ▪ Landwirtschaft
In many Third World countries agriculture still plays a major role.

crop ▪ Ernte
This year's crop of potatoes was very disappointing.

farming ▪ Landwirtschaft
After going to an agricultural college he went into farming.

fishery ▪ Fischereiwirtschaft
Fishery is very important in Scotland.

forestry ▪ Forstwirtschaft
Forestry is an important industry in Germany.

grain ▪ Korn, Getreide
Wheat is a very common type of grain in Germany.

hunting ▪ Jagdwesen
Hunting is regulated by the state.

mill ▪ Mühle
Corn is ground into flour in a mill.

mine ▪ Bergwerk, Mine
Almost all the coal mines in the Ruhr area do not produce coal any more.

mineral ▪ Mineral
Coal, salt and iron are among the minerals produced by miners.

net ▪ Netz
The fishermen kept the fish they had caught in a net.

nursery ▪ Gärtnerei, Baumschule
Charlotte bought new apple trees at a nursery.

pipe ▪ Rohr
Oil and gas are transported in pipes.

pipeline ▪ Pipeline
There is a large network of pipelines from Russia to western Europe.

pit ▪ Zeche
There used to be many pits in the North of England.

platform ▪ Plattform
Off the coast of Scotland you will find a large number of oil platforms.

plough [plaʊ] ▪ Pflug
Modern ploughs are drawn by a tractor, not by horses – and certainly not by cows.

raw material ▪ Rohstoff
The production of raw material is the key function of the primary sector.

to sow (sowed, sown/sowed) ▪ säen
Farmers sow corn in spring.

to yield ▪ hervorbringen; abwerfen
At last our experiments yielded promising results.
Our company yielded excellent profits last year.

12.3 Sekundärindustrie

construction ▪ Bau
These buildings have been under construction for almost a year.

energy ▪ Energie, Kraft
Wind, water, coal, gas and oil are our main sources of energy.

factory ▪ Fabrik
The first factories were built in England in the early 19th century.

to generate ▪ erzeugen, generieren
Electricity can be generated in various ways.

generation ▪ Erzeugung
Coal is still used for the generation of electricity.

goods (Pl.) ▪ Güter, Waren
This is to advise you that the goods ordered are ready for dispatch.

machine [məˈʃiːn] ▪ Maschine, Gerät
Most finished products are produced by machines nowadays.

metal ▪ Metall
Steel is a metal made from iron.

module ▪ Modul, Bauelement
My computer worked satisfactorily once we had introduced a new module.

nuclear ▪ Kern…, Atom…; nuklear, atomar
Nuclear energy is still rather dangerous because there is no way of storing nuclear waste safely.

plant ▪ Fabrik, Anlage
These cars are produced at our Bremen plant.

plastic ▪ Kunststoff, Plastik
For the production of plastic you require petroleum.

power ▪ Strom
Thousands of people suffered when the power supply broke down.

power station ▪ Kraftwerk
Germany has decided to do without nuclear power stations.

process ▪ Prozess, Verfahren
The process of producing aluminium requires a lot of electricity.

to produce ▪ herstellen, produzieren
Carl Benz was one of the first persons to produce cars.

product ▪ Produkt, Erzeugnis
The prices of consumer products have been rising dramatically.

production ▪ Herstellung, Produktion
We hope to increase our production of computers by 20 per cent next year.

---

builder ▪ Bauunternehmer(in)
Our architect recommended an excellent builder.

chemical ▪ chemisch, Chemie…
Germany is well known for its chemical industry.

closure ▪ Schließung, Stilllegung
Many areas have suffered from the closure of manufacturing enterprises.

concrete ['kɒŋkriːt] ▪ Beton
Concrete is still used a lot in the construction industry.

crystal ▪ Kristall
Glasses, mirrors and lamps are often made of crystal.

dairy ['daɪəri] ▪ Molkerei
Butter and cream are made in a dairy.

finished product ▪ Endprodukt
A motorcar is a good example of a finished product.

machinery ▪ Maschinen, technische Geräte
The factory was full of expensive machinery.

maker ▪ Hersteller(in)
Lamborghini is the maker of this beautiful car.

manufacturer ▪ Hersteller(in), Fabrikant(in)
Read the manufacturer's instruction carefully before using the washing machine.

manufacturing ■ Herstellungs…, Produktions…
The Midlands are a major centre of the manufacturing industry.

mass ■ Massen…
Rolls Royce cars are definitely not mass products.

mechanical ■ mechanisch, technisch
As a result of mechanical problems our production has come to a standstill.

mill ■ Fabrik
My father worked in a steel mill all his life.

to process ■ verarbeiten
In the secondary industry raw material is processed into finished products.

processing ■ Weiterverarbeitung
The processing of waste is very economical.

producer ■ Produzent(in), Hersteller(in)
General Electric is a top producer of electrical equipment.

semi-finished product ■ Halbfertigerzeugnis
Our semi-finished products are converted into finished products elsewhere.

shipbuilding ■ Schiffbau
Glasgow used to be famous for its shipbuilding industry.

smoke ■ Rauch
In manufacturing districts the air is often full of the smoke from chimneys.

solar energy ■ Sonnenenergie
Solar energy is becoming increasingly important.

to specialize in ■ sich spezialisieren auf
Our company specializes in the production of radiators.

to specify ■ genau angeben, spezifizieren
Please specify the quantity and quality of the radiators required.

specimen ■ Exemplar, Probe
We shall forward a specimen of the product ordered immediately.

to spin (spun, spun) ■ spinnen
The production process of making cloth begins with spinning the wool.

steel ■ Stahl
Steel is made from iron.

steelworks ■ Stahlwerk
Steel is produced in a steelworks.

wind energy ■ Windenergie
A lot of wind energy is produced in the North Sea.

wind farm ■ Windpark
More wind farms are being built in the North Sea to produce electricity.

12.4 Tertiärindustrie

account ■ Konto
Most people nowadays have an account with a bank.

agency ■ Agentur
Charlotte works in an agency for actors and musicians.

branch ■ Filiale
Our bank has 23 branches in seven cities.

fair ■ Messe (Ausstellung)
CEBIT in Hanover is a very important fair.

insurance ■ Versicherung
You cannot have your car registered if you do not have a car insurance.

to insure ■ versichern
If you have expensive items in your house you should insure them.

loss ■ Verlust; Schaden
Your insurance company will cover the loss of your suitcase.
Any major losses suffered should be covered by an insurance.

mass media ▪ Massenmedien
Mass media like TV and the internet are becoming increasingly important.

sale ▪ Verkauf, Absatz
As a result of the hot summer our sales of bathing costumes have increased.

service ▪ Dienstleistung; Dienstleistungs…
Providing finance for business activities is an important service.
The service sector is also called the tertiary sector.

to supply ▪ bereitstellen; (be)liefern, versorgen
Finance for this project was supplied by a major manufacturer.
We can supply you with everything you may need for your party.

supply ▪ Vorrat; Versorgung
Our store has a large supply of household goods.
Supermarkets organize the supply of the public with what they need every day.

tourism ▪ Tourismus
Tourism is a major tertiary sector industry.

trade ▪ Handel; Umsatz; Gewerbe, Branche
Foreign trade is very important.
The company enjoyed a period of lively trade.
The building trade is booming because of the low interest rates.

---

account holder ▪ Kontoinhaber(in)
At the end of the month the account holder found that he was out of funds.

account statement ▪ Kontoauszug
In our bank you will receive account statements free of charge.

bank account ▪ Bankkonto
Wages are not paid in cash. They are paid into the employees' bank accounts.

banking ▪ Bankgeschäft; Bankwesen, Bankgewerbe

Many people nowadays do their banking online.

Banking is a major industry in the service sector.

to barter ▪ Tauschhandel betreiben, tauschen

The Flintstones bartered chickens for tools.

barter ▪ Tauschhandel

Before the introduction of money people conducted trade by barter.

to borrow ▪ ausborgen, sich leihen

You can easily borrow money from us. We'll lend it to you at a low interest rate.

current account ▪ Girokonto

Your salary will be paid into your current account.

debit ▪ Soll, Lastschrift

An account statement lists all debits and credits within a period.

finance ▪ Finanzen, Geld; Finanzwirtschaft

Providing finance for investment purposes is one of the key activities of banks.

He studied Finance at university.

freight ▪ Frachtgut

Finished products are often transported by freight train or by truck.

goods (Pl.) ▪ Güter, Waren

20 per cent discount on all the goods in our store.

goods train ▪ Güterzug

Goods trains are not used as often as trucks for transporting goods.

interface ▪ Schnittstelle

A port is the interface between sea and road transport.

load ▪ Ladung, Fracht

We have a load of whisky to transport to Germany.

mail-order house ▪ Versandhaus

Amazon, the mail-order house, operates worldwide.

marketing ▪ Marketing

Without a good marketing campaign a product will not be successful.

medium (Pl.: media) ▪ Medium, Medien

The radio is still an important medium.

merchandise ▪ Handelsware

After the shop had gone bankrupt all its merchandise was sold at half-price.

merchant ▪ Kaufmann, Kauffrau

We always buy our wine from a wine merchant.

multimedia ▪ multimedial

The opening ceremony of the Olympic Games was a multimedia show.

operator ▪ Unternehmer(in)

National Express is a major coach operator, which offers long-distance travel.

portfolio ▪ Portefeuille

Many managers have a large portfolio of shares.

premium ▪ Prämie

We regret to announce an increase in your insurance premium.

publicity ▪ Publicity, Reklame, Werbung

The new Mercedes Benz A-class has been getting a lot of publicity these days.

publishing ▪ Verlagswesen

After studying literature he decided to take a job in publishing.

real estate ▪ Grundstückswesen

After taking her degree she found a job in real estate.

retail ▪ Einzelhandels…

The retail trade is the basis of the High Street.

retailer ▪ Einzelhändler(in); Einzelhandelsunternehmen

The Albrecht brothers began their career as small retailers and became two of the world's largest retailers.

saving ▪ Erspartes

I pay all my savings into a savings account.

savings bank ▪ Sparkasse

Savings banks were established in the 19th century to encourage people to save money.

shipment ▪ Lieferung

Your goods will be delivered in two separate shipments.

shipowner ▪ Reeder(in)

Cunard is the shipowner of three large cruise ships.

shipper ▪ Spediteur(in)

National Freight is a large British shipper.

shopkeeper ▪ Ladeninhaber(in)

Napoleon once said that the English were a nation of shopkeepers.

speculation ▪ Spekulation, Vermutung

Speculation is at the heart of stock exchange business.

supplier ▪ Lieferant(in)

ICI is a major supplier of chemicals.

TAN ▪ TAN

In internet banking you often require a TAN (transaction number).

tertiary sector ▪ Tertiärindustrie, Tertiärer Sektor

The tertiary sector is concerned with the distribution of goods and with services.

to trade ▪ Handel treiben

Trading within the EU is not subject to customs duties.

trade fair ▪ (Handels-)Messe

CEBIT is one of Germany's largest trade fairs.

trader ▪ Händler(in); Handelsschiff

James' grandfather was a small trader in shoes.

trading ▪ Handel, Geschäftstätigkeit

As a result of the financial crisis trading was rather disappointing.

transaction ▪ Transaktion

My bank charges me for every transaction.

transport operator ▪ Spediteur, Fuhrunternehmer
Hamish started with one truck. Now he is the country's largest transport operator.

viewer ▪ (Fernseh-)Zuschauer
Yesterday's sports programme had ten million viewers.

wholesale ▪ Großhandels…
He was the general manager of a wholesale business.

wholesaler ▪ Großhändler(in), Großhandelsunternehmen
Wholesalers sell their goods to retailers.

to withdraw (-drew, -drawn) ▪ abheben
Before going shopping he withdrew some cash from his account.

withdrawal ▪ Geldabhebung
He made five withdrawals from his account.

13. Staat, Recht, Politik

13.1 Allgemeines

approach ▪ Vorstoß
This was just another unsuccessful approach to reach an agreement.

to claim ▪ beantragen
After the birth of her first child she claimed child benefit immediately.

to control ▪ kontrollieren; regulieren
The former Soviet Union controlled almost all of Eastern Europe.
Prices are not controlled by the government.

control ▪ Macht
Hitler gained control of Germany in 1933.

to declare ▪ erklären, verkünden
The USA declared its independence in 1776.

democratic ▪ demokratisch
All the parties in our parliament are based on democratic principles.

to demonstrate ▪ demonstrieren
One of the basic human rights is the right to demonstrate.

enquiry ▪ Untersuchung
The oppostion demanded a public enquiry concerning the scandal.

to ensure ▪ sicherstellen, garantieren
The chief job of the government is to ensure the peace and welfare of its citizens.

to establish ▪ gründen, einführen
In Germany, democracy was first established in 1919.

freedom ▪ Freiheit
Everyone should have the freedom of speech.

independent ▪ unabhängig
Most colonies have become independent.

to issue ▪ in Umlauf bringen
The Bank of England is also responsible for issuing Pound Sterling banknotes.

primary (AE) ▪ Vorwahl
In every state of the USA the parties decide in primaries who is to become their presidential candidate.

proposal ▪ Vorschlag
The UN made another peace proposal, which was turned down by the conflicting parties.

to propose ▪ vorschlagen
The speaker proposed a resolution to set up a committee.

protest ▪ Protest
The late 1960s were years of student protests worldwide.

province ▪ Provinz
The Algarve is a province of Portugal.

reform ▪ Reform
Our education system requires a radical reform to make it fairer and more efficient.

regulation ▪ Regulierung, Vorschrift
The EU is rather fond of proposing ever new regulations.

to represent ▪ repräsentieren; vertreten
Parliament is supposed to represent the political will of the people.
The President represents the people.

representation ▪ Vertretung
Immigrants have representation in parliament if they are citizens of their new country.

representative (AE) ▪ Abgeordnete(r)
The US House of Representatives has 435 members and is elected every two years.

republic ▪ Republik
The USA has been a republic since 1776.

royal ▪ königlich
In Britain, the function of the royal family is basically representative.

rule ▪ Herrschaft
Until 1921 Ireland was under British rule.

system ▪ System
The English and the Scottish education systems are different.

tendency ▪ Tendenz, Neigung
There are nationalist tendencies in many countries nowadays.

voice ▪ Stimmrecht
Everybody should have a voice in this matter.

to vote ▪ wählen; abstimmen
In Britain women were given the right to vote in 1928.
Only 13 Republicans voted against the new tax plan.

vote ▪ Stimme; Abstimmung
He gave his vote to the president.
The vote on the new bill will take place on Thursday.

voter ▪ Wähler(in)
In 2014 Scottish voters decided that Scotland should remain part of the UK.

---

ally ▪ Verbündete(r)
France and Germany have been allies for more than sixty years now.

asylum ▪ Asyl
Many refugees from African countries are seeking asylum in the European Union.

autonomy ▪ Autonomie, Unabhängigkeit
South Africa achieved its autonomy in 1910.

to benefit ▪ nützen, begünstigen
Our taxation system benefits the poor.

citizen ▪ Bürger(in)
In Germany basically every adult citizen has the right to vote.

communism ▪ Kommunismus
The principles of communism were set up by Karl Marx.

communist ▪ Kommunist(in); kommunistisch
Not everybody is a communist because he lives in a communist country.

to concede ▪ zugeben; gewähren
The opposition leader conceded defeat after the election.
Parliament conceded the government further rights.

to constitute ▪ einrichten
After the revolution the rebels constituted a provisional government.

democracy ▪ Demokratie
The USA is one of the oldest democracies.

democrat ▪ Demokrat(in)
Many democrats dislike the monarchy.

to dominate ▪ beherrschen
In the early nineteenth century France dominated almost all of Europe.

to found ▪ gründen
The USA was founded in 1776.

hearing ▪ Anhörung
The hearing revealed who was responsible for the financial crisis.

to initiate ▪ einleiten, in die Wege leiten
In the UK the lawmaking process is usually initiated by the government.

liberalism ▪ Liberalismus
Liberalism was the key ideology of nineteenth-century England.

liberty ▪ Freiheit
The rebels at last achieved the liberty of their country.

nationalism ▪ Nationalismus
Nationalism is the root of many wars.

nationalist ▪ Nationalist(in)
Scotland's nationalists wish to achieve the country's independence.

neutral ▪ neutral
Switzerland has always been a neutral country.

to nominate ▪ nominieren
General Myers was nominated for the position of commander of the army.

party ▪ Partei
In the USA there are basically two parties – the Democrats and the Republicans.

plot ▪ Verschwörung
The Gunpowder Plot of 1605 is still remembered today.

proposition ▪ Aussage, These
The proposition that democracies cannot be mutual enemies has proved nonsense.

radical ▪ radikal
I'm afraid there are too many radical parties in some countries.

referendum ▪ Volksabstimmung
Some people claim that a referendum should decide major political issues.

regime ▪ Regime
The drastic political measures taken by the regime forced many citizens to emigrate.

to regulate ▪ regulieren, regeln
The European Commission has been regulating almost everything under the sun.

reign ▪ Herrschaft
Under the reign of Elizabeth I England was very powerful.

removal ▪ Absetzung
The removal of their dictator took the country's citizens several years.

republican (AE) ▪ Republikaner(in)
George W. Bush is a Republican, Barack Obama is a Democrat.

to resign ■ zurücktreten

After losing the election the Prime Minister resigned immediately.

resignation ■ Rücktritt

Everybody was shocked when they heard of the President's resignation.

resolution ■ Lösung; Beschluss; Entscheidung

All parties contributed to the resolution of the crisis.
They agreed to a resolution to give the government extra powers.
Of course, the government welcomed this resolution.

restoration ■ Wiederherstellung

The demonstrators demanded the restoration of democracy.

to restore ■ wiederherstellen

After WWII democracy was restored in western Germany.

revolution ■ Revolution

In the Revolution of 1789 the French abolished the monarchy.

revolutionary ■ Revolutionär(in)

Che Guevara and Rosa Luxemburg were revolutionaries.

to rule ■ regieren, herrschen

Until 1776 large parts of northern America were ruled by the British.

ruler ■ Herrscher(in)

Elizabeth I was one of the most powerful rulers England has ever had.

Security Council ■ Sicherheitsrat

The Security Council of the United Nations has five permanent members – China, Russia, USA, France, and the UK.

senate (AE) ■ Senate

Since the 2014 elections the Senate has had a Republican majority.

senator (AE) ■ Senator(in)

The US Senate consists of 100 senators, two from each federal state.

single market ■ einheitlicher Markt

The European Union is a single market.

socialism ▪ Sozialismus
In socialism most industries are state-owned.

socialist ▪ Sozialist(in); sozialistisch
Karl Liebknecht was a German socialist and became a communist later in his life.
The country elected a socialist prime minister.

struggle ▪ Kampf
It was after a long struggle that women achieved equal rights in western countries.

to suppress ▪ unterdrücken
The dictator suppressed the opposition.

Tory ▪ Tory
The word tory was used for an Irish rebel, now it is used for a Conservative in Britain.

to unite ▪ (sich) vereinigen, (sich) zusammenschließen
In 1776 thirteen colonies united to found the United States of America.

Veterans Day (AE) ▪ etwa: Volkstrauertag
On Veterans Day, i.e. on 11 November, people in the USA remember those who fought in a war.

13.2 Staat, nationale und internationale Institutionen, Legislative

act ▪ Gesetz
In a democracy an act is a bill passed by parliament and signed by the head of state.

administration ▪ Regierung
What is the government in Britain is the administration in the USA.

agency ▪ Behörde
The Central Intelligence Agency (CIA) is an important source of information.

army ▪ Armee; Heer
The armed forces consist of the army, the air force and the navy.
The Sixth United States Army fought in Europe during World War II.

authority ▪ Behörde
In Britain a local education authority also employs the teachers in its area.

bill ▪ Gesetzesvorlage
The House of Commons voted to pass the EU Withdrawal Bill yesterday.

budget ▪ Budget, Haushalt
On Wednesday the Chancellor will present next year's budget.

cabinet ▪ Kabinett
In Britain not every head of a government department is a member of the cabinet.

civil ▪ bürgerlich, zivil
Liberty and life are two of the most important civil rights.

code ▪ Gesetzbuch, (Verhaltens- usw.)Ordnung; Code
A code is a systematic collection of laws, e.g. the German civil code, Bürgerliches Gesetzbuch.

conference ▪ Konferenz
The 2014 Syria conference in Geneva was not successful.

council ▪ Rat
In Britain town councils provide houses for those in a difficult financial situation.

court [kɔːt] ▪ Hof
Henry VIII used to live at Hampton Court.

department ▪ Ministerium
In the UK government policy is administered through many specialized departments.

to elect ▪ wählen
Parliament is elected every four years in Germany.

election ▪ Wahl
Elections are very important in any democracy.

foundation ▪ Gründung
The Treaty of Rome in 1957 was the first step towards the foundation of the European Union.

government (AE: administration) ▪ Regierung
Democractic governments are elected by parliament, which is elected by the people.

head [hed] ▪ Oberhaupt
The Queen is the head of state in the United Kingdom.

institution ▪ Einrichtung, Institution
In the UK there is no institution like the Supreme Court in the USA.

king ▪ König
In many countries kings only serve a representative function.

legislation ▪ Gesetzgebung, Gesetze
Bills passed by parliament and signed by the Queen become current legislation.

Lower House ▪ Unterhaus
The House of Commons is also referred to as the Lower House.

majority ▪ Mehrheit
In 2017 the Conservatives did not manage to win a majority in Parliament.

minister ▪ Minister(in)
She served as a minister under the Foreign Secretary.

ministry ▪ Ministerium
She worked for several years in the Ministry of Defense.

office ▪ Amt; Ministerium
The Office of Fair Trading is a government organization.
The Foreign Office is responsible for Britain's relationship with other countries.

opposition ▪ Opposition
The Opposition demanded that the Prime Minister should resign.

parliament ▪ Parlament
The British parliament consists of the House of Lords and the House of Commons.

president ▪ Präsident(in)
The American president is the head of government.

prince ▪ Prinz; Fürst
Prince William may become King of England some time in the future.
Prince Albert is Prince of Monaco.

princess ▪ Prinzessin; Fürstin
Princess Anne was a very good horse rider.
Princess Gracia Patricia was born as Grace Kelly.

queen ▪ Königin
Queen Victoria was Queen of England from 1837 to 1901.

revenue ▪ Staatseinkünfte
Britain's tax revenue has improved a lot in recent years.

session ▪ Sitzungsperiode
The parliamentary session ends in July and begins again in September.

speaker ▪ Parlamentpräsident(in)
The Speaker opens the first sitting of the House of Commons.

treaty ▪ Vertrag, Abkommen
NATO is the abbreviation of North Atlantic Treaty Organization.

UN ▪ UNO
The UN's headquarters is in New York.

united ▪ vereinigt, vereint
The UN, the United Nations, was set up in 1945.

United Nations ▪ Vereinte Nationen
UN is the abbreviation of United Nations.

Upper House ▪ Oberhaus
The House of Lords is also sometimes called the Upper House.

amendment ▪ (Verfassungs-)Zusatz; Gesetzesänderung
People in the USA believe that the second amendment allows them to carry arms.
The opposition demanded an amendment to the bill.

base ▪ Basis, Stützpunkt
There is an air force base quite near where we live.

boundary ▪ Grenze
The Oder marks the boundary between Germany and Poland.

bureau ▪ Amt, Behörde
The FBI is the Federal Bureau of Investigation in the USA.

central bank ▪ Zentralbank
In Germany the central bank is independent of the government.

chamber ▪ Parlamentskammer
The "Bundestag" and the "Bundesrat" are the two chambers of Parliament in Germany.

chancellor ▪ (Schatz-)Kanzler(in)
The German chancellor is the head of government, in Britain the chancellor is the finance minister.

civil servant ▪ Beamte(r)
In the UK only people employed by the Crown are civil servants.

coalition ▪ Koalition
In Britain the Democratic Unionist Party and the Conservatives formed a coalition government.

colony ▪ Kolonie
In the nineteenth century most major countries had colonies on other continents.

commission ▪ Kommission
The European Commission is the EU's government.

congress ▪ Kongress
Congress is the legislative branch of the USA.

conservative ■ konservativ; Konservative(r)
Old people are generally believed to be rather conservative and to vote for Conservatives.

constituency ■ Wahlkreis
All 650 constituencies in Britain return one member of parliament.

constitution ■ Verfassung
The "Grundgesetz" is Germany's constitution.

constitutional ■ Verfassungs…, konstitutionell
The first constitutional assembly in Germany was held in Frankfurt in 1848.

convention ■ Abkommen
In 1864 the Red Cross was set up by the Geneva Convention.

councillor ■ Ratsmitglied
There were twenty Labour councillors and fifteen Conservative councillors.

declaration ■ Erklärung, Deklaration
The American Declaration of Independence was written by Thomas Jefferson.

Democrat (AE) ■ Demokrat
The Democrats and the Republicans are the two major parties in the USA.

demonstration ■ Demonstration
The opposition organized a huge demonstration against government policies.

diplomatic ■ diplomatisch
Members of the diplomatic service speak at least two foreign languages.

directive ■ Weisung, Richtlinie
Oh dear, the EU has issued another unnecessary directive.

draft ■ Entwurf
The Chancellor asked his staff to prepare a draft for next year's budget.

electoral ▪ Wahl…, Wähler
You can only vote if your name is contained in the electoral register.

emperor ▪ Kaiser
Only few countries nowadays have a king, but even fewer have an emperor.

empire ▪ (Welt-)Reich
Classical Rome was the largest empire the world had seen up to that time.

establishment ▪ Gründung; Einführung
The EU was established in 1957 as the European Economic Community.
The establishment of democracy was a major step in the development of society.

Fed ▪ US-amerikanische Bundesbank
Fed is the short form of Federal Reserve System.

federal ▪ föderalistisch, Bundes…
The USA has fifty federal states, Germany has sixteen.

federation ▪ Föderation, Bund
The European Union began as a federation of six states – Belgium, France, Germany, Italy, Luxemburg, and the Netherlands.

flag ▪ Flagge
Both the German and the Belgian flags have black, red and golden stripes.

frontier ▪ (Landes-)Grenze
In early American history the frontier marked the line between civilization and the wilderness.

to govern ▪ regieren
The aim of all governments ought to be to govern justly.

governor ▪ Gouverneur; Regierungschef eines US-amerikanischen Bundesstaates

New Zealand's Governor-General is the representative of the Queen.

Austrian-born Arnold Schwarzenegger was Governor of California.

guardian ▪ Wächter(in), Hüter(in)

The central bank is supposed to be the guardian of our currency.

House of Commons ▪ Unterhaus

As a rule, the House of Commons in Great Britain is elected every four years.

House of Lords ▪ Oberhaus

The House of Lords no longer has only aristocrats and bishops as members.

House of Representatives (AE) ▪ Repräsentantenhaus

The House of Representatives in the USA is elected every two years.

Houses of Parliament ▪ Parlament

The House of Lords and the House of Commons together are the Houses of Parliament.

imperial ▪ kaiserlich

The museum exhibits Queen Victoria's imperial crown of India.

institutional ▪ institutionell

In order to prove its efficiency the government introduced radical institutional reforms.

kingdom ▪ Königreich

The UK's full name is "The United Kingdom of Great Britain and Northern Ireland".

Labour Party ▪ Labour Party, Arbeiterpartei

The Labour Party in the UK was established in 1900.

leader ▪ (An-)Führer(in)

Margaret Thatcher was Prime Minister but not the leader of her party.

leadership ▪ Führung, Leitung
Because of her strong leadership Margaret Thatcher was known as the Iron Lady.

legislative ▪ gesetzgebend
The legislative process involves three readings of a bill in Parliament.

local authority ▪ Kommunalverwaltung
In Britain primary and secondary education are the responsibility of local authorities.

mayor ▪ Bürgermeister
Every town and city in Great Britain has an elected mayor to represent it.

mayoress ▪ Bürgermeisterin
... or a mayoress if a woman is elected to hold this office.

Member of Parliament ▪ Parlamentsabgeordnete(r)
The House of Commons has 650 Members of Parliament.

monetary ▪ monetär, Währungs...
The Bank of England, the British central bank, is responsible for Britain's monetary policy.

money supply ▪ Geldmenge
... and for the country's money supply.

MP ▪ Parlamentsmitglied
In Britain there are 650 MPs.

navy ▪ Kriegsmarine
Britain has always had a strong navy.

NHS (National Health Service) ▪ Nationaler Gesundheitsdienst
The NHS, which provides free medical services for everyone, was set up in 1948.

overall majority ▪ absolute Mehrheit
The government won the vote by a very slim overall majority.

paragraph ▪ Paragraph
Most acts of parliament have a large number of paragraphs.

parliamentary ■ parlamentarisch
Ours is a parliamentary democracy.

party leader ■ Parteivorsitzende(r)
In 2014 David Cameron was the party leader of the Conservatives.

poll ■ Wahlbeteiligung
At 61 per cent the poll was rather poor.

presidential ■ Präsidenten…, Präsidentschafts…
Hilary Clinton stood as presidential candidate in 2016.

prime minister ■ Premierminister
Margaret Thatcher was Britain's Prime Minister from 1979 to 1990.

to resolve ■ beschließen
The government resolved to spend more money on education.

scheme ■ Projekt
The government is planning to supply funds for a scheme to help exporters.

state ■ Staat
The USA consists of fifty federal states and the District of Columbia.

statute ■ Gesetz
Once a bill has become a statute it is printed in the statute book.

statutory ■ gesetzlich
Every citizen enjoys certain statutory rights.

succession ■ Folge; Nachfolge
Margaret Thatcher won three general elections in succession.
1952 is the year of Queen Elizabeth II's succession to the throne.

successor ■ Nachfolger(in)
Theresa May is David Cameron's successor.

summit ■ Gipfel(treffen)
The presidents of four countries held a summit to reach a peace agreement.

taxation ■ Besteuerung
"No taxation without representation" was a demand made by the American colonists.

territory ■ Territorium, Staatsgebiet
The territory of Liechtenstein is small.

Trades Union Congress ■ britischer Gewerkschaftsbund
The Trades Union Congress (TUC) is the equivalent of the AFL/CIO in the USA.

TUC ■ britischer Gewerkschaftsdachverband
The TUC's German equivalent is the DGB.

unanimous [ju'nænɪməs] ■ einstimmig
Unanimous decisions do not occur often in parliament.

value added tax ■ Mehrwertsteuer
There were furious debates about government plans to increase value added tax.

VAT ■ MwSt
VAT is simply the abbreviation of Value Added Tax.

veto ■ Veto
The President threatened Congress with a veto to prevent the passing of legislation.

vice president ■ Vizepräsident(in)
If the US President resigns or dies, his or her Vice President becomes President.

withdrawal ■ Zurücknehmen
The opposition demanded the withdrawal of the controversial bill.

13.3 Recht und Justiz

to appeal ■ Berufung einlegen
After the judge had passed his judgment the accused appealed against it.

appeal ▪ Berufung
The defendant's lawyers lodged an appeal against the judgment.

case ▪ (Rechts-)Fall
The judge still had three difficult cases to deal with.

charge ▪ Anklage
He faced a charge of violent conduct.

claim ▪ Anspruch
The court decided that there was nothing to support Mr Myers' claim.

client ▪ Mandant(in)
The client talked to his solicitor about his case.

to conclude ▪ entscheiden
The judge concluded that the evidence was not sufficient for the trial to proceed and closed the case.

consultation ▪ Beratung
In all difficult situations Archibald went to his lawyer for a consultation.

court [kɔːt] ▪ Gericht
He was taken to court for drunken driving.

evidence ▪ Beweis, Indiz
The evidence against the accused was so clear that the jury found him guilty.

judge ▪ Richter(in)
The judge jailed him for ten years.

judg(e)ment ▪ Urteil
The accused was pleased with the mild judgment.

justice ▪ Gerechtigkeit, Recht
The judgment was admitted to do justice to the victim of the crime.

law ▪ Gesetz, Recht; Jura
Breaking into other people's houses is clearly against the law.
She studied law in order to become a solicitor.

legal ▪ legal; gesetzlich; rechtlich
Abortion is not legal everywhere.
It is a legal requirement to be of age before you can vote.
Lawyers give their clients legal advice.

prison ▪ Gefängnis
The accused was sentenced to five years in prison.

to release ▪ freilassen
After serving five years the prisoner was at last released.

review ▪ Revision
Sometimes a higher court carries out a review of the sentence of a lower court.

right ▪ Recht
In Germany women have had the right to vote since 1919.

sentence ▪ Strafe
The judge imposed a sentence of five years imprisonment on the accused.

to take to court (took, taken) ▪ verklagen
He was taken to court for hitting and robbing an old lady.

trial ▪ Gerichtsverfahren, Prozess
It's official now: the trial of the suspected murderer begins on Thursday.

---

to accuse ▪ anklagen, beschuldigen
The thief who had broken into my flat was accused of burglary.

accused ▪ Angeklagte(r)
The accused had to swear an oath to tell the truth.

alleged ▪ mutmaßlich
The alleged criminal had left the country before the trial.

breach ▪ Verstoß
He was taken to court for breach of the law.

compensation ■ Entschädigung
Being found innocent, the prisoner received a substantial amount in compensation.

to condemn ■ verurteilen
In the past people were sometimes condemned to death for stealing a hen.

to confess ■ gestehen
The accused got off lightly because he had confessed his crime.

to convict ■ verurteilen
The accused was convicted of theft.

damages (Pl.) ■ Schadenersatz
The painter did a very bad job, so the houseowner sued him for damages.

defendant ■ Angeklagte(r)
The jury found the defendant guilty.

denial ■ Leugnen
Despite of the accused's denial of the charges the jury returned a verdict of "Guilty".

to deny ■ leugnen, abstreiten
The accused denied any responsibility for the accident.

to file ■ zu den Akten geben, einreichen
She filed a lawsuit against her ex-husband.

gaol [dʒeɪl, = jail] ■ Gefängnis
The American term "jail" is now also often used in the UK instead of "gaol".

to get off (got, got) ■ davonkommen
Although John's crimes were very serious he got off lightly.

guideline ■ Richtlinie
The law serves as a guideline for the peaceful cooperation of a country's citizens.

guilt ■ Schuld
The jury were convinced of the accused's guilt.

guilty ■ schuldig
After a very thorough discussion the jury failed to reach a verdict of "Guilty".

illegal ■ (gesetzlich) verboten, illegal
It is illegal to sell alcohol to under-18s.

to impose ■ verhängen, auferlegen
The court imposed a fine on the accused.

imprisonment ■ Gefängnisstrafe, Haft
The criminal was sentenced to five years imprisonment.

injustice ■ Ungerechtigkeit
The courts try to prevent injustice.

innocent ■ unschuldig
The defendant claimed that he was innocent.

jail (AE) ■ Gefängnis
The criminal served a five-year jail sentence.

judicial ■ gerichtlich
The judicial system in our country is rather complex.

jurisdiction ■ Jurisdiktion, Gerichtsbarkeit, Zuständigkeit
I'm afraid this case is not within the jurisdiction of our court.

jury ■ Geschworene
In this case it did not take the jury very long to reach a verdict of "Not guilty".

justification ■ Rechtfertigung
The judge asked the defendant what he could say in justification of his deed.

lawsuit ['lɔːsuːt, 'lɔːsjuːt] ■ Klage, Gerichtsverfahren, Prozess
The purchaser had been cheated by the vendor and brought a lawsuit against him.

limitation ■ Beschränkung, Einschränkung
The Magna Carta of 1215 meant a first limitation of the king's power.

magistrate ■ Richter(in)

A magistrate is a judge in a lower court and does not have to have studied the law.

offender ■ Straftäter(in)

He was sent to prison for five years because he was a notorious offender.

to pardon ■ begnadigen

After ten years in prison the criminal was at last pardoned.

pardon ■ Begnadigung

The Queen granted the criminal a pardon.

penal code ■ Strafrecht

The penal code lays down what is a crime and how it is to be punished.

penalty ■ Strafe

For a number of years the death penalty has been abolished in Europe.

plaintiff ■ Kläger(in)

The plaintiff filed a lawsuit against his neighbour.

prisoner ■ Gefangene(r)

Prisoners in this prison serve very long or even life sentences.

proof ■ Beweis

The trial did not reveal enough proof to make the jury reach a verdict of "Guilty".

prosecution ■ Anklage, strafrechtliche Verfolgung

The suspect faced a prosecution for murder.

restoration ■ Rückgabe

After the war many people demanded the restoration of their property.

to reverse ■ aufheben

The crown court reversed the judgement of the magistrate.

revision ■ Revision

The crown court carried out a revision of the former judgement.

sexual assault ■ sexueller Übergriff
He was taken to court for sexual assault.

sheriff ■ Sheriff
In the USA sheriffs are elected police officers; in England and Wales they are legal officers appointed by the Queen; in Scotland they are judges at the Sheriff Court.

to sue ■ verklagen, gerichtlich belangen
Thomas sued his neighbour for damages.

suit [suːt, sjuːt] ■ (Zivil-)Prozess; (Zivil-)Verfahren
She brought a suit against her husband for neglect.

Supreme Court ■ Oberster Gerichtshof
In both the USA and the UK the Supreme Court is the highest court.

to testify ■ als Zeuge aussagen
The witness was required to testify in court.

thief ■ Dieb(in)
The alleged thief was taken to court.

torture ■ Folter
In most civilized countries torture is illegal.

tribunal ■ (Sonder-)Gericht
Conflicts between employers and employees are dealt with by an industrial tribunal.

verdict ■ Urteil
The jury reached a verdict of "Guilty".

witness ■ Zeuge, Zeugin
The first witness was called to make his statement.

13.4 Gesetzesverstöße und Polizeiarbeit

arms (Pl.) ■ Waffen
Arms are weapons, especially bombs and guns.

bar ■ Stange; (Gitter-)Stab
The criminal had killed his victim with an iron bar.
He spent the rest of his life behind bars.

to commit ■ begehen, verüben
He was arrested because the police had observed him committing a serious crime.

crime ■ Verbrechen
Killing people is a serious crime.

criminal ■ Verbrecher(in); verbrecherisch
The police accused the criminal of another criminal offence.

to deal (dealt, dealt) ■ handeln
The police arrested him because he had dealt drugs.

fine ■ Geldstrafe
He had to pay a fine for parking in a no-parking zone.

force ■ Gewalt, Kraft
In certain circumstances the police are allowed to use force.

to guard ■ bewachen
The prisoner was guarded by two armed police officers.

guard ■ Wache, Sicherheitsbeamte(r)
The guard stood aside to allow the visitor to pass.

gun ■ Schusswaffe, Gewehr
In Britain police officers do not usually carry guns.

to investigate ■ untersuchen, ermitteln
The detectives arrived soon after the crime and started to investigate.

investigation ■ Untersuchung, Ermittlung
The investigation of this crime took a very long time.

to kill ■ töten
The police arrested a person who had apparently killed someone.

measure ■ Maßnahme
The police decided to take measures against the flood of burglaries in the city.

murder ▪ Mord
He committed the murder simply because he wanted the victim's money.

offence ▪ Straftat
It is an offence to break into other people's houses.

to prevent ▪ verhindern
However much the police try they can never prevent crime completely.

statement ▪ Aussage
The person arrested refused to make a statement to the police.

victim ▪ Opfer
The police asked the victim of the crime to describe the criminal.

violence ▪ Gewalt(tätigkeit)
After many football matches there is a lot of violence.

violent ▪ gewalttätig, brutal
The police arrested some young men because of their violent behaviour.

---

abuse ▪ Missbrauch
There have been quite a few cases of child abuse recently.

alarm ▪ Alarm
The burglars ran away when the alarm went off.

armed ▪ bewaffnet
The gangsters entered the bank armed with guns.

to arrest ▪ verhaften
The police officer caught Jack climbing out of a window and arrested him on the spot.

assault ▪ Überfall
The defendants were charged with assault.

bullet ▪ Geschoss, Kugel
The police used rubber bullets to keep the attacking crowd at a distance.

burglar ▪ Einbrecher(in)
The burglar was caught when he left the house through the broken window.

burglary ▪ Einbruch
He was arrested for burglary.

to chase ▪ jagen, verfolgen
The police chased the suspect and eventually arrested him.

clue ▪ Hinweis, Indiz
The police have no clue where to look for the criminal.

commissioner ▪ Polizeipräsident(in)
The city's Commissioner of Police resigned after a scandal involving corruption.

constable ▪ Polizist(in)
Two constables were appointed to guard the prisoner.

corruption ▪ Korruption, Bestechung
Corruption is a serious crime.

dealer ▪ Händler(in), Dealer(in)
The dealer was found to have a large quantity of illegal drugs in his bag.

to defend ▪ verteidigen, schützen
It's one of the jobs of the police to defend the country's citizens against criminals.

deputy ▪ Stellvertreter(in)
In the absence of the sheriff his deputy will take over.

detective ▪ Detektiv(in), Kriminalpolizist(in)
Two detectives searched the scene of the crime for evidence.

drunk ▪ betrunken
He was taken to court for drunk driving.

fingerprint ▪ Fingerabdruck
The police took the suspect's fingerprints.

to fire ▪ feuern, schießen
When the robber was followed by the police he fired at them without warning.

to flee (fled, fled) ■ fliehen, flüchten

After causing the accident the driver simply fled.

fraud ■ Betrug, Schwindel

The official was sacked because he had been convicted of fraud.

hold-up ■ Raubüberfall

The criminals got away with 20 million pounds after the hold-up.

inspector ■ (Polizei-)Kommissar(in)

The detective inspector arrived on the scene of the crime soon after it had happened.

to kidnap (kidnapped, kidnapped) ■ kidnappen, entführen

Charles Lindbergh's almost two-year-old son was kidnapped and killed in 1932.

killer ■ Mörder(in)

Fortunately the killer was caught very soon.

motive ■ Motiv, Beweggrund

Sweeney Todd had only one motive for murdering his customers – revenge.

to murder ■ ermorden

When the old lady refused to give the criminal any money, he simply murdered her.

murderer ■ Mörder(in)

Macheath in the "The Beggar's Opera" is a notorious murderer.

to offend ■ eine Straftat begehen

Some people will keep offending.

pickpocket ■ Taschendieb(in)

Watch out for pickpockets when you're visiting the Christmas Market.

pirate ■ Seeräuber(in), Pirat(in)

Even today there are still pirates – for instance off Somalia.

prevention ■ Vorbeugung; Vermeidung

Prevention is better than cure.

The prevention of crime is the chief function of the police.

to pursue ■ verfolgen
William ran away from the accident but an officer pursued and caught him.

to question ■ verhören
The police questioned the suspect.

raid ■ Überfall
After the raid on the bank the robbers got away with £15m.

rape ■ Vergewaltigung
Often victims of a rape suffer from this crime all their lives.

receiver ■ Hehler(in)
Oliver Twist had worked for a receiver, who sold whatever Oliver and others had stolen.

to resist ■ Widerstand leisten, sich widersetzen
The criminal tried to resist his arrest by the police.

to restore ■ zurückgeben
The police caught the thief and made him restore the stolen wallet to its owner.

to rob ■ (aus)rauben
When they returned from the party they realized that their house had been robbed.
The burglars had robbed grandfather of his valuable clock.

robber ■ Räuber(in)
Oscar Pistorius claimed that he shot his girlfriend by mistake, thinking she was a robber.

to search ■ suchen, durchsuchen
The police searched in vain for the stolen money.
The detectives searched the scene of the crime for clues.

search ■ Suche, Durchsuchung
The search for the escaped convicts was unsuccessful.
The police were given permission to carry out a search of the criminal's house.

to seize ■ beschlagnahmen
The police seized the stolen goods.

self-defence ■ Notwehr
The defendant claimed that he had shot the sheriff in self-defence.

shoplifter ■ Ladendieb(in)
Notice in a store: "Shoplifters will be prosecuted."

shotgun ■ Schrotflinte
The criminals threatened the old lady with a shotgun.

to smuggle ■ schmuggeln
The rebels had managed to smuggle arms across the border.

smuggler ■ Schmuggler(in)
Unfortunately the smugglers were not caught.

to steal (stole, stolen) ■ stehlen
They stole whatever they could lay their hands on.

to suppress ■ unterdrücken
The barrister claimed that the police has suppressed evidence revealing that the accused was innocent.

to suspect [sə'spekt] ■ verdächtigen
The police suspected that the young man had broken into a house and arrested him.

suspect ['sʌspekt] ■ Verdächtige(r)
The suspect was taken to the police station for further questioning.

suspicion ■ Verdacht
We arrest you on suspicion of murder.

suspicious ■ verdächtig
Max was arrested because he made himself suspicious.

theft ■ Diebstahl
He was accused of theft rather than burglary because he had not broken into the flat.

to trace ■ verfolgen; aufspüren
At last the police traced the criminal's escape route.
They traced him to his girlfriend's flat.

to trap ■ in die Falle locken
The police trapped the suspect and managed to arrest him at last.

violation ■ Verstoß
Child marriage is a violation of human rights.

watch ■ Wache
It is a pity that the police must still keep watch in front of synagogues.

13.5 Exekutive, öffentliche Verwaltung, Politik und Militär

action ■ Gefecht, Kampf
Ten soldiers were reported to have been killed in action.

to advance ■ vorrücken
The rebels advanced steadily toward the country's capital.

affair ■ Angelegenheit
The euro crisis is a very serious affair.

attack ■ Angriff
There have been a number of attacks on foreigners in recent weeks.

battle ■ Schlacht, Kampf
The American Civil War ended two years after the Battle of Gettysburg.

to break up (broke, broken) ■ auflösen
The army broke up the violent demonstration.

conclusion ■ Schluss, Beschluss, Entscheidung
The committee's conclusion was that the project should not be continued.

defence ■ Verteidigung, Schutz
Britain is an island. That is why it needs a strong navy as a defence against enemies.

demand [dɪ'mɑːnd] ■ Forderung
The government rejected the rebels' demands.

to free ■ befreien
The rebels fought to free their country from the dictator.

gun ▪ Geschütz
We heard the sound of guns all night.

international ▪ international
The experts met for an international conference to discuss global warming.

issue ['ɪʃuː, 'ɪsjuː] ▪ Frage, Angelegenheit
In some countries illegal immigration is a serious issue.

military ▪ militärisch
Some people think that a military intervention in a civil war does not really help.

official ▪ offiziell
Parliament launched an official inquiry into the scandal.

peace ▪ Frieden
After long negotiations the two countries at last achieved a peace agreement.

political ▪ politisch
Unemployment has always been a major political problem.

politics ⚠ ▪ Politik
Many people in nowaday's society are not interested in politics.

profit ▪ Nutzen, Vorteil
The opposition saw no profit in continuing its discussions with the government.

programme ▪ Programm
Many voters liked the political programme of the new party.

to protect ▪ schützen, verteidigen
It is a major function of the government to protect its citizens.

protection ▪ Schutz
The protection of the public from crime is the key function of the police.

relevant ▪ zuständig
The relevant official's office is on the second floor.

responsibility ■ Zuständigkeit
I'm afraid it is not our responsibility to deal with your complaint.

responsible ■ verantwortlich, zuständig
My boss is responsible for dealing with this subject.

secretary ■ Minister(in)
The Foreign Secretary is responsible for Britain's relationship with other countries.

security ■ Sicherheit
Every government's priority should be to guarantee its citizens' security.

service ■ Dienst
Education is a public service.

shot ■ Schuss
The soldiers gave up without firing a single shot.

staff ■ Stab
Her grandfather was a staff officer in the army.

strike ■ Schlag, Angriff
The government launched a strike against the rebels.

troop ■ Truppe
The general decided to withdraw his troops.

unit ■ Einheit
The government set up an anti-terrorist unit to deal with the rebels.

victory ■ Sieg
The battle at Waterloo in 1815 ended with the defeat of Napoleon.

war ■ Krieg
In the twentieth century there were two world wars.

weapon ['wepən] ■ Waffe
Entering the bank with a weapon is not allowed.

---

to abolish ■ abschaffen, aufheben
Slavery was abolished in the USA in 1865.

advance ▪ Vorrücken
At last the rebels' advance was stopped by the government troops.

air force ▪ Luftwaffe
The United States air force is very strong.

alliance ▪ Bündnis, Allianz
NATO and the Warsaw Pact were two very important alliances after WWII.

allied ▪ alliiert, verbündet
The allied forces defeated Germany in May 1945.

arrow ▪ Pfeil
In the Middle Ages soldiers used bows and arrows for shooting.

assault ▪ Angriff
Just after midnight the army launched an assault on the enemy.

bomb ▪ Bombe
Many cities were destroyed by bombs in WWII.

to command ▪ kommandieren
General Patton commanded the Seventh United States Army in WWII.

command ▪ Befehl, Führung, Kommando
The command of the entire campaign lay in the hands of General Myers.

commander ▪ Befehlshaber(in), Kommandant(in)
General McDermot was made commander of the entire operation.

compromise ▪ Kompromiss
Politicians must be experts at finding compromise solutions.

concession ▪ Zugeständnis, Konzession
The Chancellor made no concession to the opposition's demand.

to conquer ▪ erobern
In 1066 the Normans conquered England.

delegate ▪ Delegierte(r)
The government appointed her their delegate to the peace conference.

delegation ■ Delegation, Abordnung
The Prime Minister welcomed the delegation from Gabun.

division ■ Division
Every army has several divisions.

fighting ■ Kämpfe, Gefechte
There was fierce fighting on the western front.

fire brigade ■ Feuerwehr
When the house owner found that his house was on fire he called the fire brigade.

Foreign Office ■ Außenministerium
Britain's Foreign Office is located in Whitehall.

foreign policy ■ Außenpolitik
The relationship between states is the field of foreign policy.

Foreign Secretary ■ Außenminister(in)
The equivalent of the British Foreign Secretary is the Secretary of State in the USA.

immigrant ■ Einwanderer(-in)
The early non-native population of America consisted of immigrants from Europe.

to immigrate ■ einwandern
In the 1840s a large number of people from Ireland immigrated to the USA.

immigration ■ Einwanderung
Immigration to the USA is governed by strict laws.

to implement ■ einführen, umsetzen
It is not enough to pass laws – you must also implement them.

implementation ■ Vollzug, Ausführung
The implementation of peace treaties can be very difficult.

import duty ■ Einfuhrzoll
Import duties can be a major source of a country's revenue.

income tax ■ Einkommensteuer
Income tax is a major source of revenue for the state.

independence ▪ Unabhängigkeit
The American colonies achieved their independence in 1776.

intervention ▪ Intervention, Eingreifen
The strike was settled without any intervention by the government.

to invade ▪ einmarschieren, eindringen
The enemy invaded the western part of the country.

invasion ▪ Invasion
1066 is the year of the Normans' invasion of England.

knight [naɪt] ▪ Ritter
Knights played a major role in the Early Middle Ages.

to launch ▪ abschießen
The army launched a large number of rockets.

launch ▪ Abschuss
The launch of this new type of rocket proved its superior quality.

liberation ▪ Befreiung
The liberation of all slaves in the USA was not the main aim of Abraham Lincoln.

lieutenant [lef'tenənt] ▪ Leutnant
Lieutenant Smithers was promoted captain.

major ▪ Major(in)
Captain Myers was promoted major at last.

missile ▪ Rakete
The missile hit a group of civilians, killing most of them.

mission ▪ Auftrag, Einsatz
It is the army's mission to defend the country's borders.

to monitor ▪ überwachen, kontrollieren
The government monitors developments on the money market.

occupation ▪ Besetzung
WWII ended with the occupation of Germany and the defeat of Japan.

to occupy ■ besetzen, einnehmen
The United States occupied Nicaragua from 1912 to 1933, during the "Banana Wars".

to oppose ■ ablehnen, sich widersetzen
Many Ukrainians opposed the intervention of Russia.

opposite ■ gegensätzlich
The two parties pursued opposite policies.

to overcome (-came, -come) ■ siegen; besiegen
"We shall overcome", was a famous slogan in the 1960s.
After a long fight they at last overcame their enemies.

peaceful ■ friedlich
Germany's relationship with its neighbours has been peaceful since WWII ended.

pistol ■ Pistole
Army officers usually carry pistols.

politician ■ Politiker(in)
Unfortunately politicians do not generally have a good reputation.

poll ■ Umfrage
Recent polls show that the government is very popular.

to prove ■ nachweisen; sich erweisen
The police found it difficult to prove the guilt of the accused.
Restoring order has proved rather difficult.

to pursue ■ verwirklichen wollen
The country has always pursued a policy of peace.

raid ■ Angriff
Germany experienced a large number of air raids in WWII.

rebel ■ Rebell(in)
After a long struggle the government forces managed to defeat the rebels.

to rescue ■ retten, befreien
The fire brigade rescued the people trapped in their burning house.

resistance ■ Widerstand
Many French citizens joined the resistance movement against Germany in WWII.

to retreat ■ sich zurückziehen
As a result of the superior power of the enemy the army retreated.

revolver ■ (Trommel-)Revolver
Most cowboys in Westerns use revolvers for shooting.

rifle ['raɪfəl] ■ Gewehr
One of the first things soldiers must learn to do is clean and use their rifles.

riot ['raɪət] ■ Aufstand, Krawall, Unruhen
The country experienced a time of race riots.

rocket ■ Rakete
The enemy began their heavy rocket attack just after midnight.

rumour ■ Gerücht
Important decisions should not be based on rumours.

scout ■ Kundschafter(in)
The officer sent three scouts to check whether it was safe to cross t he bridge.

seal ■ Siegel
Official documents usually have a seal on them.

secret ■ geheim
This is a top secret document. Don't show it to anyone.

Secretary of State (AE) ■ Außenminister
The American Secretary of State is the equivalent of the British Foreign Secretary.

to seize ■ einnehmen
At last the army managed to seize the enemy's capital.

shield ■ (Schutz-)Schild
Medieval knights fought with a sword and a shield.

spy ■ Spion(in)
Mata Hari was accused of being a spy for a foreign country.

squad ■ Einheit; Gruppe

The police vice squad regularly uncovers immoral activities in high places.

A squad is a very small military unit.

stand ■ Einstellung

The Prime Minister is known for his conservative stand on this issue.

standby ■ Reserve

The policemen acted as standbys in case of an emergency.

submarine ['sʌbməri:n] ■ U-Boot

Submarines were already used in the American Civil War.

to submit ■ einreichen

Jacqueline's parents always submitted their tax return at the last possible moment.

to surrender ■ sich ergeben, kapitulieren

Germany surrendered on 8 May 1945.

surrender ■ Kapitulation

Japan's surrender took place on 2 September 1945.

to survey [sə'veɪ] ■ befragen

The city council surveyed all the residents who had suffered in the storm.

to suspend ■ aussetzen; suspendieren

The operation of the London Underground was suspended for two days.

The civil servant was suspended until further notice.

sword [sɔ:d] ■ Schwert

In the Middle Ages wars were still fought with swords.

tank ■ Panzer

Tanks were first used in WWI.

taxpayer ■ Steuerzahler(in)

The government must make sure that all taxpayers pay their taxes.

term ■ Amtszeit

Barack Obama's first term as president ended in 2012.

terror ▪ Terror, Schrecken

The rebels began a campaign of terror.

terrorist ▪ Terrorist(in)

Che Guevara was regarded by some as a hero, by others as a terrorist.

treasury ▪ Finanzministerium

The Treasury is one of the most important government departments.

withdrawal ▪ Rückzug, Abzug

The withdrawal of the enemy's troops came as a big surprise.

WWI, WWII ▪ Erster Weltkrieg; Zweiter Weltkrieg

WWII began only 21 years after the end of WWI.

14. Kommunikation

14.1 Allgemeines

according to ▪ zufolge, gemäß
According to the radio the weather is going to be good tomorrow.

actually ▪ wirklich, tatsächlich; eigentlich
Actually, what I wanted to say is something entirely different.

to address ▪ ansprechen
The speaker addressed his audience in a clear voice.

advice ▪ Rat
Let me give you an advice – don't do important things when you're tired.

to aim at ▪ richten an
Her remarks were clearly aimed at the opposition.

all right ▪ in Ordnung, okay
All right. Let's do it like this.

alright ▪ in Ordnung, okay
It doesn't matter whether you use the spelling "alright" or "all right".

to announce ▪ bekanntgeben, verkünden
The speaker announced that the train would be twenty minutes late.

to answer ['ɑːnsə] ▪ antworten, beantworten
I asked her where she was from, and she answered, "From Denmark".
Can please someone answer my question?

answer ['ɑːnsə] ▪ Antwort
Mary was always the first one to give the correct answer.

to argue ['ɑːgjuː] ▪ streiten, argumentieren
Stop arguing all the time.

argument ▪ Streit, Argument
There were long arguments about how to proceed.

to ask ▪ fragen
Excuse me, sir, can I ask you a simple question?

to call ▪ rufen
He called "Hello" across the street.

to comment ['kɒment] ▪ eine Bemerkung machen
George comments on everything he doesn't like.

comment ['kɒment] ▪ Kommentar, Bemerkung
She is known for her funny comments.

communication ▪ Kommunikation, Verständigung
Gestures and language are important means of communication.

conversation ▪ Gespräch, Unterhaltung
I think we should have a serious conversation about this problem.

to derive ▪ ableiten
A large percentage of words in English are derived from Latin.

to describe ▪ beschreiben
Could you please describe what exactly happened when you had the accident?

description ▪ Beschreibung
Thank you for the beautiful description of the scenery.

emphasis ▪ Betonung
In his speech the President placed much emphasis on the financial situation of the US.

to emphasize ▪ betonen
He tended to emphasize words on the wrong syllable.

er … ▪ äh …
I just wanted to ask, er, if I can have your car.

to explain ▪ erklären, erläutern
Before I tell you what to do let me briefly explain what I have in mind.

to express ▪ ausdrücken, zum Ausdruck bringen
She expressed her disappointment quite clearly.

expression ▪ Ausdruck, Äußerung
Foreigners often find it difficult to understand expressions in a local dialect.

to imply ▪ andeuten
Your statement appears to imply that you think that I am a liar.

indeed ▪ tatsächlich, wirklich; allerdings
Indeed, she acts according to her promises.
Is this what you painted yourself? – Yes, indeed.

to inform ▪ benachrichtigen, informieren
We'll inform you as soon as the product has arrived.

information ▪ Information(en), Auskunft, Angaben
Can you give me some information about your company?

to interrupt ▪ unterbrechen
Would you, please, stop interrupting me all the time!

to interview ▪ interviewen, befragen
After the election the party leaders were interviewed by journalists.

interview ▪ Interview
The interview was broadcast without the consent of the politician interviewed.

joke ▪ Witz
Occasionally it helps to tell a joke in a tricky situation.

language ▪ Sprache
German is said to be a difficult language.

to mean (meant [ment], meant [ment]) ▪ bedeuten
What does the word "offence" mean?

to mention ▪ erwähnen
In this context I would like to mention another factor.

no ▪ nein
No, this is not the way to the station.

observation ■ Bemerkung
That was a very clever observation, Mary.

of course ■ natürlich, selbstverständlich
I suppose that was Mary. – Of course it was Mary.

offence ■ Beleidigung
Oh sorry, no offence meant.

okay ■ okay, OK
Tomorrow morning at eleven? – Oh yes, that's okay.

to put (put, put) ■ ausdrücken
Let me put this differently: you've been a fool.

question ■ Frage
A fool will ask foolish questions.

to reach ■ erreichen
Where have you been? I've been trying to reach you all day.

to recommend ■ empfehlen
I would like to recommend this excellent red wine from South Africa.

reference ■ Anspielung
Was that by any chance a reference to my weight?

to repeat ■ wiederholen; nachsprechen
The professor had to repeat his explanation before everyone understood him.
Repeat this after me.

response ■ Antwort, Reaktion
"I would prefer not to" was Bartleby's response to whatever he was asked to do.

▸ **in response to** ■ in Beantwortung
We write this letter in response to your inquiry of 5 March.

to say (said [sed], said [sed]) ■ sagen
Sorry, I didn't get that. Can you say it again?

should ■ sollte(st, t, n)
The red house over there should be theirs.
If you wish to pass the test you should work a little harder.

to shout ▪ rufen, schreien
There's no need to shout. I can hear you perfectly well.

sign ▪ Zeichen
She made a sign for him to move on.

to speak (spoke, spoken) ▪ sprechen
Ron speaks German with a strong American accent.

▸ **to speak about** ▪ sprechen über
Tomorrow our local M.P. is speaking to residents about the recent flood.

▸ **to speak up** ▪ lauter sprechen
Can you speak up a little? I don't understand you.

speaker ▪ Redner(in); Sprecher(in)
Today's first speaker will be Mrs Bovary.
You will not have any problems understanding her because she is a fluent speaker of English.

speech ▪ Sprache; Sprechen
It takes about two years before children are capable of speech.
In speech we use fewer words than in writing.

statement ▪ Äußerung, Erklärung
The CEO promised to make a statement to his staff on the following day.

to talk ▪ reden, sprechen
The only thing he can do is talk, talk, talk.

to tell (told, told) ▪ sagen; erzählen; erkennen
I can't tell how many people there were.
He keeps telling stories.
They couldn't tell where the accident had happened.

thank you ▪ danke
Thank you for your good advice.

thanks ▪ danke
Thanks, darling, for ironing my shirts.

▸ **thanks a lot** ▪ herzlichen Dank
Thanks a lot for helping me with the dishes.

to understand (-stood, -stood) ▪ verstehen; begreifen
Can you speak up a little? I don't understand you.
I don't understand what you mean.

to warn ▪ warnen; ermahnen
Let me warn you of the slippery street just round the corner.
The teacher warned his pupils to be quiet.

would ▪ würde, würdest, würdet, würden; wäre, wärest, wäret, wären
If I were you I would certainly do it.
She would be so glad if you could come.

yes ▪ ja
The answer is simply, "Yes!"

---

accent ▪ Akzent
In a formal lecture speakers do not normally use a local accent.

to advise ▪ (be)raten; informieren
Can you advise me on how to proceed in this affair?
We advise you of the expected time of arrival of flight LZ 432.

aloud ▪ laut
My dentist is one of the people who think aloud.

alphabet ▪ Alphabet
There are 26 letters in the Latin alphabet.

alphabetical ▪ alphabetisch
Please arrange the tests in the alphabetical order of names.

to assure ▪ beteuern, versichern
Mary's father assured her that he would continue supporting her during her studies.

character ▪ (Schrift-)Zeichen
Chinese characters are also used in Japanese and some other Asian languages.

to cheer ▪ jubeln

When the band finished their concert everybody cheered wildly.

clause ▪ Satzteil

Sentences in lectures should not contain too many complex clauses.

commentator ▪ Kommentator(in)

She is an excellent commentator on political affairs.

to communicate ▪ mitteilen, kommunizieren

If people do not share a language they will find it difficult to communicate.

to complain ▪ sich beschweren, klagen

The hotel guests complained of noises at night.

to convey ▪ vermitteln

Convey my regards to your father, please.

to curse ▪ fluchen, schimpfen

He would curse like mad on the least provocation.

to damn ▪ verdammen

The critics damned the novel for being extremely boring.

dialogue ▪ Gespräch, Dialog

For a dialogue you require at least two speakers.

disapproval ▪ Missbilligung, Missfallen

He expressed his disapproval in no uncertain terms.

to disapprove ▪ missbilligen

The police officer disapproved of the driver's speed and told him so.

to disclose ▪ bekanntgeben, enthüllen

At last the family disclosed when the baby would be born.

discourse ▪ Diskurs

The language of political discourse is different from that of everyday discourse.

to echo ▪ wiederholen

Stop echoing my words all the time, will you?

fuck off ▪ verpiss dich, schleich dich

"Fuck off" is not a term to be used in polite society.

hyphen ▪ Bindestrich
There is a hyphen in words like "co-worker" and "co-writers".

informal ▪ ungezwungen, informell
When talking to your superiors you should not use informal language.

to interpret [ɪn'tɜːprɪt] ▪ dolmetschen
The tourist didn't speak Spanish so he needed someone to interpret for him.

intonation ▪ Intonation, Sprechmelodie
Scottish English speakers have a very distinct intonation.

irony ▪ Ironie
Irony is a form of humour in which you say things you do not mean.

letter ▪ Buchstabe
The letters in this old manuscript are not easily readable.

lower case ▪ klein geschrieben
Young people often use only lower case letters in their emails.

meaning ▪ Bedeutung, Sinn
What is the meaning of this strange word?

monotonous [mə'nɒtənəs] ▪ monoton
His monotonous voice made listening to him difficult.

to murmur ▪ murmeln
She was so shy that she only murmured in reply to the question.

to mutter ▪ murmeln, brummen
I haven't done you any harm. So why are you muttering?

native speaker ▪ Muttersprachler(in)
My sister's English was so good that she spoke it almost like a native speaker.

obliged ▪ verpflichtet (sein)
I'm much obliged for your help.

pardon ▪ Entschuldigung
Pardon, what is your name again?

phrase ■ Redewendung, Ausdruck
The phrase "How do you do?" does not mean what the individual words suggest.

to pose ■ stellen
They took care to pose the question carefully.

to pretend ■ behaupten
Charles pretended that he had lost his keys.

to pronounce ■ aussprechen
Learning to pronounce the words of a foreign language correctly can be difficult.

pronunciation ■ Aussprache
I find the pronunciation of Russian very difficult.

to question ■ befragen
The interviewer questioned the applicant concerning her professional qualifications.

to reckon ■ annehmen
I reckon you're Mary's friend – right?

remark ■ Bemerkung
That was a very clever remark, Kate.

to respond ■ reagieren, antworten
Henry shouted Sybil's name but she did not respond.

rhetoric ['retərɪk] ■ Rhetorik, Redekunst
Churchill's "Blood, Sweat and Tears"-speech was a brilliant piece of rhetoric.

rhetorical [rɪ'tɒrɪkəl] ■ rhetorisch
In poetry a lot of rhetorical devices are used.

rubbish ■ Mist, Unsinn
Oh no. That is complete rubbish.

to scream ■ schreien
Seeing the approaching train, I screamed a warning to our taxi-driver.

shit! ▪ Scheiße!, Mist!
Saying "shit!" is not polite.

slang ▪ Slang, gruppenspezifische Sprache
I don't understand this military slang.

so do I ▪ ich auch
I always go to Holland for my holiday. – So do I.

to swear [sweə] (swore, sworn) ▪ fluchen
Stop swearing in front of the children.

syllable ▪ Silbe
The word "anger" has two syllables.

synonym ▪ Synonym
"Shut" is a synonym for "closed".

tense ▪ Tempus, Zeitform
Strictly speaking, there are only two tenses in English – the present and the past.

that is ▪ das heißt
As a senior citizen you are entitled to a discount, that is if you are over sixty.

to translate ▪ übersetzen
Translating literature and legal texts is a very tricky business.

translation ▪ Übersetzung
A word-for-word translation is usually nonsense.

understatement ▪ Untertreibung
The English are very good at the art of understatement.

upper case ▪ groß geschrieben
Some people use upper case letters to stress certain words.

verbal ▪ mündlich, verbal
Verbal communication tends to be less formal than written communication.

vocabulary ▪ Vokabular, Wortschatz
The speaker's vocabulary was impressive.

vowel ■ Vokal
The pronunciation of French and English vowels is entirely different.

warning ■ Warnung
The authorities issued a warning about a serious flood.

welcome: you're welcome ■ gern geschehen
Thanks for looking after little Joan. – You're welcome.

what about …? ■ was ist mit …?
What about John? Is he coming as well?

to whisper ■ flüstern
Can you please stop whispering? I can't really concentrate.

whistle ['wɪsəl] ■ Pfeifen, Pfiff
The criminal warned his friend with a short, sharp whistle.

14.2 Begrüßung und Abschied

bye-bye ■ (auf) Wiedersehen
Bye-bye, sweetheart.

goodbye ■ auf Wiedersehen, auf Wiederhören
Don't forget that at the end of an interview you are supposed to say goodbye.

to greet ■ begrüßen
Small children often do not like greeting visitors properly.

hello ■ hallo, guten Tag
Many people nowadays say "hello" rather than "good morning" or "good evening".

hey ■ hallo, he
Hey, wait a minute.

hi ■ hey, hallo
My mother didn't like me saying "hi" rather than "good morning".

how are you? ▪ wie geht es dir/Ihnen?
I haven't seen you for ages. How are you?

see you! ▪ bis bald!
Sorry, I've got to go shopping for a few minutes. – See you!

so long (AE) ▪ bis dann
Instead of "goodbye" the Americans say "so long".

take care! ▪ mach(t)'s gut!
Okay then. Take care!

to welcome ▪ begrüßen, willkommen heißen
First of all I would like to welcome you all.

welcome ▪ willkommen; Willkommen
Welcome to our party.
Henry was given a very warm welcome when he returned after his long illness.

---

how do you do? ▪ guten Tag, angenehm
As a rule you only say "How do you do?" the first time you meet somebody.

Mister ▪ Herr
If you address a man you don't know, don't say "Mister" but "Sir".

Mistress ▪ Frau
If you address a woman you don't know, don't say "Mistress" but "Madam".

pleased ▪ erfreut
You often say "I'm pleased to meet you" when you've been introduced to someone.

to shake hands (shook, shaken) ▪ sich die Hand geben
The British usually shake hands when they meet for the first time.

so what? ▪ ja und?
You're late again! – So what?

touch ▪ Kontakt
Let's keep in touch.

▸ to get in touch with ■ sich in Verbindung setzen mit
After the accident the driver got in touch with the other driver's family.

to wave ■ winken
They waved them goodbye.

14.3 Verbot und Erlaubnis, Bitte und Ablehnung, Notwendigkeit

to admit ■ hineinlassen; zulassen
Visitors are not admitted after the show has begun.
The committee decided that Mary should be admitted to the club.

to allow ■ erlauben, ermöglichen
At King's College, Cambridge, students are not allowed to walk on the college lawns.

attention ■ Achtung
Attention! The show will begin soon.

to beg ■ betteln, bitten
Stop begging for more wine. You've had enough.

can (could, could) ■ können
You can have it if you really want it.

certainly ■ sicherlich
Might I borrow this book? – Yes, certainly. Take it for as long as you like.

to claim ■ fordern
The speaker claimed his listeners' full attention.

come on! ■ Komm(t) schon!, Los!
The train has arrived. Come on or we'll miss it!

to demand ■ verlangen, fordern
The opposition demanded the resignation of the Prime Minister.

to force ■ zwingen
The board forced their CEO to resign.

to grant ▪ gewähren

At last we were granted permission to build our house.

have to (had, had) ▪ müssen

You have to be very good and lucky to never get into trouble.

importance ▪ Wichtigkeit, Bedeutung

Loyalty is of very high importance in personal relationships.

important ▪ wichtig

The tertiary sector has become more important than the secondary sector.

to let (let, let) ▪ lassen

Please, Dad, let me go to the party tonight.

may ▪ (vielleicht) können; dürfen

I may be able to do this but I'm not quite sure.

May I come in, sir?

might ▪ könnte (eventuell); dürfte

I dont think it's true, but I admit it might be.

Might I come in, Sir?

must ▪ müssen

It's late, we must hurry.

must not ▪ nicht dürfen

You must not enter here.

necessary ▪ notwendig, nötig

It is necessary that you work hard for your exam.

to order ▪ anordnen, befehlen

The headmistress ordered the girls to wear skirts covering their knees.

order ▪ Anordnung, Befehl

The CEO's order was to carry out an investigation of the scandal.

ought to ▪ (eigentlich etwas) sollen

You do not have to do this but you ought to.

please ▪ bitte

Can you pass me the sugar, please?

power ▪ Berechtigung
The general was given the power to attack the enemy.

private ['praɪvət] ▪ privat
"Strictly private! No admission."

to reject ▪ ablehnen
Stirling University rejected his application for admission.

to remind s.o. ▪ jdn. erinnern
The teacher reminded her pupils that there would be a test soon.

request ▪ Bitte, Antrag
His request to be granted asylum was turned down.

to require ▪ benötigen; verlangen, vorschreiben
Our organization requires an entirely new structure.
The police requires you to register with them if you move here.

requirement ▪ Erfordernis; Voraussetzung
It is a legal requirement that you pay tax.
Oliver met the requirements for admission to Oxford university.

shall ▪ sollen
The Bible says, "You shall not kill."
Shall I bring you a cup of tea?

to speak to (spoke, spoken) ▪ sprechen mit
Could I speak to the CEO, please?

to take a seat (took, taken) ▪ Platz nehmen
Do come in and take a seat, please.

unimportant ▪ unwichtig
What matters is being healthy and happy. Everything else is unimportant.

unnecessary ▪ unnötig
In making this experiment don't take any unnecessary risks.

---

admission ▪ Zutritt, Zulassung
Strictly no admission for people under eighteen.

to approve ▪ zustimmen, genehmigen

This is to inform you that we have approved your proposal.

to ban ▪ ausschließen; verbieten

Smokers are banned from this restaurant.

Our landlord bans ball games in the garden.

to command ▪ befehlen

He commanded that the entrance to the castle should be blocked.

constraint ▪ Zwang, Beschränkung, Einschränkung

He insisted on doing everything his own way – he wouldn't tolerate any constraints.

licence ▪ Lizenz, Erlaubnis, Genehmigung

James Bond has a licence to kill.

to license ▪ lizensieren, erlauben

In the end, the authorities licensed the publication of the controversial book.

needn't ▪ nicht (zu tun) brauchen

He's not your boss. You needn't do what he tells you to do.

to object [əb'dʒekt] ▪ dagegen sein, Einwände haben

Many people objected to being treated like criminals.

to owe ▪ schulden

I think you owe me an apology.

pass ▪ Passierschein

If you want to leave the camp you require a pass.

permission ▪ Erlaubnis, Genehmigung

The prisoners were granted permission to walk in the yard for an hour.

to permit ▪ erlauben, gestatten

Staff are permitted to use the company's sports facilities.

piss off! ▪ hau ab!, verpiss dich!

Piss off! is not something you say in polite society. It is rather vulgar.

to plead [pliːd] ▪ (dringend) bitten
After two hours of waiting in the police station I pleaded to be allowed to go.

refusal ▪ Ablehnung; Verweigerung; Absage
He was sent a letter of refusal by the local council.
She disliked the hospital's refusal to allow her to visit her husband.
Her application was rejected without any reason for the refusal.

to request ▪ bitten, auffordern
Spectators are requested to remain seated during the performance.

to restrict ▪ beschränken, einschränken
The number of spectators in the theatre is restricted to 600 only.

restriction ▪ Begrenzung, Einschränkung
A lot of restrictions apply concerning what you are allowed to import into the USA.

shut up! ▪ halt(et) die Klappe!
You've been talking nonsense for two hours and I'm sick of it all. So just shut up!

statute ▪ Statut, Satzung
The college statutes do not permit students to walk on the lawn.

to submit o.s. ▪ sich unterwerfen; sich unterziehen; sich anpassen
Ben always has difficulties submitting himself to regulations.
Liz had to submit herself to an operation.
They had problems submitting themselves to the new rules.

to turn down ▪ ablehnen
The boss turned down her request for a pay rise.

to urge ▪ drängen, zureden
Although her husband urged her to give up smoking she kept smoking until she died.

urgent ▪ dringend
Given your health, losing weight is very urgent.

wait a minute! ■ Moment mal!
Wait a minute! What was the cook doing when the murder occurred?

14.4 Meinung, Diskussion, Vorträge, Berichte

account ■ Bericht
The witness gave a very clear account of what he had observed.

aspect ■ Gesichtspunkt, Blickwinkel
Now let me look into another aspect of this fascinating subject.

to assume ■ annehmen
I assume we all share the same perspective.

to claim ■ behaupten
The speaker claimed that what the other party had said was untrue.

to close ■ beenden
Let me close my speech with a few final remarks.

to conclude ■ (be)enden, (be)schließen
Ladies and gentlemen, allow me to conclude my lecture with a few personal remarks.

context ■ Zusammenhang, Kontext
The speaker explained that his remark had referred to a different context.

to contribute ■ beitragen, beisteuern
He always contributed something useful to every discussion.

contribution ■ Beitrag
Thank you very much for your valuable contribution to our discussion.

debate ■ Debatte, Diskussion
There was a long debate before everyone agreed.

to discuss ■ diskutieren, erörtern
Let's discuss how to get out of our financial trouble.

discussion ▪ Diskussion
After a long discussion the two parties agreed on a compromise.

except ▪ außer, es sei denn
This door must be kept closed, except in case of fire.

to formulate ▪ formulieren, ausarbeiten
If you wish to be understood, you must formulate your point clearly.

forum ▪ Forum
Many discussions take place in forums.

however ▪ jedoch, dennoch, aber
I agree. However, I would like to point out that we must also consider another point.

idea ▪ Idee, Gedanke; Ahnung
That is a good idea. It'll solve our problem.
I have no idea what you are talking about.

to matter ▪ von Bedeutung sein
In this context your argument really matters a lot.

▸ **that doesn't matter** ▪ das macht nichts

to mean (meant [ment], meant [ment]) ▪ meinen
If she said so you can be sure that she means it.

nevertheless ▪ dennoch, trotzdem
Our problems are difficult. Nevertheless we must try to solve them.

not really ▪ eigentlich nicht
I do not really think that you are right.

opinion ▪ Meinung
It is my firm opinion that animals must not be treated cruelly.

opposition ▪ Gegensatz
The speaker was in clear opposition to the previous speaker.

perhaps [pə'hæps, præps] ▪ vielleicht
I still have my doubts but perhaps you are right.

▸ **to protest** ▪ potestieren
I must protest most strongly against your decision.

to reply ▪ antworten, erwidern
He always waits very long before replying to a letter.

sentence ▪ Satz
Speak in complete sentences if you wish to be understood.

speech ▪ Ansprache
He delivered a brilliant speech at his daughter's wedding.

standard ▪ üblich, Standard…
Scientific texts are usually written in standard English.

to state ▪ aussprechen; nennen
Could you, please, briefly state what you have in mind?
State your conditions.

subject ▪ Thema
The subject of his speech is "The health industry in Germany."

to suggest ▪ vorschlagen; andeuten
The speaker suggested dealing with the question of finance at a later stage.
Are you suggesting that there is no alternative to your thesis?

suggestion ▪ Vorschlag; Andeutung
At this point I would like to make a suggestion.
I reject any suggestion that our attitude might be wrong.

theme ▪ Thema
The theme of this conference is "The Health Industry".

therefore ▪ deshalb
I see we cannot reach an agreement now. Therefore I suggest meeting again later.

view ▪ Standpunkt
"In my view things were better in the past", said the old man.

word ▪ Wort
During the entire debate he did not say a single word.

angle ■ Blickwinkel
I would like to look into this subject from a different angle.

approval ■ Anerkennung, Zustimmnung
The speaker's lecture met with general approval.

to assert ■ behaupten
I do not quite agree with what my colleague has just asserted.

besides ■ außerdem, überdies
Besides, I'd like to say that I agree entirely with you.

to cite ■ zitieren
In all her speeches she likes to cite authorities.

to clarify ■ klarstellen
Before reacting to the other speeches the chairwoman clarified her position.

complexity ■ Komplexität, Vielschichtigkeit
Our teacher explains subjects of great complexity in a manner that we understand him.

controversial ■ umstritten, kontrovers
During the panel discussion quite a few controversial opinions were voiced.

controversy ■ Kontroverse
There is still a controversy among experts about the reasons for global warming.

to convince ■ überzeugen
The speaker managed to convince his audience of the truth of his statement.

to debate ■ debattieren
It was only after debating for hours that the committee reached an agreement.

to exaggerate ■ übertreiben
If you wish to convince your hearers you must not exaggerate.

framework ▪ Gerüst, Rahmen
Before beginning with my speech I would like to point out its general framework.

to hesitate ▪ zögern
Before answering a difficult question the minister tends to hesitate a little.

to highlight ▪ hervorheben
If you want this point to be clearly understood you must highlight it properly.

to hint at s.th. ▪ etwas andeuten
The speaker also hinted at the problem of putting into practice his idea.

illustration ▪ Erläuterung, Veranschaulichung
Let me give you an illustration of what I have in mind.

item ▪ Punkt
Let's proceed to the next item on the agenda.

to justify ▪ rechtfertigen
There is nothing to justify cruelty to animals.

moreover ▪ außerdem, überdies, zudem
This attitude is not moral. Moreover, it is against the law.

namely ▪ nämlich
There is only one thing that matters in a business, namely success.

notion ▪ Vorstellung, Begriff
I do share the notion that women and men have equal rights.

objection ▪ Einwand, Widerspruch
The opposition had no objection to the government's proposal.

oh dear! ▪ meine Güte!; oje!
Oh dear! You can't really mean it.

on the one hand … on the other hand ▪ einerseits … andererseits
On the one hand there is some truth in what you claim, on the other hand I disagree with some of your statements.

panel ▪ Gremium
The panel discussed the uses and misuses of medicine.

to pause ▪ eine (kurze) Pause machen
The speaker paused in order to stress the point he was going to make.

to persuade ▪ überreden; überzeugen
Against her long-held convictions he persuaded her to eat meat.
I am not persuaded that we need to change our strategy.

persuasion ▪ Überredung; Überzeugung
Advertising is called the gentle art of persuasion.
It is my persuasion that every human being has the same rights.

point of view ▪ Blickwinkel, Ansicht, Einstellung
From my point of view your approach is not acceptable.

to point out ▪ hinweisen auf
Let me point out the contradictions in your statement.

to reinforce ▪ untermauern, bestätigen
Recent events, I'm afraid, rather reinforce my position.

repetition ▪ Wiederholung
Make sure that there are not too many repetitions in your speech.

reply ▪ Antwort, Erwiderung
The company's reply to my question was less than satisfactory.

to stress ▪ betonen, hervorheben
The Education Secretary stressed the importance of a sound education.

topic ▪ Thema, Gegenstand
The topic of today's lecture is "Jane Austen's novels".

to underline ▪ betonen
The Minister underlined that his decision on the matter was final.

to voice ▪ zum Ausdruck bringen
She voiced her dissatisfaction in no uncertain terms.

to yell ▪ laut schreien
Some listeners yelled in protest against the speaker.

14.5 Bewertung, Widerspruch, Übereinstimmung

actual ▪ eigentlich, konkret, genau
Are you quite sure that those were his actual words? – Yes. That is what he said.

to admit ▪ zugeben
The speaker admitted that what he had said was not true.

to agree ▪ zustimmen, übereinstimmen
I couldn't have put it better myself. I agree with everything you have said.

agreement ▪ Übereinstimmung
I'm afraid we are not in agreement on this question.

bad (worse, worst) ▪ schlecht, schlimm
This is really a bad idea.
The weather is worse than ever.
This the worst essay I have ever read.

bloody ▪ verdammt
You're a bloody fool – that's what you are!

boring ▪ langweilig
We saw a very boring film on the weekend.

criticism ▪ Kritik
If there was one thing he didn't like it was criticism.

to decide ▪ (sich) entscheiden
The audience found it difficult to decide which of the two speakers was right.

decision ▪ Entscheidung
After a long discussion the parties at last reached a decision.

difficult ▪ schwierig
As a young person he was really difficult. He constantly got into trouble.

easy ▪ leicht
It's so easy. It's child's play.

fine ■ schön; glänzend; fein
At last the winter is over and we've got fine and warm weather.
That was a really fine performance.
She drew a fine line.

fortunately ■ glücklicherweise
Fortunately we still made it on time for the concert although our train was late.

good (better, best) ■ gut
She speaks very good English.
On our second meeting he made a better impression.
The best vacation we ever had was in Spain.

to grant ■ zugeben
Eric granted that Joan was right.

great ■ groß; toll, klasse
The Great Fire of London in 1666 destroyed a large part of the city.
Shakira's concert was really great.

interesting ■ interessant
Thank you very much – you have raised a very interesting question.

just ■ gerecht, berechtigt
The insurance company decided that Harry's claim was just.

logical ■ logisch
I'm afraid that what you're saying is not logical.

poor ■ armselig, schlecht
The students' performance in this test was rather poor.

right ■ richtig
Is London the capital of ther UK? – Yes, that's right.

▸ **you are right** ■ du hast recht

silly ■ albern, dumm
Kevin was known for his silly remarks.

slight ■ gering, leicht
There has been a slight improvement in the company's results.

substantial ▪ überzeugend
The speaker supported his theory by substantial arguments.

super ▪ super, klasse, spitze
That rock concert was really super!

ultimate ['ʌltəmət] ▪ beste(r, s), optimal, vollendet; umwerfend, unvergleichlich; letzte(r, s), ultimativ
Shakespeare is regarded by many as the ultimate dramatist.
Surfing is the ultimate experience.
Her ultimate goal was to become a professor.

very ▪ sehr
That is a very good proposal.

wrong [rɒŋ] ▪ falsch
I'm sorry to say that this is wrong.

▸ **you are wrong** ▪ du hast unrecht

---

acceptance ▪ Aufnahme, Akzeptanz
Hindemith's music did not enjoy wide acceptance.

to admire ▪ bewundern
Maria Callas was widely admired for her singing.

amazing ▪ erstaunlich, unglaublich
What Mozart achieved with his music is really amazing.

to appreciate s.o./s.th. ▪ jdn./etwas schätzen
Sartre was a widely appreciated philosopher.

astonishing ▪ erstaunlich, verblüffend
Glenn Gould's skill as a pianist was quite astonishing.

to attribute ▪ zuschreiben
He attributed the success of the project entirely to himself.

awful ▪ furchtbar, schrecklich
The effects of the hurricane were really awful.

brilliant ▪ großartig, brillant
Yes, that's the way we'll do it. That was a brilliant idea, Jack.

complex ['kɒmpleks] ■ komplex, kompliziert
This is rather a complex question. We certainly can't deal with it on the spot.

complicated ■ kompliziert
This problem is far too complicated for me to deal with.

to contradict ■ widersprechen
As a young boy I was quite stubborn. I always contradicted my father.

to criticise ■ kritisieren
He was severely criticised for his racist remarks.

crucial ■ entscheidend, äußerst wichtig
Next Thursday's meeting is crucial. So make sure that you can come.

cruel ■ grausam
It is cruel to make animals suffer.

curious ■ sonderbar
Look at that person over there. Doesn't he look very curious in that outfit?

to deserve ■ verdienen
She played so well that she really deserved to win.

to differ ■ verschiedener Meinung sein
Sorry, I beg to differ.

to disagree ■ nicht übereinstimmen; anderer Meinung sein
The management disagreed with the union's proposal to shorten working hours.
Sorry, but I disagree.

dramatic ■ einschneidend
Last year's heat wave had a very dramatic effect on farmers.

enormous ■ enorm, gewaltig
This year's floods have had enormous economic consequences.

evaluation ■ Schätzung, Einschätzung
After a careful evaluation of your performance we have decided to promote you.

extraordinary ■ außergewöhnlich
He was caught driving at an extraordinary speed.

extreme ■ äußerste(r, s), extrem
The temperature in Death Valley can be extreme.

flat ■ langweilig
The film was so flat that most people left the cinema before the end.

glory ■ Ruhm, Ehre; Pracht
Shakespeare's works are often regarded as the glory of English literature.
In spring you can admire the flowers in all their glory.

grand ■ prächtig, großartig
That was a grand performance. The artist played five extra pieces after the concert.

gross ■ grob, ekelhaft
Some of the comedian's jokes were rather gross – so we left the theatre.

harmful ■ schädlich
I think that any form of extremism is very harmful.

horrible ■ schrecklich
He killed his whole family? – What a horrible thing to do!

horror ■ Entsetzen, Grauen, Horror
The sight of the accident filled us with horror.

incredible ■ unglaublich
This factory produces an incredible amount of smoke.

to judge ■ beurteilen, einschätzen
The teacher had problems judging Christopher's performance properly.

marvellous ■ wunderbar, großartig
Yesterday's concert was really marvellous.

mysterious ■ geheimnisvoll, rätselhaft
What is going on in this company is rather mysterious.

nightmare ■ Alptraum

The team's performance was a real nightmare.

nonsense ■ Unsinn, Quatsch

I've never heard such nonsense in all my life.

notorious ■ berüchtigt

He regarded the previous speaker as a notorious liar.

offensive ■ anstößig

Liza did not like Tom because he always made offensive remarks.

outstanding ■ hervorragend

The Chancellor's speech was outstanding.

to question ■ bezweifeln

I question the truth of your statement.

respectable ■ respektabel, gut

As far as I am concerned this was a very respectable achievement.

sensation ■ Sensation

The singer's performance was quite a sensation.

sensational ■ sensationell, spektakulär

The young athlete's performance was really sensational.

singular ■ einzigartig

The artist's performance was really singular.

so-called ■ so genannt

So-called experts give you a lot of useless advice.

splendid ■ wunderbar, glänzend

That was a splendid performance.

standing ■ Status, Ansehen, Ruf

Sir Simon Rattle is a conductor of the highest standing.

stunning ■ toll, fantastisch

Germany achieved a stunning World Cup victory over Brazil.

Such is life! ■ So ist das Leben!

Such is life! We must take things the way they come.

to suit [su:t, sju:t] ■ stehen; gefallen
Oh, how lovely. That black dress really suits you.
The warm and dry climate in southern Spain suits me.

superb [sju:'pɜ:b] ■ vorzüglich, ausgezeichnet, hervorragend
The food in this restaurant is indeed superb.

superficial ■ oberflächlich
This book on twentieth century wars is really superficial.

terrible ■ furchtbar, schrecklich
There was a terrible thunderstorm in our area last night.

terrific ■ großartig, fantastisch
I think our team's performance was terrific.

unacceptable ■ inakzeptabel, nicht tragbar
Smoking while other people are eating is completely unacceptable.

unbelievable ■ unglaublich
The artist's performance was simply unbelievable.

to undermine ■ untergraben
Don't try to undermine my authority.

undoubtedly ■ zweifellos
Paul is undoubtedly very clever, but he could be more modest about it.

unfortunately ■ unglücklicherweise, leider
We missed our plane because unfortunately our train was late.

unique [ju:'ni:k] ■ einzigartig
Albert Einstein was a unique scientist.

well-done ■ gut gemacht
Well-done, young lady. That was excellent.

14.6 Schriftliche Äußerungen, Briefe, Dokumente

to address ■ adressieren
Don't forget to address the letter properly.

address ▪ Adresse, Anschrift
Please put your address on the back of the envelope.

to attach ▪ beilegen
Please study the attached document carefully.

to concern ▪ betreffen
Letters sometimes begin with the expression, "To whom it may concern".

to confirm ▪ bestätigen
This is to confirm that the product has arrived.

dash ▪ Gedankenstrich
A dash separates two closely related parts of a sentence: "Speak more loudly – I can't hear you".

full stop (AE: period) ▪ Punkt
Make sure that you put a full stop at the end of a sentence.

to include ▪ beifügen
We have included a confirmation of your booking with this letter.

ink ▪ Tinte
Our printer has run out of ink.

inquiry ▪ Erkundigung, Anfrage
We have received your inquiry of 5 January 2014.

letter ▪ Buchstabe
I can't read this. It is written in Greek letters.

Madam ▪ meine Dame, gnädige Frau
Dear Sir/Madam, I am writing about my enquiry of 5 November.

Miss ▪ Fräulein
The address "Miss" is just as little used as "Fräulein" in Germany.

Mr ▪ Herr
On letters you use the abbreviation "Mr" for "Mister".

Mrs ▪ (verheiratete) Frau
... and Mrs, i.e. "Mistress", for a married woman.

Ms ▪ Frau
The abbreviation Ms refers to any woman – whether married or not.

note ▪ Notiz, Mitteilung, Nachricht
The boss left a note on her secretary's desk.
Please give me a note when the item is available again.

paper ▪ Papier
Do you want to write something? – I'll give you some paper.

period (AE) ▪ Punkt
Where the English use the term "full stop", Americans say "period".

to receive ▪ erhalten, empfangen
We have received your order for fifty shirts (order number 246/135).

to refer [rɪˈfɜː] (referred; referring) ▪ sich beziehen
I refer to your letter of 26 October.

reference [ˈrefərəns] ▪ Aktenzeichen
In replying to our letter please quote our reference.

to sign ▪ unterzeichnen, unterschreiben
The two presidents signed the peace agreement.

Sir ▪ Herr
"Dear Sir" is used when you don't know the addressee's name.

text ▪ Text
Immanuel Kant's texts are notoriously difficult to understand.

to write ▪ schreiben
Although she was only five she was already able to write.

written ▪ geschrieben
What counts is your written word.

---

abbreviation ▪ Abkürzung, Kürzel
"PDF" is an abbreviation for "Portable Document Format"

bracket ▪ Klammer
Extra information is often put in brackets.

c/o ▪ z. Hd., zu Händen
If you wish to reach a specific addressee in a company you may use c/o (care of) before the person's name.

colon ▪ Doppelpunkt
You usually put a colon before explanations, quotations, and lists.

comma ▪ Komma
In English commas are not used quite as often as in German.

complaint ▪ Beschwerde, Klage
Mary wrote a letter of complaint to the hotel manager because of the noise.

to complete ▪ vervollständigen, ausfüllen
You need to complete this form before we can deal with your complaint.

to correspond ▪ in Briefverkehr stehen
Even if you are on holiday you can still correspond with the company.

e.g. ▪ zum Beispiel
"e.g." is derived from Latin "exempli gratia", which means "for instance".

etc. (Lat.: et cetera) ▪ usw., und so weiter
In our library you will find detective stories, novels, dictionaries, etc.

example ▪ Beispiel; Muster
Let me give you an example of how to write an official letter.
This is a classic example of a well written business letter.

▸ for example ▪ zum Beispiel
He listed a number of related topics – for example home trade and foreign trade.

exclamation mark ▪ Ausrufungszeichen
The exclamation mark is used to express anger or surprise.

format ▪ Format
Letters of application must be written in a good format to be successful.

i.e. ▪ d. h.
"i.e." is derived from Latin "id est", which means "that is".

to insert ▪ einfügen

Anything that is not of vital importance should be inserted in brackets.

instance ▪ Beispiel, Fall

They found many instances of corruption in his official documents.

▸ for instance ▪ etwa, zum Beispiel

We ought to invite a key speaker, for instance the headmaster.

journal ▪ Tagebuch

My mother-in-law has been keeping a journal for the past sixty years.

layout ▪ Layout

Her boss had quite clear ideas concerning the layout of official letters.

leaflet ▪ Broschüre, Prospekt; Flugblatt

For more information please refer to the instruction leaflet.
Before the election the party members handed out leaflets in public places.

notebook ▪ Notizbuch

He always had a notebook and a pen in his coat.

on behalf of ▪ im Namen von

I am writing this letter on behalf of Mr Myers.

paragraph ▪ Absatz

Texts should have enough paragraphs. They help readers to read the text.

pen ▪ Füller, Tintenstift

A pen is still often used to write a letter to a friend.

pencil ▪ Bleistift

Use a pencil for drawing lines and for making notes.

phrase ▪ Satz

In order to keep your text clear you should avoid long phrases.

plain ▪ klar

Official letters ought to be written in a plain style everyone can understand.

to print ■ in Druckschrift schreiben
Please print your name under the signature.

print ■ Druckschrift
Liz wrote all her essays in print.

prompt ■ umgehend
We would be grateful for a prompt reply to our enquiry.

question mark ■ Fragezeichen
Don't forget to put a question mark after a question.

receipt [rɪ'siːt] ■ Eingang, Erhalt
Herewith we confirm the receipt of your letter of 25 June.

recommendation ■ Empfehlung
Sybil's boss gave her a letter of recommendation when she left the company.

regarding ■ in Bezug auf, bezüglich
My boss wrote a letter regarding his business partner's strange attitude.

semicolon ■ Semikolon
Semicolons are used more in English than in German.

signature ■ Unterschrift
Without a signature a document is usually not valid.

Sincerely yours ■ Mit freundlichen Grüßen
A formal letter to someone you know and address by name is usually concluded by "Sincerely yours" or "Yours sincerely".

stroke ■ (Schräg-)Strich
The abbreviation c/o can be read as "c stroke o".

to underline ■ unterstreichen
Jennifer underlines every word she thinks is important.

Yours faithfully ■ Hochachtungsvoll
Letters beginning with "Dear Madam/Sir" are concluded with "Yours faithfully".

Yours sincerely ■ Mit freundlichen Grüßen
In other cases you can use "Yours sincerely".

15. Mengen und Maße, Zahlen

15.1 Mengen und Maße

additional ▪ zusätzlich
Any additional baggage must be paid for.

all ▪ alle, alles; ganz
All human beings should enjoy the same human rights.
That's all for today.
His face was all red.

almost ▪ beinahe, fast
This barrel holds almost 150 litres.

any ▪ ein(e, er, es); welch(e, er, es); jede(r, s); etwas
This is a very difficult question. I wonder if any of you can answer it.
Are any of the books here for sale?
Which apple can I take? Take any you like.
There's not a lot left, but still – would you like any more?

at least ▪ mindestens, wenigstens
He earns at least €50,000 a year.

bit ▪ Stück; Teil
There's still a bit left of the cake.
The cup fell on the floor and there were bits of china everywhere.

▸ **a bit** ▪ ein bisschen
There's still a bit left of the cake.

centimetre ▪ Zentimeter
A centimetre is about two fifths of an inch.

to contain ▪ enthalten
This bottle contains 0.75 litres of wine.

content ['kɒntent] ▪ Rauminhalt
The content of this barrel is 1.5 cubic metres.

degree ■ Maß, Grad
In Death Valley temperatures can easily reach 50 degrees Celsius.

double ■ doppelt
This recipe is for four. For eight, use double the amount.

empty ['empti] ■ leer
It doesn't matter whether a glass is half full or half empty.

enough [ɪ'nʌf] ■ genug, genügend
There is not enough beer in this glass. Fill it up, please.

entire ■ gesamt, ganz, vollständig
Just look at that! The dog has eaten the entire cake.

extent [ɪk'stent] ■ Ausdehnung, Grad
The extent of the damage caused by the flood is not clear yet.

extra ■ extra, übrig
I have a couple of apples extra. You can have them.

Fahrenheit ■ Fahrenheit
32 degrees Fahrenheit are zero degrees Celsius.

few ■ wenige
Only few candidates managed to solve the problem.

▸ **a few** ■ ein paar
There are a few things I would like to discuss with you.

foot (Pl.: feet) ■ Fuß (30,48 cm)
There are twelve inches in a foot.

full ■ voll, gefüllt
He always made sure that all his guests had full glasses.

gram(me) ■ Gramm
For this dish we need 250 grams of butter.

half [hɑːf] ■ halbe(r, s)
500 grammes are half a kilogramme.

half [hɑːf] (Pl.: halves [hɑːvz]) ■ Hälfte
There were two world wars in the first half of the 20th century.

hardly ▪ kaum

When the guests had finished eating there was hardly anything left of the food.

inch ▪ Inch (2,45 cm), Zoll

There are twelve inches in a foot, and 3 feet in a yard.

lack ▪ Mangel

The boss complained about the lack of good workers in his company.

length ▪ Länge

The length of a tennis court is exactly 78 feet, i.e. 23.79 metres.

to limit ▪ begrenzen, einschränken

The number of visitors admitted is limited to twenty.

litre ▪ Liter

In Britain, a litre is the equivalent of 1.76 pints.

long ▪ lang

Five years are a long time and forty kilometres are a long distance.

lot ▪ Menge, Masse

5 million euros are rather a lot of money.

▸ **a lot** ▪ viel

Jamie always talks a lot.

▸ **a lot of** ▪ viele

A lot of people had the flu last winter.

many (more, most) ▪ viele

Maria Theresia had many children – sixteen in fact.

to measure ['meʒə] ▪ messen

He measured the distance from our house to that of our neighbours.

measure ['meʒə] ▪ Maß

The bridegroom had his suit made to measure.

metre ▪ Meter

A metre has three feet and 3.4 inches.

mile ▪ Meile

A mile has 1609 metres.

much (more, most) ■ viel
We don't have much money. I wish we had more but what I value most is to have a happy life.

nearly ■ fast, beinahe
The glass is nearly empty.

no ■ kein(e, r, s)
There is strictly no admission before the interval.

▸ **no way!** ■ ausgeschlossen!, auf keinen Fall!
No way, you can't get in here.

none ■ keine(r, s)
I'm afraid I found none of the items on the list.

only ■ nur
At the end of every month we usually have only little money left.

part ■ Teil
That is, I'm afraid, only part of the story.

partly ■ teilweise
My glass is only partly full. Can you fill it up please?

piece ■ Stück, Teil
Would you like another piece of cake?

proportion ■ Anteil; Verhältnis
The proportion of people in employment must increase.
The proportion of female to male students should be 1 to 1.

quarter ■ Viertel; Quartal, Vierteljahr
The train leaves at a quarter past nine, i.e. at 9.15.
First quarter profits were up by ten per cent compared to the same period last year.

to reduce ■ verringern; verkleinern
The manager announced that the club would have to reduce its team.
The room was too small for the large photograph. So it had to be reduced.

rest ■ Rest, Übriges
You can have the rest of what is in the pot if you like.

scale ▪ Maßstab; Skala; Ausmaß

On a one-inch map the scale is one inch per mile, i.e. approximately 1:64,000.

This instrument has a metric scale.

The scale of our losses has taken us by surprise.

scales (Pl.) ▪ Waage

The scales clearly showed that I had not lost any weight.

set ▪ Satz

Cups and saucers are usually sold as sets.

several ▪ einige, verschiedene

A lot of men have several suits.

single ▪ einzige(r, s); einzelne(r, s); einstellig

She did not speak one single word all evening.

Smoking is the single most important cause of cancer.

The failure rate in this test is down to single figures.

some ▪ einige; etwas

Could you buy some potatoes for this dish, please?

Could I please have some more of the pudding?

something ▪ etwas

I'm sure there's something to eat in the fridge.

stone ▪ Stone (Gewicht)

A stone is equal to 14 pounds, i.e. 14 times 453.59 grammes or 6.35 kilogrammes.

substantial ▪ bedeutend; beträchtlich

The company paid a substantial amount to take over one of its rivals.

When we moved in we had to carry out substantial renovations.

sufficient ▪ ausreichend, genügend

We must make sure that there is sufficient food for everyone.

total ▪ Gesamtsumme; gesamt

You owe us a total of £455.50.

Total sales this year reached a record high.

up to ▪ bis zu
This bucket will hold up to three gallons.

various ▪ verschiedene
There are various types of flour.

volume ▪ Volumen; Umfang; Lautstärke
The volume of this container is 5 gallons.
The volume of traffic on a Friday afternoon is incredible.
Please turn down the volume.

whole [həʊl] ▪ ganz
I don't believe it. He ate the whole plate of pasta himself.

yard ▪ Yard
A yard has thirty-six inches, i.e. 91.5 cm.

---

accurate ['ækjərət] ▪ genau
It is not enough to send us an estimate. What we need is the accurate figure.

acre ▪ Acre (0,405 Hektar)
An acre is about half as large as a football field.

altogether ▪ insgesamt
There are altogether fifteen people in this group.

amount ▪ Betrag, Menge
$ 500,000 is rather a large amount.

approximate [ə'prɒksəmət] ▪ ungefähr
The approximate content of this bottle is 1.5 litres.

average ▪ Durchschnitt; durchschnittlich
People in our company earn $ 45,000 on average.
The average German drinks about 100 litres of beer per year.

barely ▪ kaum
Many of the refugees speak barely any English when they arrive.

bunch ▪ Bündel, Strauß; Haufen, Menge
You can bring a bunch of grapes or a bunch of flowers.
There were a bunch of mothers waiting outside the schoolyard.

complete ■ vollständig, komplett
The participants are now complete.

to constitute ■ ausmachen
Women constitute more than fifty per cent of the population.

density ■ Dichte
The population density in the Netherlands is very high.

equivalent [ɪ'kwɪvələnt] ■ gleichwertig, entsprechend
An English pound is equivalent to 453.59 grammes.

fraction ■ Bruch, Bruchteil
In poor countries people earn only a fraction of what they need.

gallon ■ Gallone
In the UK a gallon has 4.546 litres, an American gallon has 3.785 litres.

kilogram(me) ■ Kilogramm
There are about 2 pounds and 3 ounces in a kilogram(me).

kilometre ■ Kilometer
There are approximately 1094 yards in a kilometre.

to lack ■ fehlen; nicht haben
Unfortunately we lack the money to buy a new car.

little (less, least) ■ wenig
There was little water left in his glass, less in mine and least in John's.

lump ■ Klumpen
Melt a lump of butter in the pan.

mass ■ Masse
Mix the ingredients and put the mass into a large pot.

maximum ■ Maximum
The maximum speed of this car is 110 mph.

measurement ■ Maß; Messung
The dressmaker took the lady's measurement before making her wedding dress.
The measurement of a little child's temperature can be difficult.

milligram(me) ▪ Milligramm
A milligramme is the thousandth part of a gramme.

millimetre ▪ Millimeter
A millimetre is the thousandth part of a metre.

minimum ▪ Minimum; Mindest…
Ten correct answers out of twenty are the minimum you must achieve.
The minimum amount to be paid in is $ 50.

minority ▪ Minderheit
An increasing number of fathers look after their children while the mothers pursue their careers.

moderate ['mɒdərət] ▪ mittlere(r, s), gemäßigt
As a clerk you cannot expect to enjoy more than a moderate income.
The climate in the UK is mostly moderate.

numerous ▪ zahlreich
Despite trying numerous diets he did not lose any weight.

ounce ▪ Unze
A pound has 16 ounces, i.e. 16 times 28 grammes (or 453.59 grammes).

particle ▪ Teilchen, Partikel
There were tiny particles of dust everywhere.

per cent (AE: percent) ▪ Prozent
5 per cent of 250 is 12.5.

percent (AE) ▪ Prozent
"Percent" is the American spelling of "per cent".

percentage ▪ Prozentsatz
The percentage of Germans who cannot read or write is approximately 4 per cent.

pile ▪ Haufen, Stapel
You'll find your book on top of the pile of books in my study.

pint [paɪnt] ▪ Pint
A UK pint has 0.568 litres, the American pint has 0.473 litres.

plenty ■ reichlich, viel
There was plenty of food and drink at the party.

pound ■ Pfund
A pound has 16 ounces, i.e. 453.59 grammes.

quantity ■ Menge, Quantität
Please advise us whether the required quantity of the article ordered is available.

reserve ■ Reserve
We'd better stop eating so much. Our reserves are running low.

roughly ■ ungefähr, grob geschätzt
Mary thinks that the bucket holds roughly five gallons.

somewhat ■ etwas, ein wenig
It's somewhat warmer today than yesterday.

spare ■ übrig
We have a spare room for the occasional guest.

surplus ■ Überschuss; überschüssig
We achieved a moderate surplus last month.
We still have some surplus funds available.

ton ■ Tonne
In Britain a ton has 2,240 pounds, i.e. 1,016 kilograms, in the USA 2,000 pounds.

tonne ■ Tonne
A tonne has 1,000 kg.

vast ■ riesig
In order to improve our situation we require vast amounts of money.

wealth [welθ] ■ Fülle
There is a wealth of useful material on this subject.

to weigh ■ wiegen
When Herbert was young he weighed only 12 stones, i.e. 76 kilogrammes ...

weight ■ Gewicht
... and now he is always trying to lose weight.

15.2 Zahlen und Arithmetik

zero ['zɪərəʊ] ■ Null
The number 1,000 has three zeros.

▸ bei Telefonnummern, Kontonummern usw.: O [əʊ]
James Bond is agent number 007, pronounced "double oh – seven".

one ■ eins

first ■ erste(r, s)

▸ **first of all** ■ zuerst, als allererstes
Before we start something new, first of all we need to get our finances in order.

two ■ zwei

second ■ zweite(r, s)

three ■ drei

third ■ dritte(r, s)

four ■ vier

fourth ■ vierte(r, s)

five ■ fünf

fifth ⚠ ■ fünfte(r, s)

six ■ sechs

sixth ■ sechste(r, s)

seven ■ sieben

seventh ■ siebte(r, s)

eight ■ acht

eighth ■ achte(r, s)

nine ■ neun

ninth [naɪnθ] ■ neunte(r, s)

ten ■ zehn

tenth ■ zehnte(r, s)

eleven ■ elf, Elf

eleventh ▪ elfte(r, s)

twelve ▪ zwölf

twelfth ⚠ ▪ zwölfte(r, s)

thirteen ▪ dreizehn

thirteenth ▪ dreizehnte(r, s)

fourteen ▪ vierzehn

fourteenth ▪ vierzehnte(r, s)

fifteen ▪ fünfzehn

fifteenth ▪ fünfzehnte(r, s)

sixteen ▪ sechzehn

sixteenth ▪ sechzehnte(r, s)

seventeen ▪ siebzehn

seventeenth ▪ siebzehnte(r, s)

eighteen ▪ achtzehn

eighteenth ▪ achtzehnte(r, s)

nineteen ▪ neunzehn

nineteenth ▪ neunzehnte(r, s)

twenty ▪ zwanzig

twentieth ▪ zwanzigste(r, s)

twenty-one ▪ einundzwanzig

twenty-first ▪ einundzwanzigste(r, s)

thirty ▪ dreißig

thirtieth ⚠ ▪ dreißigste(r, s)

forty ▪ vierzig

fortieth ▪ vierzigste(r, s)

fifty ▪ fünfzig

fiftieth ▪ fünfzigste(r, s)

sixty ▪ sechzig

sixtieth ▪ sechzigste(r, s)

seventy ■ siebzig
seventieth ■ siebzigste(r, s)
eighty ■ achtzig
eightieth ■ achtzigste(r, s)
ninety ■ neunzig
ninetieth ■ neunzigste(r, s)
hundred ■ hundert
hundredth ■ hundertste(r, s)
two hundred ■ zweihundert
two hundreth ■ zweihundertste(r, s)
thousand ■ tausend
thousandth ■ tausendste(r, s)
million ■ Million
billion ■ ⚠ Milliarde
A billion is a thousand million, i.e. 1,000,000,000.

---

to add ■ addieren; hinzufügen
If you add 2 and 2 the result is 4 and if you add another 2 the result is 6.
Let me add that I am very convinced we will reach our aim.

addition ■ Addition; Hinzufügung
4805 plus 6838 is 11,643. The addition is correct.
This yoghurt is produced without the addition of artificial colouring.

▸ **in addition to** ■ zusätzlich, darüber hinaus
Could you also buy some wine in addition to bread and cheese?

to divide ■ dividieren
If you divide one foot by twelve the result is one inch.

figure ■ Zahl
Henry was not very good at figures.

firstly ■ erstens

Firstly you are late and secondly you are wrong.

minus ■ minus, weniger

Five minus three is two.

number (Abk.: No.) ■ Zahl; Nummer

Three is my lucky number.

Their room number is 431.

▸ **a number of ...** ■ einige, ein paar, eine Reihe von

plus ■ plus, und

Five plus five is ten.

point ■ Punkt

The figure 1.5 is read as one-point-five.

▸ **That's the point!** ■ Darum geht's!

product ■ Produkt

Sixteen is the product of four times four.

secondly ■ zweitens

Firstly it's very cold and secondly it's wet.

sum ■ Summe

The sum of seven and four is eleven.

---

to deduct ■ abziehen

If you deduct five from eleven the result is six.

digit ■ Ziffer

One hundred is a figure with three digits.

dozen ['dʌzən] ■ Dutzend

The group consisted of a dozen members.

even ■ gerade

Numbers which can be divided by 2 are even numbers.

multiple ■ Vielfaches

18 is a multiple of 2, 3, 6, and 9.

to multiply ■ multiplizieren

If you multiply five by six the result is thirty.

nought ▪ Null

The figure 0.5 is read "nought point five" or simply "point five".

odd ▪ ungerade

1, 3, 5 etc. are odd numbers.

ratio ▪ Verhältnis

The ratio between girls and boys in our class is 5 to 3.

to reckon ▪ schätzen; berechnen

I didn't really count the guests at the party. I reckon there were fifty of them.

Experts reckon the rate of economic growth next year to be 2.5 per cent.

to subtract ▪ subtrahieren

If you subtract five from ten the result is five.

16. Zeit und Raum, Farben und Formen

16.1 Zeit, Termine

Wochentage

Monday ■ Montag
▸ **on Monday** ■ am Montag
▸ **on Mondays** ■ montags
Tuesday ■ Dienstag
Wednesday ['wenzdi] ■ Mittwoch
Thursday ■ Donnerstag
Friday ■ Freitag
Saturday ['sætədi] ■ Samstag, Sonnabend
Sunday ■ Sonntag

Monate

January ■ Januar
▸ **on 20 January** ■ am 20. Januar
▸ **the month of January** ■ der Monat Januar
February ■ Februar
March ■ März
April ■ April
May ■ Mai
June ■ Juni
July ■ Juli
August ■ August

September ▪ September
October ▪ Oktober
November ▪ November
December ▪ Dezember

Jahreszeiten

spring ▪ Frühling
Spring was rather cold and wet this year.
summer ▪ Sommer
Summer is my favourite season.
autumn ['ɔːtəm] (AE: fall) ▪ Herbst
Autumn, also called fall in the USA, begins on 22 September.
fall (AE; BE: autumn) ▪ Herbst
Fall in New England can be beautiful.
winter ▪ Winter
Last year's winter was very mild.

---

a.m. ▪ morgens
"a.m." is derived from Latin "ante meridiem", which means "before midday".
afternoon ▪ Nachmittag
The weather was so good that we went for a walk in the afternoon.
age ▪ Zeitalter
The Elizabethan age is sometimes also called the Shakespearean age.
ago ▪ vor; (lange) her
Elephants do not forget anything, even if it happened many years ago.
That was long ago.
already [ɔːl'redi] ▪ schon, bereits
In winter it is getting dark already at 5 p.m.

always ['ɔːlwəz, 'ɔːlweɪz] ▪ immer; ständig
In the past trains used to be always on time.
He's terrible. He's always talking!

ancient ['eɪnʃənt] ▪ alt, antik
Mary knows a lot about ancient history. She's published books on ancient Rome.

annual ▪ jährlich
Our annual meeting is always on the first Monday in March.

appointment ▪ Verabredung, Termin
I'm sorry I can't come, I have an appointment with my doctor.

at once ▪ sofort
Don't do it some time. Do it at once.

back ▪ zurück
We can never turn the clocks back.

before ▪ zuvor
I've never seen that before.

to begin (began, begun) ▪ anfangen, beginnen
University courses usually begin at 9 a.m.

beginning ▪ Anfang, Beginn
At the beginning of his career he worked as an actor at a small theatre.

brief ▪ kurz
Could you take a brief look at this document?
A minute is a brief period of time.

by ▪ bis
The essay has to be handed in by Monday.

century ▪ Jahrhundert
In the twentieth century mankind experienced two world wars.

constant ▪ (an)dauernd
The constant noise from the air condition disturbed us very much.

daily ■ täglich
Many young people nowadays do not read a daily newspaper any longer.

date ■ Datum
The date of Christmas Day is 25 December.

dawn ■ Morgendämmerung
In Summer, the time span between dawn and dusk is almost 17 hours.

day ■ Tag
A year usually has 365 days.

decade ['dekeɪd] ■ Jahrzehnt
In recent decades the internet has become extremely important.

during ■ während
Millions of people died during WWII.

dusk ■ (Abend-)Dämmerung
There is daylight from dawn to dusk.

early ['ɜːli] ■ früh, frühzeitig
If you wish to see the sun rise, you must get up very early.

end ■ Ende, Schluss
At the end of this programme we'll go to bed.

evening ■ Abend
In our country it only gets dark after ten in the evening in June.

eventually ■ schließlich, endlich
After being awaited for two hours his friend turned up eventually.

ever ■ immer, schon mal
Have you ever been to America? – Yes, twice, and I liked it very much.

for ■ für; seit
This present is for you.
I've been waiting for hours.

forever ■ auf ewig, immer
I will love you forever.

former ■ ehemalig, früher

In former times many countries were governed by a king or queen.

fortnight ■ vierzehn Tage, zwei Wochen

This year we're going on holiday to Switzerland for a fortnight.

future ■ Zukunft; zukünftig

We don't know what the future will bring. Our future situation may be better – or worse.

hour ['aʊə] ■ Stunde

An hour has sixty minutes.

immediate [ɪ'miːdiət] ■ unmittelbar

We thank you very much for your immediate reply to our enquiry.

initial ■ anfänglich, erste(r, s)

After I had recovered from my initial shock I knew what to do.

just ■ gleich; gerade

Wait a minute. I'm just coming.

I was just going to leave when Mary rang.

to last ■ dauern

Classes at German universities usually last 90 minutes.

last ■ letzte(r, s)

Christmas is the last holiday in the year.

late ■ spät

Late in the afternoon it began to rain heavily.

▸ **don't be late** ■ komm(t) nicht zu spät

length ■ Dauer

Tom played loud music for the length of two hours in the middle of the night.

midday ■ Mittag

We usually have our main meal at midday.

midnight ■ Mitternacht

The party went on till late after midnight.

minute ['mɪnɪt] ■ Minute

The train is due to arrive at five minutes past eleven.

moment ■ Moment, Augenblick
We got into our car and a moment later it began to rain.

month ■ Monat
Next month we will go to Italy.

morning ■ Morgen
I hate getting up in the morning.

never ■ nie
I've never seen anything like this before.

New Year ■ Neujahr
Happy New Year everyone.

next ■ nächste(r,s)
Next year we're going to Florida for a holiday.

night ■ Nacht
It's March now and nights are getting shorter.

no longer, not any longer ■ nicht mehr
I can't be bothered to care any longer. I've too often tried to help them.

noon ■ Mittag
Our shop is open on Sundays from 9 until noon.

now ■ jetzt, nun
We've worked all day. It's time for a break now.

only ■ erst
He's only 20, so he isn't allowed to buy alcoholic drinks in the USA.

p.m. ■ nach 12 Uhr mittags
We usually have lunch at 1 p.m., which means "post meridiem".

past ■ frühere(r, s); Vergangenheit; nach
All the past presidents of the country are buried in this church.
In the past we used to eat much more meat than today.
It is five minutes past ten.

pause ■ Pause
There was a brief pause before the next speaker began his speech.

period ▪ Zeitspanne
Generally the weather is going to be dull with a few sunny periods in the North.

phase ▪ Phase, Abschnitt
After failing his exam he went through a difficult phase.

present ▪ gegenwärtig; Präsens
It will take some time to solve our present problems.
Stories are usally told in the past, not in the present.

previous ▪ vorig, vorherig
They were still recovering from the effects of the party on the previous evening.

prospect ▪ Aussicht; Wahrscheinlichkeit
The prospect for good weather on the weekend is quite good.
The prospects for a recovery in the near future are rather poor.

recent ▪ kürzlich; neueste(r, s), jüngste(r, s)
This is a photo I took on a recent trip to Malta.

to remain ▪ (ver)bleiben
The weather will remain cold and windy in the next few days.

second ▪ Sekunde
A minute has sixty seconds.

short ▪ kurz
Fortunately the meeting was quite short.

since ▪ seitdem; seit
I moved from Munich to Cologne in 2010 and haven't returned since.
Eric has been in retirement since 2015.

sometimes ▪ manchmal
Henry sometimes wondered what he was doing before he met Catherine.

soon ▪ bald; früh
I'm sure the situation will soon improve.
Can't you come on Sunday? Thursday is too soon for us.

start ■ Anfang
We missed the bus and were late for the start of the concert.

still ■ noch
Ron was still working when it was getting dark.

subsequent ■ anschließend, später
Subsequent events showed that the general's fears were right.

to succeed ■ nachfolgen
Barack Obama succeeded George W. Bush.

sudden (Adj.) ■ plötzlich, jäh
Unfortunately there was a sudden change in the weather.

suddenly (Adv.) ■ plötzlich
Suddenly the door flew open and Mr X entered the room.

sunrise ■ Sonnenaufgang
Farmers often have to start working before sunrise.

sunset ■ Sonnenuntergang
... and sometimes they do not stop before sunset.

sunshine ■ Sonnenschein
You can have more than sixteen hours of sunshine at the beginning of summer.

then ■ dann
First I'll take a shower and then I'll clean my teeth.

throughout ■ während
He was sick throughout the entire month of February.

till (= until) ■ bis
I'll give you exactly till Friday to do this job.

time ■ Zeit; (erstes usw.) Mal
There is a time for everything under heaven, an old book says.
Tony saw his old friend for the first time after twenty years.

▸ **in time** ■ rechtzeitig
We arrived just in time.

▸ **Once upon a time ...** ■ Es war einmal ...
Many folk tales begin with the words, "Once upon a time".

▸ **to tell the time** ▪ sagen, wie spät es ist
Excuse me, can you tell me the time?

today ▪ heute
"Today" is the title of a widely read newspaper in the USA.

tomorrow ▪ morgen
Don't do tomorrow what you can do today.

tonight ▪ heute Abend
Would you like to come for dinner tonight?

towards [tə'wɔːdz, AE: tɔːrdz] ▪ gegen
The party will be over towards midnight.

until ▪ bis
The weather will remain cold and wet until Friday.

upon ▪ bei
Upon arrival at the airport you will be met by our representative.

to wait ▪ warten
At last you're here! I've been waiting for you since 2 p.m.

week ▪ Woche
Last week we were very busy and this week isn't any better.

weekend ▪ Wochenende
That is why we are looking forward to the weekend.

when ▪ wann; als; wenn
When will you be coming to visit us?
I was very small when I was young.
You can go when the lights turn green.

while ▪ Weile
Can you wait a while, please? I won't be long.

will ▪ werden
You will find additional information on the internet.

year ▪ Jahr
There are twelve months in a year.

yesterday ▪ gestern
Yesterday was 4 November 2014.

yet ▪ schon; bis jetzt, noch
Is it time to go to bed yet?
She hasn't come yet.

afterwards ▪ danach, später
Henry had to be taken to hospital but recovered soon afterwards.

to age ▪ altern, älter werden
I'm afraid Henry has aged considerably in the past couple of months.

at present ▪ gegenwärtig
We can't deliver this product at present, because it is out of stock.

to await ▪ erwarten
We have eagerly awaited this meeting.

BC (Before Christ) ▪ v. Chr., vor Christus
Rome was founded in 753 BC.

by now ▪ inzwischen, mittlerweile
You should know by now that crime doesn't pay.

calendar ▪ Kalender
Check the 2018 calendar to find on which day your birthday falls that year.

to cease ▪ aufhören, enden
During the wet season it hardly ever ceases raining in India.

chronological ▪ chronologisch
In the chronological order of the months of the year January is the first.

consistent ▪ (be)ständig
The weather was terrible yesterday. It was cold, windy and there was a consistent drizzle.

constant ▪ dauernd, konstant
There was a constant drizzle all afternoon.

contemporary ■ zeitgenössisch
Some people say that contemporary classical music can be disturbing.

era ■ Ära, Zeitalter
The Victorian era in the UK is the time between 1837 and 1901.

finally ■ schießlich, zuletzt
The expedition were relieved when finally they saw the light.

interval ■ Abstand
The explosions took place at an interval of only five minutes.

lately ■ kürzlich, in letzter Zeit
There hasn't been much rain lately.

latter ■ spätere(r, s)
There are going to be thunderstorms in the latter part of the day.

meanwhile ■ inzwischen, unterdessen
Allow the soup to boil for ten minutes. Meanwhile prepare the salad.

medieval [medi'iːvəl] ■ mittelalterlich
Many cathedrals in Britain were built in medieval times.

Middle Ages ■ Mittelalter
The Middle Ages ended between the fourteenth and the sixteenth centuries.

millennium ■ Jahrtausend
The third millennium began on 1 January 2001.

nowadays ■ heutzutage
Nowadays many couples live together without being married.

permanent ■ dauerhaft, permanent
I've never had a permanent job so far.

to predict ■ vorhersagen
There are people who believe they can predict the future.

primitive ■ frühzeitlich
In primitive societies trade was first conducted by barter.

prior to ■ vor, bevor
All bills must be paid prior to departure.

recently ■ kürzlich, neulich, vor Kurzem; in letzter Zeit
I had a medical check-up recently.
I haven't been feeling well recently.

simultaneous ■ gleichzeitig, simultan
Lightning and thunder occurred almost simultaneously.

temporary ■ vorübergehend, befristet
After being unemployed for a while he had to put up with a temporary job.

timing ■ Timing, Wahl des richtigen Zeitpunkts
Paul's timing is remarkable. He is never late for an appointment.

Victorian ■ viktorianisch
The Victorian age takes its name from Queen Victoria, who ruled from 1837 to 1901.

weekly ■ wöchentlich
There has been a weekly improvement in our situation.

whenever ■ wann auch immer, sobald, jedesmal wenn
Our dog begins to bark whenever someone knocks on the door.

16.2 Häufigkeit, Dauer

again ■ wieder, noch einmal
Sorry, can you say that again?

common ■ üblich, gewöhnlich
Rain is common on the British west coast.

concentration ■ Häufung
There is a concentration of luxury homes in this area of the city.

frequent ■ häufig
There are frequent train connections to Waterloo.

occasional ■ gelegentlich
We go to London for the occasional visit to our children.

often ▪ oft, häufig
People say that it often rains in England.

once [wʌns] ▪ einmal; sobald; einst
It happened only once.
Once you are eighteen you are legally an adult.
Many tales begin with the words, "Once upon a time there was . . .".

▸**once again** ▪ noch einmal
Sorry, I didn't quite get you. Could you please say that once again?

▸**once more** ▪ noch einmal, ein weiteres Mal
I've told you three times already. I'll tell you once more, then not again.

rare ▪ selten, rar
Fortunately it is very rare for me to be ill.

regular ▪ regelmäßig, regulär
Rain is a quite regular occurrence in the west of Britain.

seldom ▪ selten
Our children keep complaining that we are so seldom at home.

twice ▪ zweimal

---

coincidence [kəʊˈɪnsɪdəns] ▪ Zufall
It was a coincidence that I met John yesterday. We certainly hadn't planned to meet.

continuous ▪ ständig, ununterbrochen
We've had continuous rain all day.

duration ▪ Dauer, Länge
Some people think that operas should not exceed four hours' duration.

everyday ▪ alltäglich, Alltags...
A pizza used to be an everyday dish in Italy.

frequency ▪ Häufigkeit, Frequenz
With alarming frequency the student made the same silly mistake.

irregular ▪ unregelmäßig
Trains do not use this line often. They only pass at irregular intervals.

norm ▪ Norm
In the past it used to be the norm to live together only when one was married.

to persist ▪ andauern
The country's financial problems have been persisting for several years.

run ▪ Dauer, Periode
We had a long run of mild weather last winter.

16.3 Räumliche Verhältnisse

above [ə'bʌv] ▪ oben; über
Seen from above the scenery is remarkable.
If your temperature rises above 40 degrees Celsius you should see a doctor.

across ▪ gegenüber; quer über
The supermarket is right across the road.

against ▪ gegen, an
Can you lean the picture against the wall, please? We'll hang it up later.

ahead [ə'hed] ▪ vor, voraus
I can't keep up with you, just go ahead.

along ▪ entlang, längs
He liked to jog along the canal because the path was even.

anywhere ▪ irgendwo; überall; überall hin
There are no special seats. Just sit anywhere.
You can buy clothes anywhere in High Street.

around ▪ ringsherum, umher; um … herum
A trip around the world is rather expensive.
The church stood in the middle of the square with beautiful trees all around.
My parents live just around the corner.

away ▪ weg, entfernt
The beach is just five minutes away.

▸ **away from** ▪ entfernt von
They lived miles away from the nearest road.

behind ▪ hinter; hinten
There is a huge park behind the castle.
At half time, our team was three goals behind.

below ▪ unten; unter; unterhalb
Our neighbours in the flat below are very nice people.
Sales figures for our new product remained below expectations.

beside ▪ neben
He wanted to sit beside his friend at the party.

between ▪ zwischen
Stuttgart is located between Frankfurt and Munich.

beyond ▪ jenseits
We enjoyed the lovely view of "Mount Doom" beyond the lake.

bottom ▪ Boden; untere(r, s)
The bottom of the pan was full of fat.
The book is on the bottom shelf.

broad ▪ breit
Near New Orleans the Mississippi is very broad.

by ▪ bei; in der Nähe von; vorbei
He lives in a house by the river.
They drove by our house and had to turn.

central ▪ zentral, Haupt…
Poland is a country in central Europe and Warsaw, its capital, has a large central station.

centre ▪ Zentrum, Mittelpunkt

Only few people still believe that Earth is the centre of the universe.

close ▪ nah

Can you tell me where the station is? – Oh yes, it's quite close, right up the road.

deep ▪ tief

Don't jump into the water. It's very deep.

direction ▪ Richtung

The last time I saw my husband he was walking in the direction of the city centre.

distance ▪ Entfernung; Abstand; Strecke

Our hotel was within walking distance of the beach.

The distance from our hotel to the beach was only half a mile.

Over long distances flying is more comfortable than going by car.

down ▪ nach unten; herunter, entlang

I hear a noise in the living room. Let's go down and check.

Just walk down the road. The Café Royal is right at the end.

east ▪ Osten

Everywhere in the world the sun rises in the east.

eastern ▪ östlich, Ost…

The eastern parts of Germany enjoy better weather than eastern France.

edge ▪ Rand

We built our house right at the edge of the forest.

elsewhere ▪ woanders, anderswo

I can't find my notebook where it usually is – I must have put it elsewhere.

everywhere ▪ überall; überall hin

The Tyrol has a good infrastructure. You'll find restaurants and hotels practically everywhere.

The old couple went everywhere together.

to extend ■ sich erstrecken; verlängern
Europe extends from the Atlantic coast of France to the Urals Mountains in Russia.
You can of course extend the ladder – by one metre in fact.

far ■ weit (entfernt)
I can't walk all the way to the hotel. It's too far from here.

forward ■ vorwärts, voran
Vernon never stood still or went backwards. He always went forward.

▸ **to look forward to** ■ sich freuen auf
Mary looked forward to receiving the prize for her essay.

from ■ aus, von
I come from Germany. And where are you from?

further ■ weiter, ferner
Glasgow is further away from Stirling than Edinburgh is.

global ■ weltweit, global
Rising sea levels are a major global problem.

here ■ hier
I've been living here for thirty years now.

high ■ hoch
Mount Everest is the highest mountain in the world.

in ■ in
I've lived in London all my life but now I am thinking about moving into another city.

inside ■ innen, innerhalb; drinnen
We stayed inside because it was so cold.

into ■ in … hinein
We went into Hyde Park for a walk.
Don't put your hand into the machine while it is working.

left ■ linke(r, s)
He shot a goal with his left foot.

▸ **on the left** ▪ auf der linken Seite, links
In Malta you drive on the left, as you do in Britain.

level ▪ waagerecht, eben
Our lawn was completely level.

low ▪ niedrig
In Siberia, winter temperatures can be very low.

narrow ▪ eng, schmal
This road is too narrow for my car to pass.

near ▪ nahe, in der Nähe
Buckingham Palace is near Trafalgar Square.

north ▪ Norden
In the north of Canada it can be very cold in winter.

▸ **north of** ▪ nördlich von

northern ▪ nördlich
The northern areas of the country are much colder than the southern ones.

nowhere ▪ nirgendwo (hin), nirgends
Nowhere would I like to be more than here.

off ▪ weg (von), entfernt (von); von, aus
The ship sank five miles off the coast.
We'll have to get off the bus at the next stop.

on ▪ auf; an
The food is on the table.
The train is arriving on platform six.

onto ▪ auf
With a crash the vase fell onto the floor.

out ▪ draußen; heraus
The children were out all day.
You are not supposed to be here. Get out immediately.

out of ▪ außerhalb
After only a few seconds the train was out of sight.

outside ▪ draußen; außerhalb
It has stopped raining. Let's go and play outside.
We waited outside the factory until our fathers came out.

over ▪ hinüber, herüber; drüben
Let's ask our neighbours over for a cup of tea.
Their house is over there.

place ▪ Ort, Platz
Do you know of a place for me to stay?

to take place (took, taken) ▪ stattfinden
The referendum on Scotland's independence took place on 18 September 2014.

point ▪ Stelle
This is precisely the point where I met my future wife for the first time.

position ▪ Platz, Stelle, Lage; Stellung
The position of the lost plane was not known.
Ladies and gentlemen, please ensure that your seat is in an upright position.

presence ▪ Anwesenheit
Your presence at the trial is required.

present ▪ anwesend
All the managers were present when the discussion started.

range ▪ Reichweite
I didn't hear the birds sing because they were outside my hearing range.

to reach ▪ reichen
The water reached almost to the roof of the house.

right ▪ rechte(r, s)
I hurt my right leg in the accident.

▸ **on the right** ▪ auf der rechten Seite, rechts
In Germany and most other EU countries you drive on the right.

size ■ Größe
What's the size of your new house?

somewhere ■ irgendwo; irgendwohin
There must be a place for us somewhere.
Let's go somewhere else. It's too noisy here.

south ■ Süden
Munich is in the south of Germany.

▸ **south of** ■ südlich von

southern ['sʌðən] ■ südlich
It's much warmer in the southern parts of the country.

space ■ Raum; Abstand; Platz
Don't forget to leave a space between words.
At last Jack found a space for his car.

spot ■ Flecken
This is a lovely spot. Let's rest here a little.

square ■ Platz
Trafalgar Square is the address of the National Gallery.

there ■ da, dort; dorthin
You'll find the book over there on my desk.
If you don't want to read it any more just put it there.

through ■ durch (hindurch)
He walked through the door.

throughout ■ überall
He is famous throughout the country.

to ■ nach; zu; bis
We're going to France for a holiday next year.
Let's go to the supermarket to buy some food.
This tram line goes to Desire.

top ■ oberes Ende; Spitze
You'll find their house at the top of the street.
Last season our team was top of the league.

▸ **on top of** ■ oben auf
You'll find the book on top of the pile of books on the table.

towards [tə'wɔːdz, AE: tɔːrdz] ■ in Richtung; nahe
He kept looking towards the door.
You'll find the book towards the end of the shelf.

under ■ unter
Our dog always hides under a table when there is a thunderstorm.

up ■ oben; nach oben; hinauf
Father is up in his study.
Just go up the stairs and you'll find him.
He climbed up the ladder.

upon ■ auf
The secretary placed the document upon her boss's desk.

upper ■ obere(r, s); höhere(r, s); Ober…
They live on the upper floor of this house.
Mark lives on one of the upper floors of this house.
The House of Lords is also called the Upper House.

west ■ Westen
The sun sets in the west.

western ■ westlich
Nevada is in the western part of the USA.

where ■ wo; wohin
Where is Hoboken? Just opposite Manhattan.
Where are you going? I'm going for a walk.

wide ■ breit; weit
Many roads in Dartmoor are hardly wide enough for two cars to pass.
In Kansas there are wide open spaces.

---

apart ■ abseits, für sich
The housekeeper's flat is apart from the main building.

▸ apart from ■ abgesehen von
Dieter eats everything apart from fish.

▸ **to tell apart** ▪ auseinanderhalten
It was difficult to tell the twins apart.

aside ▪ beiseite, zur Seite
She laid aside her knitting and took up a book.

backwards ▪ rückwärts, nach hinten
Could you step backwards a little so that the others can pass?

beneath ▪ unterhalb, unter
You will find your safety belt beneath your seat.

depth ▪ Tiefe
Lake Michigan has a maximum depth of 281 metres.

dimension ▪ Dimension, Abmessung
The Sahara is a desert of tremendous dimensions.

distant ▪ fern
We heard the waves from the distant shore.

extension ▪ Erweiterung, Verlängerung
Fortunately the site was so large that they could build an extension.

external ▪ äußerlich, Außen…
This paint is only for external use.

gap ▪ Lücke, Spalt
Our baby has a gap between two teeth.

height [haɪt] ▪ Höhe
I can't walk up here. I have a fear of heights.

horizontal ▪ horizontal
The sea stretched in a horizontal line under a cloudless sky.

indoors ▪ drinnen, im Haus; hinein
When it was cold I liked to play tennis indoors.
After running about in the snow we went indoors to get warm again.

inner ▪ innere(r, s), Innen…
The palace had a beautiful inner garden.

interior ▪ Innere(r, s), Innenausstattung
The interior of the palace was rather disappointing.

layer ▪ Schicht

The soil consisted of several different layers of earth.

to locate ▪ ausfindig machen, lokalisieren, orten

It is not difficult to locate mobiles when they are being used.

nearby ▪ in der Nähe, nahe gelegen

You can have your meals in a good restaurant nearby.

next to ▪ neben

Our house is right next to the church.

opposite ['ɒpəzət] ▪ gegenüber liegend

The two parties sat at opposite ends of the table.

outdoors ▪ draußen

Mary and Ann like playing outdoors very much.

outer ▪ äußere(r, s), Außen...

Most people like living in one of the outer suburbs.

past ▪ an ... vorbei; hinter

He walked past me without speaking to me.

The letterbox is right past the church.

remote ▪ entfernt, abgelegen

Our hotel is in a very remote area so you will find it very relaxing.

setting ▪ Umgebung; Schauplatz

Our hotel is in a beautiful setting.

The Belgian village of Waterloo was the setting of Napoleon's defeat.

shallow ▪ flach, seicht

Don't jump in. The water is rather shallow.

shelter ▪ Unterstand

At last they found a shelter in the forest.

sideways ▪ seitlich

The hikers had to walk sideways in order to be able to pass others.

stand ▪ Stellung

The burglar took a stand at the corner so that he could easily get away.

to stretch ▪ sich dehnen, sich erstrecken

Russia stretches from the Ukraine in the west to China in the east.

to surround ▪ umgeben; umzingeln

The square is surrounded by beautiful Georgian houses.

The soldiers surrendered because they were surrounded by the enemy.

underground ▪ unterirdisch

Even the London tube does not always run underground.

underneath ▪ unter; darunter

The experts discovered the remains of an old castle underneath the new building.

He wore a sweater with nothing underneath.

underwater ▪ Unterwasser…

Diving is basically an underwater sport.

upright ▪ senkrecht, aufrecht

Will passengers please make sure that their seats are in the upright position.

upside down ▪ verkehrt herum

If you hold your book upside down you will find it difficult to read it.

upwards ▪ nach oben

Look upwards! There are hundreds of geese flying to Africa.

vast ▪ weit

The Duke of Sutherland owns vast areas of land in northern Scotland.

vertical ▪ vertikal

In a house walls are usually vertical.

wherever ▪ wo auch immer; wohin auch immer

Wherever you are don't forget me.

Wherever you go remember me.

widespread ['waɪdspred] ▪ weitverbreitet

Last year there were widespread fires in California.

width ■ Weite; Breite
The width of the Mojave Desert is very impressive.
In New Orleans the Mississippi has a width of some 900 metres.

worldwide ■ weltweit
Mozart's music is known almost worldwide.

zone ■ Zone
The north of Italy is located in an earthquake zone.

16.4 Farben, Formen, Helligkeitsstufen

black ■ schwarz
Many old people used to wear black in the past.

blue ■ blau

bright ■ hell
It was a bright morning in summer.

brown ■ braun

circle ■ Kreis
Every point on the line of a circle is equally far away from its centre.

colour ■ Farbe
Traffic lights show three colours: red, amber and green.

corner ■ Ecke
A triangle has three corners.

dark ■ dunkel; Dunkelheit
When she left the house, she realized that it had become entirely dark outside.
My brother was afraid to go out in the dark.

darkness ■ Dunkelheit
We couldn't distinguish anything clearly in the darkness.

golden ■ golden, Gold…

green ■ grün

grey ▪ grau

hollow ▪ hohl
Some birds build their nests in hollow trees.

light ▪ Licht; hell
There was a dim light at the end of the tunnel.
At last the evenings are getting lighter.

line ▪ Linie

loud ▪ grell
She liked wearing clothes in loud colours.

orange ▪ orangefarben

point ▪ Spitze
I cut myself on the point of a needle.

rectangle ▪ Rechteck
A football field has the shape of a rectangle.

red ▪ rot

round ▪ um … herum; rund
They sat round the table.
Our dinner table is round, not square.

square ▪ Quadrat; quadratisch
A square has four equal sides and four right angles.
I prefer a round table to a square one.

straight ▪ gerade; glatt
The road across the desert is completely straight.
She has very straight hair.

▸ **straigth ahead** [ə'hed] ▪ geradeaus
Just walk straight ahead and you'll be at the station in five minutes.

violet ▪ violett

white ▪ weiß

yellow ▪ gelb
In autumn the leaves on the trees turn yellow.

amber (bei Ampeln) ■ gelb
When the lights turn amber you are supposed to stop.

coloured ■ farbig, bunt
Some people prefer black-and-white photographs to coloured ones.

cube ■ Würfel
A cube is a body which consists of six squares meeting at right angles.

faint ■ matt, zart, schwach
There was still some faint light on the horizon.

oval ■ oval, eiförmig
The US President's office is called oval office because of its shape.

pale ■ blass, fahl
You're quite pale. Are you ill?

parallel ■ parallel
Parallel lines never meet.

pink ■ rosa
Pink is for girls, and blue is for boys, or isn't it?

purple ■ purpurrot, lila, violett
Any colour which is a mixture of red and blue is called purple.

shade ■ Tönung
This is a strange shade of yellow.

shape ■ Gestalt, Form
This building has rather a strange shape – it looks like a castle from a fairytale.

shiny ■ glänzend
Mrs McIntyre polished the table to make it really shiny.

sphere ■ Kugel
Footballs and tennis balls have the shape of a sphere.

triangle ■ Dreieck
In a triangle the sum of all angles is 180.

17. Eigenschaften, Ereignisse, Reihenfolge, Art und Weise

17.1 Allgemeine Eigenschaften, Zustände, Gemeinsamkeiten und Unterschiede

advantage ■ Vorteil
It is certainly an advantage to speak the language of the country you travel to.

▸ **to take advantage of** (took, taken) ■ nutzen
You should take advantage of this generous offer.

arrangement ■ Anordnung
Everybody was fascinated by the beautiful flower arrangement.

as well ■ auch
They liked eating fish and meat as well.

as well as ■ ebenso … wie
Philip arrived with two suitcases as well as a travelling bag.

basic ■ grundsätzlich, fundamental
Freedom of speech is one of the basic human rights.

bitter ■ bitter
I can't drink this beer. It's much too bitter.

cold ■ kalt; Kälte
It was so cold outside that everyone wore a coat to protect them against the cold.

to combine ■ kombinieren, zusammenstellen
When you write an essay it is not enough to combine other authors' theories.

common ■ gemeinsam, allgemein
What they have in common is the love of their country.

condition ■ Zustand
After the long winter many roads were in a dreadful condition.

considerable ▪ erheblich, beträchtlich
After his illness he put on a considerable amount of weight.

constant ▪ konstant
Make sure that you maintain a constant temperature in your flat.

to contrast ▪ gegenüberstellen
In "Romeo and Juliet" Shakespeare contrasts the behaviour of Benvolio and Tybalt.

contrast ['kɒntrɑːst] ▪ Gegensatz, Kontrast
There is a sharp contrast between the rich and the poor in this country.

cool ▪ kühl
We always like it cool in our bedroom.

critical ▪ kritisch
The situation in our neighbouring country has become rather critical.

danger ['deɪndʒə] ▪ Gefahr
In recent years the danger of strong winds and floods has been increasing.

difference ▪ Unterschied
It doesn't make a difference whether he shoots with his right or his left foot.

different ▪ verschieden, unterschiedlich
Tom and Mary are different characters. He is very shy and she will talk to everyone.

dirt ▪ Schmutz, Dreck
When we arrived at our holiday cottage we were disgusted by all the dirt we saw.

dirty ▪ dreckig, schmutzig
Our room was so dirty that we told the hotel management to do something about it.

dry ▪ trocken
This summer has been very dry so far. It has hardly rained at all.

effective ■ effektiv, wirksam
Penicillin is not an effective drug if your disease is caused by a virus.

either ■ jede(r, s) von beiden
It doesn't matter which one you buy. You can take either.

either ... or ■ entweder ... oder
Either you stop telling lies or I'll never believe you again.

else ■ sonst, andere(r, s)
Can anybody else suggest an answer?

equal ■ gleich
Men and women should have equal rights everywhere.

essential ■ wesentlich
Water is essential for life on earth.

exact ■ exakt, genau
The exact time is 11.55 p.m.

excellent ■ hervorragend, exzellent
My car is excellent. I haven't had a problem with it in ten years.

familiar ■ vertraut, gewohnt
The students were familiar with the professor's strictness.

famous ■ berühmt
Maradona used to be a famous football player.

firm ■ stabil, fest
Our sofa cushions are very firm.

fit ■ ⚠ geeignet
This stuff is not fit to be eaten.

free ■ frei
We can be glad to live in a free country.

general ■ allgemein, generell
As a general rule, men and women have the same rights.

▸ **in general** ■ im Allgemeinen
Our performance this season has in general been quite good.

good ■ (der, die, das) Gute
Dad always tried to do good.

handy ■ ⚠ handlich, praktisch
A screwdriver can be a very handy thing to have.

hard ■ hart; schwer; heftig (⚠ auch Adv.)
Diamonds are among the hardest materials known.
She found it very hard to do all the work alone.
One of the kids hit him hard on the head.

heavy ■ schwer
Can you help me carry this? It's far too heavy for me.

hot ■ heiß
It was so hot outside that we stayed indoors.

huge ■ riesig, (riesen)groß
The little girl had huge blue eyes.

kind ■ Art, Sorte
They have all kinds of plants in their garden.

known ■ bekannt, anerkannt
Alec Guinness used to be a well-known actor.

light ■ leicht
She was as light as a feather.

like ■ wie
Luke looks exactly like his elder brother Mike.
Like her sister, she went to a private school.

link ■ Verbindung, Glied
There is an obvious link between politics and literature.

modern ■ modern
My brother has a taste for modern art.

natural ■ natürlich
People have a natural tendency to forget things they don't like.
It is only natural that parents want to support their kids.

neither ■ keine(r, s) von beiden; auch nicht
Neither of the two girls knew how to do it.

neither … nor ■ weder … noch
Neither Joan nor Isabel were able to solve the problem.

new ■ neu
Quite a few new novels have been published this year.

nor ■ und auch nicht
I have no idea what to do. – Nor have I.

normal ■ normal, üblich
At last the two countries resumed normal diplomatic relationships.

not ■ nicht, kein
This is not a real examination. It's just a test.

obvious ■ offensichtlich
It is quite obvious that the weather is becoming warmer from year to year.

order ■ Ordnung, Zustand; Reihenfolge
My colleague's office was never in good order.
List these historical events in chronological order.

powerful ■ mächtig
The USA is a powerful nation.

precise ■ präzise, exakt
The precise time is 11.55 a.m.

proper ■ echt, richtig; anständig
That's what I call a proper meal!
Eating your food with your fingers is not considered proper behaviour.

pure ■ rein, pur; sauber
You can't drink this. It's pure alcohol.
You can't drink this water. It's not pure.

quality ■ Eigenschaft
We must analyze the qualities of the material before using it for our new product.

rapid ▪ schnell, rasch
The doctors were astonished at my father's rapid recovery after the operation.

real ▪ wirklich, real; echt
Mark Twain's real name was Samuel Langhorne Clemens.
It's a pity my ring was stolen, but at least it was not real gold.

relative ▪ ⚠ von Bedeutung, relevant
I'm sorry, but this is not relative to the problem under discussion.

risk ▪ Risiko, Gefahr
His motto is, "No risk – no fun".

rough ▪ uneben
After the long winter the country roads were very rough.

safe ▪ sicher, ungefährlich
It's not safe to walk on the ice yet. It's too thin.

secure ▪ sicher
As a teacher you usually have a secure job.

separate ['sepərət] ▪ unterschiedlich
The school for the boys and that for the girls are in separate buildings.

serious ▪ ernst
The consequences of Monday's accident were quite serious.

severe ▪ schwer; ernst
I'm afraid you've got a rather severe cold.
WWII had severe consequences for the whole world.

sharp ▪ scharf
Be careful. This knife is very sharp.

significant ▪ beachtlich, bedeutend, signifikant
Unfortunately, no significant progress has been reported from the peace talks.

similar ▪ ähnlich
Mary and Joan are twins but they do not look similar.

simple ▪ einfach
Working with this tool is quite simple.

situation ▪ Lage, Situation
They found themselves in a tricky situation.

soft ▪ weich; zart; sanft, leise
Lynn couldn't sleep because the bed was too soft for her.
Babies usually have a very soft skin.
The guests were entertained by soft music in the background.

sorry ▪ traurig, jämmerlich
The house was in a sorry state.

sort ▪ Sorte, Art
What sort of cups do you collect?

sour [saʊə] ▪ sauer
I had to pay ten euros for a glass of sour wine.

specific ▪ genau
What exactly are you driving at? Can you be a little more specific?

state ▪ Zustand
After his accident Justin was in a state of complete confusion.

strange ▪ fremd(artig), sonderbar
I felt rather strange among all those people I didn't know.
His behaviour has always struck me as rather strange.

strong ▪ fest
This lock is very strong. It will keep out any burglar.

suitable ['suːtəbəl, 'sjuːtəbəl] ▪ geeignet, passend
That miniskirt is not really suitable for a wedding.

sweet ▪ süß
I do not like my coffee sweet.

true ▪ wahr, richtig
Tick the true option.

type ▪ Typ, Art, Sorte; Marke
What type of computer would you advise me to buy?

unfit ▪ ungeeignet
The lobster was once considered unfit for human consumption.

unnatural ▪ unnatürlich; ungewöhnlich
Last July's weather was very wet, which is rather unnatural.

unreasonable ▪ unvernünftig; übertrieben
Going out in cold weather without warm clothes is unreasonable.
It is unreasonable to expect that she would work extra hours without extra pay.

useful ▪ nützlich, praktisch
Computers are very useful.

usual ▪ gewöhnlich
There will be more rain than usual next month.

violence ▪ Heftigkeit
The violence of the thunderstorm took us all by surprise.

violent ▪ heftig
The violent storm blew away the roof of our school.

warm ▪ warm
In Florida the sea is quite warm even in February.

wet ▪ nass, feucht; regnerisch
Our clothes got all wet when the rain started.
The weather in Florida can be rather wet – and very hot – in August.

worth ▪ wert; Wert
This ring is worth several thousand dollars.
The new fridge has already proved its worth.

---

adequate ['ædɪkwət] ▪ angemessen, ausreichend, genügend
You earn € 6000 a month? – I'd say that is adequate.

artificial ▪ künstlich
She preferred artificial fur to real fur.

bare ▪ kahl
Most hills in Britain are bare. The trees were used for building ships in the past.

comparable ■ vergleichbar

Apples and pears are not really comparable.

to compare ■ vergleichen

In one of his sonnets Shakespeare compares a lady to a summer day.

comparison ■ Vergleich

You cannot make a comparison between entirely different things.

comprehensive ■ umfassend

Experts are supposed to have a comprehensive knowledge of their field.

concrete ■ konkret, eindeutig

Despite our long discussion we were not able to achieve a concrete result.

convenient ■ bequem, praktisch

Our house is in a convenient location – everything we need is within easy reach.

correlation ■ Beziehung, Zusammenhang

Quite a few people claim that there is no correlation between wealth and happiness.

to correspond ■ (sich) entsprechen, übereinstimmen

John and Conny, I'm afraid your essays correspond so closely that I cannot accept them.

dangerous ['deɪndʒərəs] ■ gefährlich

The doctrine that war is only the continuation of politics is rather dangerous.

decoration ■ Dekoration, Schmuck

The decorations in the ballroom were splendid.

delicate ['delɪkət] ■ heikel

We have to be very careful because the subject is rather delicate.

to differ ■ sich unterscheiden

The two brothers did not differ very much. It was difficult to tell them apart.

disadvantage ▪ Nachteil, Benachteiligung
Not being able to read and write is a serious disadvantage if you are looking for a job.

distinct ▪ verschieden; deutlich
There are several distinct types of this plant.
I have a distinct feeling that there's going to be a thunderstorm.

distinctive ▪ charakteristisch
Honesty is her distinctive feature.

dust ▪ Staub
Nobody had cleaned the house for ages so that everything was covered in dust.

effectiveness ▪ Wirkung, Effektivität
The effectiveness of this new medecine is very doubtful.

efficiency ▪ Leistungsfähigkeit, Effizienz
We can only license this new medecine if its efficiency exceeds that of similar medecines.

evident ▪ offensichtlich
Sorry, but the available data make it quite evident that you are wrong.

explicit ▪ deutlich, klar, eindeutig
Her teacher was always quite explicit in her instructions.

false ▪ falsch; künstlich
Words that apparently are identical in English and German but have a different meaning are called "False Friends", such as "handy" (handlich, praktisch) or "billion" (Milliarde).
He's got false teeth.

fantastic ▪ fantastisch, wunderbar
I've never heard any music like this before. It was fantastic!

feature ▪ Merkmal, Eigenschaft
One of the main features of this house is its splendid view of the sea.

fierce ▪ heftig, wild, stürmisch
There was a fierce wind when we got to the beach.

flexible ▪ biegsam

Steel is not really very flexible.

fragile ▪ zerbrechlich

Be careful with this very old cup. It is highly fragile.

fragment ▪ Bruchstück, Splitter, Fragment

Oh dear. The cup's broken. Could you help me pick up the fragments?

genuine ['dʒenjuɪn] ▪ echt

If you bought that gold chain at such a low price you can't expect it to be genuine.

harmless ▪ harmlos

Not all dogs are harmless.

ideal ▪ ideal

With a canal and a motorway nearby, this is the ideal place for a new factory.

identical ▪ identisch

Twins are not always identical.

imitation ▪ Nachahmung, Imitation

It's not a real fur. It's an imitation.

inflammable ▪ leicht entzündbar

Don't smoke while filling up your car because petrol is highly inflammable.

intensive ▪ intensiv

The victim of the accident had to be admitted into an intensive care unit.

invalid ▪ ungültig

Don't tap in an invalid PIN.

keen ▪ heftig; begeistert

I felt a very keen pain in my back.

He has always been a keen tennis player.

loose ▪ lose, locker

Daddy, my tooth feels loose.

massive ▪ massiv; schwer

Big Ben is a massive bell in the Elizabeth Tower.

After the accident the driver had massive health problems.

to match ▪ zusammenpassen

Heather's parents always said that red and blue do not really match.

merit ▪ Verdienst, Leistung

The novel may have had many readers but its merits as a work of art are limited.

mess ▪ Durcheinander, Chaos; Dreck

He could not find anything because his room was in a complete mess.

Please, clean up your dog's mess.

mixture ▪ Mischung, Gemisch

This salad is a mixture of potatoes, bacon, onions and mayonnaise.

nasty ▪ scheußlich, gräßlich

What's that nasty smell in this room?

outline ▪ Kontur

It was so dark that I could only see the outline of the building.

pleasant ['plezənt] ▪ angenehm

This year's April was very pleasant.

precious ['preʃəs] ▪ wertvoll

Gold and silver are precious metals.

prominent ▪ auffallend

Norwich Cathedral has a very prominent position in the city.

remarkable ▪ bemerkenswert, beachtlich

The mountains are called the Remarkables, which is what they are.

reservation ▪ Vorbehalt

I support your proposal without reservations.

respectively ▪ beziehungsweise

The apples and pears cost £1.50 and £2 per pound respectively.

ridiculous [rɪˈdɪkjələs] ▪ lächerlich

None of his friends took him seriously because he kept making ridiculous remarks.

second-hand ▪ gebraucht, Gebraucht…

These second-hand shoes are almost new.

sensitive ▪ heikel

This is rather a sensitive subject.

significance ▪ Bedeutung

It was only long after Van Gogh's death that his significance was recognized.

smooth ▪ glatt

There was no wind and the sea was completely smooth.

solemn [ˈsɒləm] ▪ feierlich

The music composed for this occasion was very solemn.

solid ▪ fest; massiv; stabil

At last they reached solid ground.

Her wedding ring was solid gold.

The house is so solid that not even a hurricane can damage it.

steady [ˈstedi] ▪ fest; kontinuierlich

Their relationship can only be described as steady.

The weather was a nightmare. There was steady rain for a whole week.

steep ▪ steil

Jonathan was not able to cycle up the hill because it was too steep.

sticky ▪ klebrig; stickig; schwierig

Do not touch it yet. It is still sticky.

Please, open a window. It's rather sticky in here.

This is rather a sticky situation.

stiff ▪ steif; hart

All my muscles are stiff after all this running.

I never wear a shirt with a stiff collar.

straightforward ▪ einfach

That was a surprisingly straightforward solution.

strict ▪ genau
In the strict sense of the word this is not correct.

substitute ▪ Ersatz
Pills are no substitute for good food.

subtle ['sʌtl] ▪ fein, subtil
She has a very subtle sense of humour.

tight ▪ knapp, dicht
Our timetable is rather tight.

tough [tʌf] ▪ strikt
Richard's boss is very tough.

transparent ▪ durchsichtig, transparent
In most cases glass is transparent.

tremendous ▪ gewaltig
Our region experienced a tremendous thunderstorm last night.

tricky ▪ kompliziert
I'm afraid this riddle is too tricky for me.

uncertain ▪ unbeständig; unbestimmt, unsicher
This summer the weather was rather uncertain.
She expressed her anger in no uncertain terms.

universal ▪ allgemein, universell
It is rather optimistic to hope for universal peace on earth.

unlike ▪ unähnlich; anders als
No wonder they are unlike. After all, they are not identical twins.
Unlike her brother she is very friendly.

unpleasant [ʌn'plezənt] ▪ unangenehm
Because of the railworkers' strike our journey was rather unpleasant.

unsteady [ʌn'stedi] ▪ nicht stabil; instabil; zittrig
I can't sit on this chair. It's unsteady.
The weather last week was rather unsteady.
She was so sad that her voice was unsteady.

unusual ▪ ungewöhnlich; außergewöhnlich
Being late for an appointment is unusual for Jim.
He had to make an unusual effort to pass his exam.

useless ▪ sinnlos; unbrauchbar
Trying to persuade Harry is useless.
We need a new computer because our old one is useless.

vague [veɪg] ▪ vage, unbestimmt
I don't know what to make of him. He is always so vague about everything.

valid ▪ begründet
The judge accepted the objection because he regarded it as valid.

valuable ▪ wertvoll
Gold and diamonds are regarded as very valuable.

to vary ▪ variieren, verschieden sein; sich verändern
Employment figures in the various parts of the country vary considerably.

vice versa ▪ umgekehrt
John does not like Mary – and vice versa.

wonderful ▪ wunderbar, wundervoll
Shakespeare's "Hamlet" is a wonderful play.

17.2 Geschehen, Ereignisse

accident ▪ Zufall
She found her friend's house just by accident.

to arise (arose, arisen) ▪ sich ergeben
I shall certainly apply for a pay rise if the opportunity arises.

catastrophe [kə'tæstrəfi] ▪ Katastrophe
Japan is still suffering from the consequences of the nuclear catastrophe in 2011.

change ▪ Veränderung
There's been a radical change in the country's political climate.

conference ▪ Besprechung
I'm afraid you can't speak to Mr Stevenson. He's at a conference until 3 p.m.

damage ▪ Schaden
Burning too much coal causes serious damage to the environment.

to drop ▪ fallen (lassen)
He dropped his mobile and it fell into the water.

to fall (fell, fallen) ▪ fallen
Martin broke his leg when he fell from a tree.

▸ **to fall asleep** ▪ einschlafen

▸ **to fall down** ▪ hinfallen

▸ **to fall ill** ▪ krank werden

▸ **to fall in love** ▪ sich verlieben

fall ▪ Fall
Humpty Dumpty sat on a wall, / Humpty Dumpty had a great fall …

fire ▪ Feuer
In very dry weather there is always the risk of fire.

▸ **to catch fire** ▪ Feuer fangen

flood ▪ Flut, Hochwasser
In the rainy season there are often floods in India and Bangladesh.

to flow ▪ fließen
The Rhine flows into the North Sea near Rotterdam.

to happen ▪ geschehen, sich ereignen
Your car's damaged. What's happened?

impact ▪ Aufprall; Auswirkung
The bridge was severely damaged by the impact of the car.
Global warming has a severe impact on mankind.

implication ▪ Auswirkung, Implikation
You must always be aware of the implications of what you do.

▸ **good luck!** ▪ viel Glück!

matter ■ Angelegenheit
Mass unemployment is a serious matter.

occasion ■ Gelegenheit, Anlass
I hope we'll meet again on some other occasion.

to occur ■ vorkommen
The accident occurred at the corner of High Street and Market Street.

opportunity ■ Gelegenheit, Chance
When Frederick was offered a new job, he took the opportunity at once.

possibility ■ Möglichkeit
There is a distinct possibility that your decision is correct.

to start ■ beginnen, anfangen; starten
I'm starving. Let's start eating.
The race starts at 3.30 p.m.

to stick (stuck, stuck) ■ klemmen
Can you help me? The window keeps sticking.

---

to burst (burst, burst) ■ platzen, brechen
The dam burst and caused severe flooding.

crash ■ Unfall, Absturz
More than a hundred people died in the plane crash yesterday.

to damage ■ beschädigen, schaden
Harry's car was badly damaged in the accident.

destruction ■ Zerstörung
The tornado resulted in the destruction of entire villages.

disaster ■ Katastrophe, Unglück
The flooding of eastern Germany in 2013 was a very severe natural disaster.

to echo ■ widerhallen
The thunder was echoed from the other side of the valley.

escape ▪ Flucht

The prisoners managed their escape by digging a tunnel under the prison wall.

expansion ▪ Zunahme

The rapid expansion of the city's population caused serious problems.

to explode ▪ explodieren

When a bomb exploded in the city centre the government reacted immediately.

explosion ▪ Explosion

The bomb explosion in front of the government building caused a severe political crisis.

exposure ▪ Aussetzung; Entlarvung

The members of the expedition suffered from their exposure to the extreme cold.

The manager suffered very much from the media's exposure of his fraud.

flame ▪ Flamme

If you see flames in your house call the fire brigade immediately.

to flash ▪ aufblitzen

At first we saw lightning flash on the horizon and then there was a thunderstorm.

to float ▪ schwimmen, treiben, oben bleiben

Unfortunately a lot of rubbish is floating on the oceans.

incident ▪ Vorfall, Ereignis

The election took place without any serious incidents.

occurrence ▪ Begebenheit

Ambrose Bierce wrote short stories about occurrences during the Civil War.

outcome ▪ Ergebnis, Resultat

When the government started the tax reform they were not sure about its outcome.

to pop ▪ platzen
Little Mary cried because her balloon had popped.

pop ▪ Knall
To most ears, the pop of champagne cork is a welcome sound.

shipwreck ▪ Schiffbruch
The shipwreck was caused by the crew's negligence.

shock ▪ Stoß
The shock of the explosion was felt several miles away.

slam ▪ Knall
I heard the slam of a door just after midnight.

to slide (slid, slid) ▪ rutschen; gleiten
Oil prices have been sliding for some time.
The snake slid along the path.

to slip ▪ ausrutschen
She slipped on a banana skin and broke her left arm.

smash ▪ Krachen; Unfall
Mike heard a loud smash just after midnight.
There was car smash just outside his house.

to swell (swelled, swollen) ▪ anschwellen
The heavy rain in the past weeks has made the river swell.

to wave ▪ wehen, flattern
The flags were waving in the wind.

17.3 Entwicklung, Reihenfolge

after ▪ nach
After the break he continued his talk about politics.

also ▪ auch, außerdem, darüber hinaus
When I was young I had to learn Latin first and then also English and later French.

and so on ▪ und so weiter
In this class we'll talk about trees, bushes, flowers, and so on.

another ■ noch ein(e, er, s)
Could I have another glass of beer, please?

back ■ zurück
He moved abroad for a while but he came back soon.

to become (became, become) ■ werden
He wants to become a teacher.

to cause ■ verursachen
Smoking causes serious damage to your health.

cause ■ Grund, Anlass
The present political conditions are the cause of so much trouble.

to change ■ (sich) verändern
The new president will change the country.
You've changed a lot since I last saw you.

consequence ■ Folgerung, Konsequenz
As a consequence of global warming sea levels are expected to rise.

to continue ■ fortfahren; fortsetzen
The lecturer was so dizzy that he was unable to continue.
After a short break they continued their discussion.

effect ■ Auswirkung, Effekt
Before developing new machines you ought to study their effects on human beings.

to fade ■ schwächer werden, verblassen
Unfortunately the colours in this beautiful dress are fading.

growth ■ Zunahme
China is still experiencing a rapid growth of its population.

to imply ■ mit sich bringen
Having children implies a lot of responsibilities.

to improve ■ (sich) verbessern
The food in this restaurant has improved very much.

improvement ■ Verbesserung
There has been a marked improvement in John's performance.

to increase [ɪn'kriːs] ■ zunehmen, wachsen; vergrößern, vermehren

The average age of human beings has increased very much.
We don't manage to increase our property.

increase ['ɪnkriːs] ■ Zunahme, Wachstum

The twentieth century witnessed a sharp increase in global temperatures.

inevitable ■ unvermeidlich, zwangsläufig

If you wish to pass this test it is inevitable that you work hard.

primary ■ hauptsächlich, primär

The primary function of governments is to secure the well-being of its citizens.

prime ■ Haupt…, wesentlich

Smoking is the prime cause of lung cancer.

progress ['prəʊgres] ■ Fortschritt

The twentieth century witnessed a lot of technical progress.

ready ■ fertig, bereit

Dinner's ready now, children.

road ■ Weg

At last our company is on the road to recovery.

row ■ Reihe

They lost five matches in a row.

sequence ■ Folge, Reihenfolge

The traditional sequence of events is marriage first and children later.

sign ■ Anzeichen

There are some signs that the patient may be recovering at last.

to spread [spred] (spread, spread) ■ sich ausbreiten; sich erstrecken

The news of peace spread like fire.
Pisgah National Forest spreads over an area of 500,000 acres.

stage ■ Stufe, Phase, Stadium
I'm afraid that at this stage I cannot say whether the negotiations will be successful.

towards ■ zu
There is a clear tendency towards more strikes.

turn ■ Wende
Things are taking a very unpleasant turn.

---

to alter ■ ändern
When Rip van Winkle returned to his village he found it completely altered.

at first ■ zuerst, am Anfang
At first he resisted the temptation but then he gave in.

at last ■ endlich, schließlich
After long months of fruitless efforts he succeeded at last.

consequently ■ folglich
The past winter was very cold. Consequently our fuel bill will be very high.

continuing ■ andauernd
We also counted on the continuing support of our parents.

decay ■ Verfall
The country was in a state of decay for a long time before it recovered.

to decrease [dɪˈkriːs] ■ abnehmen, zurückgehen
The birthrate in Germany has been decreasing since WWII.

to enhance ■ verbessern, stärken
Diagrams and transparencies usually enhance the effectiveness of lectures.

to expand ■ zunehmen
China's population has been expanding rapidly.

gain ■ Anstieg
The company recorded a gain in profits in the past year.

gradual ▪ allmählich, schrittweise

There has been a gradual improvement in our company's performance.

gradually ▪ allmählich, nach und nach

Our situation has been gradually getting worse.

hence (Adv.) ▪ daher

This product is very much in demand – hence its high price.

to involve ▪ beinhalten, zur Folge haben; voraussetzen

This job involves a lot of hard work.

Becoming a professor involves a lot of hard work and quite some intelligence.

to line up ▪ eine Schlange bilden, sich aufstellen

Hundreds of people lined up at the box office to buy tickets.

modification ▪ Änderung, Modifikation

The engineer introduced some modifications to the machine.

to modify ▪ ändern, modifizieren

Herewith we advise you that we have modified our terms of delivery.

to persist ▪ weitermachen

Despite many protests he persisted with his speech.

premise ['premɪs] ▪ Voraussetzung, Prämisse

The basis of our project is the premise that the economic climate remains favourable.

principal ▪ Haupt…, hauptsächlich

Corruption is the principal reason for the country's decline.

prior ▪ früher, vorherig, Vor…

Prior versions of this software do not run on my computer.

to proceed ▪ fortschreiten; fortfahren; vorrücken

The operation was proceeding smoothly.

The speaker coughed briefly and then proceeded with his speech.

After taking her A levels she proceeded to university.

to progress [prə'gres] ▪ vorankommen, Fortschritte machen; fortschreiten

The expedition was progressing very slowly because of the rain.
After talking about politics the speakers progressed to talking about art.

removal ▪ Beseitigung, Entfernung

The removal of red wine stains is a difficult matter.

to render ▪ werden lassen

The pain was so intense that it rendered him helpless.

to renew ▪ erneuern

The police renewed their efforts to restore peace in the city.

to reverse ▪ rückgängig machen

The surgeon told the patient that the operation could not be reversed.

to ruin ▪ ruinieren, verderben

The crop was ruined by the wet summer.

to spoil (spoilt/spoiled, spoilt/spoiled) ▪ verderben, schlecht werden

Our fridge has stopped working, and all the food spoilt.

to strengthen ▪ stärken

In order to be successful we must strengthen our relationships with our rivals.

successive ▪ aufeinanderfolgend

Margaret Thatcher won three successive general elections.

switch ▪ Wechsel, Austausch

There's been a switch in the leadership of this company recently.

to transform ▪ verwandeln

If we don't transform our system we'll lose the support of our customers.

transformation ▪ Umgestaltung, Umwandlung

The transformation of our society will take some time.

transition ■ Übergang, Wechsel
The transition from a Conservative to a Labour government was quite smooth.

trend ■ Tendenz, Trend
The trend towards increasing global warmth is continuing, I'm afraid.

turning point ■ Wendepunkt
The fall of the Berlin wall was a turning point in the history of Germany.

17.4 Einordnung, Auswahl

about ■ etwa, ungefähr
That building is about 200 metres tall.

alternative ■ Alternative
There is no alternative to wind and solar power if we wish to reduce global warming.

another ■ ein anderer, eine andere, ein anderes
It was so noisy where we lived first that we soon moved to another area.

category ■ Kategorie, Klasse
Food and drink belong to different categories of food.

extra ■ besonders
If I want to pass this test I'll have to work extra hard.

fairly ■ ziemlich
This was fairly well done.

instead ■ statt(dessen), an Stelle von
Can I please have tea instead of coffee.

level ■ Niveau, Höhe
The two players were not on the same level of skills.

to list ■ auflisten, verzeichnen
You must list alphabetically all the books you have consulted.

list ▪ Liste, Verzeichnis
There is a long list of things to do next week.

main ▪ hauptsächlich, Haupt…
Ecuador is the world's main exporter of bananas.

maybe ▪ ungefähr, vielleicht
He drove at a speed of maybe 70 mph.

mere ▪ bloße(r, s); nur
The mere fact that the conference has not been cancelled is a success.
She was a mere girl and still her parents wanted her to marry.

middle ▪ mittlere(r, s)
Matthew achieved a position in the middle management of his company.

next ▪ dann
First there was silence. Next, I heard soft music.

original ▪ ursprünglich, original
The original manuscripts of Shakespeare's works have never been found.

other ▪ andere(r, s)
My brother likes Fielding's "Tom Jones" better than most of his other works.

▸ **every other** ▪ jede(r/n, s) zweite(r/n, s)
I go swimming every other day.

priority ▪ Priorität, Vorrang
Of all our tasks the protection of our population has the clear priority.

rather ▪ ziemlich
Your performance is not really good, it is even rather poor.

relative ▪ jeweilige(r, s)
The relative merits of these materials need to be investigated.

relevant ▪ relevant
Yours was the most relevant remark made so far.

same ▪ der-, die-, dasselbe, dieselben
My brother's children and mine went to the same school.

to select ▪ auswählen
Of all the applicants the company selected me for the post of personnel officer.

selection ▪ Auswahl, Wahl
One of the key functions of a personnel officer is the selection of new staff.

series ▪ Reihe(nfolge)
Of the series of fifteen tests we made, only the last one was successful.

to serve ▪ genügen
These two boards will serve as a table.

special ▪ besondere(r, s)
He is quite a special character.

together ▪ zusammen
Can we do the job together? I can't do it alone.

too ▪ auch; zu (sehr)
If Simon is invited, I'd like to come too.
These shoes are too small for me. Could I please try on size 10?

total ▪ völlig, total
The conference was a total catastrophe.

---

inferior ▪ minderwertig, unterlegen
We cannot accept this product because it is of inferior quality.

in part ▪ teilweise, zum Teil
The bankruptcy of the company was in part due to the general economic situation.

latter ▪ zweite(r, s), letztere(r, s)
If I have to choose between Arsenal and Chelsea I distinctly prefer the latter.

lesser ▪ geringer, unbedeutender
It is difficult to decide which of the two options is the lesser evil.

magnificent ■ großartig
Beethoven's violin concerto is magnificent.

major ■ bedeutend, wichtig
General Electric is a major company.

marginal ■ marginal, geringfügig
The difference in the performance of these two engines is only marginal.

minor ■ nebensächlich, mindere(r, s)
Fortunately she suffered only minor injuries in the accident.

model ■ Muster
She was a model of good manners.

notably ■ insbesondere, vor allem
This rule applies to everyone, but notably to young people.

partial ■ teilweise
Florence introduced a partial ban of cars during the summer season.

particular ■ bestimmte(r, s), besondere(r, s)
Do you have anything particular in mind?

▸ in particular ■ insbesondere
Henry likes all types of literature, but in particular sentimental novels.

prominent ■ prominent, führend
Winston Churchill was one of the most prominent British politicians in the 20th century.

rank ■ Rang
The exhibition included a large number of first rank pictures.

secondary ■ sekundär, zweitrangig
Some people say that earning a lot of money is of only secondary importance.

sheer ■ bloß, pur, rein
The sheer size of Brazil is amazing – it's 23 times as large as Germany.

sole ▪ einzig, alleinig

In Britain the eldest son was usually the sole heir of his father's property.

to sort out ▪ aussortieren

Let's sort out all the records we do not listen to any longer.

to split (split, split) ▪ verteilen

In an Ltd some of the profits are split among the shareholders.

superior to ▪ überlegen

This wine is superior to the one we had yesterday.

supreme ▪ höchste(r, s), oberste(r, s); äußerste(r, s)

The president of the USA is also its supreme military commander.

It was only by a supreme effort that I managed not to fall asleep.

underlying ▪ zugrunde liegend, grundlegend

The underlying reason for your poor results is simply your laziness.

unexpected ▪ unerwartet

Brazil's 1 to 7 World Cup defeat by Germany was completely unexpected.

upwards ▪ aufwärts

I'm afraid we'll have to revise the costs of the project upwards.

17.5 Art und Weise

absolute ▪ absolut, vollständig

I'm afraid that what you say is absolute nonsense.

anyhow ▪ sowieso; irgendwie

Give me the letter. I'll be going to the post office anyhow.

He didn't bother about what clothes to wear. He would just dress anyhow.

anyway ▪ sowieso, ohnehin

You needn't go shopping. I'll be going to the supermarket anyway.

apparent [ə'pærənt] ■ offensichtlich; scheinbar
She slammed the door for no apparent reason.
Mary had a look of apparent innocence, although we all thought she was guilty.

appropriate ■ angemessen
I'm afraid I can't accept this essay. It is not written with the appropriate care.

as ■ so, wie
Love your neighbour as you love yourself.

at all ■ überhaupt
He said he didn't like that at all.

especially ■ besonders
Don't forget your umbrella – especially if you travel to the west coast.

even ■ sogar, selbst, noch
We'd even have gone for a walk in much worse weather.

likely ■ wahrscheinlich
According to experts the economic situation is likely to improve.

manner ■ Art, Weise
They treated their guests in a very friendly manner.

method ■ Methode
He had his own personal method of dealing with problems.

quite ■ ganz, ziemlich
Your essay is not excellent but it is quite good.

really ■ tatsächlich, wirklich
The Tower of London is really a very old building.

so ■ so
He was so nice to me. I could hardly believe it.

sort of ■ irgendwie
The tree over there looks sort of strange.

that ■ so
Of course you can walk there. It isn't that far.

though ■ doch, jedoch
He's had a lot of trouble with his heart. He hasn't stopped smoking though.

thus ■ so; somit
Thus far and not a step further.
We have not been successful. Thus we'll have to live with the consequences.

way ■ Methode, Art
Sorry, but this is not the right way to do it.

with ■ mit; bei
Yesterday I saw Tom with Sophia in the park.
He is thirty and still lives with his parents!

---

accordingly ■ entsprechend
The job is very complex and should therefore be paid accordingly.

as for ■ was … betrifft
As for classical music I have no taste for it.

barely ■ karg
When we first moved in, the flat was barely furnished.

definitely ■ eindeutig, definitiv
What you say is definitely not correct.

deliberate ■ absichtlich
The police claimed that the accident had been the result of the driver's deliberate manoeuvre.

fundamental ■ wesentlich, grundlegend
The management's fundamental mistakes led to the company's bankruptcy.

furthermore ■ darüber hinaus
Furthermore I would like to point out that there is also another side of the coin.

implicit ■ indirekt, implizit
I cannot help regarding your statement as an implicit attack on my position.

impressive ■ beeindruckend, eindrucksvoll

After the war the country achieved an impressive recovery.

in accordance with ■ in Übereinstimmung mit, entsprechend

Anyone who does not act in strict accordance with the rules will be dismissed.

in relation to ■ in Bezug auf

What do you have to say in relation to the incident in question?

inadequate ■ unangemessen, unzureichend

I'm afraid your essay is inadequate and its low mark is thus justified.

means ■ Mittel

The mobile is the most popular means of communication among young people.

mode ■ Art, Methode

The car is by far the most important mode of transport nowadays.

notably ■ auffallend

She is a notably clever little girl.

oral ■ mündlich

Your final exam also includes an oral element.

overall ■ gesamt, allgemein

The overall performance of our staff last year was excellent.

pretty ■ ziemlich

I'm afraid your performance was pretty terrible, John.

radical ■ rigoros

The steps taken by the police to fight extremists were radical.

random ■ willkürlich, wahllos, zufällig

Take any random sample of people and see what their answers are.

scarcely ■ kaum

Our parents had scarcely enough money to buy a car.

somehow ■ irgendwie

The mechanic didn't really know how to fix the car but he managed somehow.

straightforward ■ direkt

He answered the question in a straightforward manner.

thereby ■ dadurch, damit

Some businesses sell their goods cheap, thereby improving their position sales.

thorough ■ gründlich, genau

As a scientist you must be very thorough in whatever you do.

thoroughly ■ gründlich; völlig

The doctor examined his patient thoroughly.

Phil thought that Liz was thoroughly wrong.

uncontrolled ■ unkontrolliert

He has a rather uncontrolled way of spending his money

unlikely ■ unwahrscheinlich

The weather is unlikely to improve in the next few days.

virtually ■ praktisch, eigentlich, so gut wie

After he had lost his job he was virtually bankrupt.

18. Artikel, Pronomina

a / an (vor Vokal: an apple, an hour) ■ eine(r, s)
In the zoo we saw a lion and an elephant.

anybody ■ jede(r, s); jemand
It's child's play. Anybody can do this.
This is very tricky. Can anybody solve this riddle?

anyone ■ jede(r, s); jemand
Anyone who believes that money can buy happiness is wrong.
Does anyone happen to know when the next bus goes?

anything ■ etwas; alles
I'm so thirsty. I haven't had anything to drink for hours.
Whatever there was on the table she would eat anything.

both ■ beide
You can take both books if you like.

▸ **both ... and** ■ sowohl ... als auch
David Cameron was both Prime Minister and party leader.

each ■ jede(r, s) (aus einer bestimmten Menge)
Each of these five children will get an ice cream.

each other ■ einander
We've never played tennis against each other.

every ■ jede(r, s) (aus einer unbestimmten Menge)
Every human being ought to enjoy the same rights.

everybody ■ alle, jeder
I do not expect everybody to like what I have to say.

everyone ■ alle, jeder
Will please everyone listen to what I am saying?

everything ■ alles
Cook what you like. I eat everything.

he ■ er
He promised to come on Thursday, but he didn't turn up.

her ■ ihr
She is very much in love with her friend.

hers ■ ihre(r, s)
Is this Mary's car? – Yes, it's hers.

herself ■ selbst; sich
Joan made this box herself. Nobody helped her.
She hurt herself when peeling the potatoes.

him ■ ihm, ihn
Even if you don't like him you should at least send him a birthday card.

himself ■ selbst; sich
As he couldn't do the job himself he had to ask for help.
He had hurt himself when trying to jump over the fence.

his ■ sein, seine(r, s)
Mozart died before he had finished his "Requiem".

how ■ wie, auf welche Weise
Good morning, madam. How can I help you?

I ■ ich
It's cold? – Okay, I'll shut the window.

it ■ es
The book is on the table in the living room. Could you please, bring it to me?

its ■ sein
The country still suffers from its lack of experts.

itself ■ selbst; sich
The cat had to find food itself.
The cat cleaned itself for quite some time.

me ■ mich, mir
Could you pass me the sugar, please?

mine ■ meine(r, s)
It's not your car. It's mine.

my ▪ mein
Would you, please, stop telling jokes about my friends?

myself ▪ mich selbst, mir selbst, ich selbst
You don't need to help me. I can do it myself.

nobody ▪ niemand
Nobody knew how to solve the problem.

no one ▪ niemand
When she arrived at the hotel there was no one to help her.

nothing ▪ nichts
There was nothing they could do for me.

one ▪ man
One can hardly say that everything John says is correct.

one another ▪ eineinander, gegenseitig
Friends are supposed to help one another.

oneself ▪ sich; selbst
This is the ideal place to base oneself for a lovely holiday.
One can easily do that oneself.

our ▪ unser
Nero is the name of our dog.

ours ▪ unsere(r, s)
No, not this one. The yellow house is ours.

ourselves ▪ uns selbst; wir selbst
We must help ourselves and not rely on other people.
We can do this ourselves. We don't need any help.

own ▪ mein, dein, sein, unser, euer, ihr eigene(r, s)
That's my own car you're laughing at, you know.
The beautiful house over there is my own.

she ▪ sie
She does not like shopping.

somebody ▪ jemand
Yes, I saw somebody run away but I don't know who it was.

someone ▪ jemand
Can, please, someone shut the door?

such ▪ solche(r, s), solche ein(e)
Oh no. I don't want to talk to him. He's such a fool.

that ▪ das, jene(r, s)
No, it's not this house, it's that one over there.

the [ðə; vor Vokal: ði: the egg, the hour] ▪ der, die, das
Do you see the boy over there?

▸**the … the** ▪ je … desto
The more I see you, the more I love you.

their ▪ ihr
Their house is the red one over there.

theirs ▪ ihre(r, s)
Is that your parents' car? Yes, it's theirs.

them ▪ sie (Akk.); ihnen
If you see them tell them I'd like to see them.
This is your parents' book. Can you please give it to them?

themselves ▪ selbst; sich selbst
They can't solve the riddle themselves.
His motto is "God helps those who help themselves".

these ▪ diese (hier)
Can you please give me these apples, not those over there?

they ▪ sie
They were walking hand in hand in the park.

this ▪ diese(r, s); dies
Could you give her this racket, not that one?
This is the way I like it.

those ▪ diese (dort)
These apples are sour, could I have some of those over there?

us ▪ uns
Let us hope that it is not going to rain.

we ▪ wir
We can do it if we really try.

what ▪ was; was für ein(e)
What can I do for you?
What nonsense!

whatever ▪ egal was, was auch immer
Whatever the weather we'll go for a walk.

which ▪ welche(r, s)
Which of the three pieces of cake would you like?

who [huː] ▪ wer; der, den, die, das
Who is that boy over there?
Who do you mean? – The boy in the green sweater.

whoever [huːˈevə] ▪ wer auch immer
Just look at the two boys over there. Whoever they are they are certainly handsome.

whom [huːm] ▪ wen, wem; den, dem; die, der
Whom do you have in mind? Charles, whom I lent some money.
He is the boy whom I saw last week at the party and whom I gave my address.
She is the girl with whom I danced yesterday and whom I'm meeting tonight.

whose [huːz] ▪ wessen; dessen/deren
Whose car is the Porsche outside? – It belongs to the girl whose friend is just crossing the street.

you ▪ du, dir, dich; ihr, euch; Sie, Ihnen
You are the best friend I have ever had. I make you this present because I like you.
You are the guys I've been looking for. I have something important to tell you.
You are the gentlemen I wanted to meet. I have some vital information for you.

your ▪ dein, euer, Ihr
Your children are very nice.

yours ▪ deine(r, s), Ihre(r, s), eure(r, s); der deine/Ihre

This is not my exercise book, it's yours.

I will be yours for ever.

yourself (Pl.: -selves) ▪ selbst, dich (selbst), euch (selbst); sich (selbst)

Please do it yourself.

This concerns yourself/yourselves.

Just try to keep yourself/yourselves informed of all the details of this programme.

19. Weitere Präpositionen

about ■ über
Can you tell me something about this author, please?

among ■ unter, zwischen, bei
She lived among country folk all her life.

as to ■ betreffend, bezüglich
As to the delivery date, we'll let you know as soon possible.

at ■ an, in, bei
The train at platform 3 is about to depart. Stand back, please!
My boss is at a meeting.

because of ■ wegen
Because of the rain we stayed at home.

but ■ außer
No one but Heather answered the question correctly.

by ■ mit; von
Of course you can pay by bank card.
This cake was made by Anne.

despite ■ trotz
Despite the bad weather many people came to the open air concert.

due to ■ aufgrund, infolge, wegen
Due to bad weather we had to cancel our party.

in ■ hinein
He always puts too much sugar in his coffee.

including ■ einschließlich
This is the full price – of course including tax.

in terms of ■ bezüglich, hinsichtlich, was … betrifft
Jamie Oliver is an expert in terms of cooking.

of ■ von
The languages of Malta are Maltese and English.

on ■ über
Wilbur Sanders wrote a major book on Shakespeare.

out of ▪ aus
All our chairs made are out of wood.

over ▪ über
He kicked the ball over the goal.

per ▪ pro, je, für
The average income per head has not increased a lot in recent years.

such as ▪ wie (etwa)
That amount should cover our expenses, such as petrol, food, and accommodation.

why ▪ warum
Why does Mum always have to do the dirty work?

within ▪ innerhalb; binnen
There are four schools within an area of 3 miles around our house.
The bill is to be paid within ten days.

without ▪ ohne
Don't come here without the money I lent you.

---

concerning ▪ bezüglich, betreffend
I have an enquiry concerning our order of 20 June.

in favour of ▪ zugunsten, für
I am in favour of helping people in need to help themselves.

in spite of ▪ trotz
In spite of his broken leg he went to work as usual.

in the light of ▪ angesichts, unter Berücksichtigung
In the light of recent findings we ought to change our plans.

other than ▪ ander(e)s als, außer
Other than Mary there was no one in the classroom when the teacher entered.

via ['vaɪə] ▪ über
The train to Hamburg goes via Hanover.

20. Konjunktionen

although ▪ obwohl
We won the match although two of our players were sent off in the first half.

and ▪ und
American runners finished first and second in the race.

as ▪ als, während; da
The telephone rang just as I was having breakfast.
As I was busy I couldn't answer the phone.

as if ▪ als ob, als wenn
He behaved as if he didn't know what to do.

as though ▪ als ob
He looks as though he's been working all night.

because ▪ weil
I'll take an umbrella because it looks like rain.

before ▪ bevor; vor
Can you help me before you go?
"Is this a dagger which I see before me?"

but ▪ aber
I would like to come but I've got an appointment at the same time.

either ▪ auch (nicht)
I'm glad you don't like him. I don't like him either.

even if ▪ selbst wenn
Even if you wish me to stay at home I will go to the party.

even though ▪ obwohl
She did not take an umbrella even though it was raining hard.

for ▪ denn
. . . for he's a jolly good fellow . . .

if ▪ wenn, falls; ob
If you work very hard you have a chance of passing this test.
I don't know if I'll be able to go on holiday this year.

in order to ▪ um zu

He stopped eating sweets in order to lose weight.

or ▪ oder

You can still decide whether to study English or French.

otherwise ▪ sonst, ansonsten

Please hurry. Otherwise we will come too late.

so ▪ daher

I am very tired, so I will go to bed.

so that ▪ damit, so dass

He spoke a little louder so that grandfather could hear him.

than ▪ als

John is taller than I am.

that ▪ dass; weil

I suggest that we should go on holiday over Christmas.

Of course I'd like to go to the party, but I can't. It's just that I've got no time.

though ▪ obwohl

Henry went for a long walk though it was raining heavily.

unless ▪ außer wenn

You'll have to pay the full price unless you are a senior citizen.

whereas ▪ während, wohingegen

Whereas people in northern Italy are well-off, those in the south tend to be poor.

whether ▪ ob

He wasn't sure whether he had locked the door.

while ▪ während; obwohl; wohingegen

Can you, please, stop talking while I am trying to concentrate?

While I can see your problems I would like you to see mine as well.

That pot costs £100 while this one over here costs only £30.

as long as ▪ solange; wenn

She said she'd come to the party as long as nobody smoked.

as soon as ▪ sobald

I'll come as soon as I have finished my homework.

in case ▪ falls

Dial 999 in case there is a fire.

in that ▪ darin, dass …

The sailor was lucky in that he was saved by a passing steamer.

now that ▪ jetzt, wo …

Now that my father is a pensioner he travels a lot.

provided ▪ vorausgesetzt

I'll come to your party provided that Mary can come as well.

since ▪ da, weil

Since the Prime Minister lost the election he resigned.